*I met the girl
under full-bloomed cherry blossoms,
and my fate has begun to change.*

10

WITHDRAWN

Naoshi Arakawa

STORY & CHARACTERS

The autumn of his 12th year, Kōsei Arima's mother died, causing him to lose the ability to play the piano. He lost his purpose, and his days lost all color. But in the spring when he was 14 met the exceptionally quirky violinist Kaori Miyazono.

As he accompanies Kaori and plays solo in the Maihō piano competition, Kōsei's days gradually fill with color. And then, when Kaori fails to appear at the gala concert, he takes the stage alone. As the boy plays Love's Sorrow, Kōsei is released from his mother's curse, and he makes up his mind to walk the path of a musician.

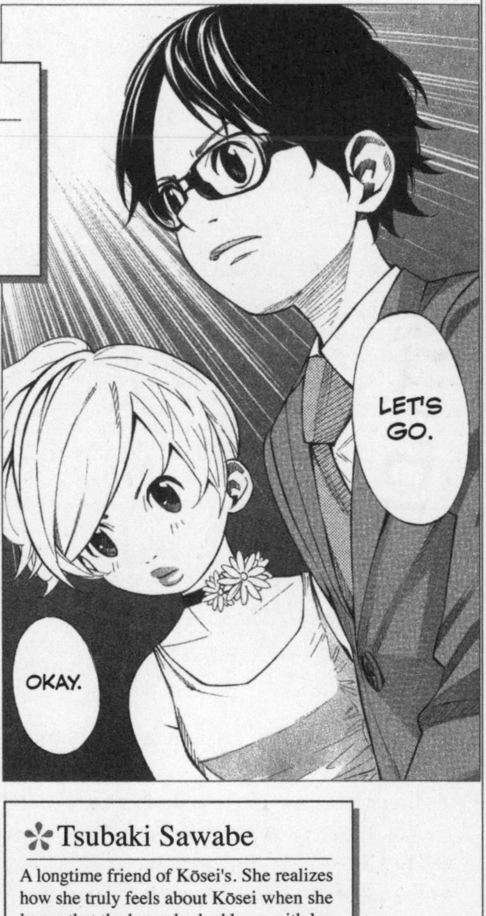
LET'S GO.
OKAY.

Kōsei Arima

An ex-piano prodigy who lost his ability to play when his mother died. After meeting Kaori, he returns to the path of music.

Nagi Aizato

A girl who appeared before Hiroko Seto and Kōsei out of nowhere and demanded training. In reality, she is Nagi Aiza, the younger sister of Takeshi Aiza.

Tsubaki Sawabe

A longtime friend of Kōsei's. She realizes how she truly feels about Kōsei when she learns that the boy who had been with her all her life will be moving far away.

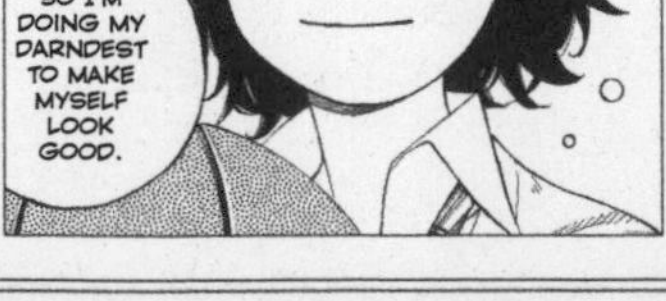
I DON'T WANT HIM TO SEE ME LIKE THAT.
SO I'M DOING MY DARNDEST TO MAKE MYSELF LOOK GOOD.

SO

GIVE ME

ONE MORE CHANCE.

LITTLE

STAR

PLEASE.

A CHANCE TO STAND AT YOUR SIDE.

HOW I

✻ Kaori Miyazono

A quirky violinist. She fainted before the gala concert and is now in the hospital.

...

ARE SO CRUEL.

YOU

Meanwhile, Kaori, having failed to appear at the gala concert, was once again in a hospital bed. Kōsei wonders what he can do for the despondent girl. He wracks his brains and eventually decides to play a piano duet with Nagi at Kuru Fest, conveying his feelings to Kaori through music. "Please. Play with me, one more time." Kaori breaks into a tearful smile at Kōsei's heartfelt request.

contents

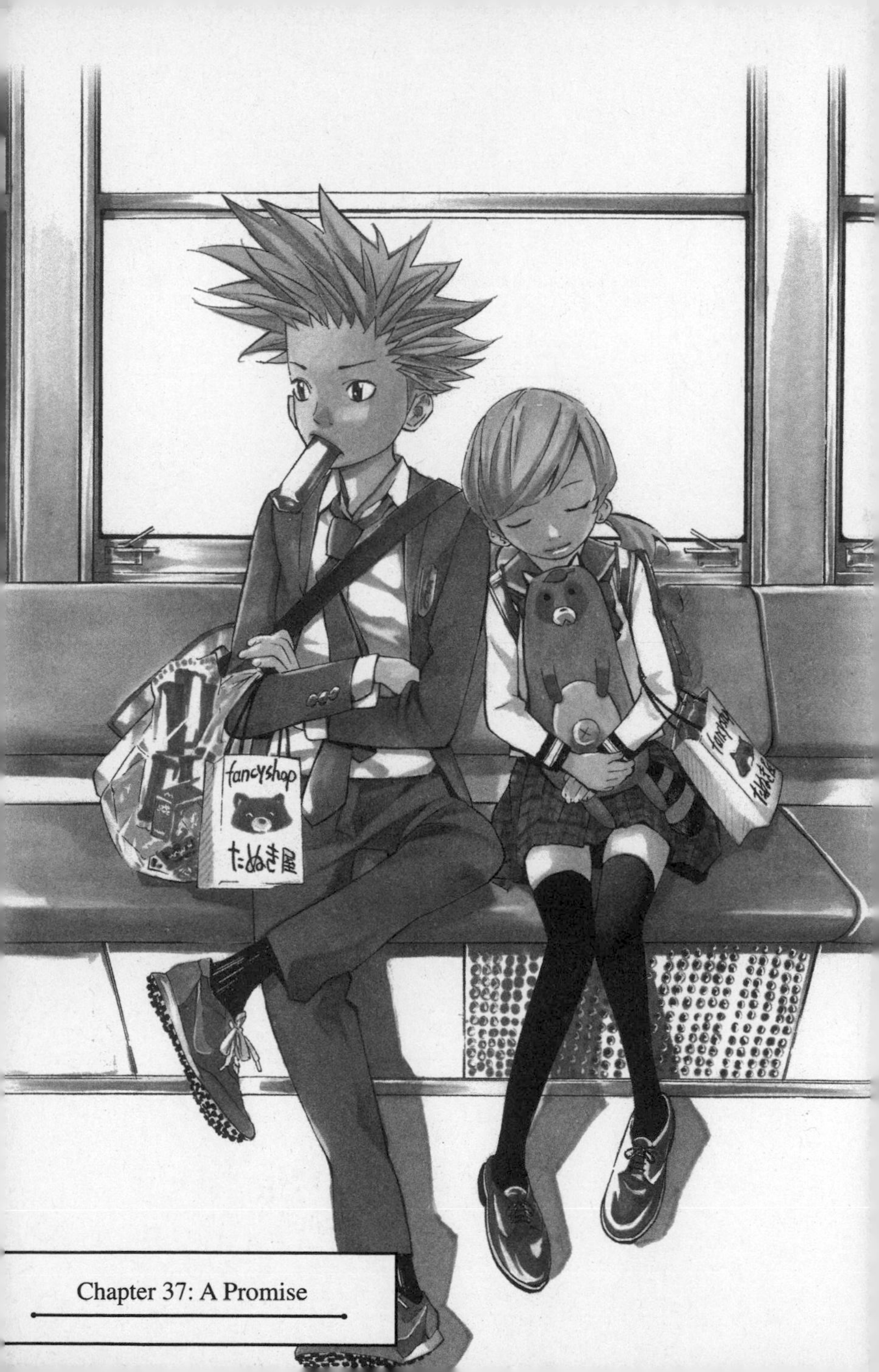
fancyshop
たぬき屋

Chapter 37: A Promise

Your Lie in April

I met the girl under full-bloomed cherry blossoms, and my fate has begun to change.

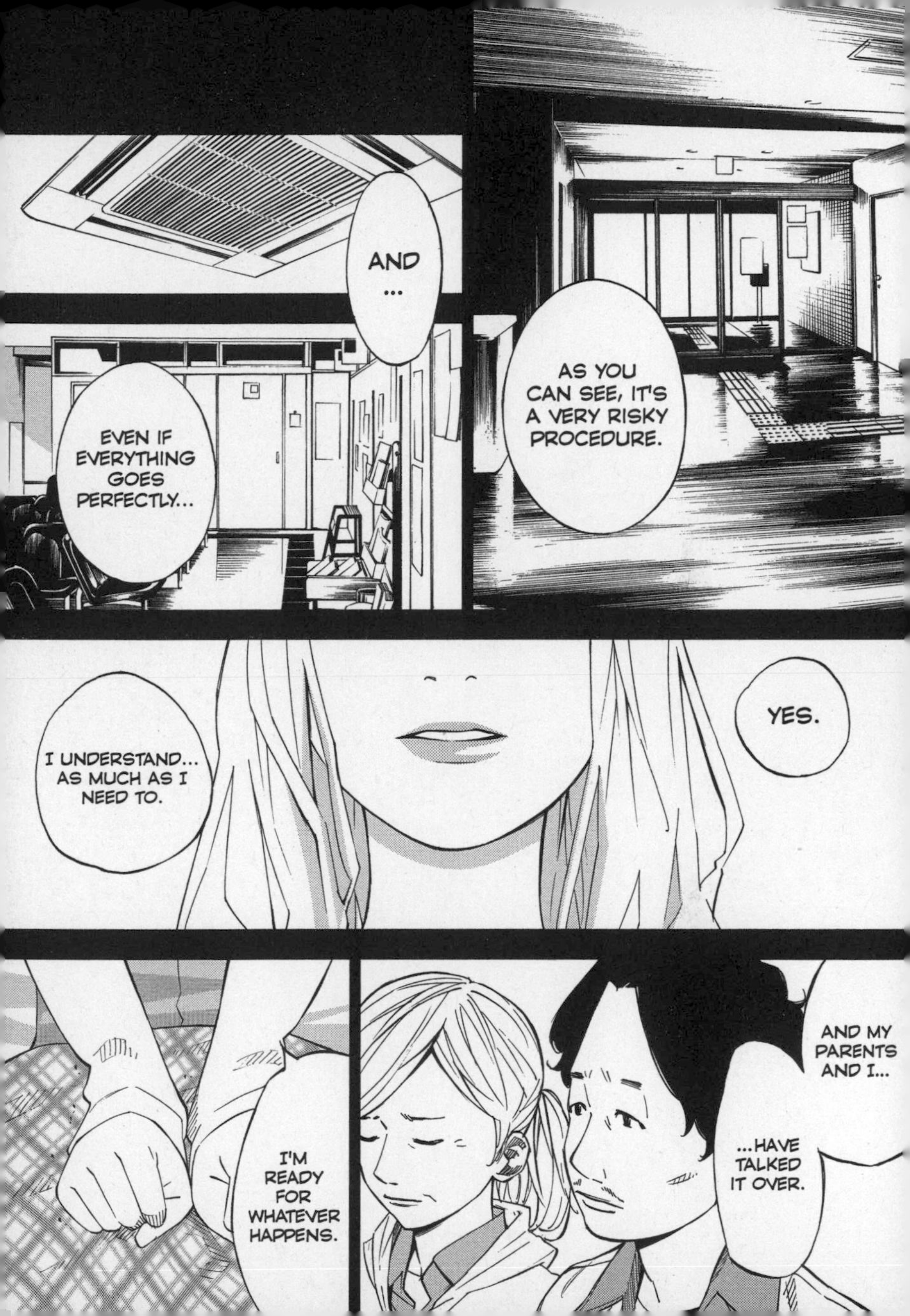
AS YOU CAN SEE, IT'S A VERY RISKY PROCEDURE.
AND ...
EVEN IF EVERYTHING GOES PERFECTLY...
YES.
I UNDERSTAND... AS MUCH AS I NEED TO.
AND MY PARENTS AND I...
...HAVE TALKED IT OVER.
I'M READY FOR WHATEVER HAPPENS.

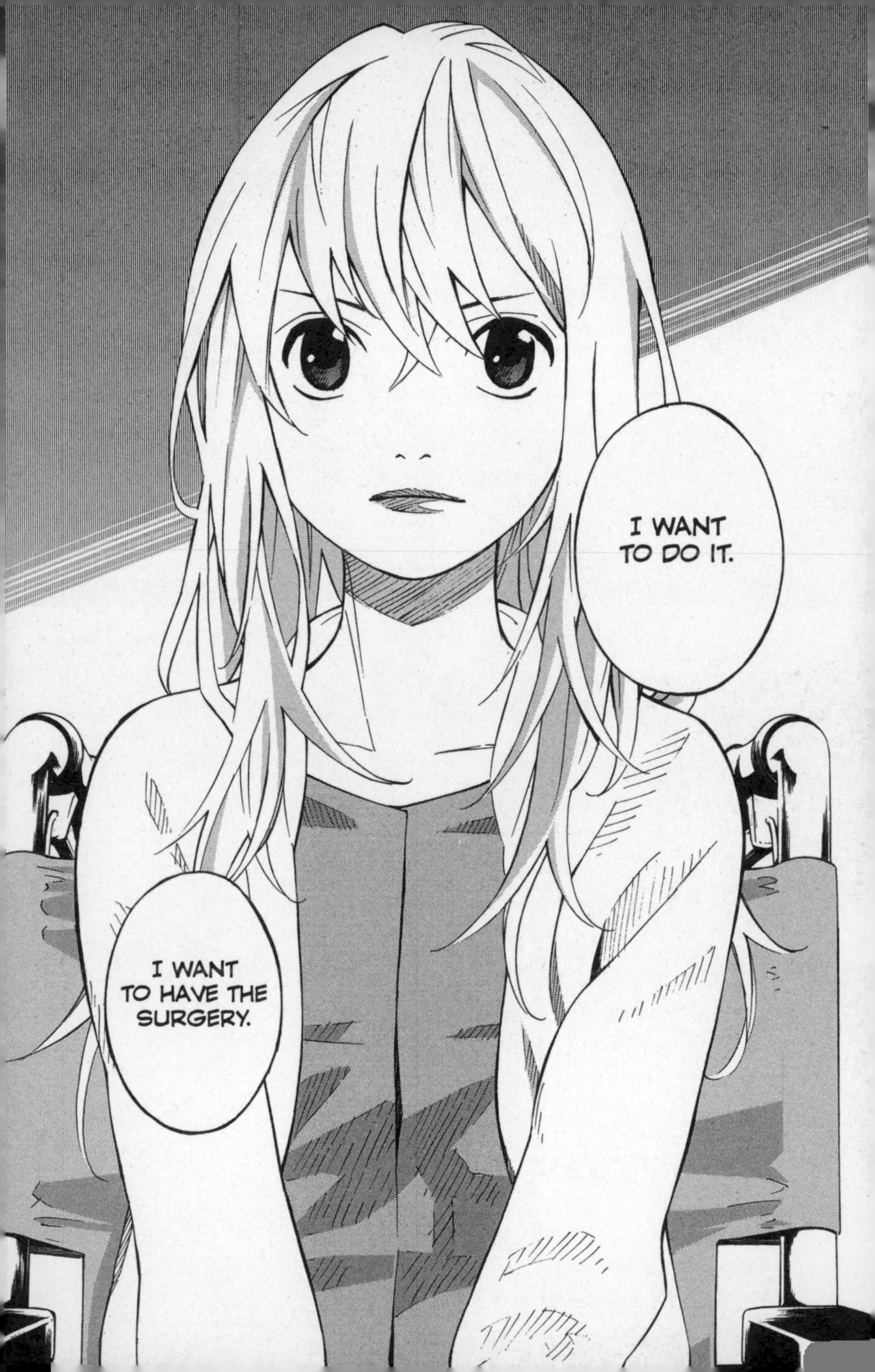
I WANT TO DO IT.
I WANT TO HAVE THE SURGERY.

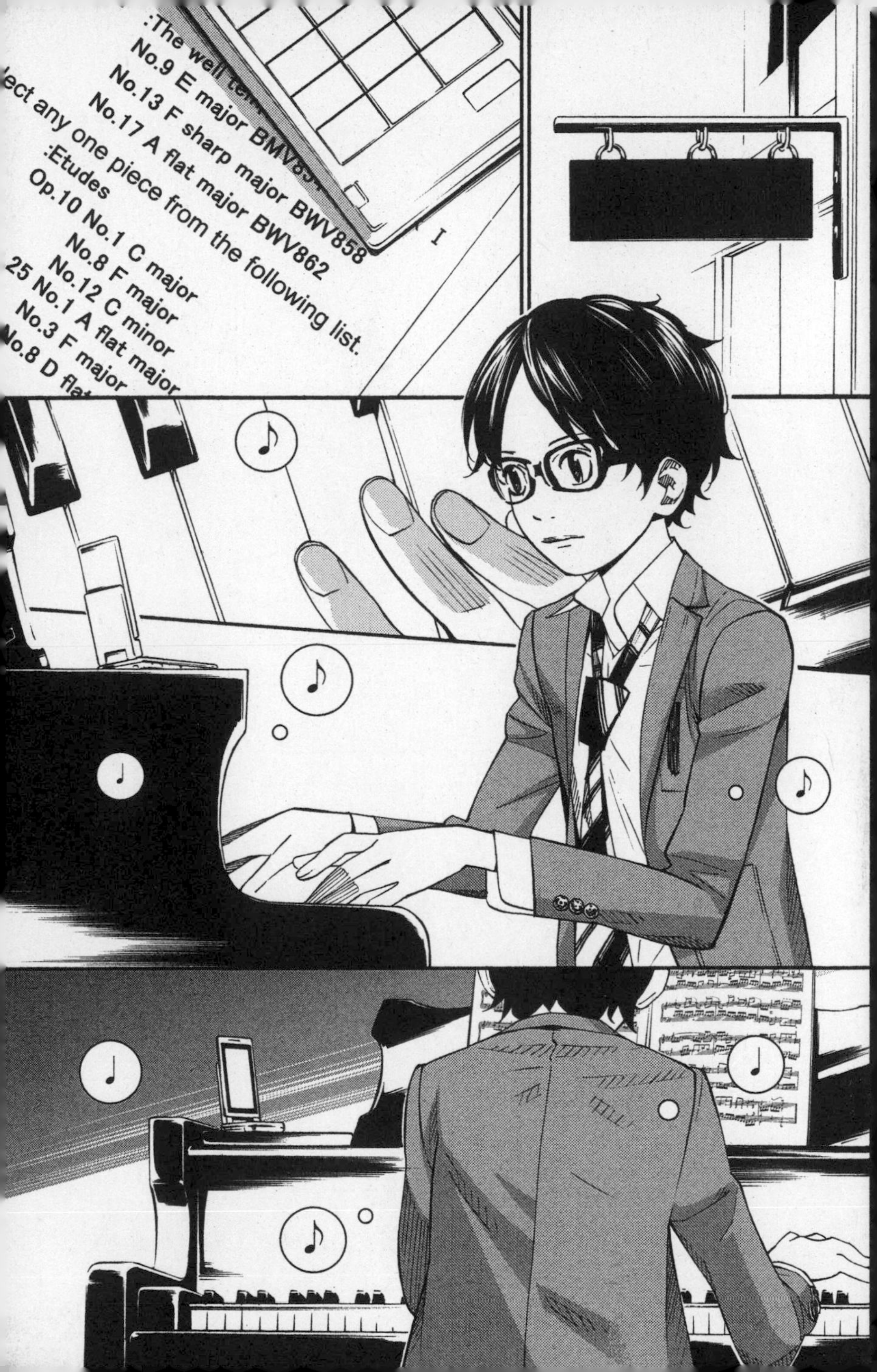
:The well tem
No.9 E major BWV85
No.13 F sharp major BWV858
No.17 A flat major BWV862
ect any one piece from the following list.
:Etudes
Op.10 No.1 C major
No.8 F major
No.12 C minor
25 No.1 A flat major
No.3 F major
No.8 D fla

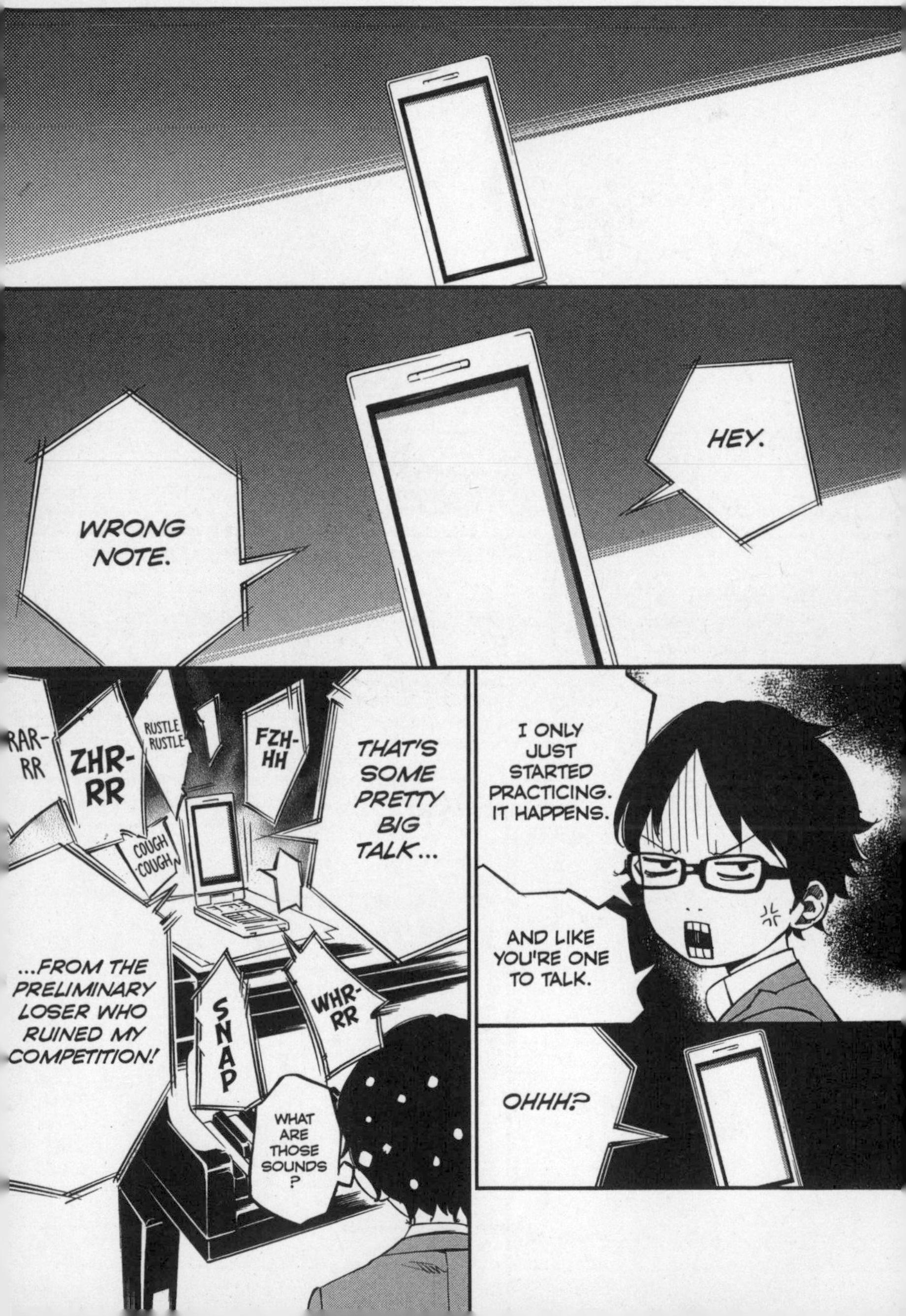
HEY.
WRONG NOTE.
I ONLY JUST STARTED PRACTICING. IT HAPPENS.
AND LIKE YOU'RE ONE TO TALK.
OHHH?
THAT'S SOME PRETTY BIG TALK...
FZH-HH
RUSTLE RUSTLE
ZHR-RR
RAR-RR
COUGH COUGH
...FROM THE PRELIMINARY LOSER WHO RUINED MY COMPETITION!
WHR-RR
SNAP
WHAT ARE THOSE SOUNDS?

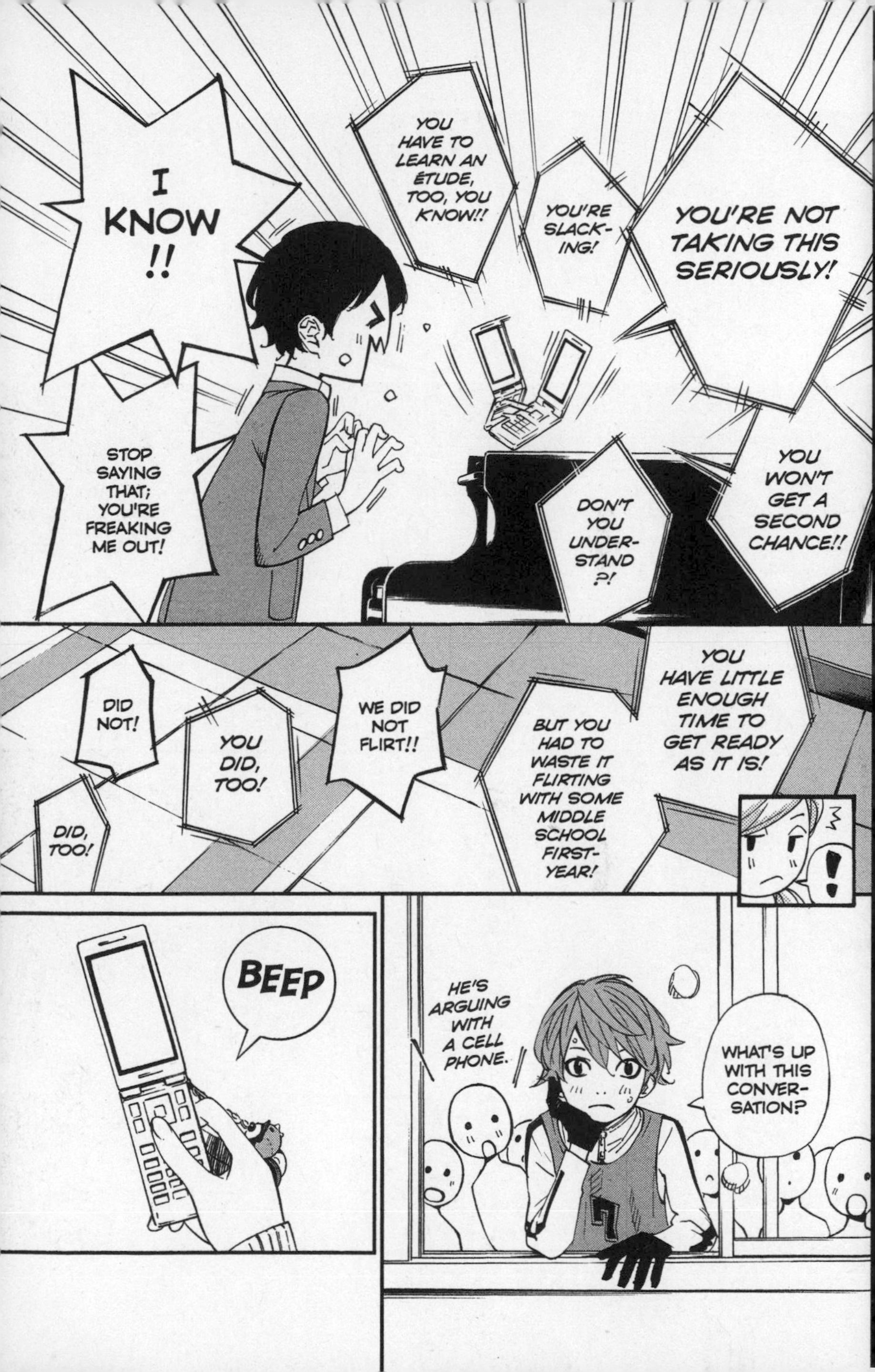
YOU'RE NOT TAKING THIS SERIOUSLY!
YOU'RE SLACKING!
YOU HAVE TO LEARN AN ETUDE, TOO, YOU KNOW!!
YOU WON'T GET A SECOND CHANCE!!
DON'T YOU UNDERSTAND?!
I KNOW!!
STOP SAYING THAT; YOU'RE FREAKING ME OUT!
YOU HAVE LITTLE ENOUGH TIME TO GET READY AS IT IS!
BUT YOU HAD TO WASTE IT FLIRTING WITH SOME MIDDLE SCHOOL FIRST-YEAR!
WE DID NOT FLIRT!!
YOU DID, TOO!
DID NOT!
DID, TOO!
WHAT'S UP WITH THIS CONVERSATION?
HE'S ARGUING WITH A CELL PHONE.
BEEP

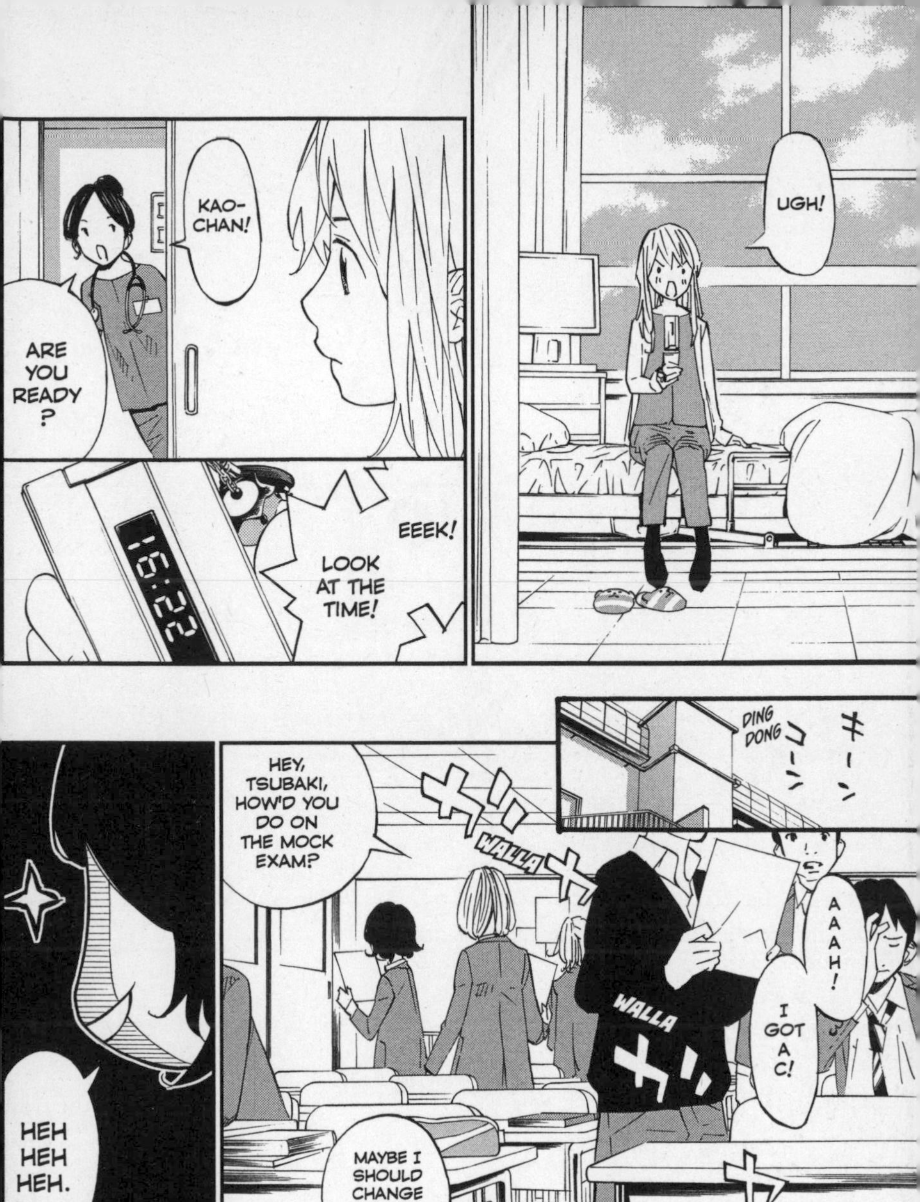
UGH!
KAO-CHAN!
ARE YOU READY?
EEEK!
LOOK AT THE TIME!
DING DONG
キーン コーン
AAAH!
I GOT A C!
WALLA
HEY, TSUBAKI, HOW'D YOU DO ON THE MOCK EXAM?
WALLA
MAYBE I SHOULD CHANGE MY FIRST CHOICE.
HEH HEH HEH.

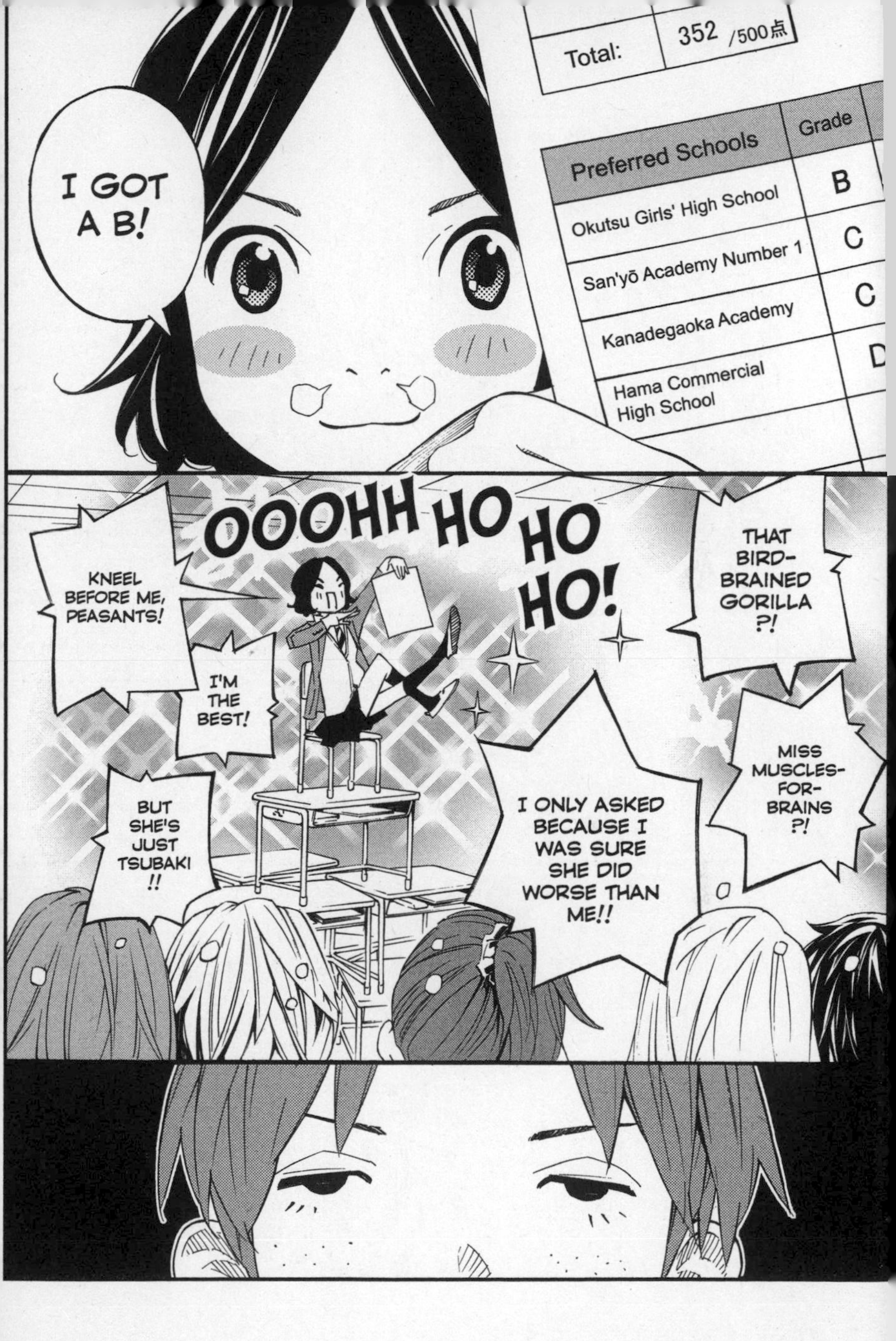
Total: 352 /500点
Preferred Schools
Grade
Okutsu Girls' High School B
San'yō Academy Number 1 C
Kanadegaoka Academy C
Hama Commercial High School D
I GOT A B!
THAT BIRD-BRAINED GORILLA?!
OOOHH HO HO HO!
KNEEL BEFORE ME, PEASANTS!
MISS MUSCLES-FOR-BRAINS?!
I'M THE BEST!
I ONLY ASKED BECAUSE I WAS SURE SHE DID WORSE THAN ME!!
BUT SHE'S JUST TSUBAKI!!

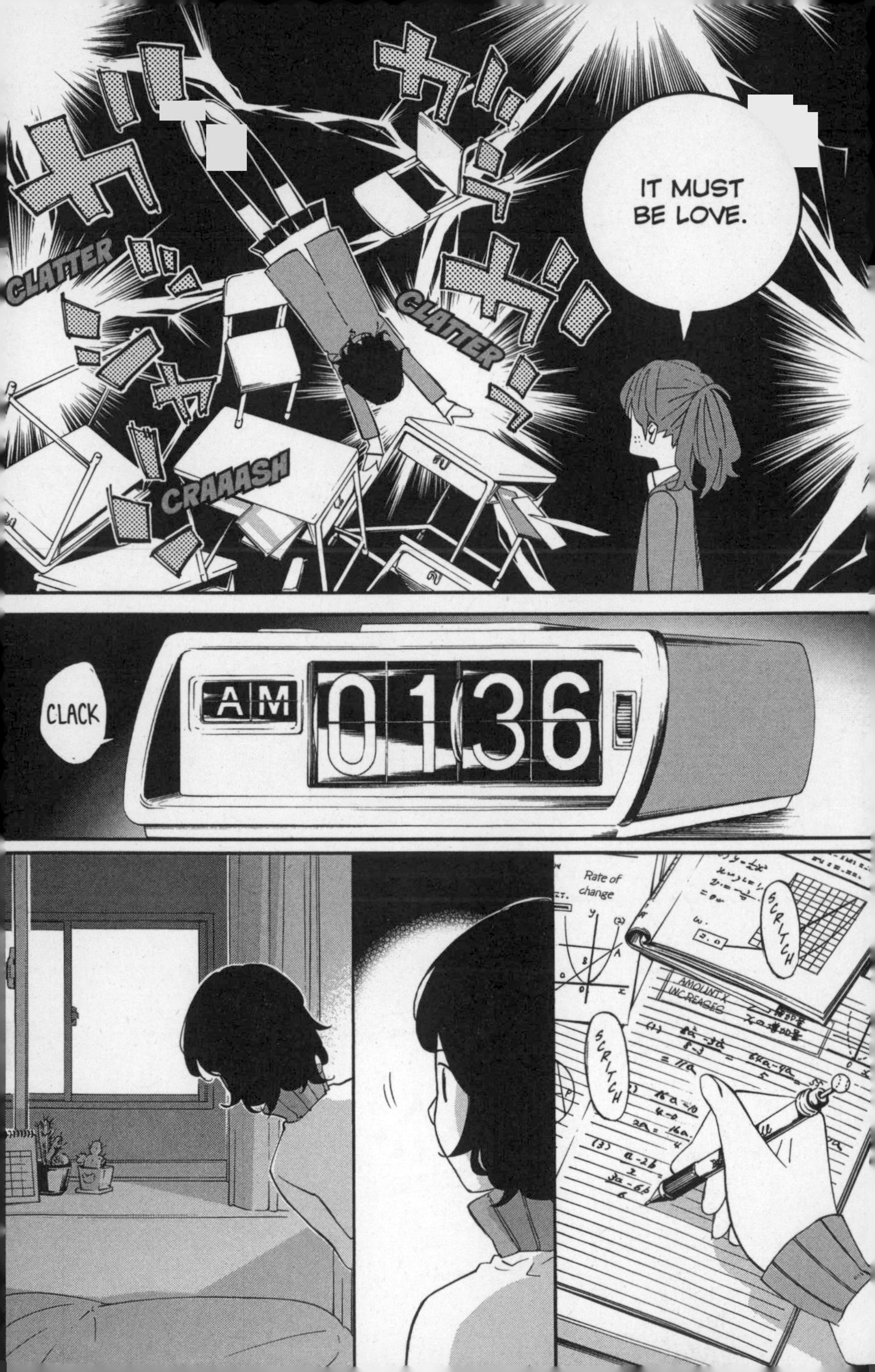
IT MUST BE LOVE.
CLATTER
CLATTER
CRAAASH
CLACK
AM 0136
Rate of change
SCRITCH
AMOUNT X INCREASES
SCRITCH

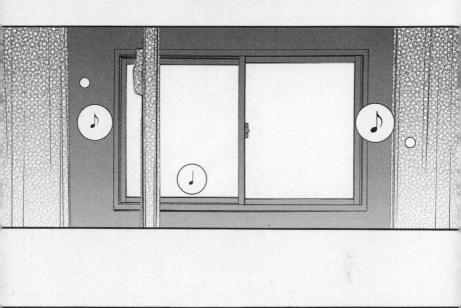

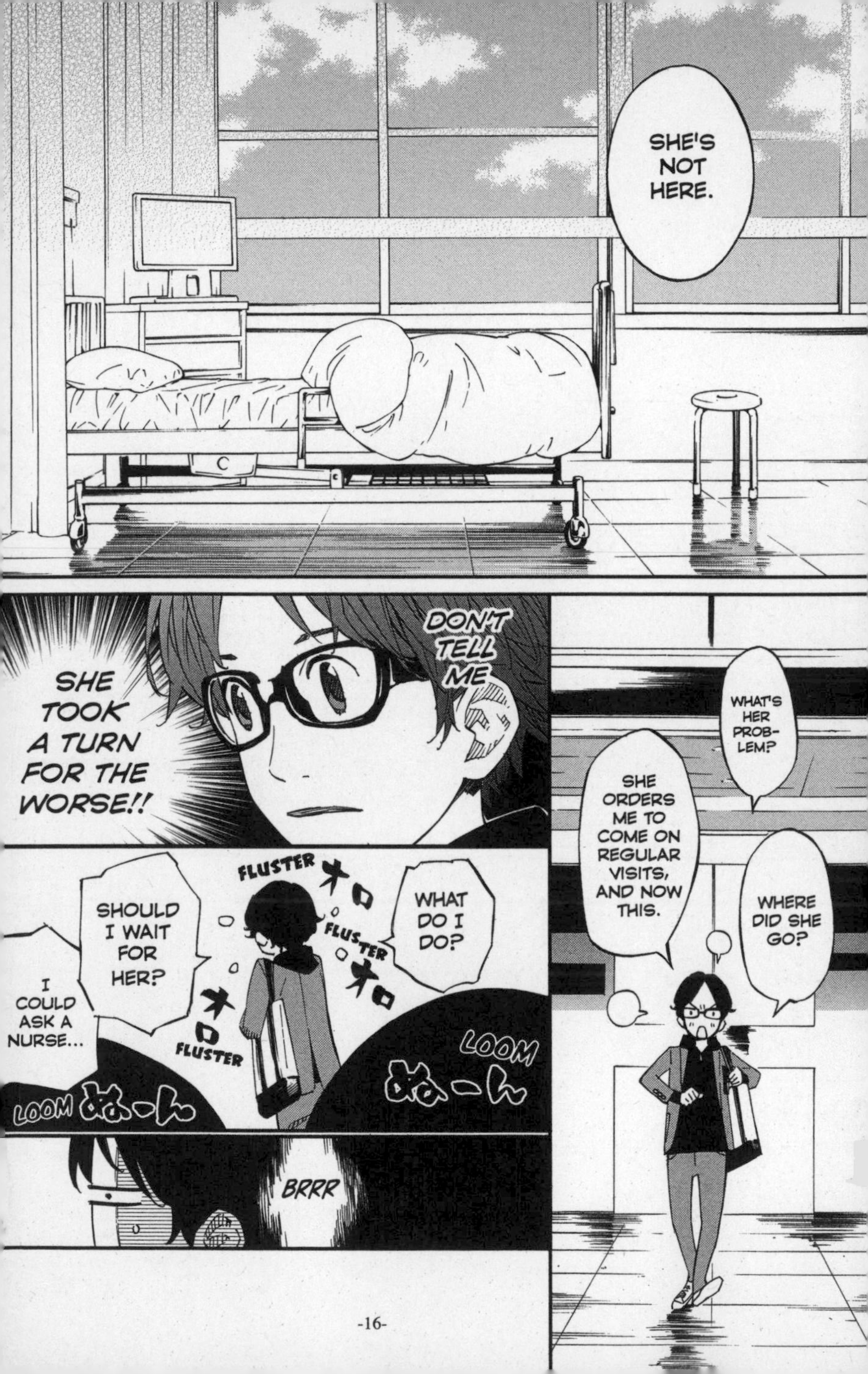
SHE'S NOT HERE.
WHERE DID SHE GO?
WHAT'S HER PROB-LEM?
SHE ORDERS ME TO COME ON REGULAR VISITS, AND NOW THIS.
DON'T TELL ME
SHE TOOK A TURN FOR THE WORSE!!
WHAT DO I DO?
FLUSTER オロ
FLUSTER オロ
SHOULD I WAIT FOR HER?
オロ FLUSTER
I COULD ASK A NURSE...
LOOM ぬーん
LOOM ぬーん
BRRR

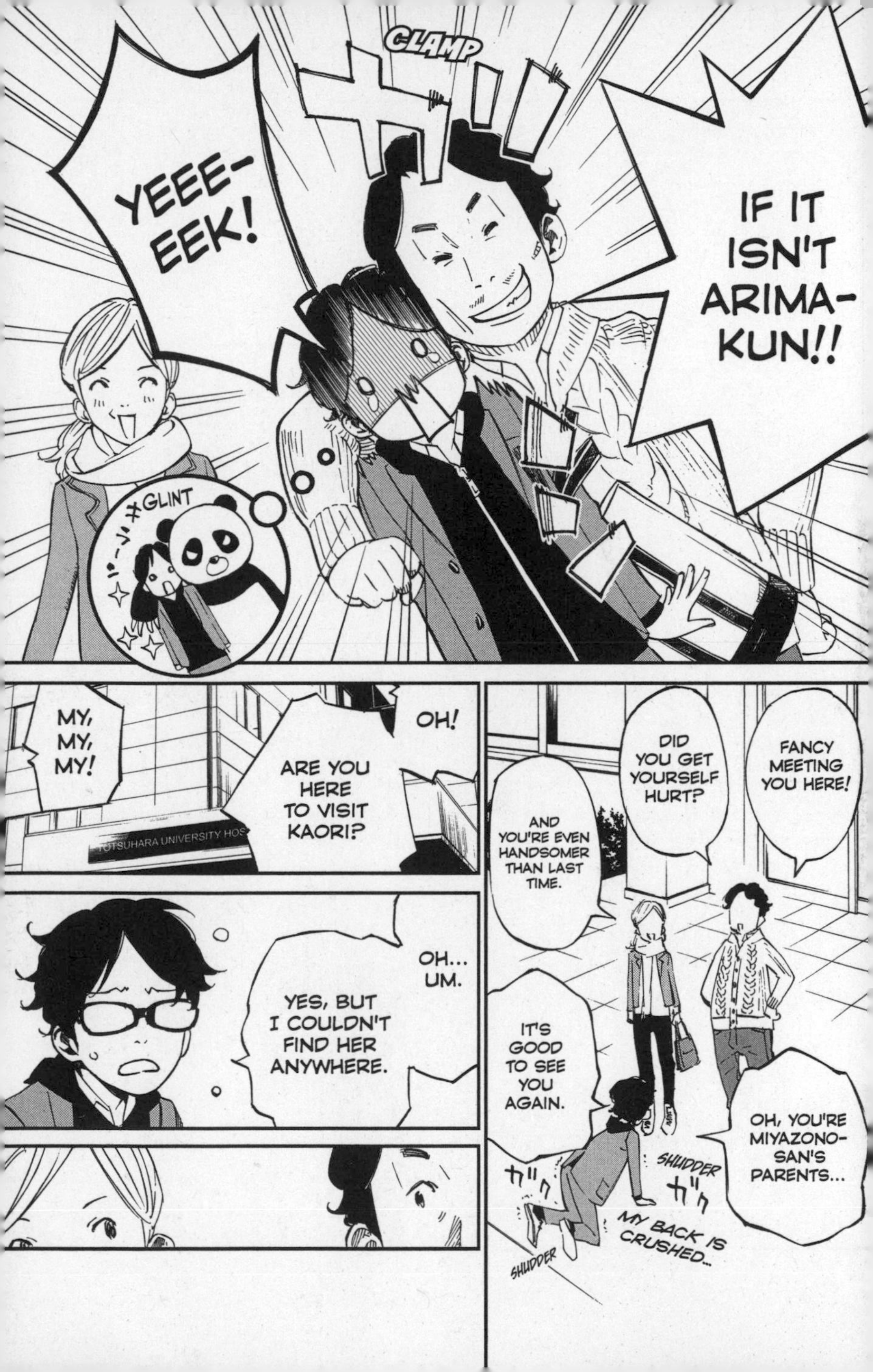

CLAMP
IF IT ISN'T ARIMA-KUN!!
YEEEE-EEK!
GLINT
FANCY MEETING YOU HERE!
DID YOU GET YOURSELF HURT?
AND YOU'RE EVEN HANDSOMER THAN LAST TIME.
OH, YOU'RE MIYAZONO-SAN'S PARENTS...
IT'S GOOD TO SEE YOU AGAIN.
SHUDDER
MY BACK IS CRUSHED...
SHUDDER
OH!
ARE YOU HERE TO VISIT KAORI?
MY, MY, MY!
TOTSUHARA UNIVERSITY HOS
OH... UM.
YES, BUT I COULDN'T FIND HER ANYWHERE.

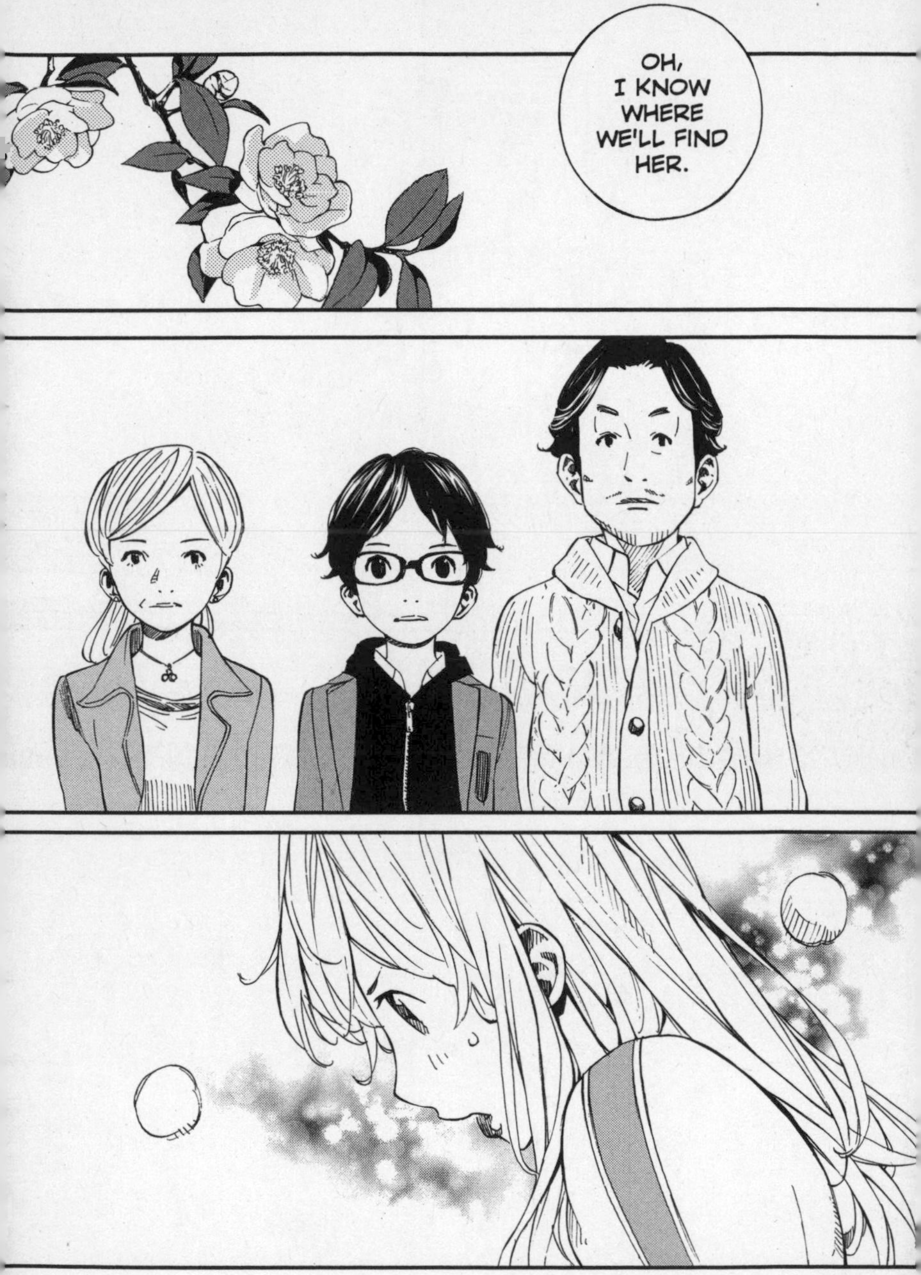
OH, I KNOW WHERE WE'LL FIND HER.

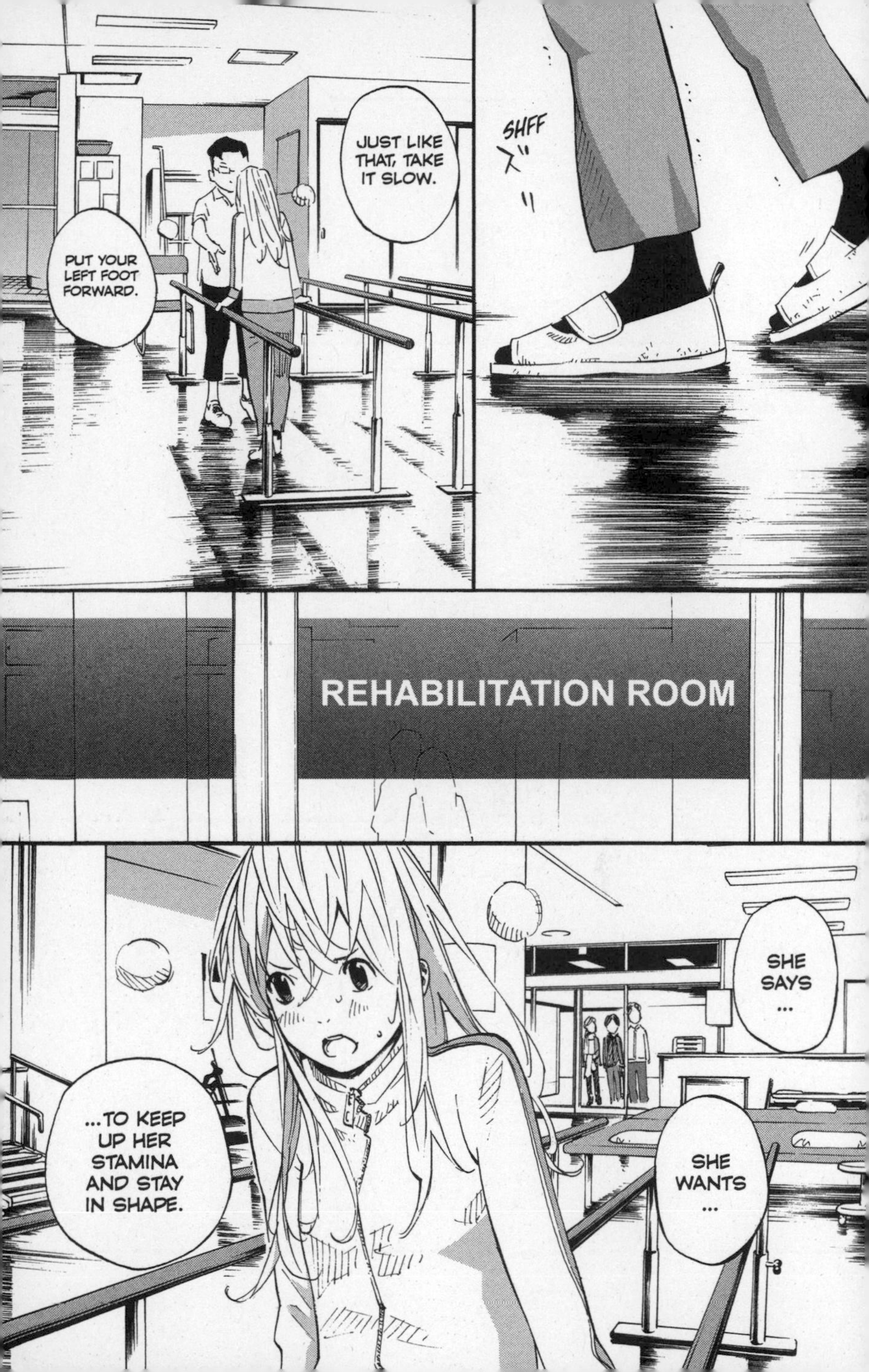
SHFF
ズリ
JUST LIKE THAT, TAKE IT SLOW.
PUT YOUR LEFT FOOT FORWARD.
REHABILITATION ROOM
SHE SAYS ...
SHE WANTS ...
...TO KEEP UP HER STAMINA AND STAY IN SHAPE.

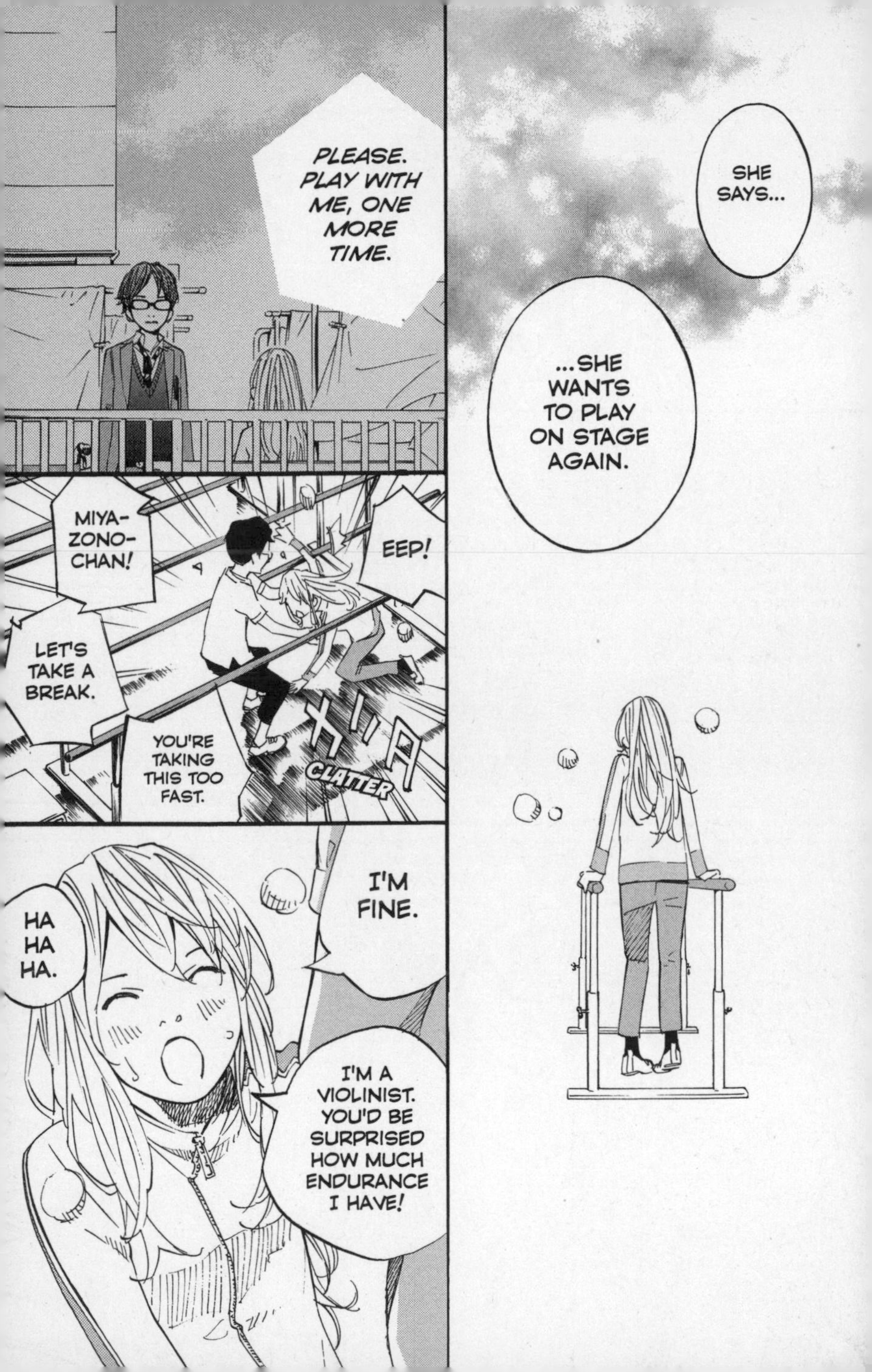
SHE SAYS...
...SHE WANTS TO PLAY ON STAGE AGAIN.
PLEASE. PLAY WITH ME, ONE MORE TIME.
EEP!
MIYA-ZONO-CHAN!
CLATTER
YOU'RE TAKING THIS TOO FAST.
LET'S TAKE A BREAK.
I'M FINE.
HA HA HA.
I'M A VIOLINIST. YOU'D BE SURPRISED HOW MUCH ENDURANCE I HAVE!

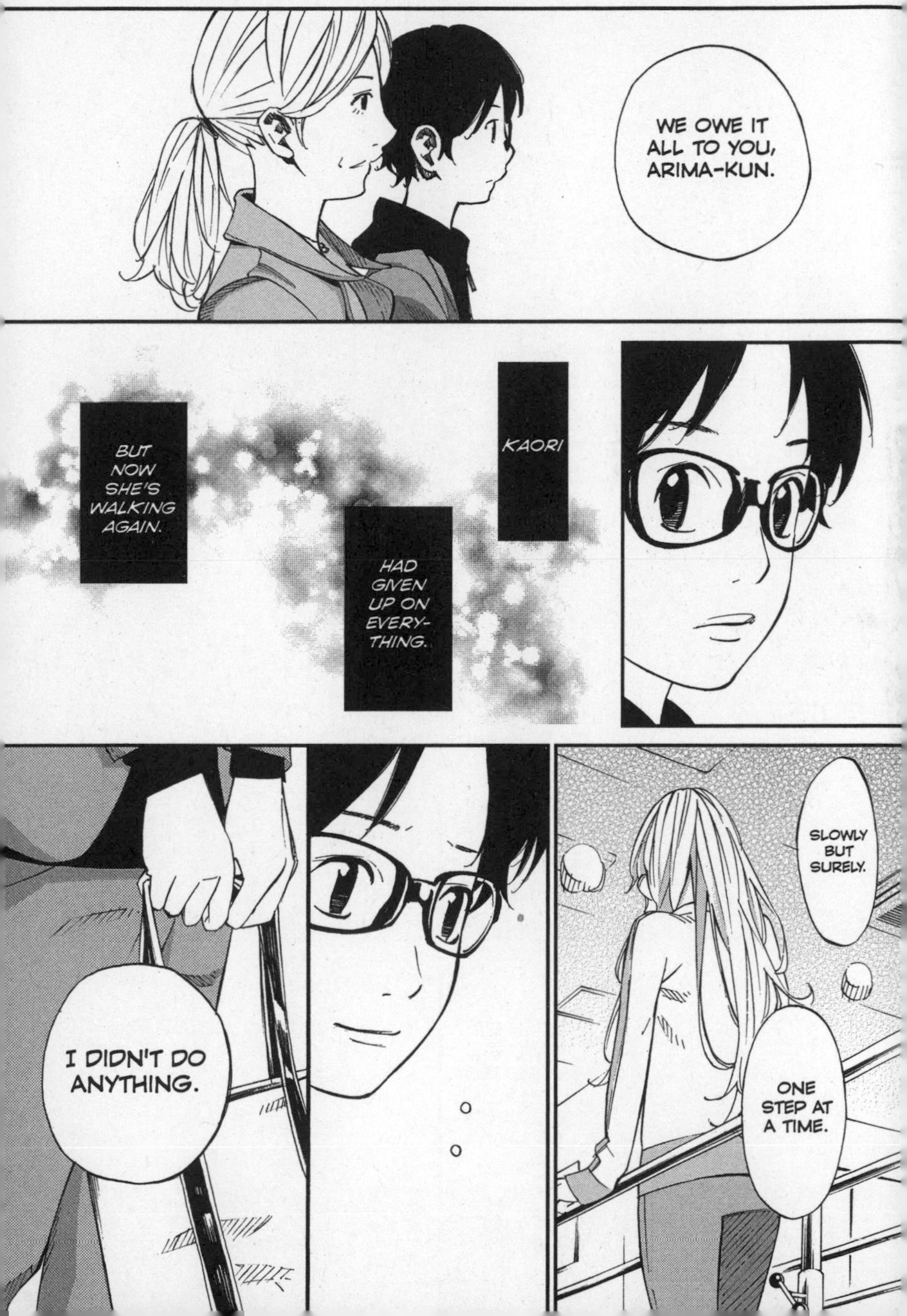
WE OWE IT ALL TO YOU, ARIMA-KUN.
KAORI
HAD GIVEN UP ON EVERY-THING.
BUT NOW SHE'S WALKING AGAIN.
SLOWLY BUT SURELY.
ONE STEP AT A TIME.
I DIDN'T DO ANYTHING.

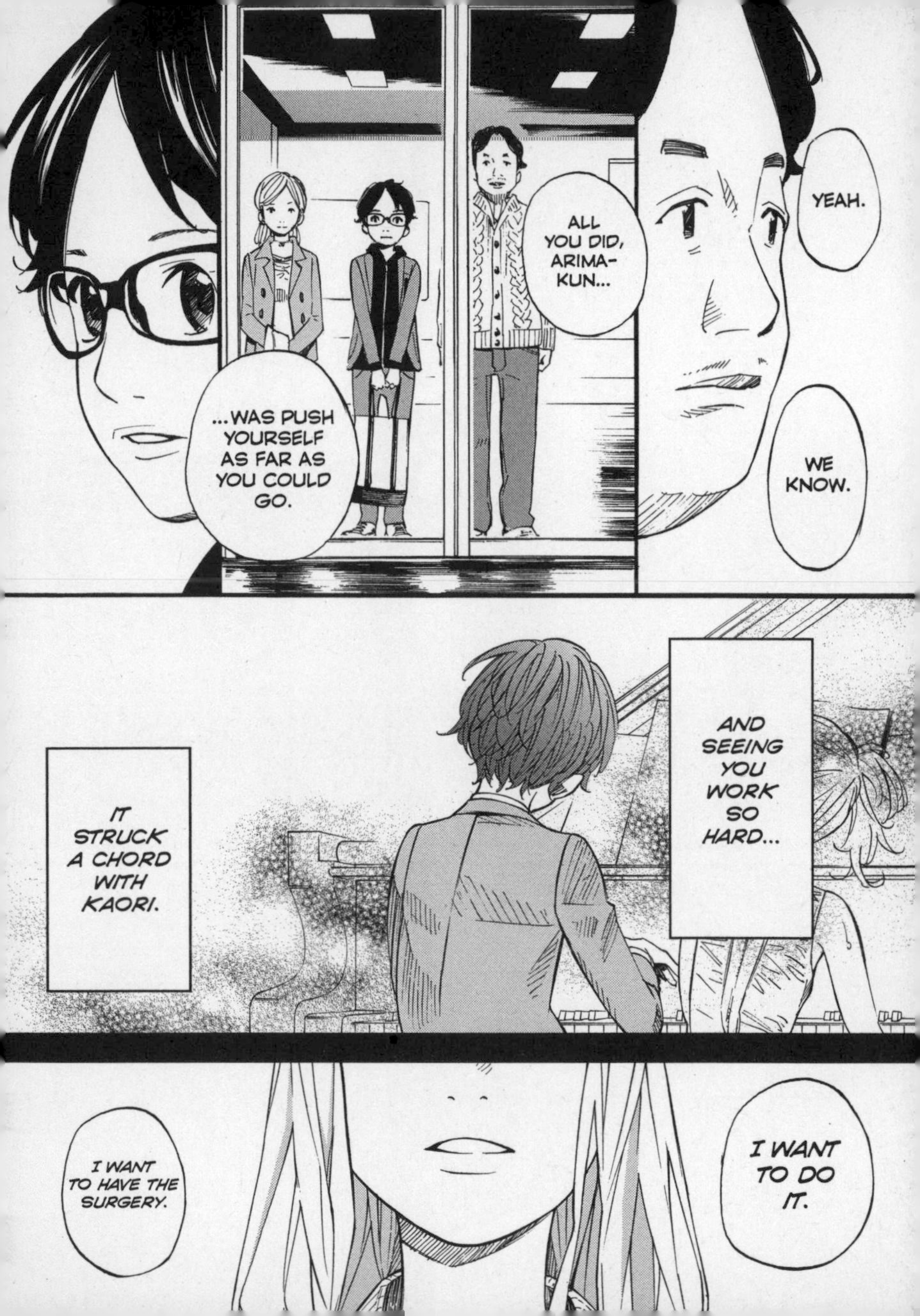
YEAH.
WE KNOW.
ALL YOU DID, ARIMA-KUN...
...WAS PUSH YOURSELF AS FAR AS YOU COULD GO.
AND SEEING YOU WORK SO HARD...
IT STRUCK A CHORD WITH KAORI.
I WANT TO DO IT.
I WANT TO HAVE THE SURGERY.

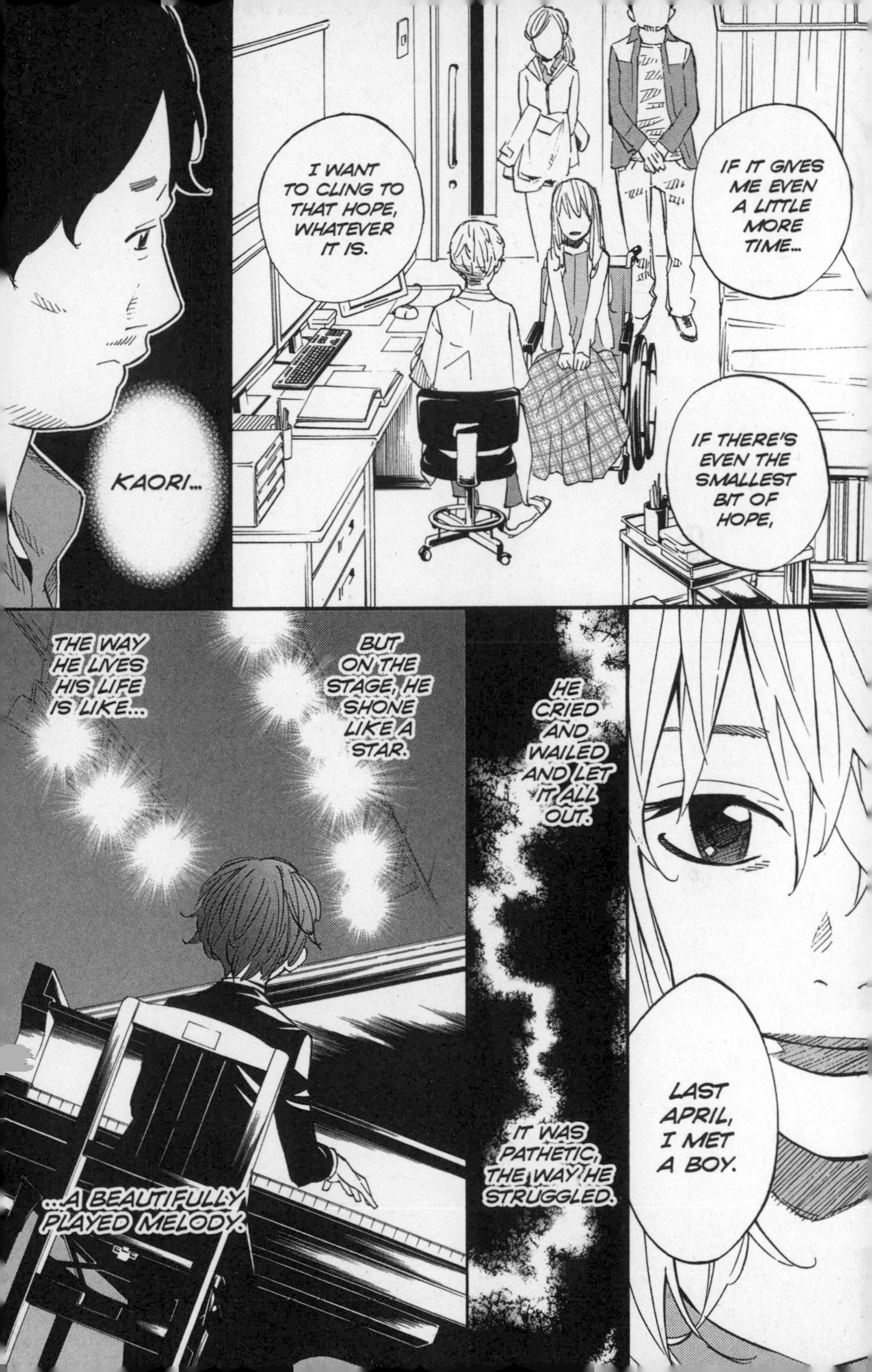
IF IT GIVES ME EVEN A LITTLE MORE TIME...
I WANT TO CLING TO THAT HOPE, WHATEVER IT IS.
IF THERE'S EVEN THE SMALLEST BIT OF HOPE,
KAORI...
LAST APRIL, I MET A BOY.
HE CRIED AND WAILED AND LET IT ALL OUT.
IT WAS PATHETIC, THE WAY HE STRUGGLED.
BUT ON THE STAGE, HE SHONE LIKE A STAR.
THE WAY HE LIVES HIS LIFE IS LIKE...
...A BEAUTIFULLY PLAYED MELODY.

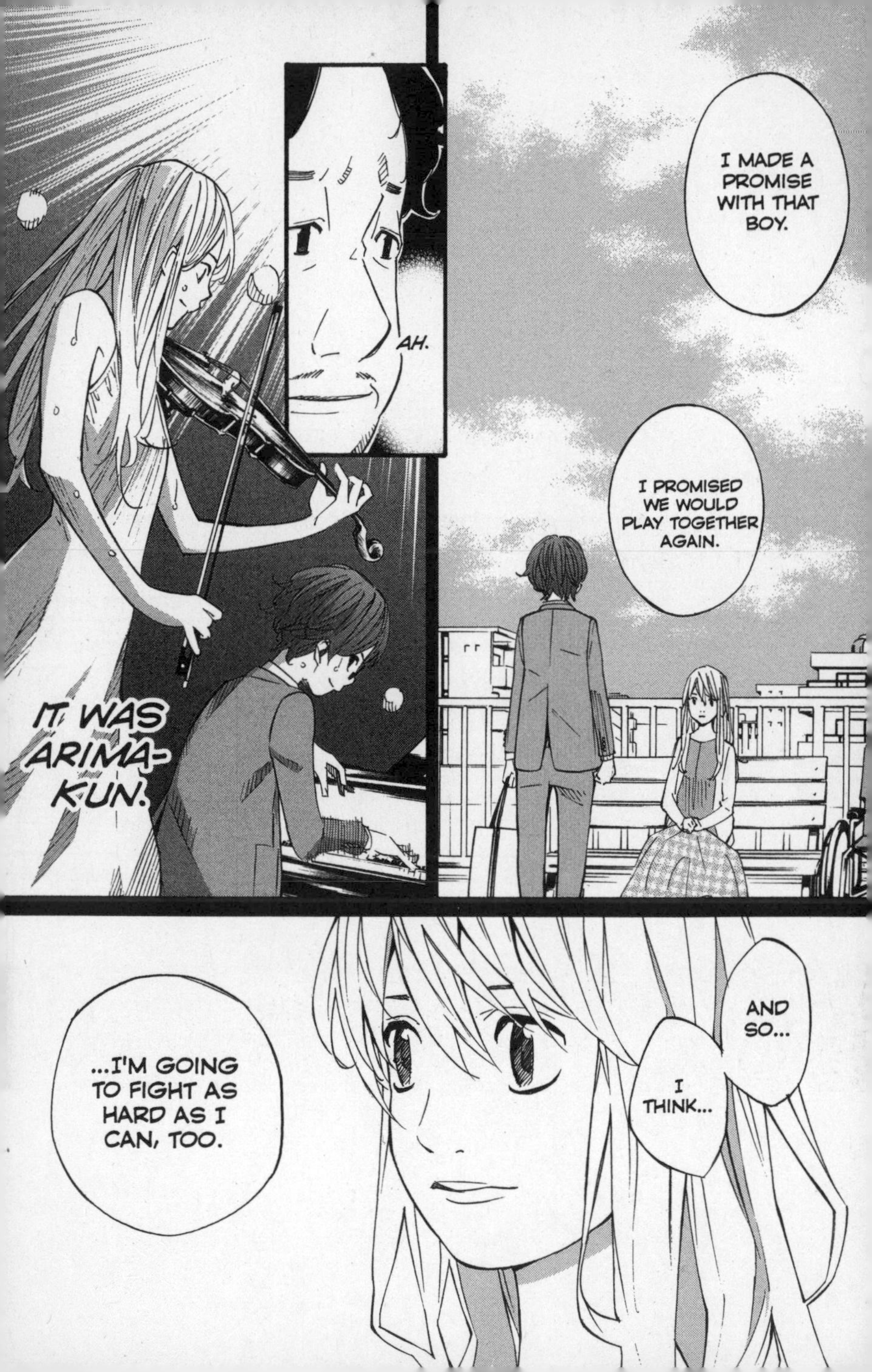
I MADE A PROMISE WITH THAT BOY.
I PROMISED WE WOULD PLAY TOGETHER AGAIN.
AH.
IT WAS ARIMA-KUN.
AND SO...
I THINK...
...I'M GOING TO FIGHT AS HARD AS I CAN, TOO.

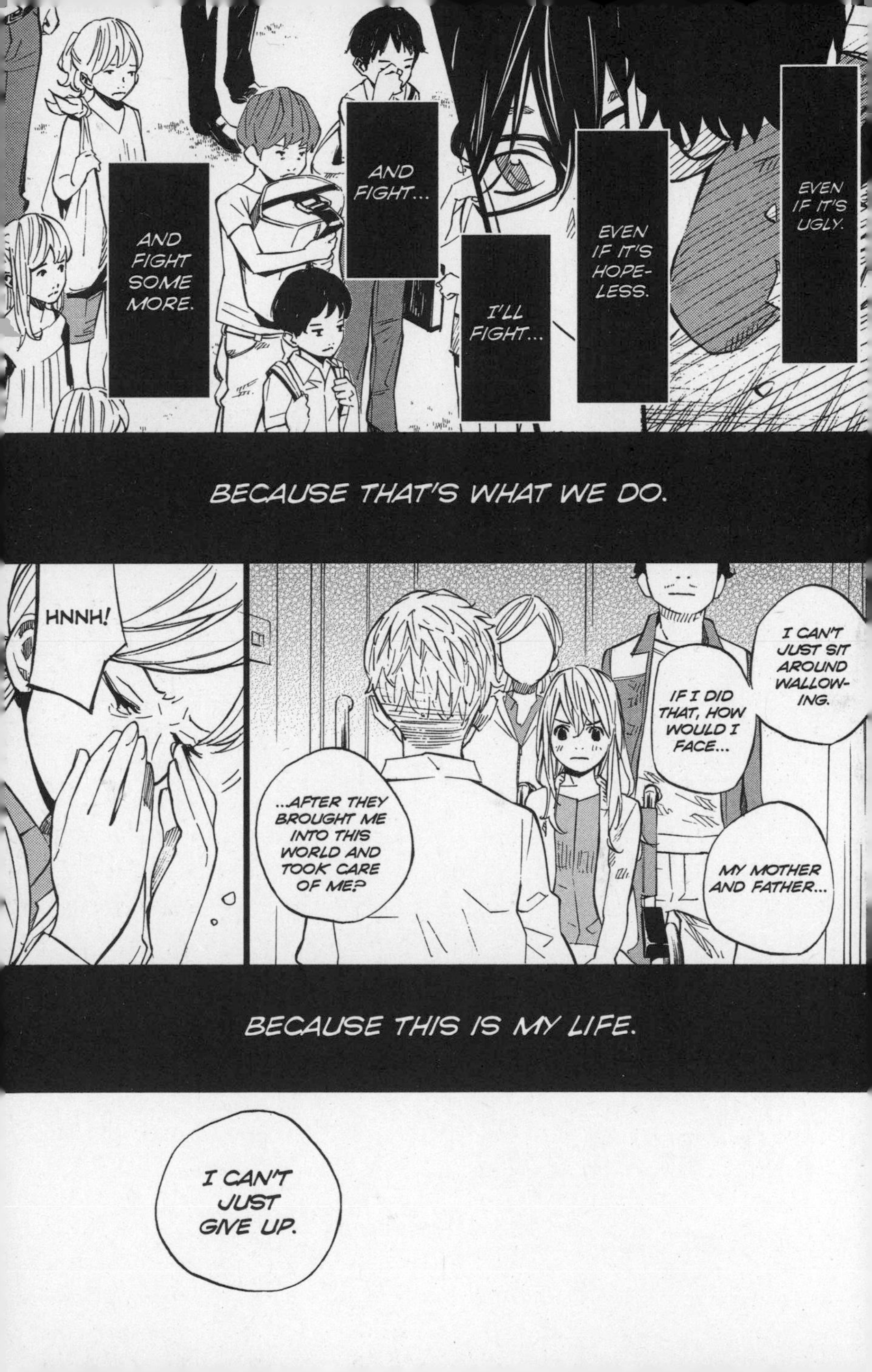
EVEN IF IT'S UGLY.
EVEN IF IT'S HOPE-LESS.
I'LL FIGHT...
AND FIGHT...
AND FIGHT SOME MORE.
BECAUSE THAT'S WHAT WE DO.
I CAN'T JUST SIT AROUND WALLOW-ING.
IF I DID THAT, HOW WOULD I FACE...
MY MOTHER AND FATHER...
...AFTER THEY BROUGHT ME INTO THIS WORLD AND TOOK CARE OF ME?
HNNH!
BECAUSE THIS IS MY LIFE.
I CAN'T JUST GIVE UP.

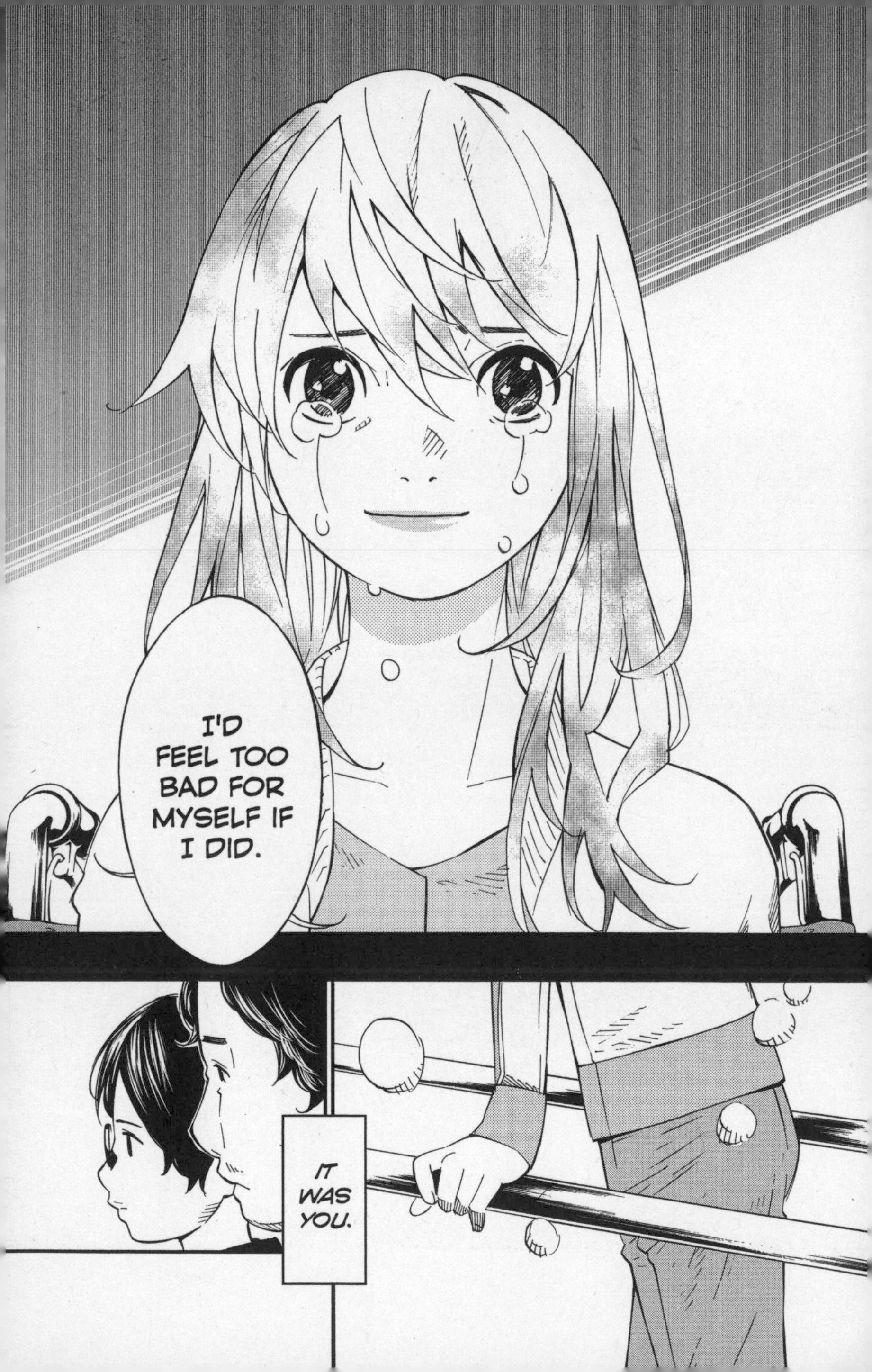
I'D FEEL TOO BAD FOR MYSELF IF I DID.
IT WAS YOU.

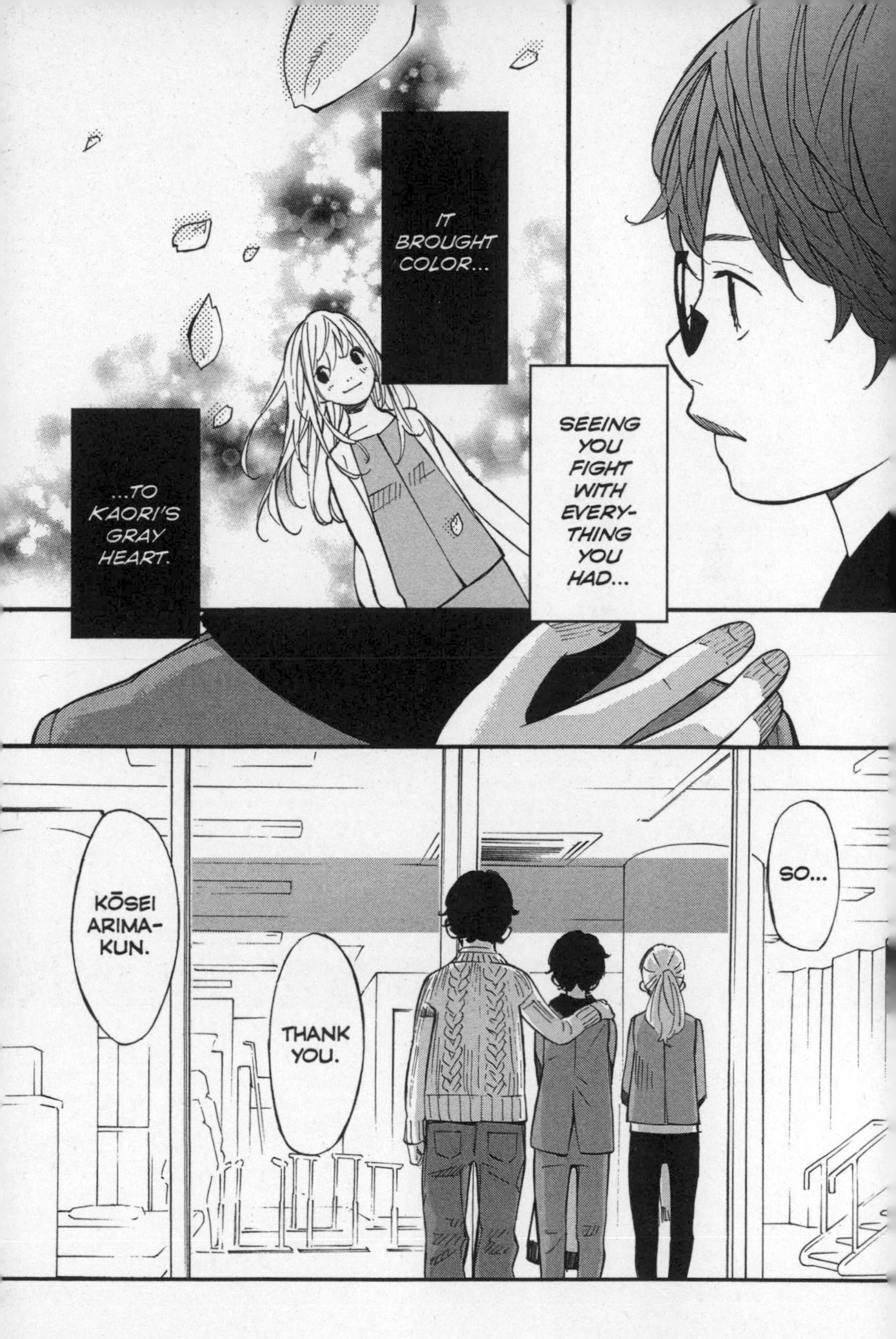
SEEING YOU FIGHT WITH EVERY-THING YOU HAD...
IT BROUGHT COLOR...
...TO KAORI'S GRAY HEART.
SO...
KŌSEI ARIMA-KUN.
THANK YOU.

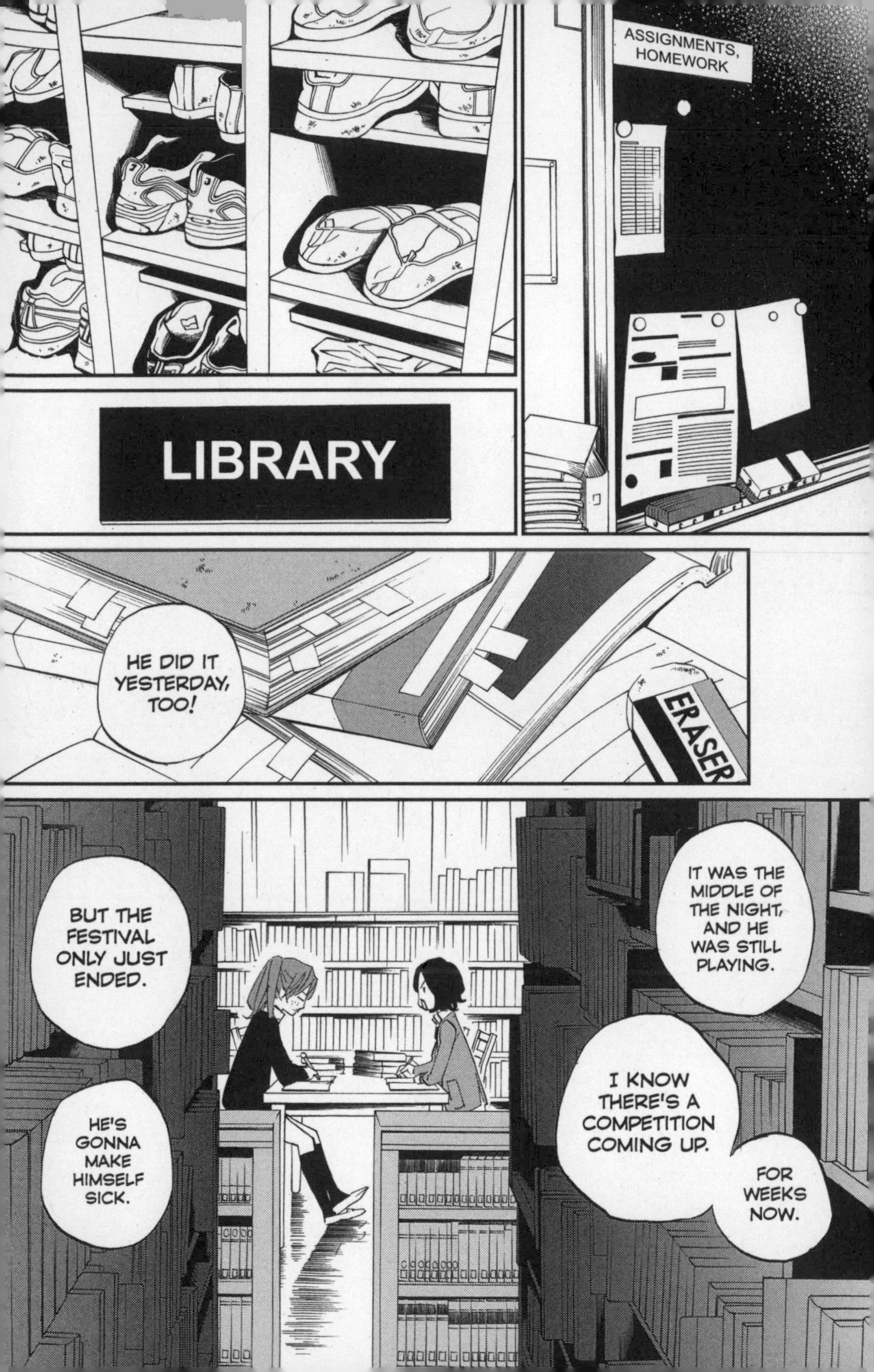
ASSIGNMENTS, HOMEWORK
LIBRARY
HE DID IT YESTERDAY, TOO!
ERASER
IT WAS THE MIDDLE OF THE NIGHT, AND HE WAS STILL PLAYING.
BUT THE FESTIVAL ONLY JUST ENDED.
I KNOW THERE'S A COMPETITION COMING UP.
FOR WEEKS NOW.
HE'S GONNA MAKE HIMSELF SICK.

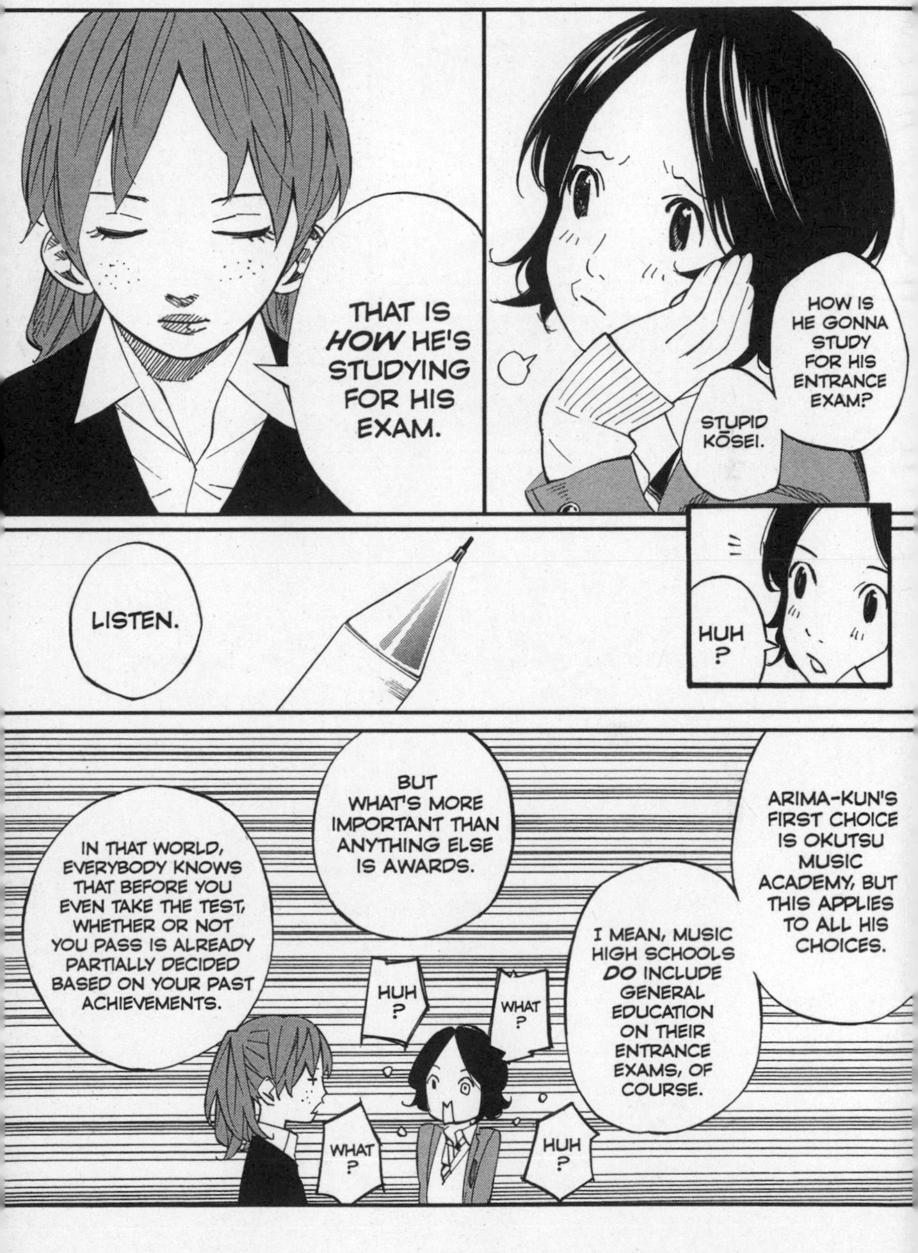
HOW IS HE GONNA STUDY FOR HIS ENTRANCE EXAM?
STUPID KŌSEI.
THAT IS *HOW* HE'S STUDYING FOR HIS EXAM.
HUH?
LISTEN.
ARIMA-KUN'S FIRST CHOICE IS OKUTSU MUSIC ACADEMY, BUT THIS APPLIES TO ALL HIS CHOICES.
I MEAN, MUSIC HIGH SCHOOLS *DO* INCLUDE GENERAL EDUCATION ON THEIR ENTRANCE EXAMS, OF COURSE.
BUT WHAT'S MORE IMPORTANT THAN ANYTHING ELSE IS AWARDS.
IN THAT WORLD, EVERYBODY KNOWS THAT BEFORE YOU EVEN TAKE THE TEST, WHETHER OR NOT YOU PASS IS ALREADY PARTIALLY DECIDED BASED ON YOUR PAST ACHIEVEMENTS.
WHAT?
HUH?
HUH?
WHAT?

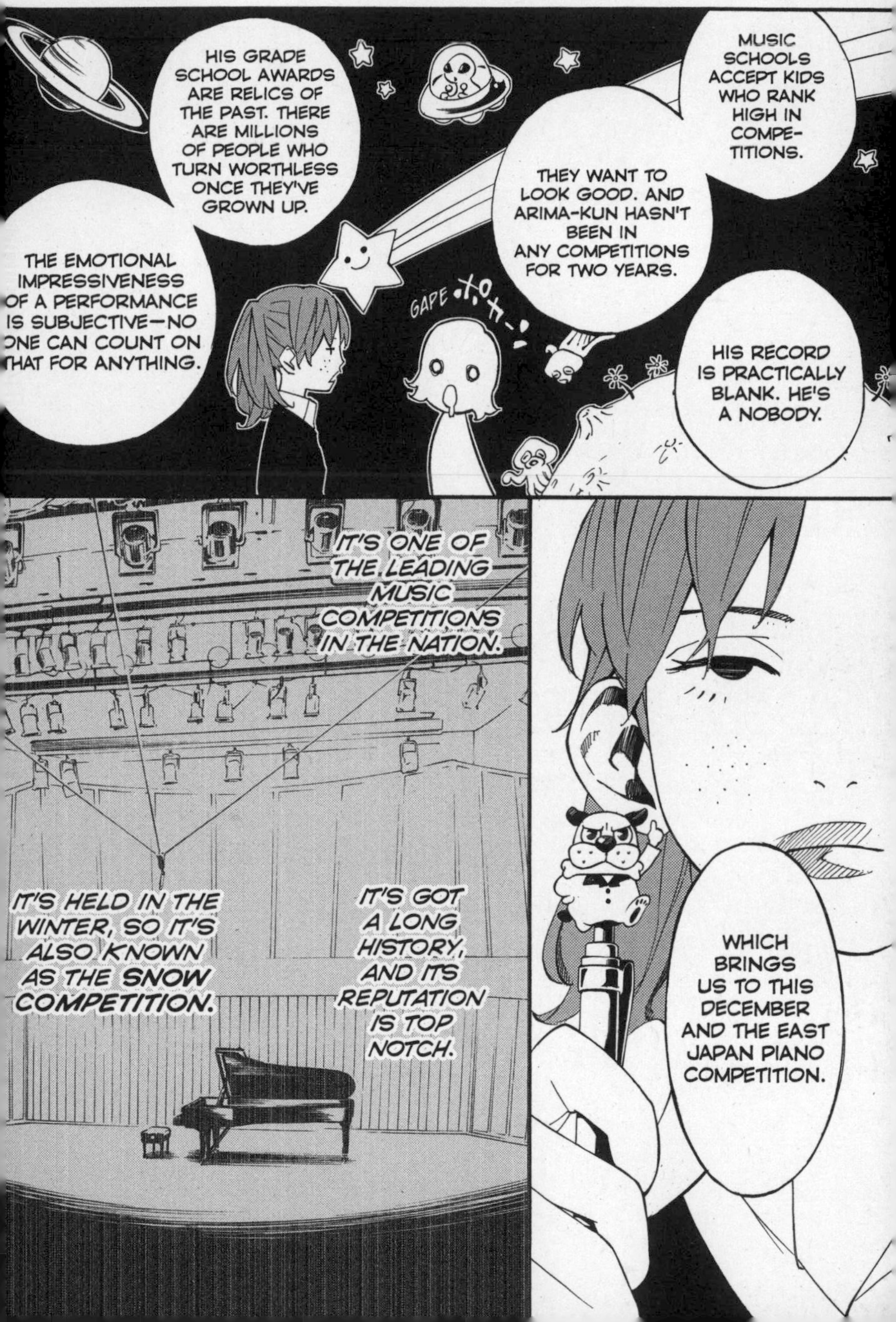
MUSIC SCHOOLS ACCEPT KIDS WHO RANK HIGH IN COMPE-TITIONS.
THEY WANT TO LOOK GOOD. AND ARIMA-KUN HASN'T BEEN IN ANY COMPETITIONS FOR TWO YEARS.
HIS RECORD IS PRACTICALLY BLANK. HE'S A NOBODY.
HIS GRADE SCHOOL AWARDS ARE RELICS OF THE PAST. THERE ARE MILLIONS OF PEOPLE WHO TURN WORTHLESS ONCE THEY'VE GROWN UP.
GAPE
THE EMOTIONAL IMPRESSIVENESS OF A PERFORMANCE IS SUBJECTIVE—NO ONE CAN COUNT ON THAT FOR ANYTHING.
WHICH BRINGS US TO THIS DECEMBER AND THE EAST JAPAN PIANO COMPETITION.
IT'S ONE OF THE LEADING MUSIC COMPETITIONS IN THE NATION.
IT'S GOT A LONG HISTORY, AND ITS REPUTATION IS TOP NOTCH.
IT'S HELD IN THE WINTER, SO IT'S ALSO KNOWN AS THE SNOW COMPETITION.

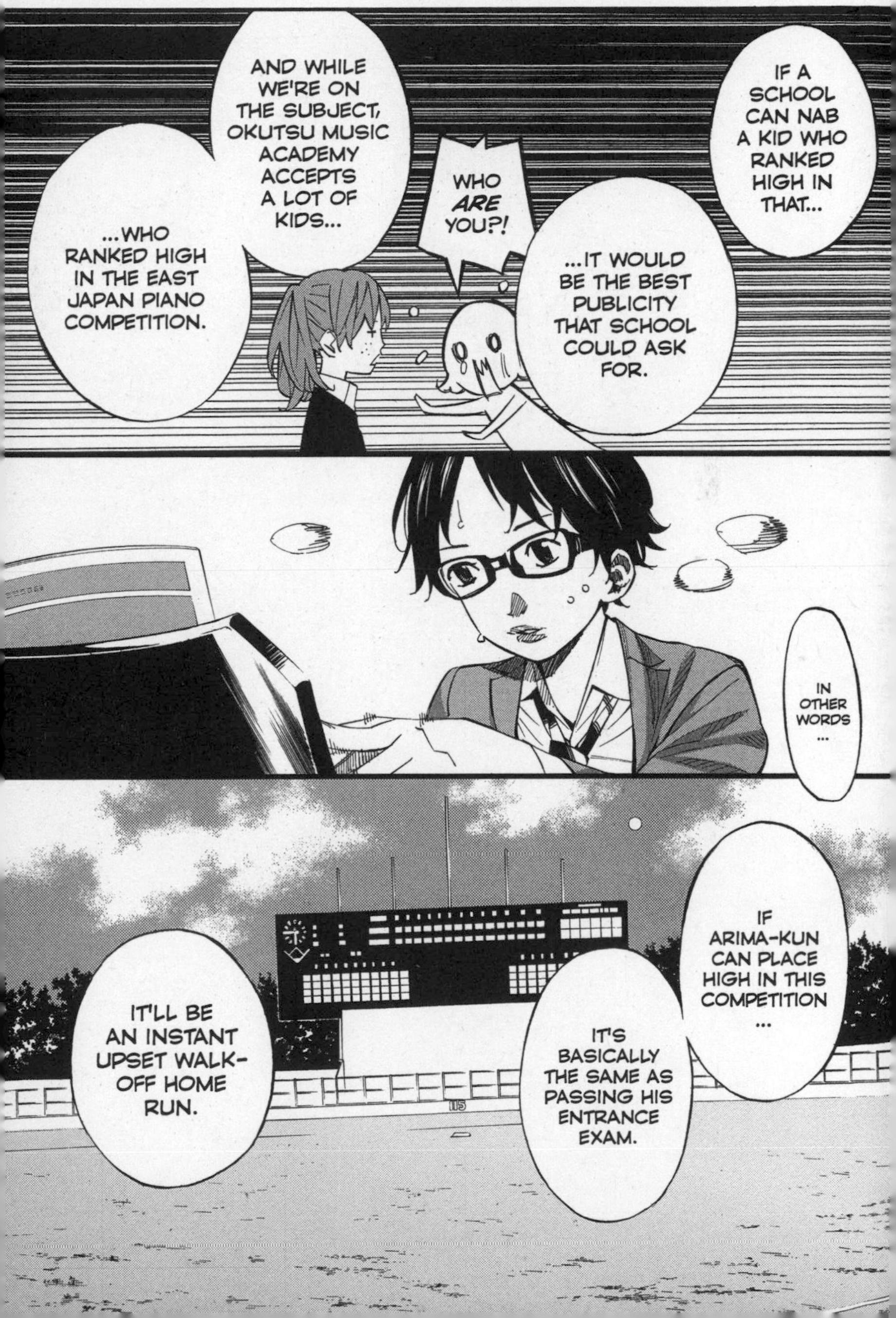
IF A SCHOOL CAN NAB A KID WHO RANKED HIGH IN THAT...
...IT WOULD BE THE BEST PUBLICITY THAT SCHOOL COULD ASK FOR.
WHO *ARE* YOU?!
AND WHILE WE'RE ON THE SUBJECT, OKUTSU MUSIC ACADEMY ACCEPTS A LOT OF KIDS...
...WHO RANKED HIGH IN THE EAST JAPAN PIANO COMPETITION.
IN OTHER WORDS...
IF ARIMA-KUN CAN PLACE HIGH IN THIS COMPETITION...
IT'S BASICALLY THE SAME AS PASSING HIS ENTRANCE EXAM.
IT'LL BE AN INSTANT UPSET WALK-OFF HOME RUN.

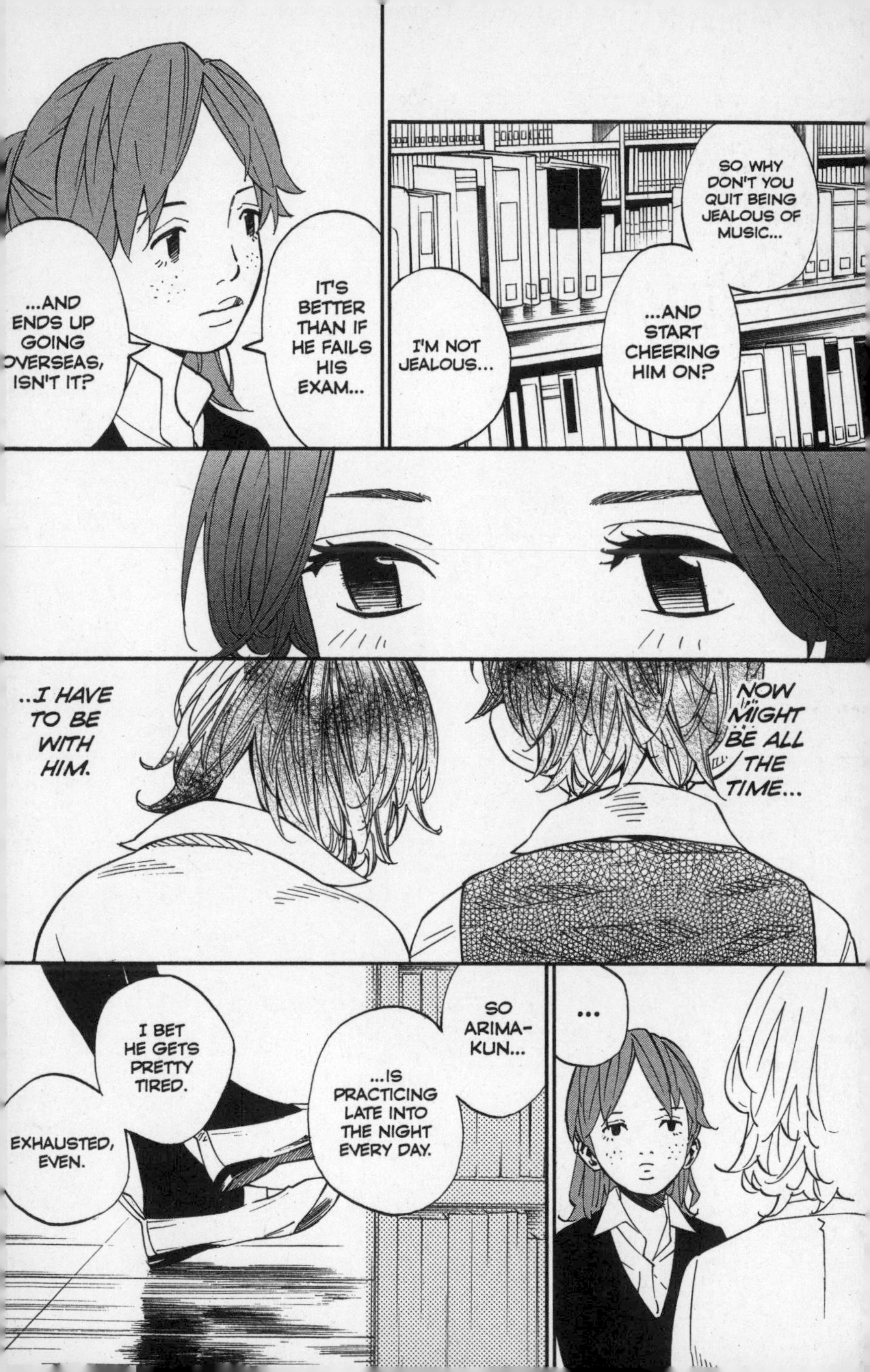
SO WHY DON'T YOU QUIT BEING JEALOUS OF MUSIC...
...AND START CHEERING HIM ON?
I'M NOT JEALOUS...
IT'S BETTER THAN IF HE FAILS HIS EXAM...
...AND ENDS UP GOING OVERSEAS, ISN'T IT?
NOW MIGHT BE ALL THE TIME...
...I HAVE TO BE WITH HIM.
...
SO ARIMA-KUN...
...IS PRACTICING LATE INTO THE NIGHT EVERY DAY.
I BET HE GETS PRETTY TIRED.
EXHAUSTED, EVEN.

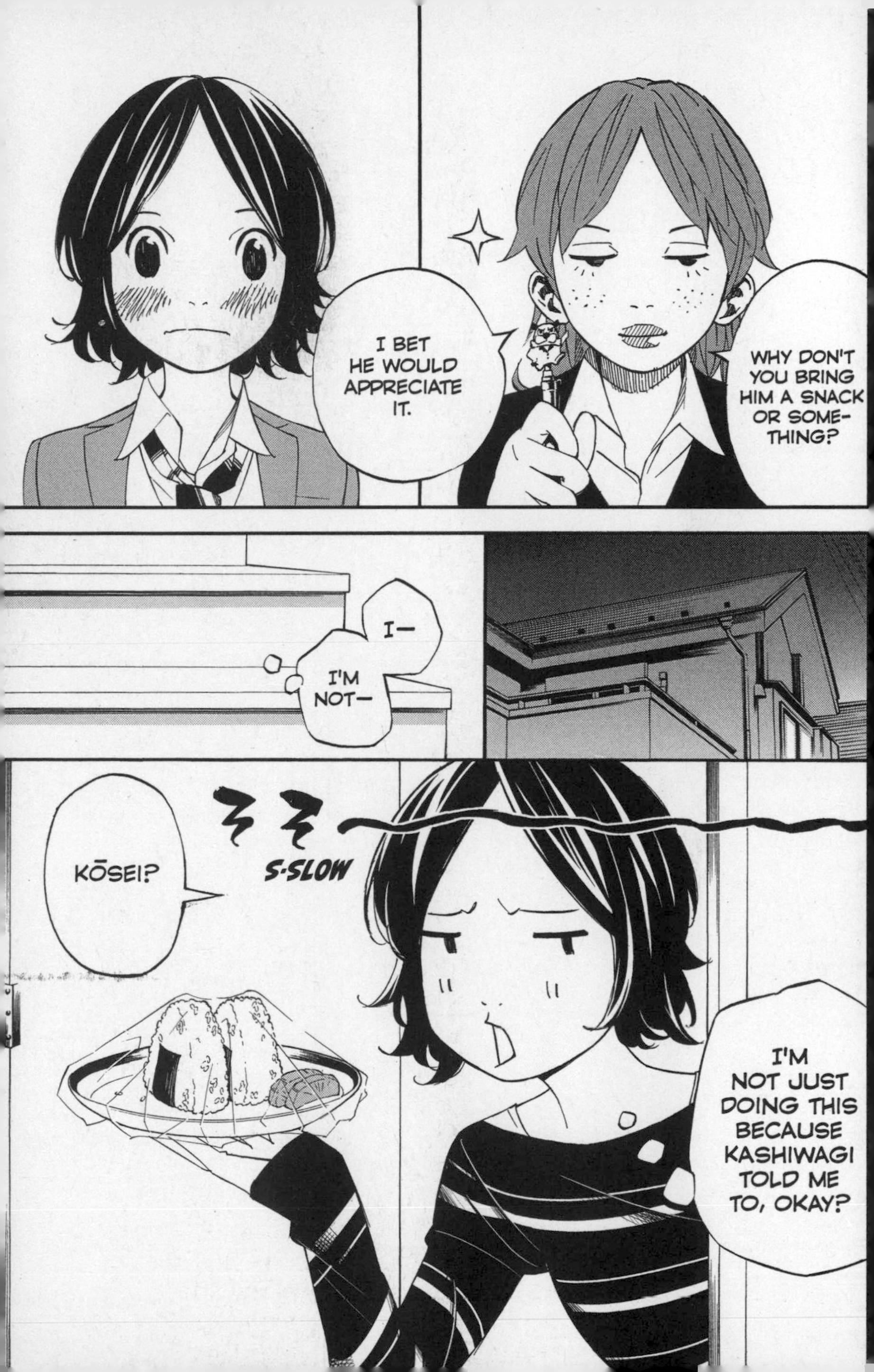
WHY DON'T YOU BRING HIM A SNACK OR SOME-THING?
I BET HE WOULD APPRECIATE IT.
I—
I'M NOT—
KŌSEI?
S-SLOW
I'M NOT JUST DOING THIS BECAUSE KASHIWAGI TOLD ME TO, OKAY?

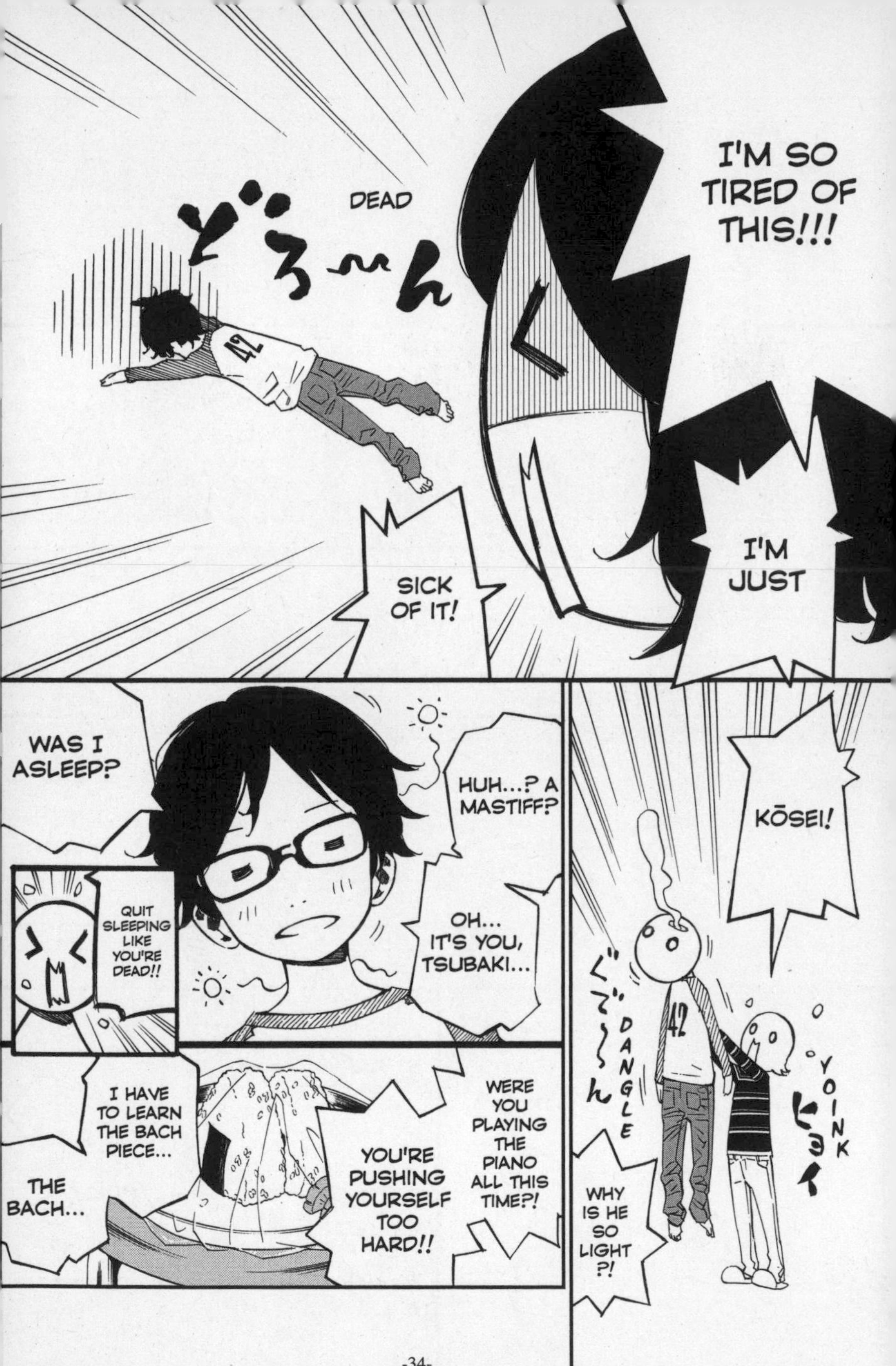
I'M SO TIRED OF THIS!!!
どろ〜ん
DEAD
I'M JUST
SICK OF IT!
KŌSEI!
ぐで〜ん
DANGLE
ヒョイ
YOINK
WHY IS HE SO LIGHT?!
HUH...? A MASTIFF?
OH... IT'S YOU, TSUBAKI...
WAS I ASLEEP?
QUIT SLEEPING LIKE YOU'RE DEAD!!
WERE YOU PLAYING THE PIANO ALL THIS TIME?!
YOU'RE PUSHING YOURSELF TOO HARD!!
I HAVE TO LEARN THE BACH PIECE...
THE BACH...

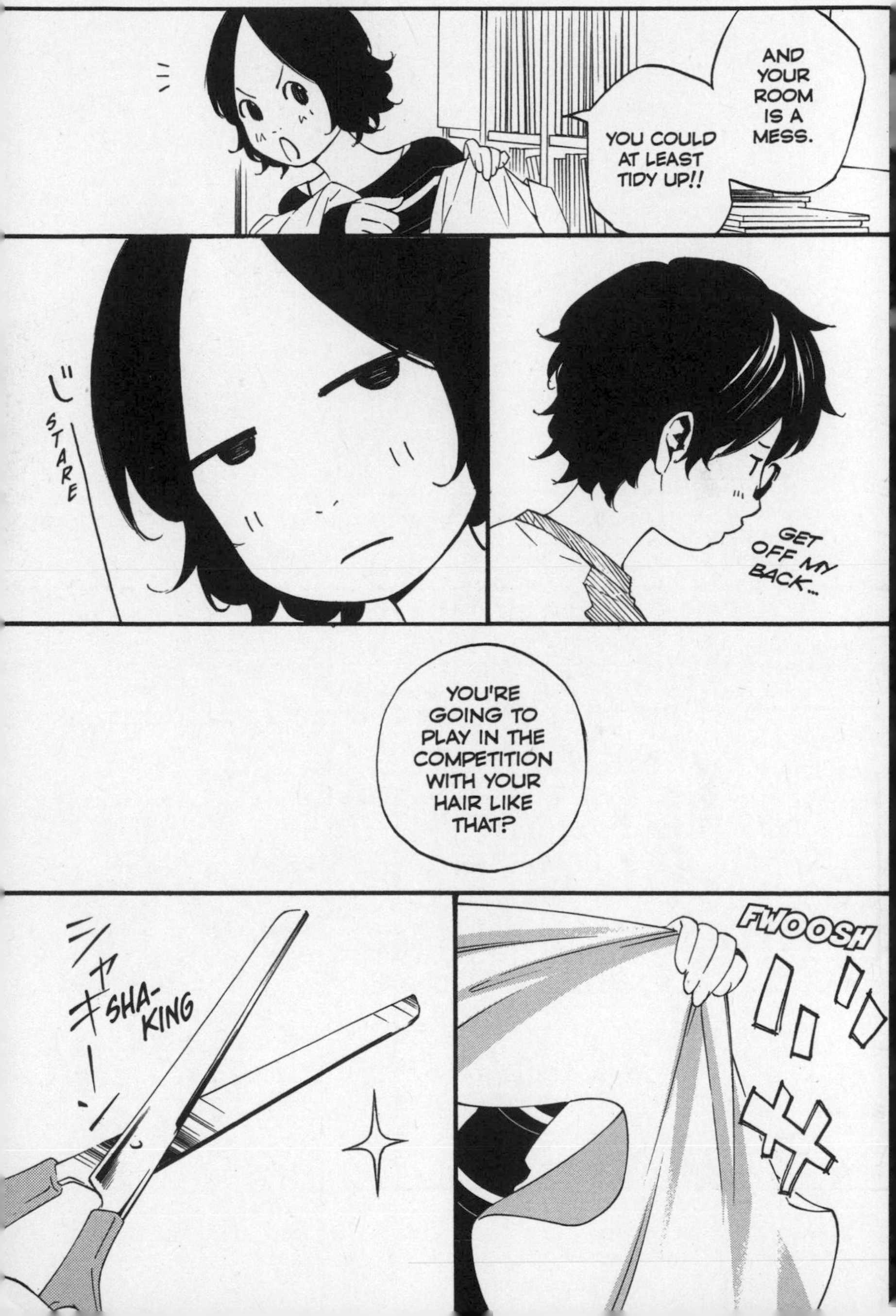
AND YOUR ROOM IS A MESS.
YOU COULD AT LEAST TIDY UP!!
GET OFF MY BACK...
じ
STARE
YOU'RE GOING TO PLAY IN THE COMPETITION WITH YOUR HAIR LIKE THAT?
FWOOSH
SHA-KING

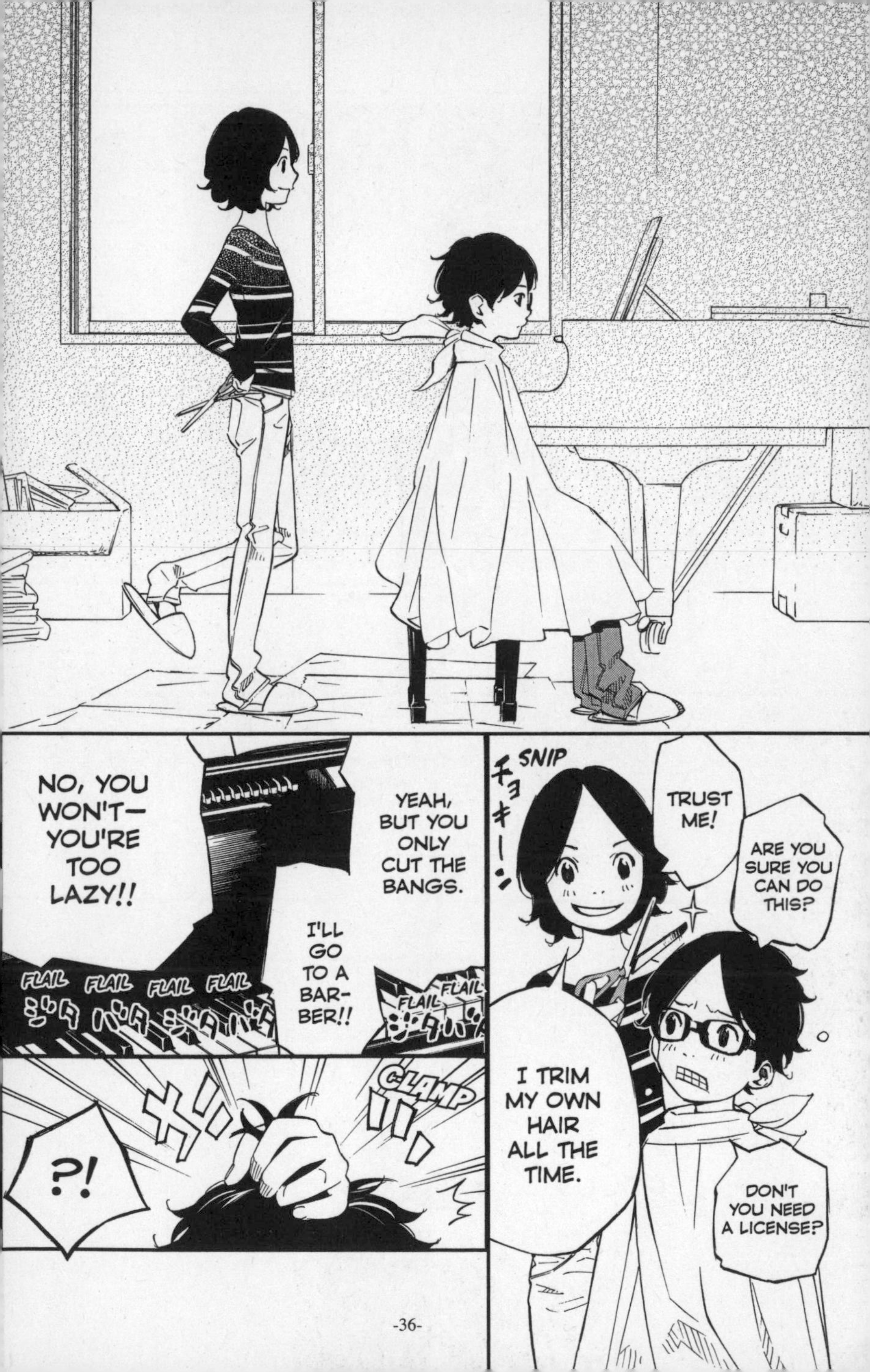
ARE YOU SURE YOU CAN DO THIS?
TRUST ME!
SNIP
DON'T YOU NEED A LICENSE?
I TRIM MY OWN HAIR ALL THE TIME.
YEAH, BUT YOU ONLY CUT THE BANGS.
I'LL GO TO A BAR-BER!!
NO, YOU WON'T—YOU'RE TOO LAZY!!
FLAIL FLAIL
FLAIL FLAIL FLAIL FLAIL
CLAMP
?!

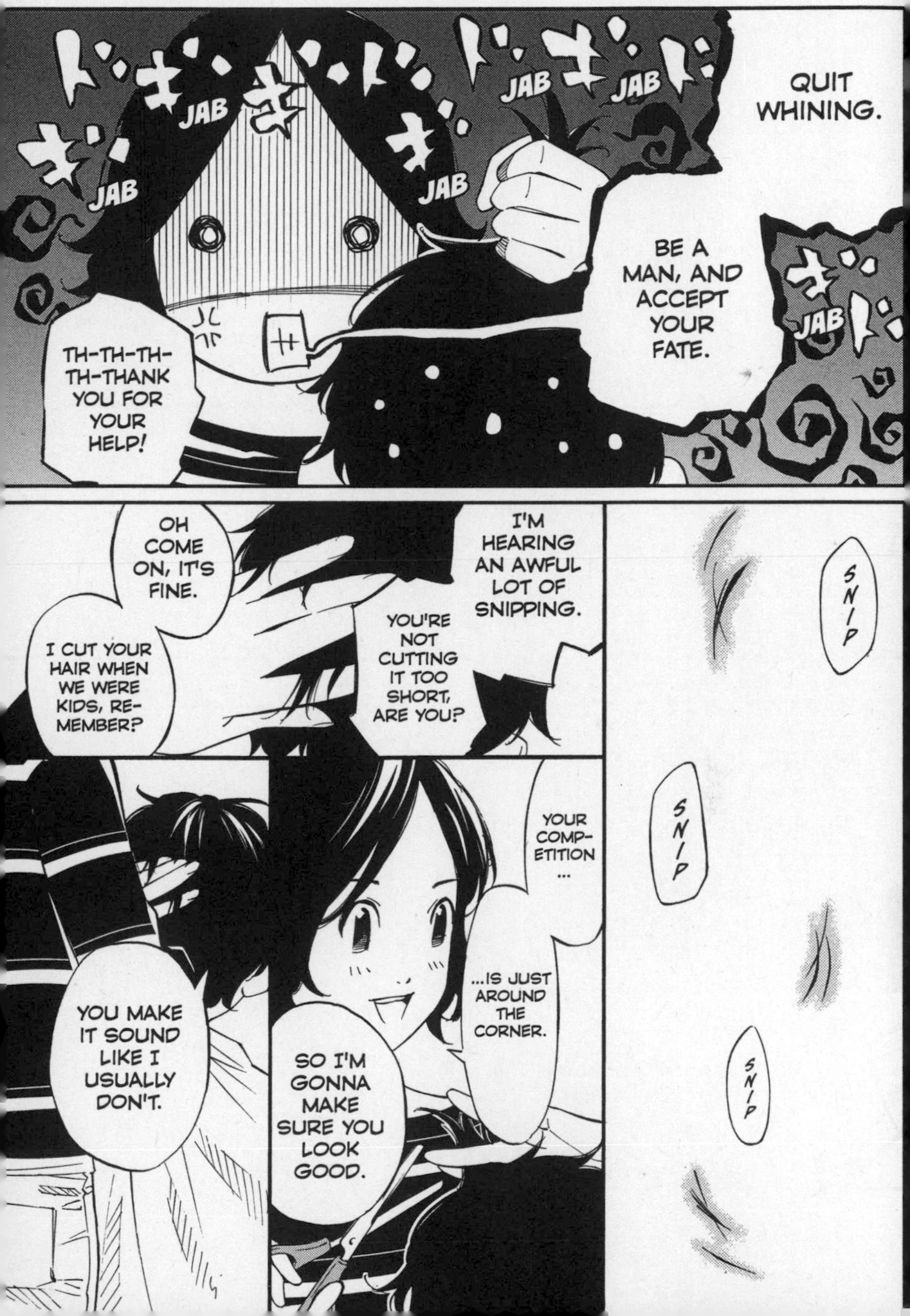
QUIT WHINING.
BE A MAN, AND ACCEPT YOUR FATE.
JAB
JAB
JAB
JAB
JAB
JAB
TH-TH-TH-TH-THANK YOU FOR YOUR HELP!
SNIP
SNIP
SNIP
I'M HEARING AN AWFUL LOT OF SNIPPING.
YOU'RE NOT CUTTING IT TOO SHORT, ARE YOU?
OH COME ON, IT'S FINE.
I CUT YOUR HAIR WHEN WE WERE KIDS, RE-MEMBER?
YOUR COMP-ETITION ...
...IS JUST AROUND THE CORNER.
SO I'M GONNA MAKE SURE YOU LOOK GOOD.
YOU MAKE IT SOUND LIKE I USUALLY DON'T.

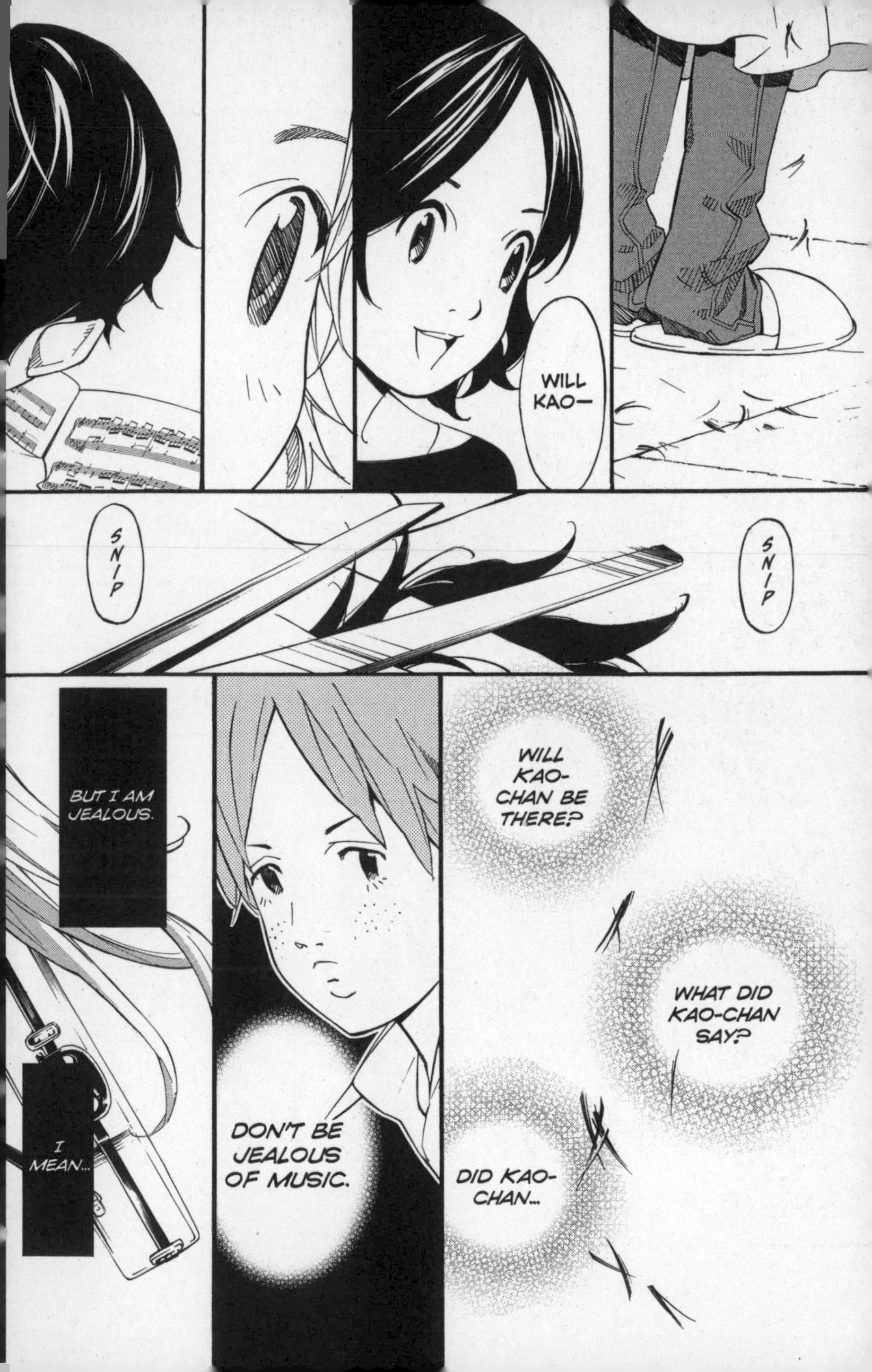
WILL KAO—
SNIP
SNIP
WILL KAO-CHAN BE THERE?
WHAT DID KAO-CHAN SAY?
DID KAO-CHAN...
DON'T BE JEALOUS OF MUSIC.
BUT I AM JEALOUS.
I MEAN...

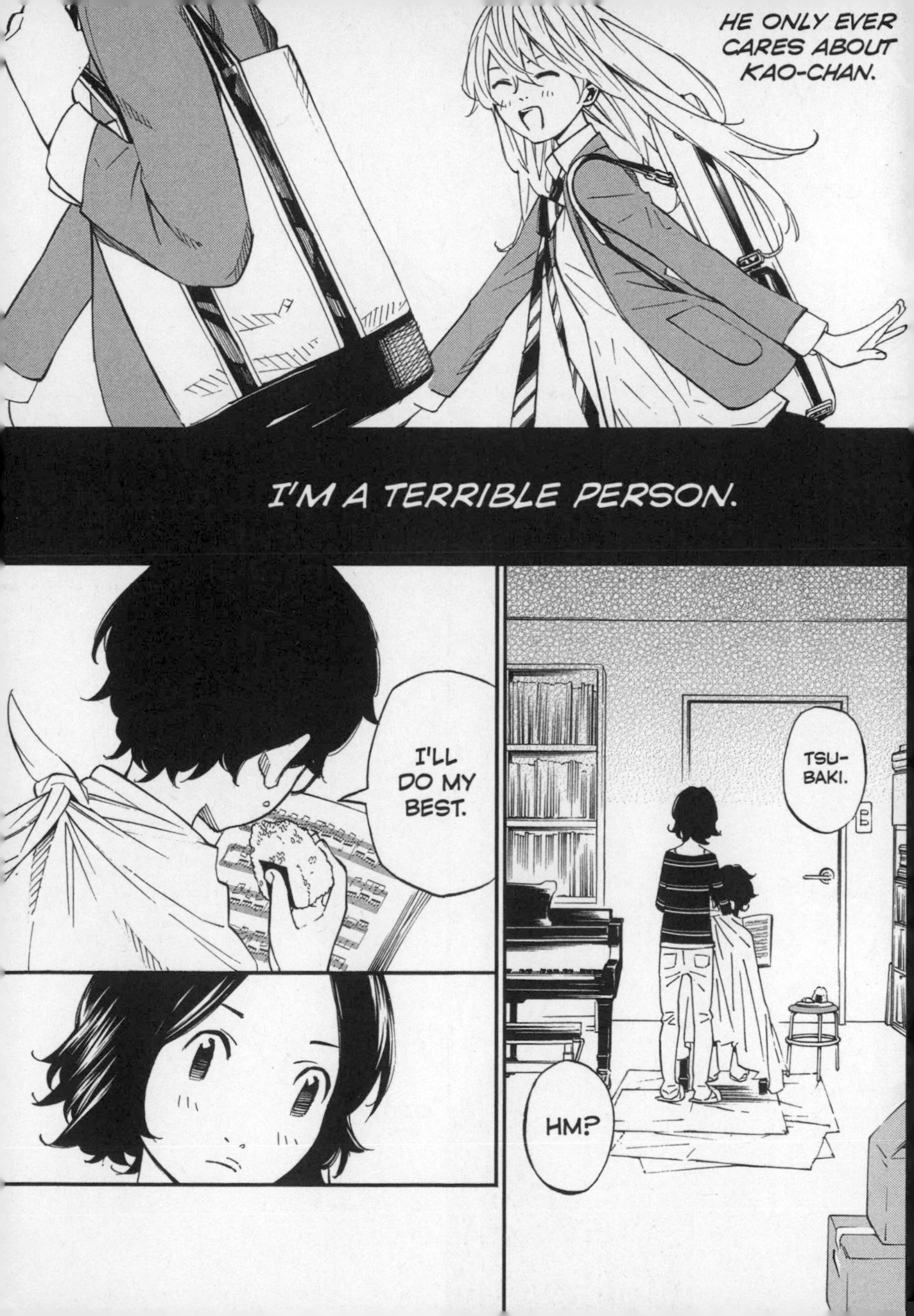
HE ONLY EVER CARES ABOUT KAO-CHAN.
I'M A TERRIBLE PERSON.
TSU-BAKI.
HM?
I'LL DO MY BEST.

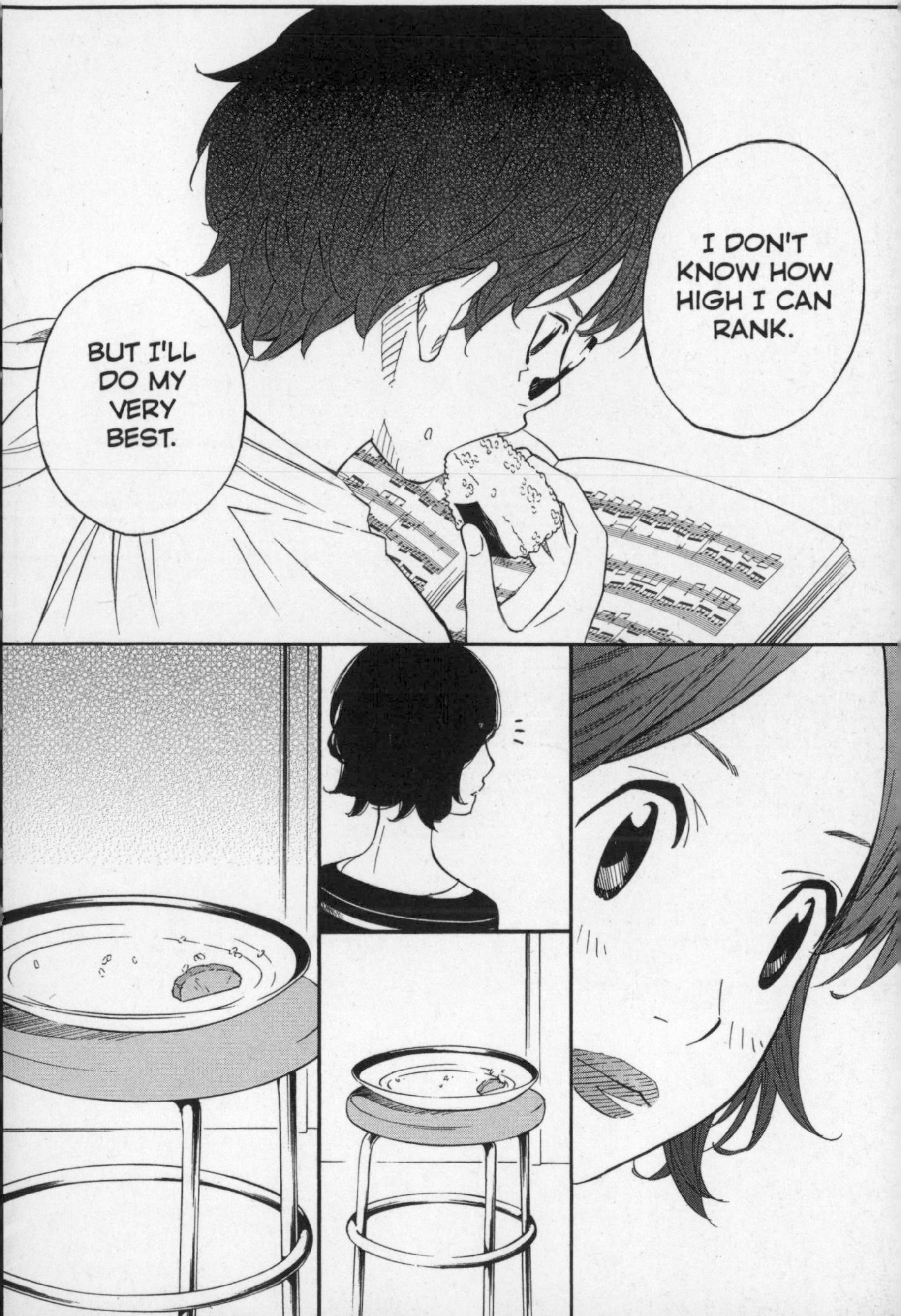
I DON'T KNOW HOW HIGH I CAN RANK.
BUT I'LL DO MY VERY BEST.

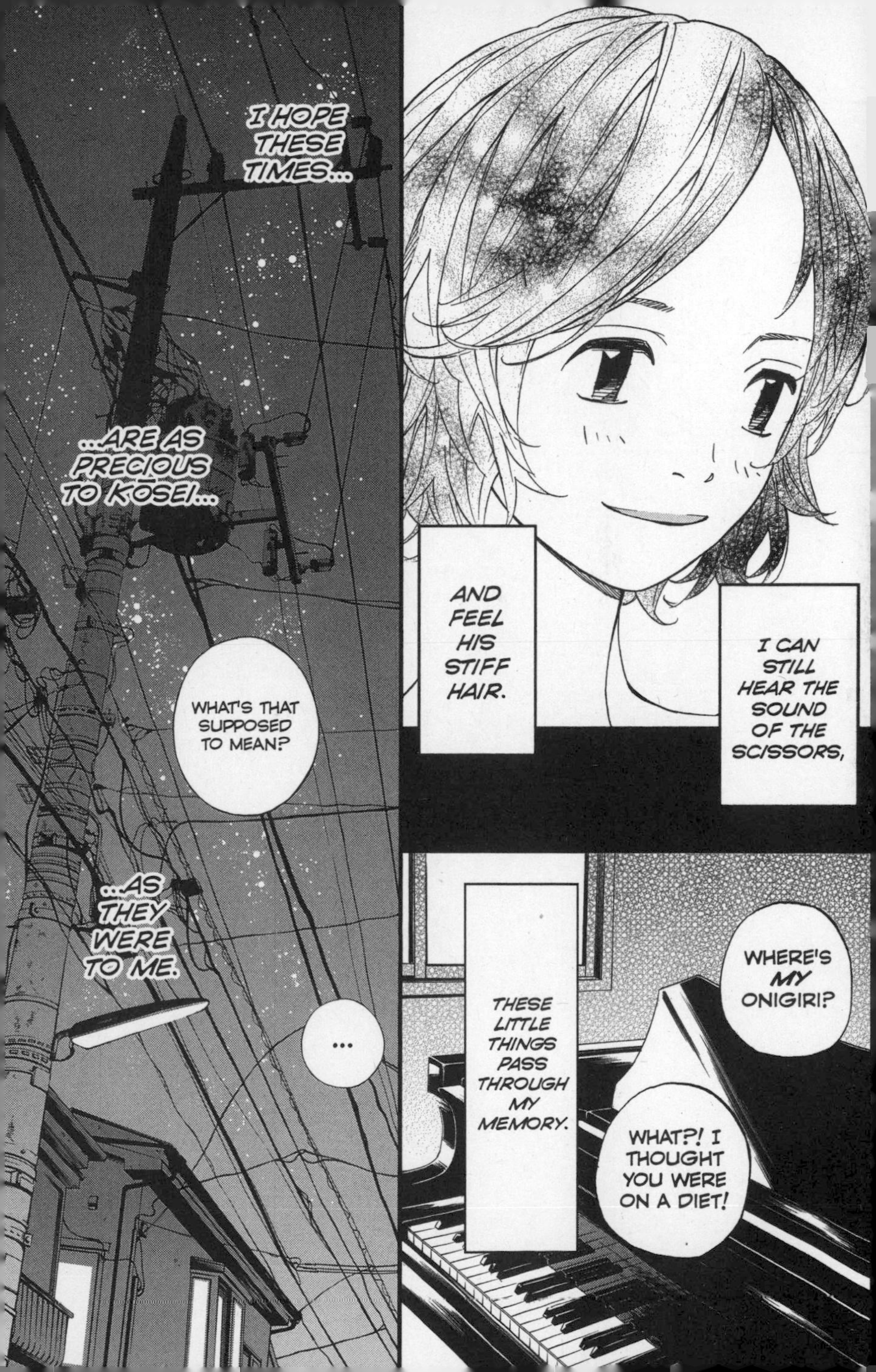
I CAN STILL HEAR THE SOUND OF THE SCISSORS,
AND FEEL HIS STIFF HAIR.
WHERE'S MY ONIGIRI?
WHAT?! I THOUGHT YOU WERE ON A DIET!
THESE LITTLE THINGS PASS THROUGH MY MEMORY.
I HOPE THESE TIMES...
...ARE AS PRECIOUS TO KŌSEI...
WHAT'S THAT SUPPOSED TO MEAN?
...AS THEY WERE TO ME.
...

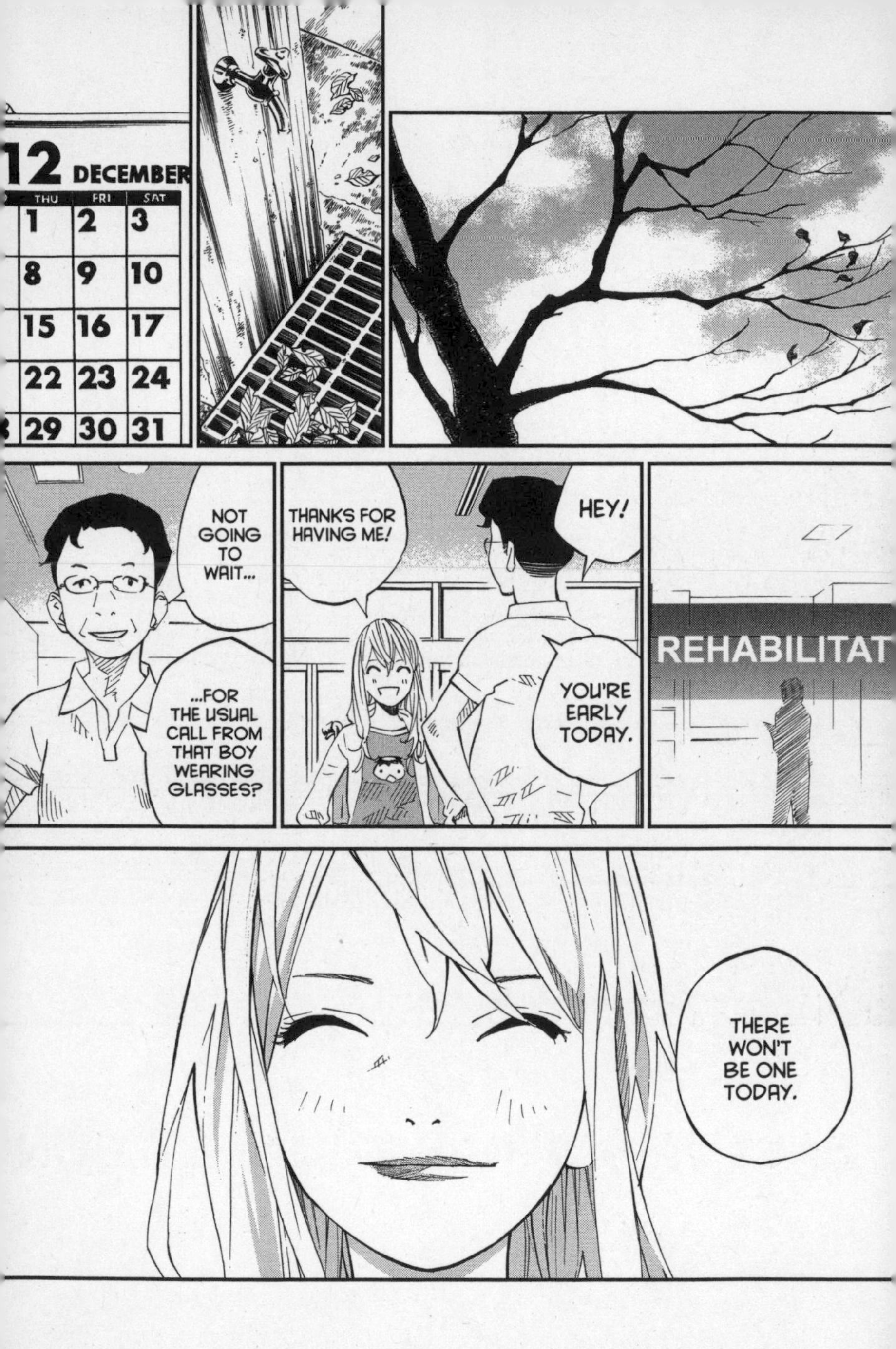
12 DECEMBER
THU FRI SAT
1 2 3
8 9 10
15 16 17
22 23 24
29 30 31
REHABILITAT
HEY!
YOU'RE EARLY TODAY.
THANKS FOR HAVING ME!
NOT GOING TO WAIT...
...FOR THE USUAL CALL FROM THAT BOY WEARING GLASSES?
THERE WON'T BE ONE TODAY.

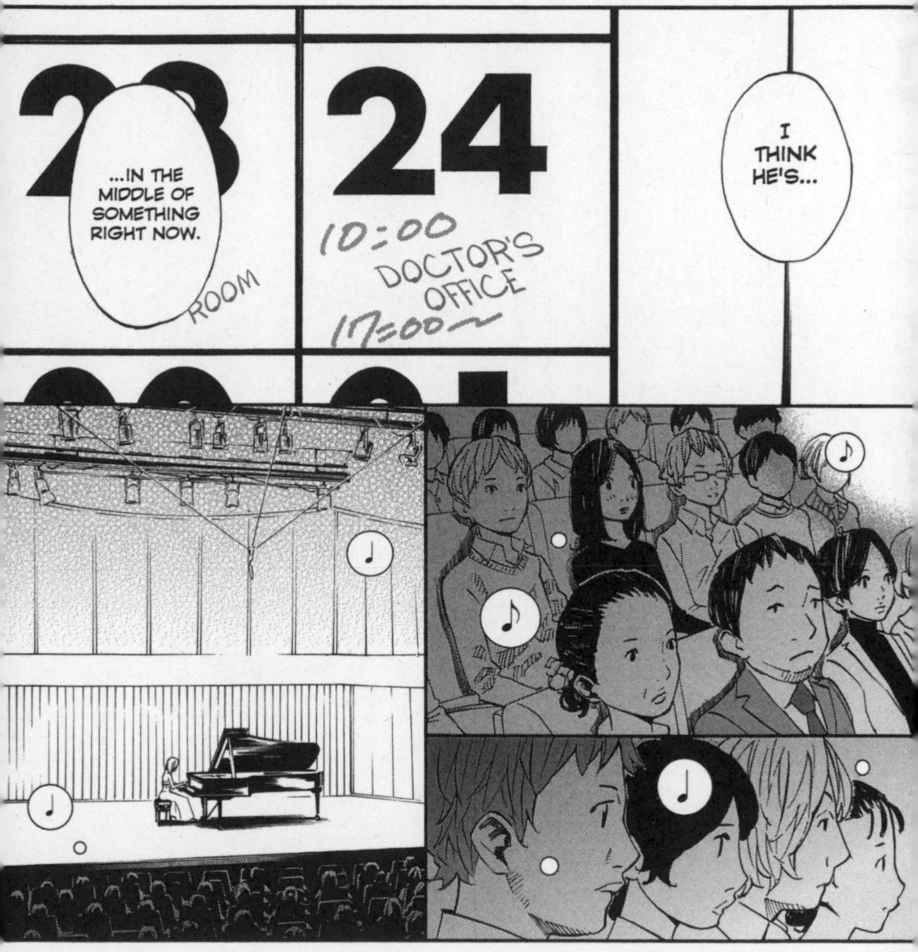
I THINK HE'S...
24
10:00
DOCTOR'S OFFICE
17:00~
...IN THE MIDDLE OF SOMETHING RIGHT NOW.
ROOM

EAST JAPAN PIANO COMPETITION

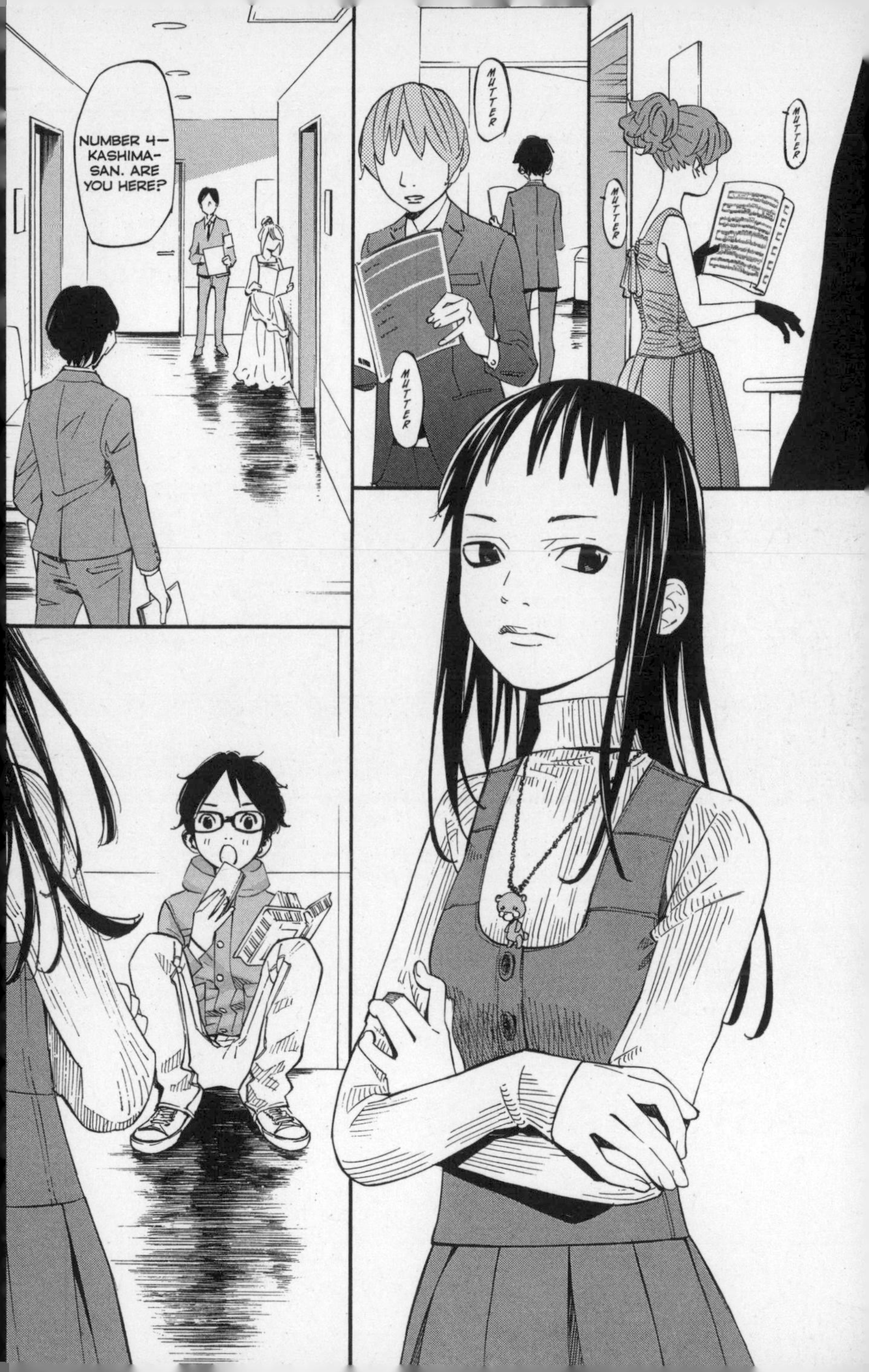
MUTTER
MUTTER
MUTTER
MUTTER
NUMBER 4—KASHIMA-SAN. ARE YOU HERE?

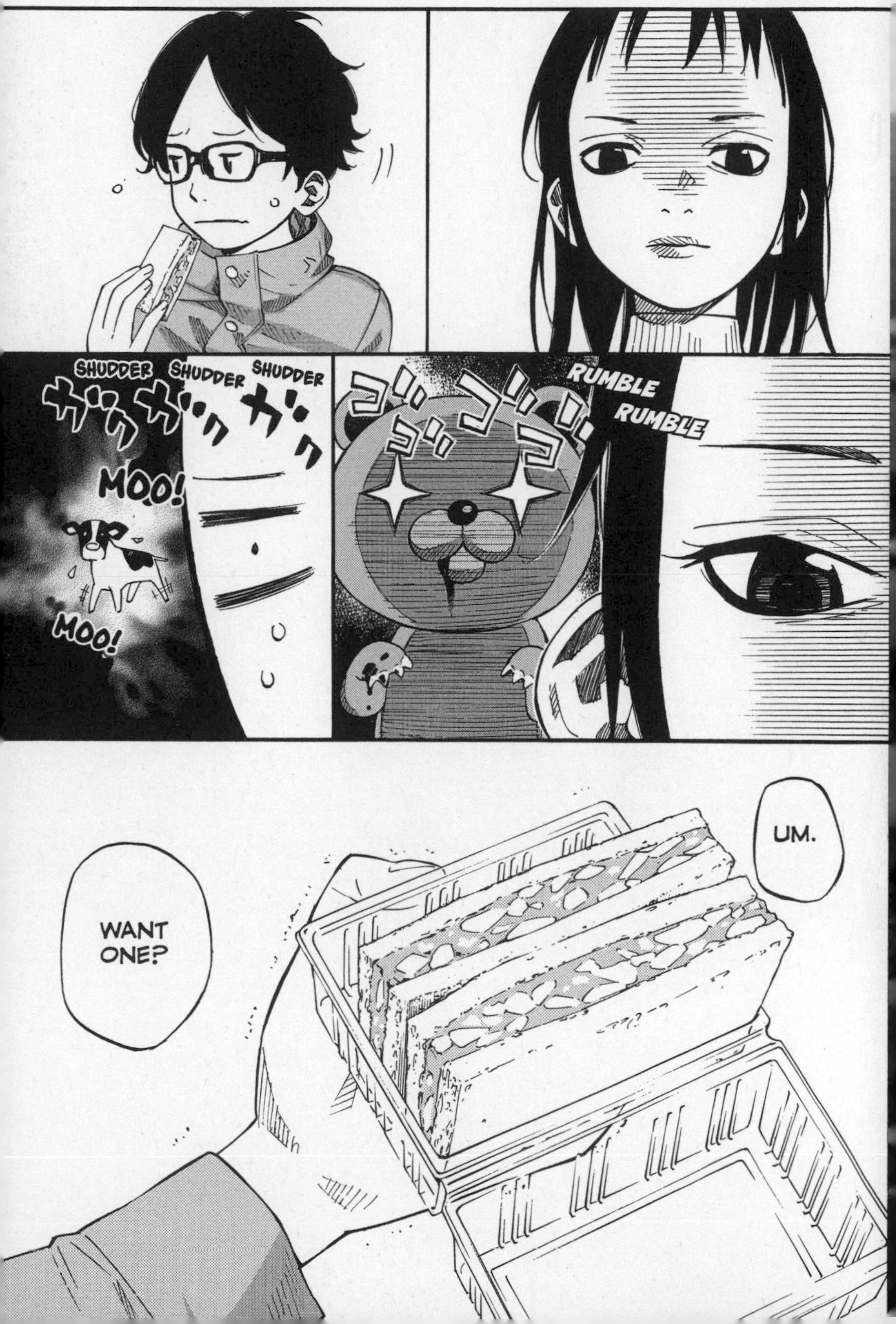
RUMBLE
RUMBLE
SHUDDER
SHUDDER
SHUDDER
MOO!
MOO!
UM.
WANT ONE?

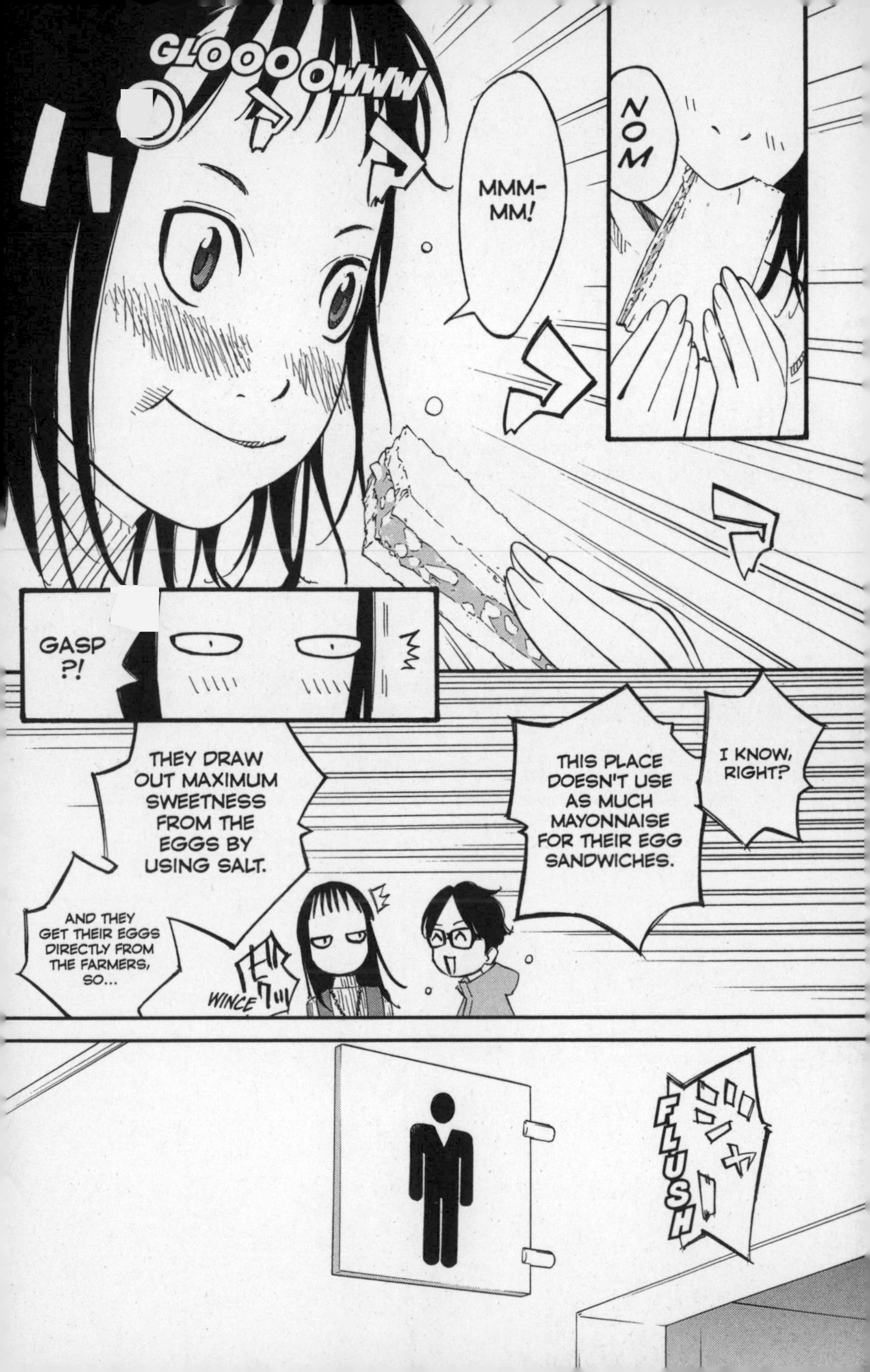
NOM
MMM-MM!
GLOOOOWWW
GASP ?!
I KNOW, RIGHT?
THIS PLACE DOESN'T USE AS MUCH MAYONNAISE FOR THEIR EGG SANDWICHES.
THEY DRAW OUT MAXIMUM SWEETNESS FROM THE EGGS BY USING SALT.
AND THEY GET THEIR EGGS DIRECTLY FROM THE FARMERS, SO...
WINCE
FLUSH

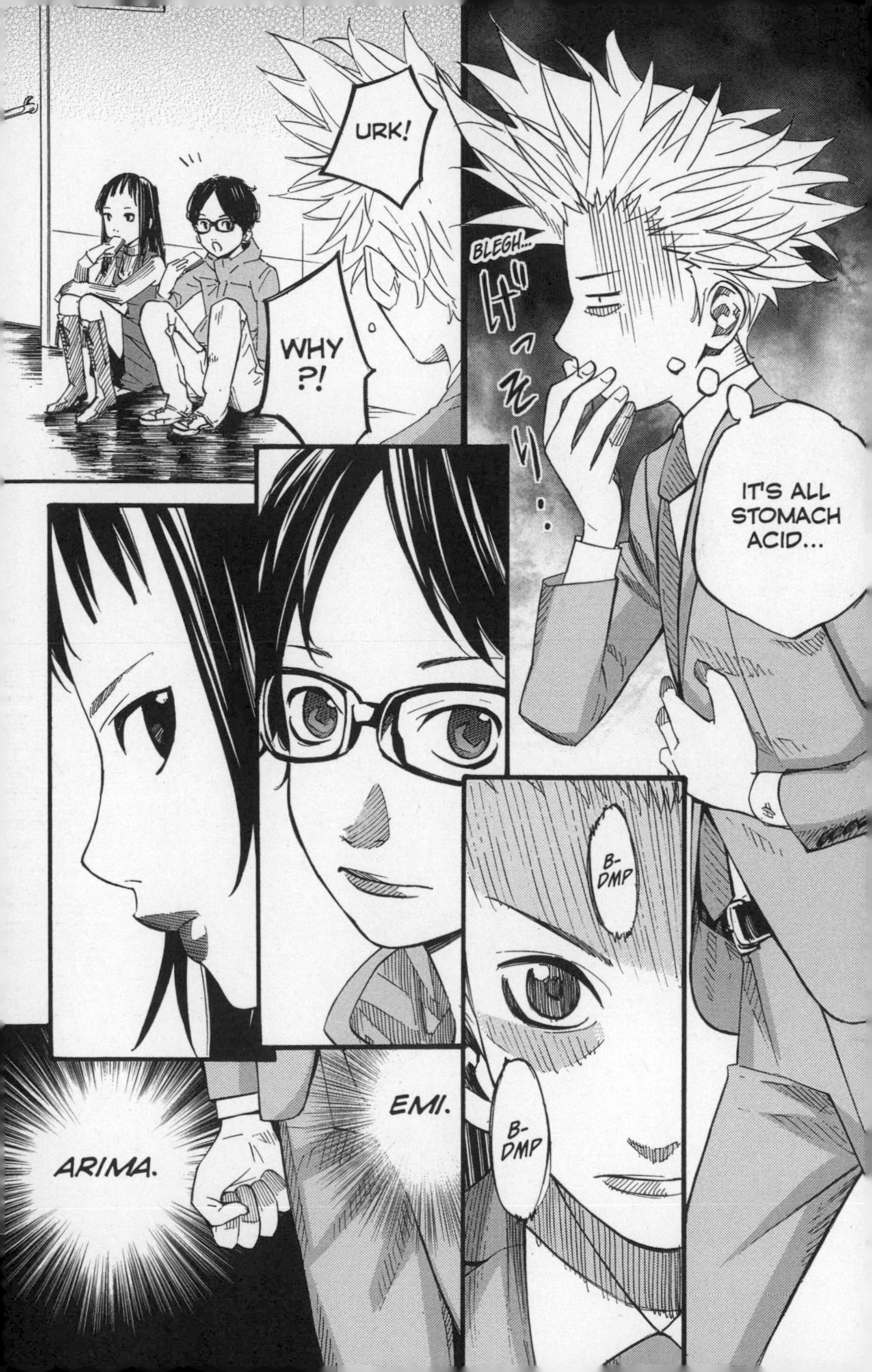
BLEGH...
IT'S ALL STOMACH ACID...
URK!
WHY?!
B-DMP
B-DMP
EMI.
ARIMA.

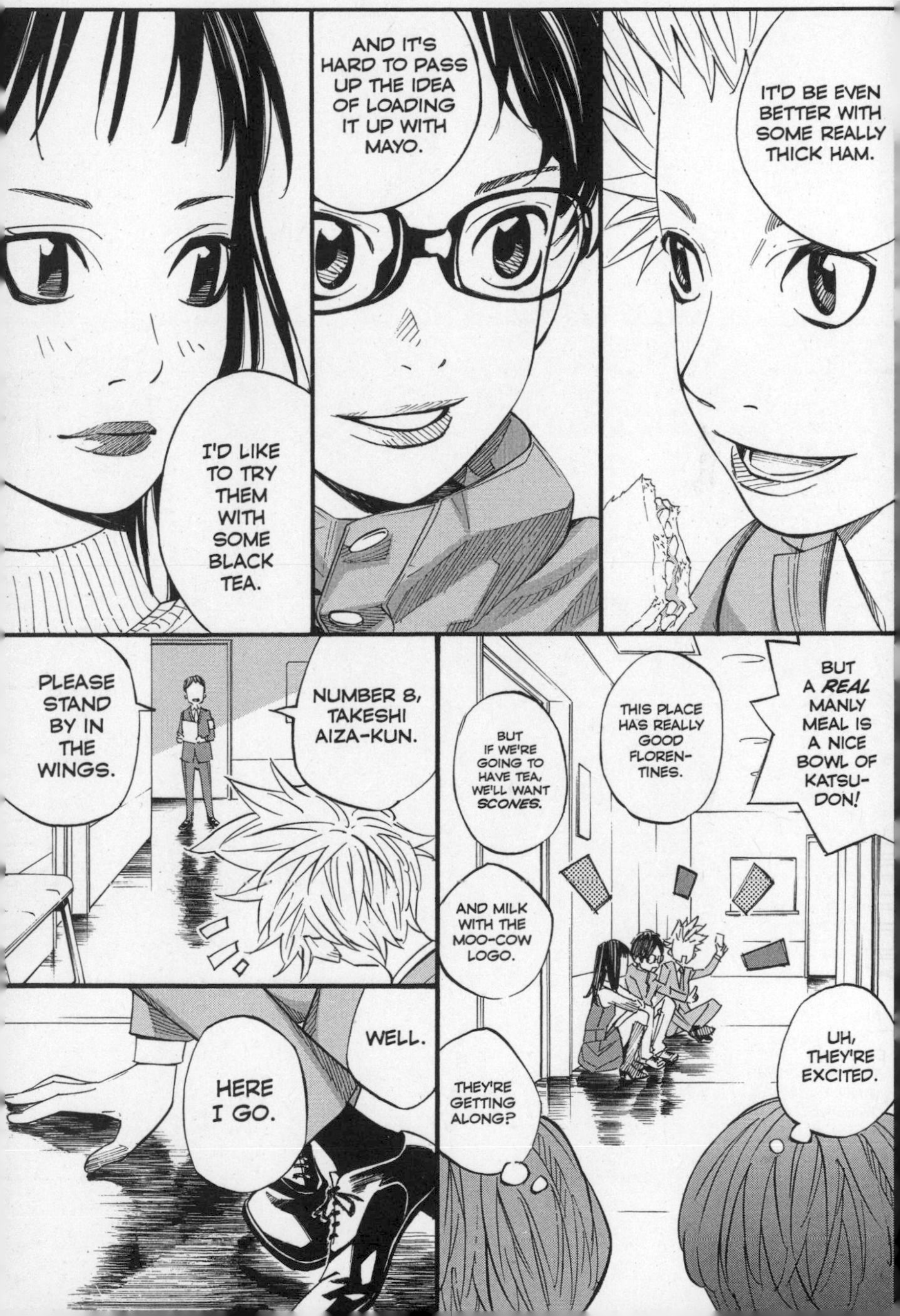
IT'D BE EVEN BETTER WITH SOME REALLY THICK HAM.
AND IT'S HARD TO PASS UP THE IDEA OF LOADING IT UP WITH MAYO.
I'D LIKE TO TRY THEM WITH SOME BLACK TEA.
BUT A *REAL* MANLY MEAL IS A NICE BOWL OF KATSU-DON!
THIS PLACE HAS REALLY GOOD FLOREN-TINES.
BUT IF WE'RE GOING TO HAVE TEA, WE'LL WANT *SCONES*.
AND MILK WITH THE MOO-COW LOGO.
UH, THEY'RE EXCITED.
THEY'RE GETTING ALONG?
NUMBER 8, TAKESHI AIZA-KUN.
PLEASE STAND BY IN THE WINGS.
WELL.
HERE I GO.

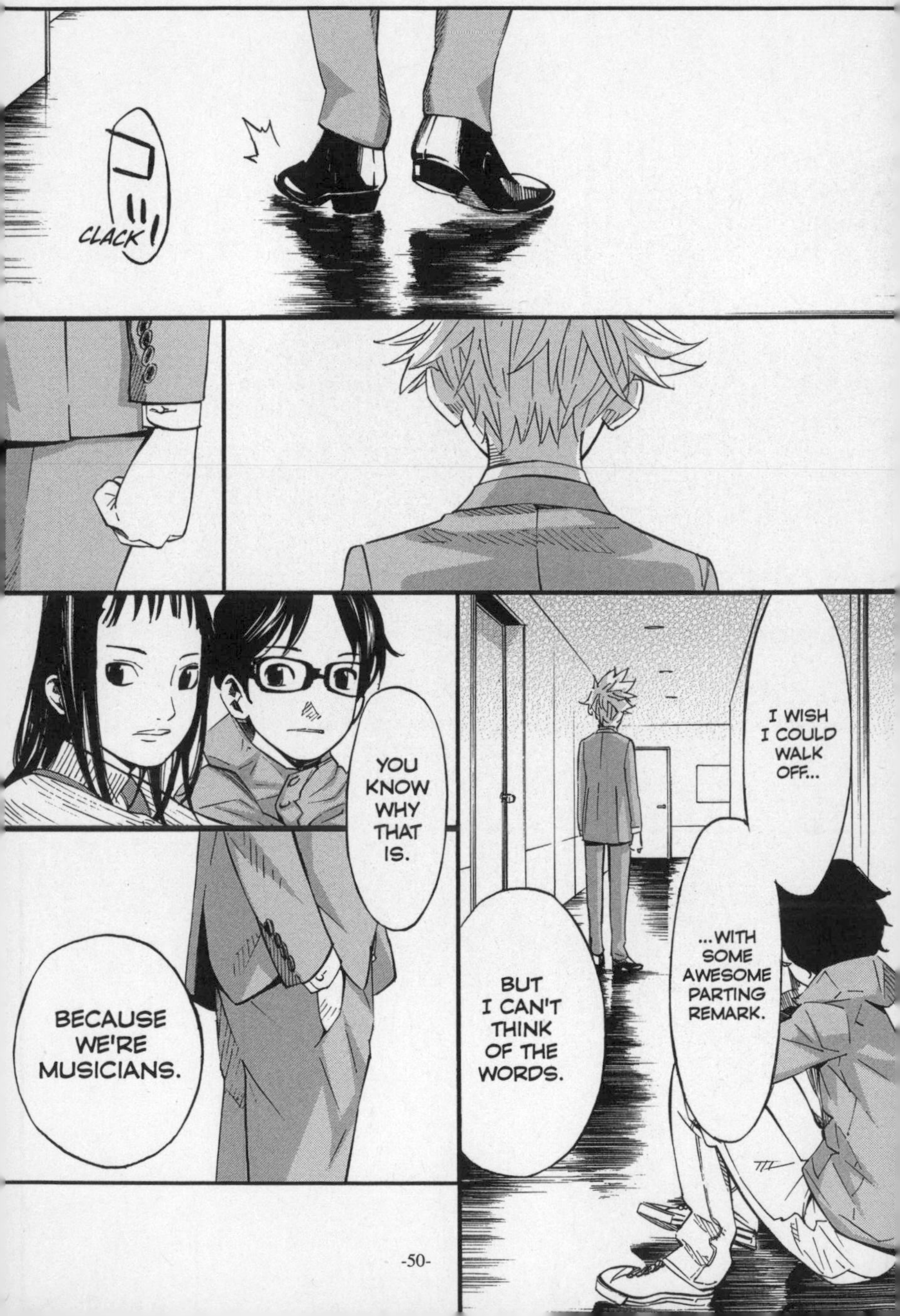
CLACK
I WISH I COULD WALK OFF...
...WITH SOME AWESOME PARTING REMARK.
BUT I CAN'T THINK OF THE WORDS.
YOU KNOW WHY THAT IS.
BECAUSE WE'RE MUSICIANS.

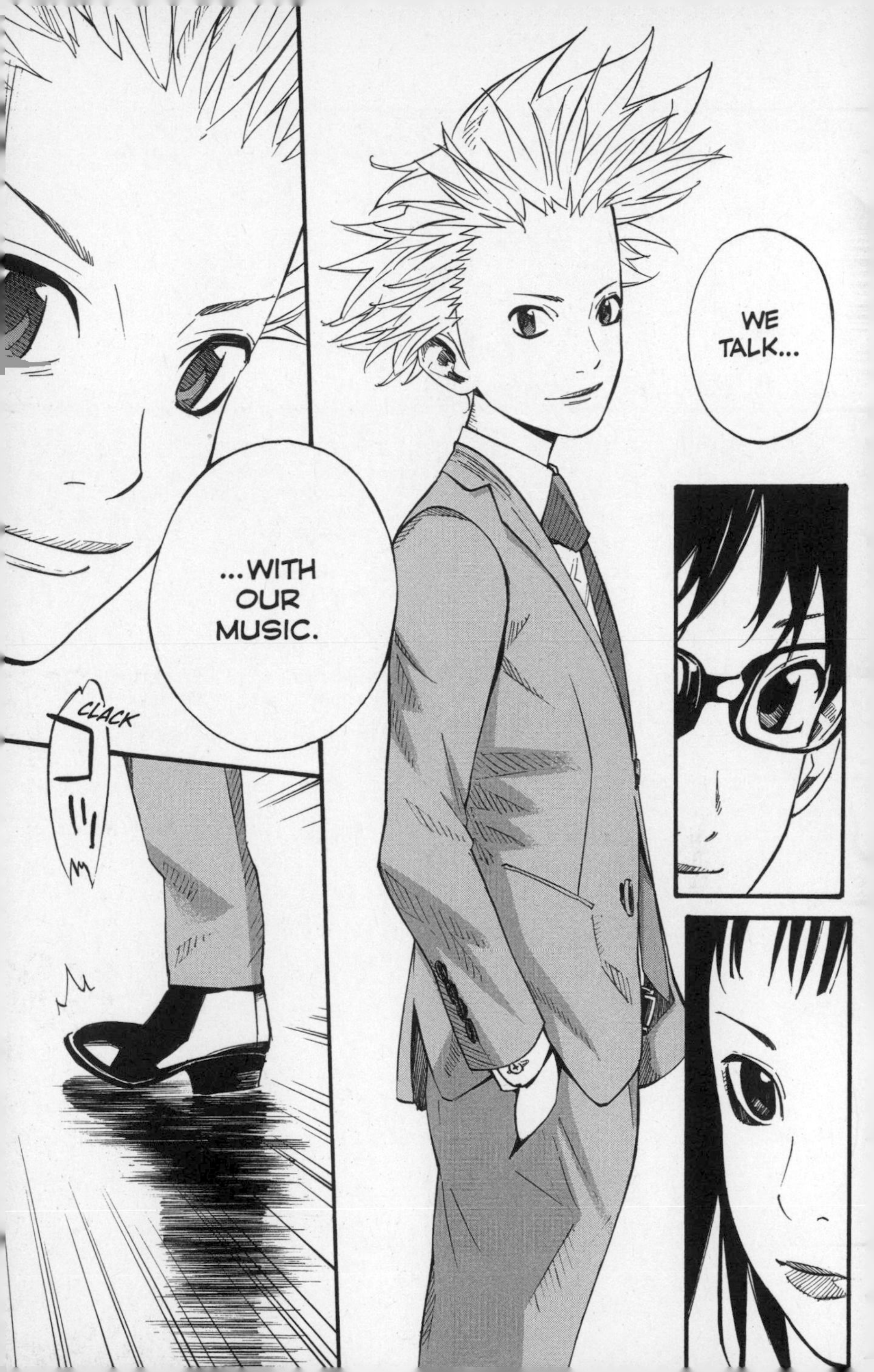
WE TALK...
...WITH OUR MUSIC.
CLACK

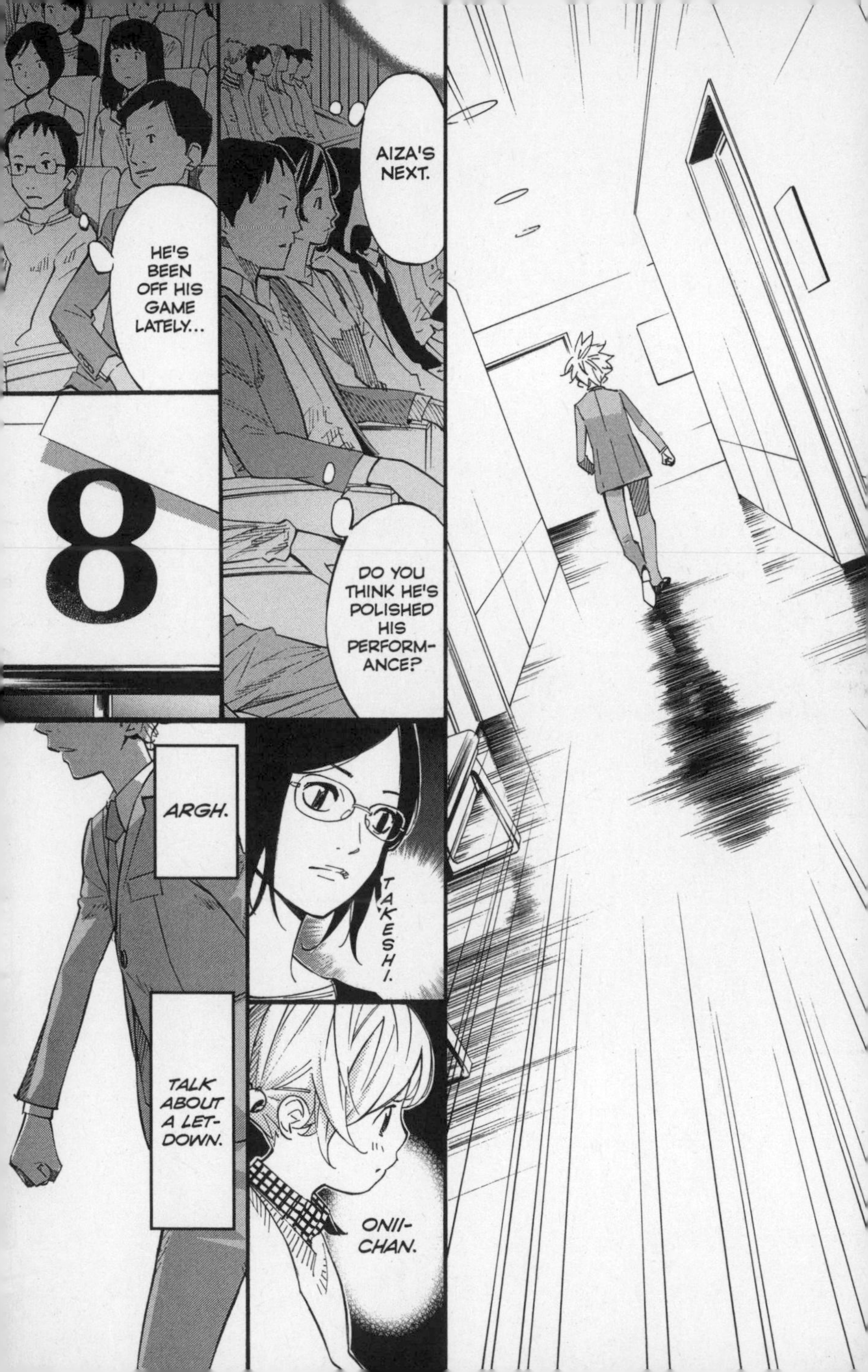
AIZA'S NEXT.
DO YOU THINK HE'S POLISHED HIS PERFORMANCE?
HE'S BEEN OFF HIS GAME LATELY...
8
TAKESHI.
ONII-CHAN.
ARGH.
TALK ABOUT A LET-DOWN.

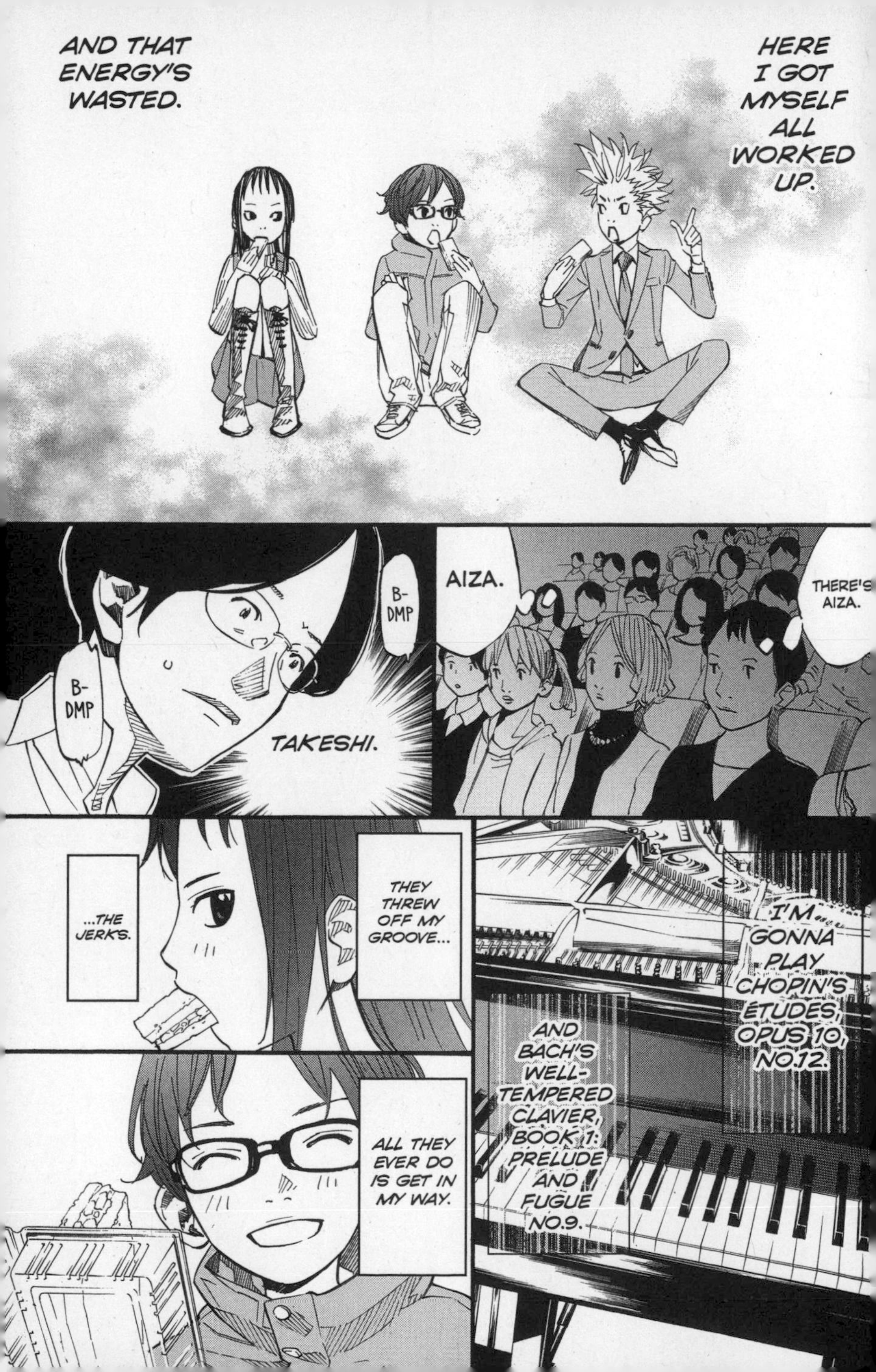
HERE I GOT MYSELF ALL WORKED UP.
AND THAT ENERGY'S WASTED.
THERE'S AIZA.
AIZA.
B-DMP
B-DMP
TAKESHI.
I'M GONNA PLAY CHOPIN'S ÉTUDES, OPUS 10, NO.12.
AND BACH'S WELL-TEMPERED CLAVIER, BOOK 1: PRELUDE AND FUGUE NO.9.
THEY THREW OFF MY GROOVE...
...THE JERKS.
ALL THEY EVER DO IS GET IN MY WAY.

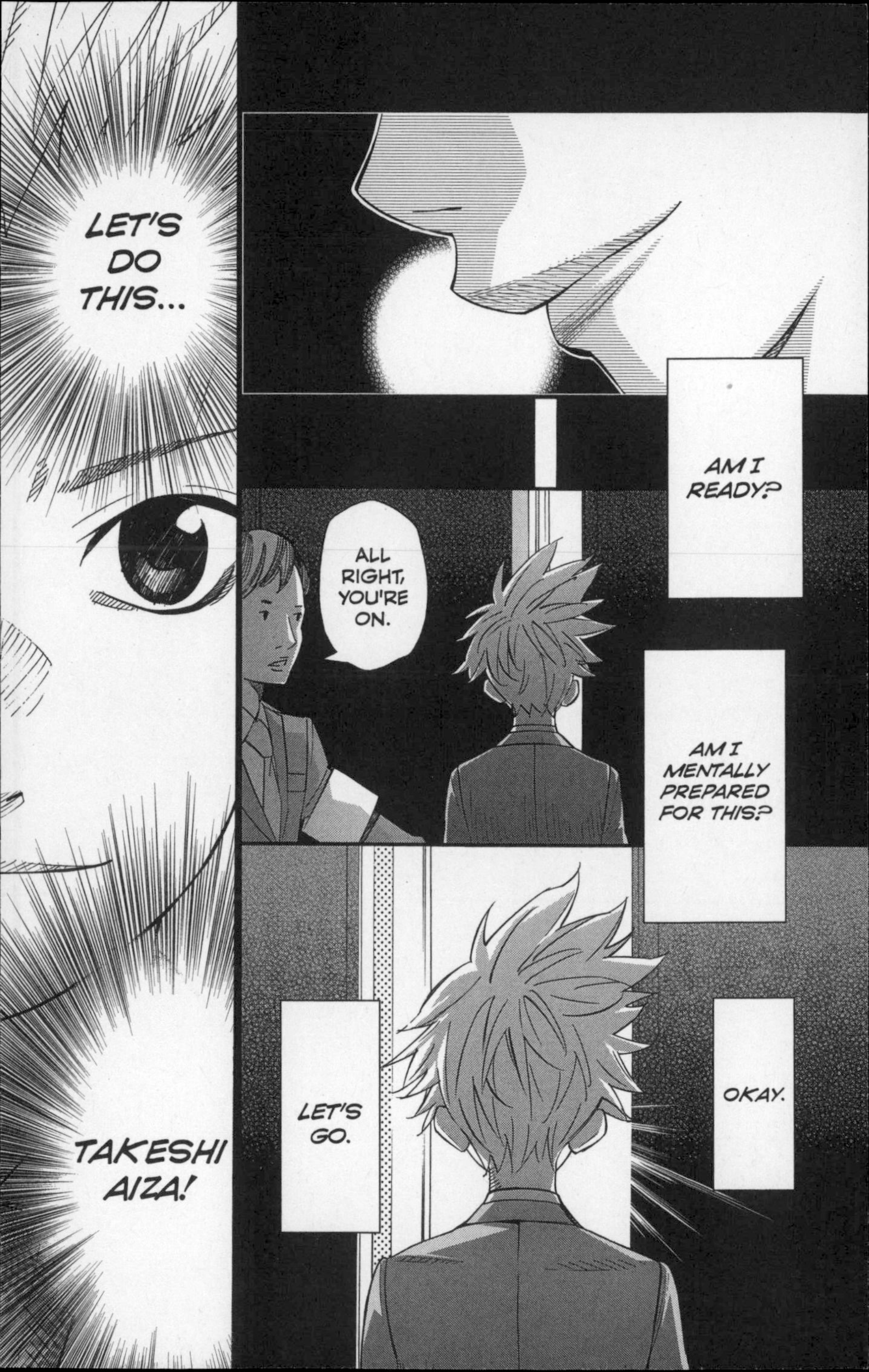
AM I READY?
ALL RIGHT, YOU'RE ON.
AM I MENTALLY PREPARED FOR THIS?
OKAY.
LET'S GO.
LET'S DO THIS...
TAKESHI AIZA!

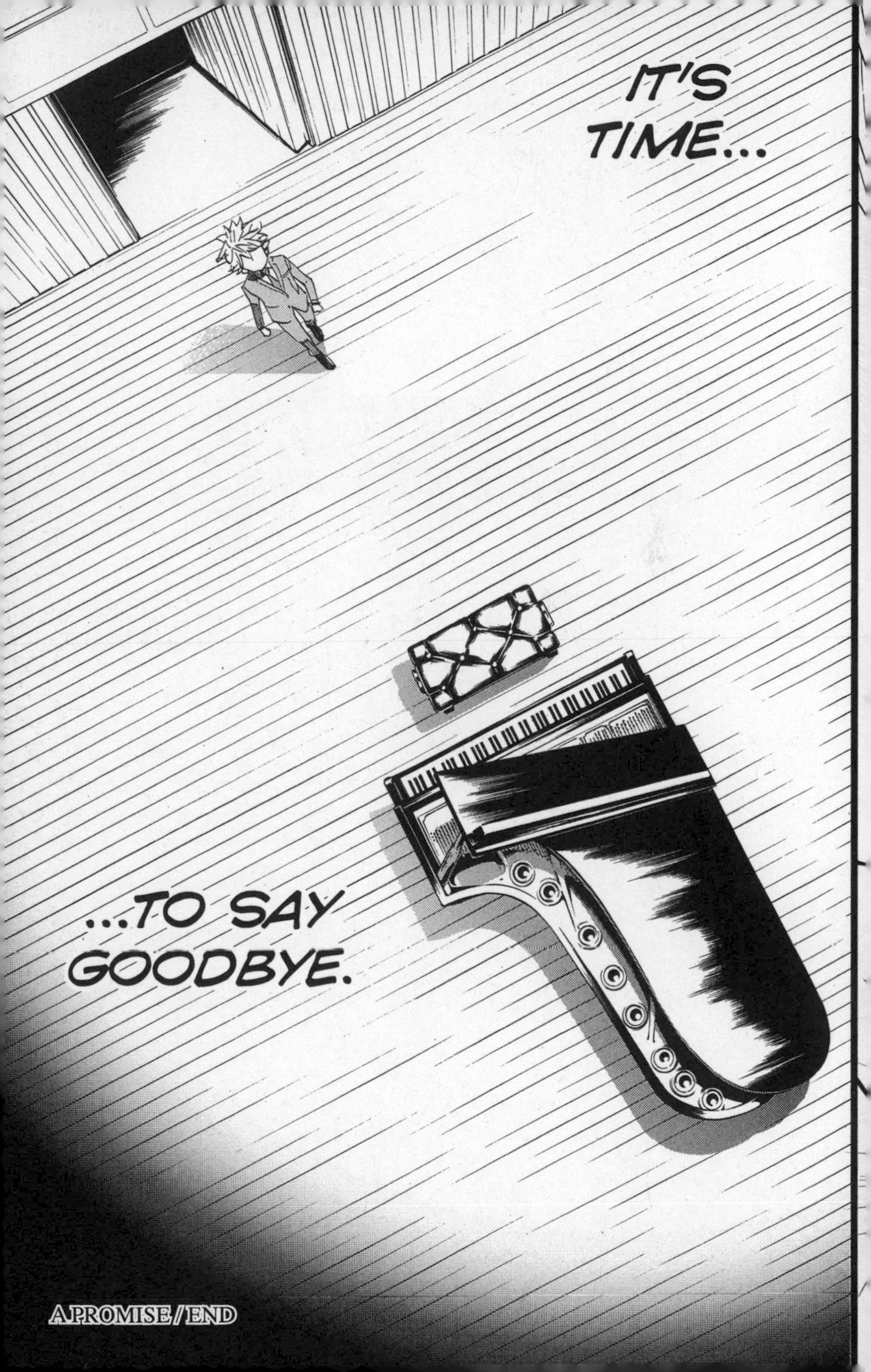
IT'S TIME...
...TO SAY GOODBYE.
A PROMISE / END

Your Lie in April

I met the girl under full-bloomed cherry blossoms, and my fate has begun to change.

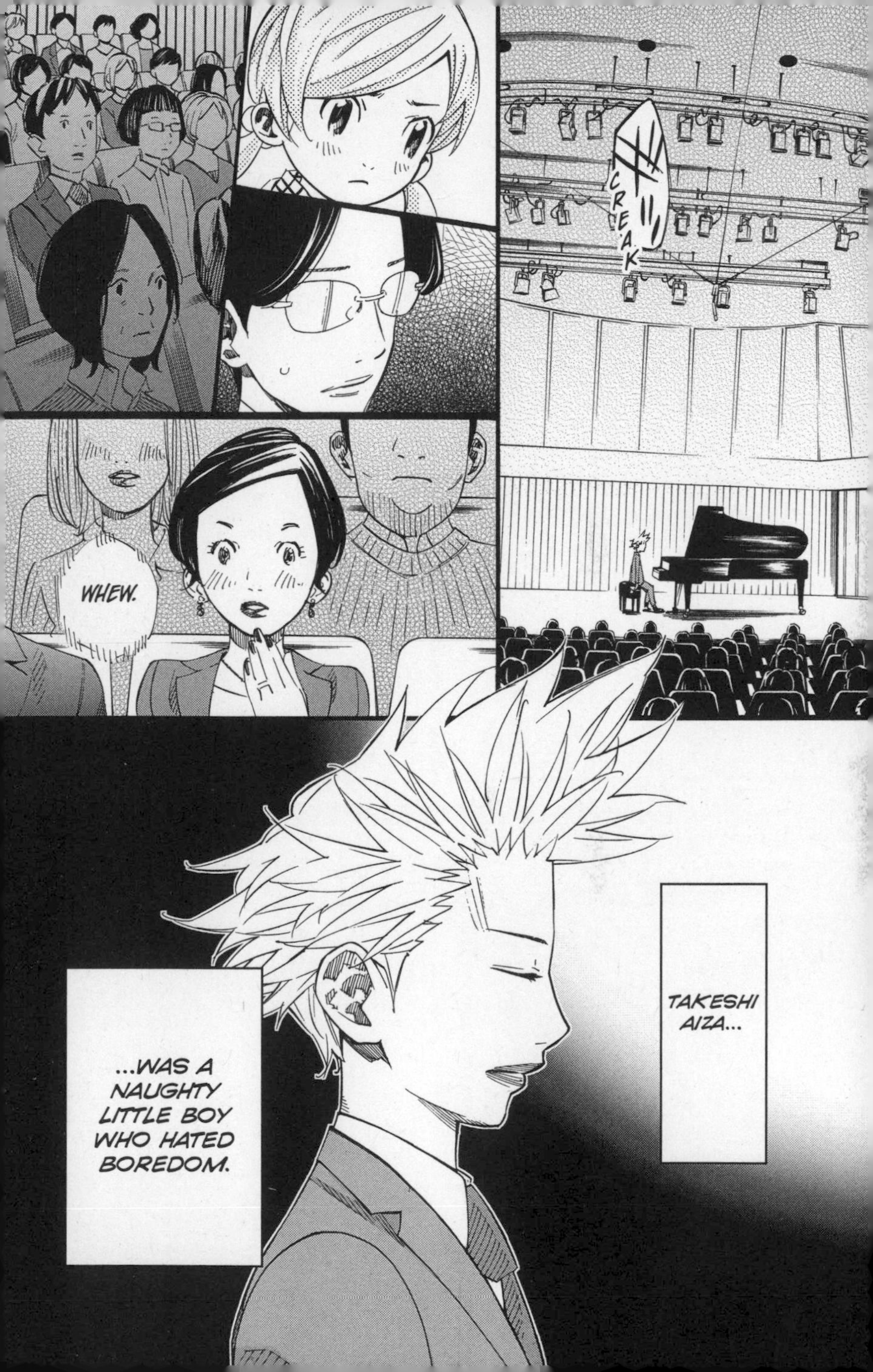
CREAK
WHEW.
TAKESHI AIZA...
...WAS A NAUGHTY LITTLE BOY WHO HATED BOREDOM.

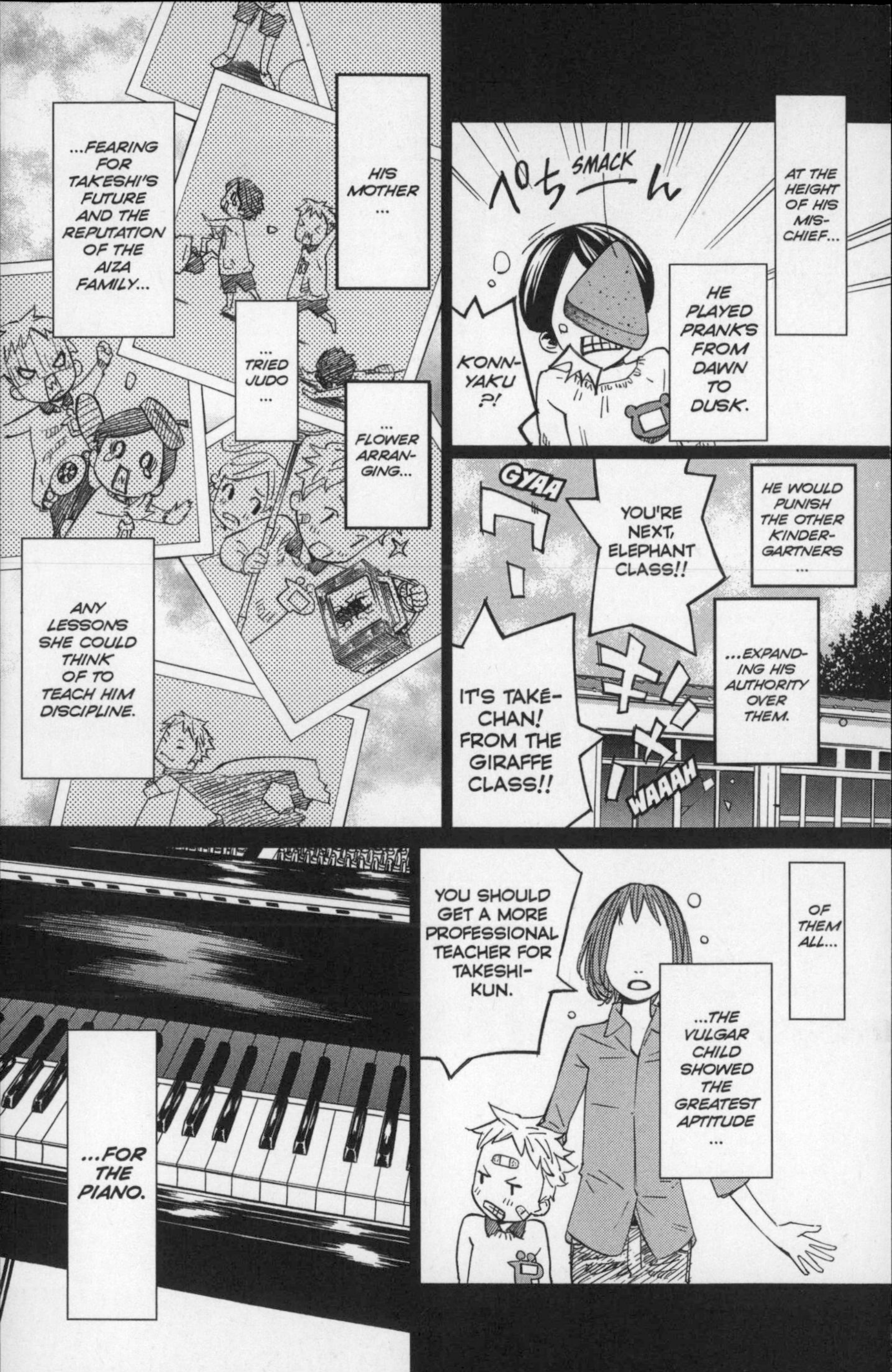
AT THE HEIGHT OF HIS MISCHIEF...
HE PLAYED PRANKS FROM DAWN TO DUSK.
SMACK
KONNYAKU?!
HE WOULD PUNISH THE OTHER KINDERGARTNERS...
GYAA
YOU'RE NEXT, ELEPHANT CLASS!!
...EXPANDING HIS AUTHORITY OVER THEM.
IT'S TAKE-CHAN! FROM THE GIRAFFE CLASS!!
WAAAH
HIS MOTHER...
...FEARING FOR TAKESHI'S FUTURE AND THE REPUTATION OF THE AIZA FAMILY...
...TRIED JUDO...
...FLOWER ARRANGING...
ANY LESSONS SHE COULD THINK OF TO TEACH HIM DISCIPLINE.
OF THEM ALL...
...THE VULGAR CHILD SHOWED THE GREATEST APTITUDE...
YOU SHOULD GET A MORE PROFESSIONAL TEACHER FOR TAKESHI-KUN.
...FOR THE PIANO.

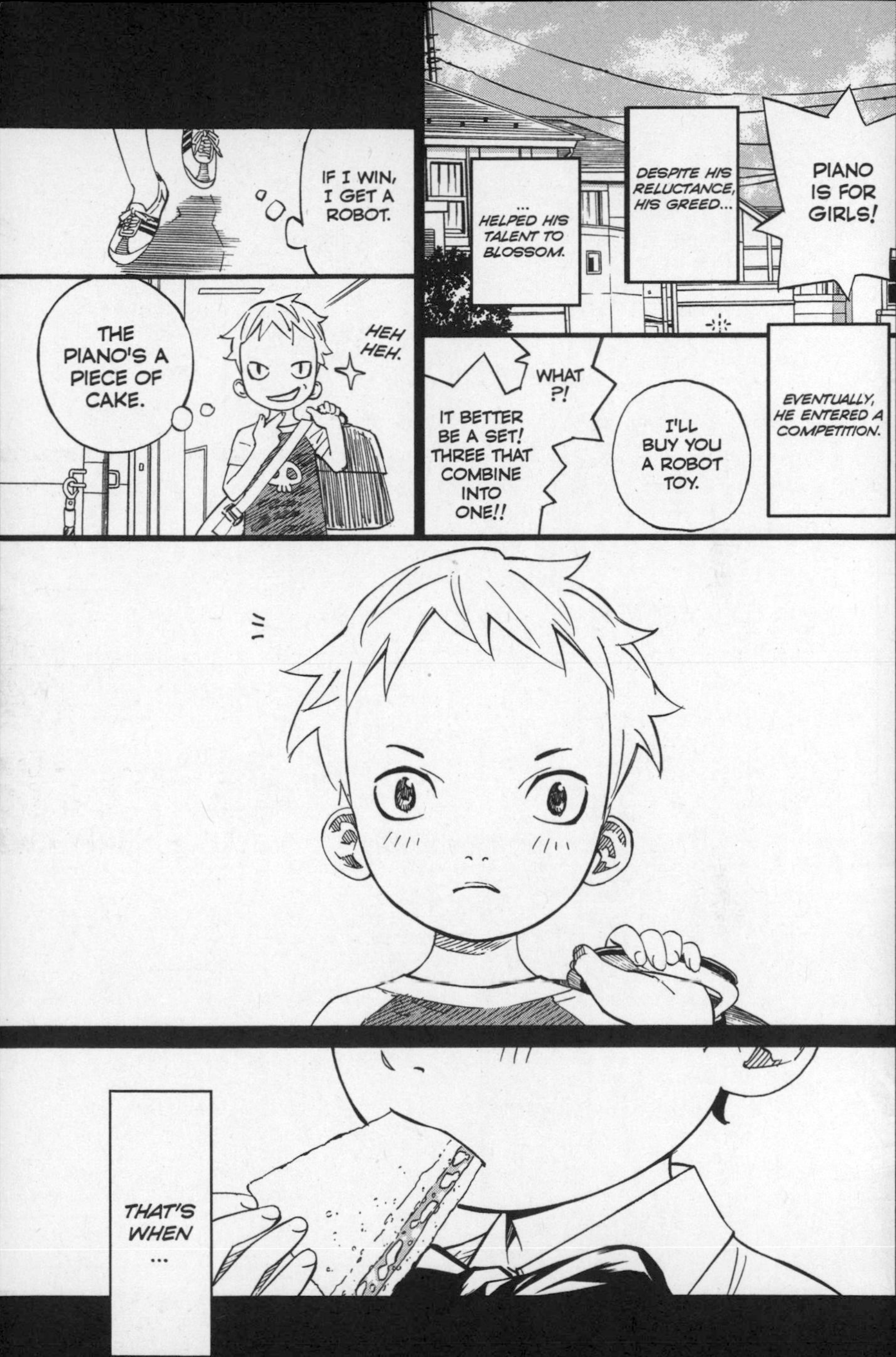
PIANO IS FOR GIRLS!
DESPITE HIS RELUCTANCE, HIS GREED...
... HELPED HIS TALENT TO BLOSSOM.
EVENTUALLY, HE ENTERED A COMPETITION.
I'LL BUY YOU A ROBOT TOY.
WHAT ?!
IT BETTER BE A SET! THREE THAT COMBINE INTO ONE!!
IF I WIN, I GET A ROBOT.
HEH HEH.
THE PIANO'S A PIECE OF CAKE.
THAT'S WHEN ...

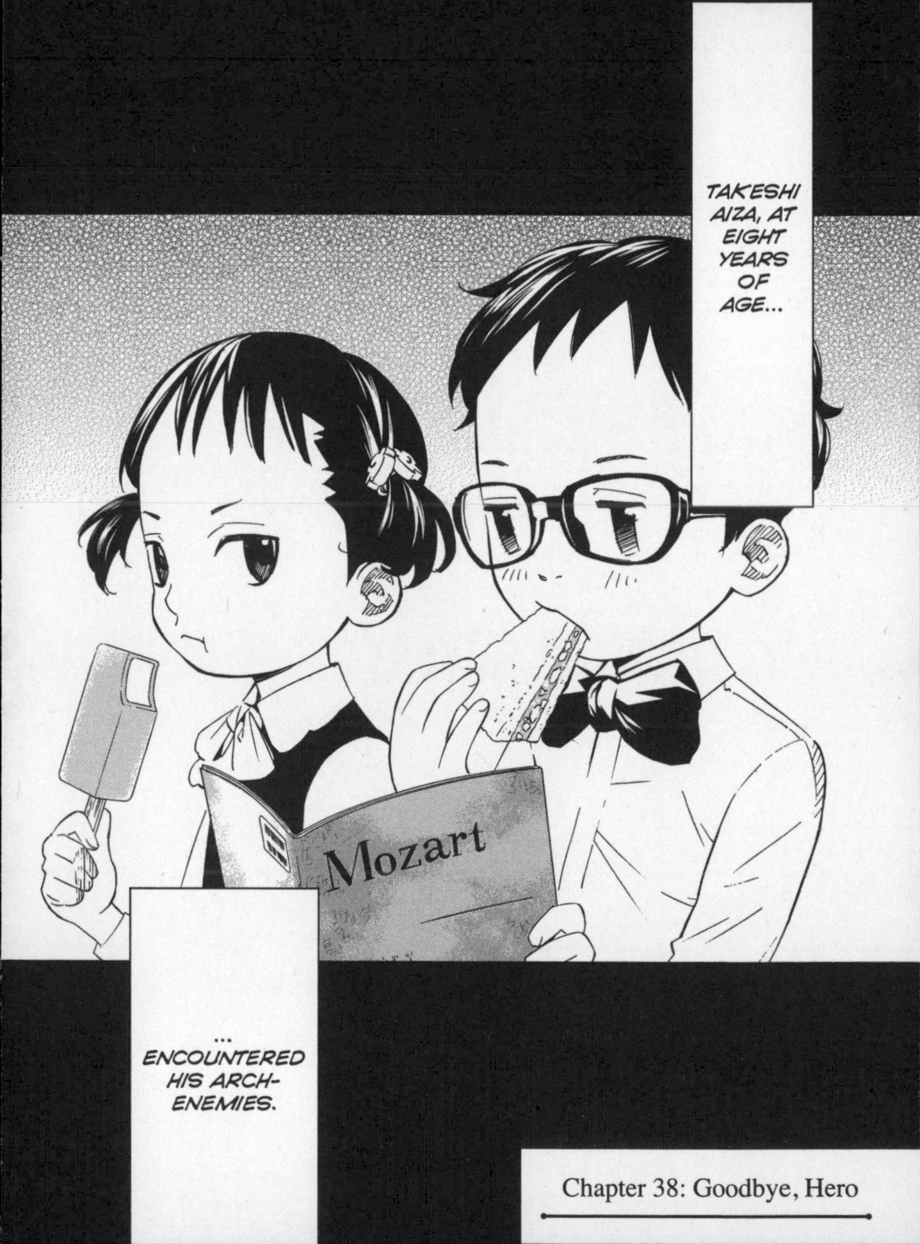
TAKESHI AIZA, AT EIGHT YEARS OF AGE...
Mozart
... ENCOUNTERED HIS ARCH-ENEMIES.
Chapter 38: Goodbye, Hero

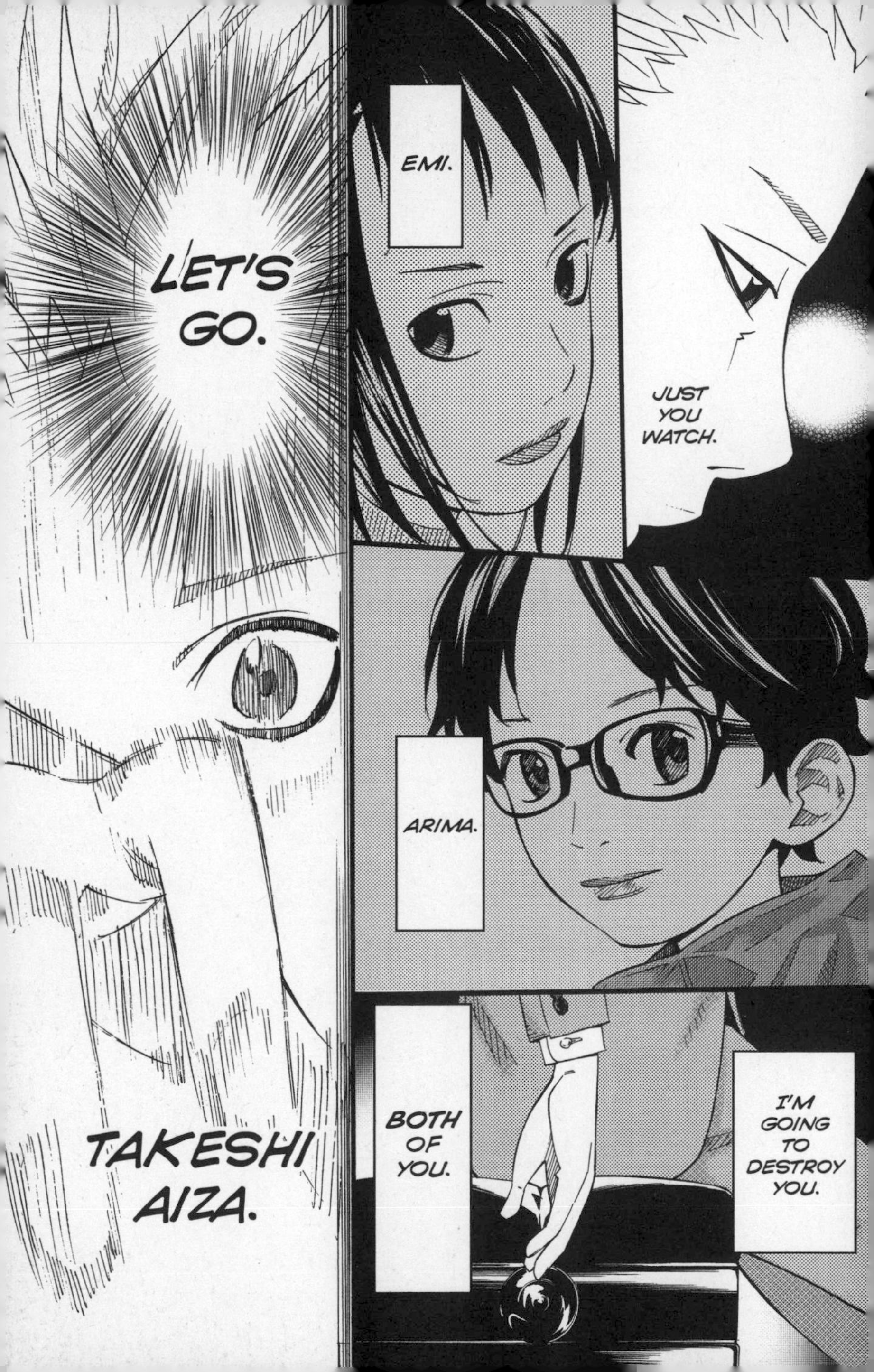
JUST YOU WATCH.
EMI.
ARIMA.
I'M GOING TO DESTROY YOU.
BOTH OF YOU.
LET'S GO.
TAKESHI AIZA.

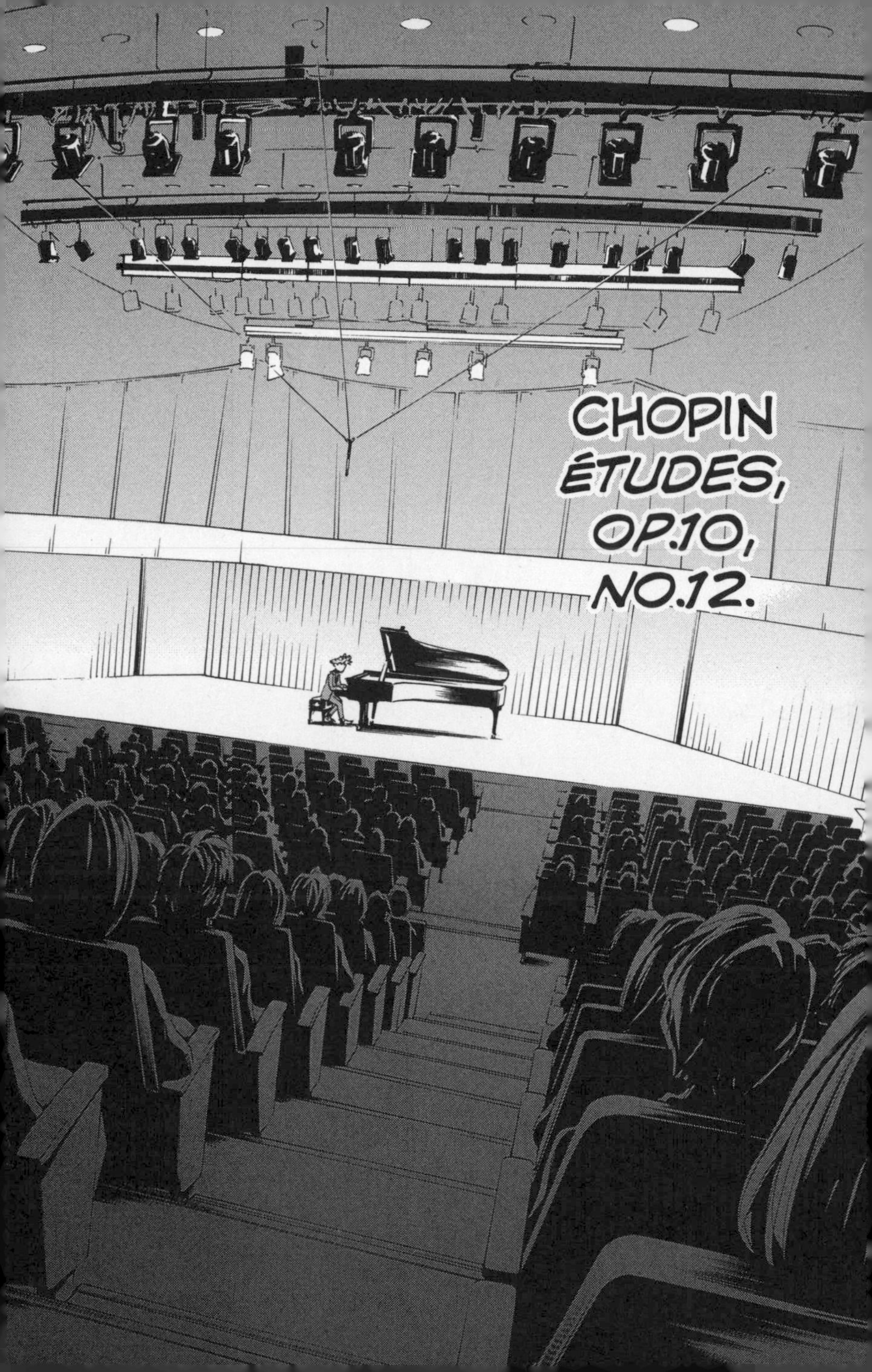
CHOPIN ÉTUDES, OP.10, NO.12.

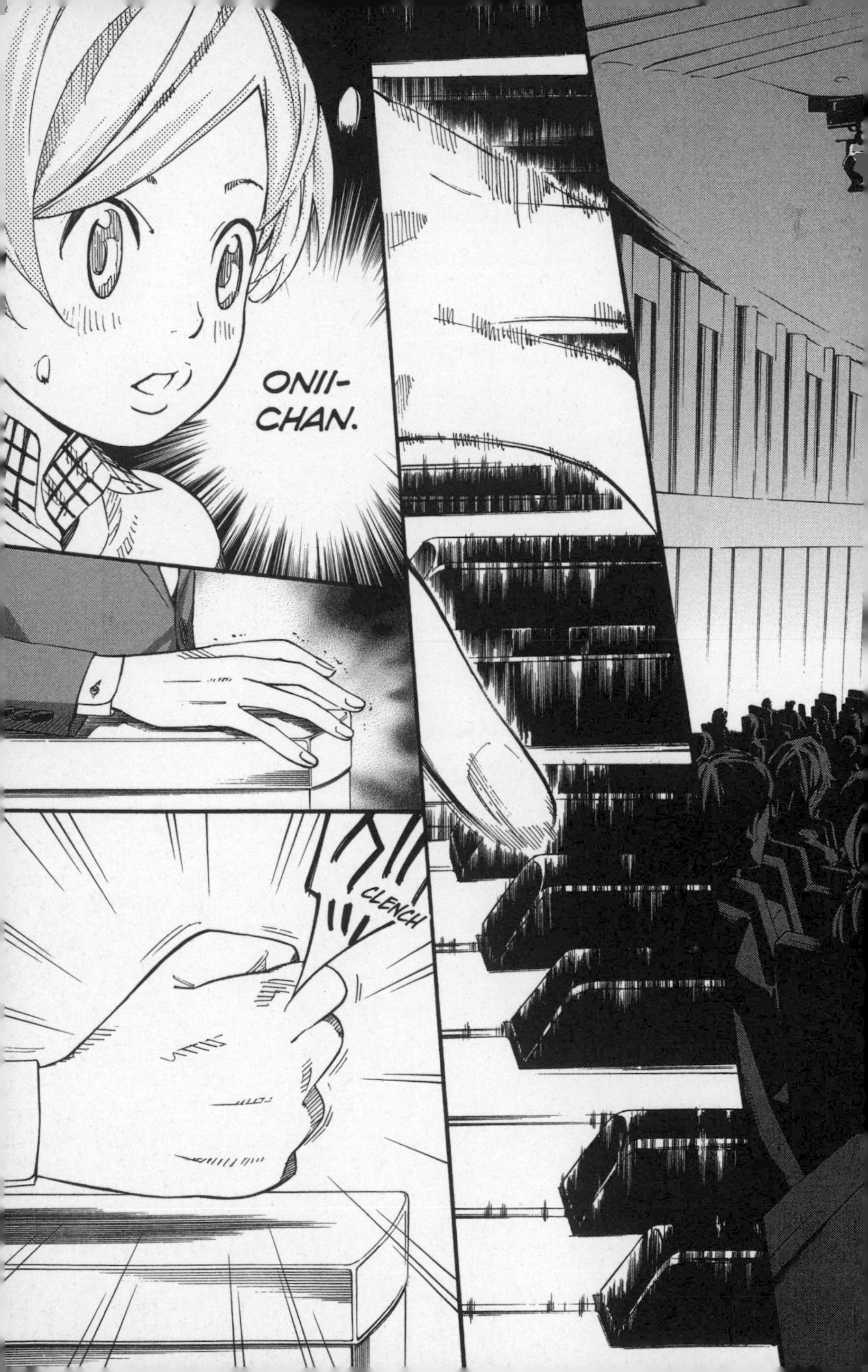
ONII-
CHAN.
CLENCH

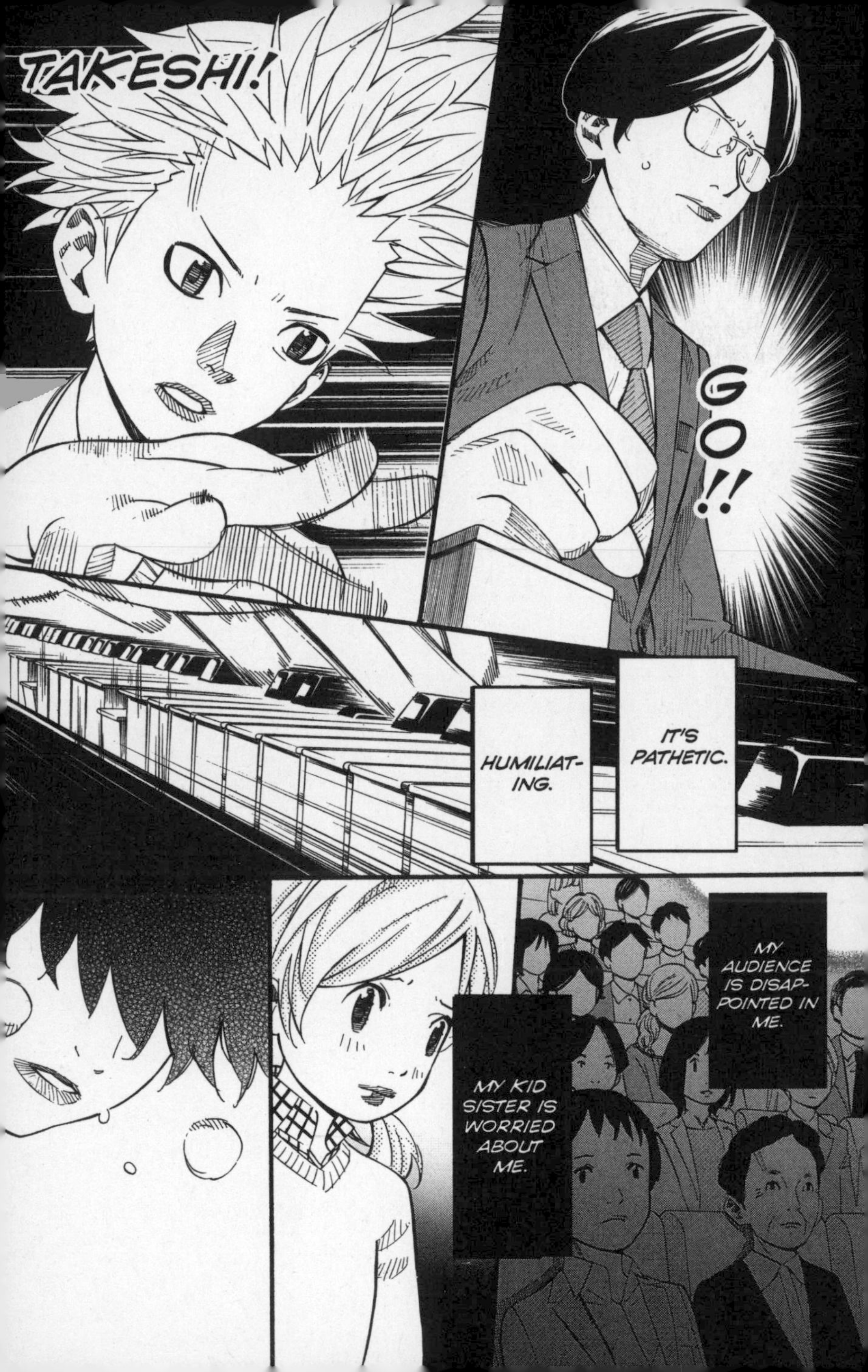
GO!!
TAKESHI!
IT'S PATHETIC.
HUMILIATING.
MY AUDIENCE IS DISAPPOINTED IN ME.
MY KID SISTER IS WORRIED ABOUT ME.

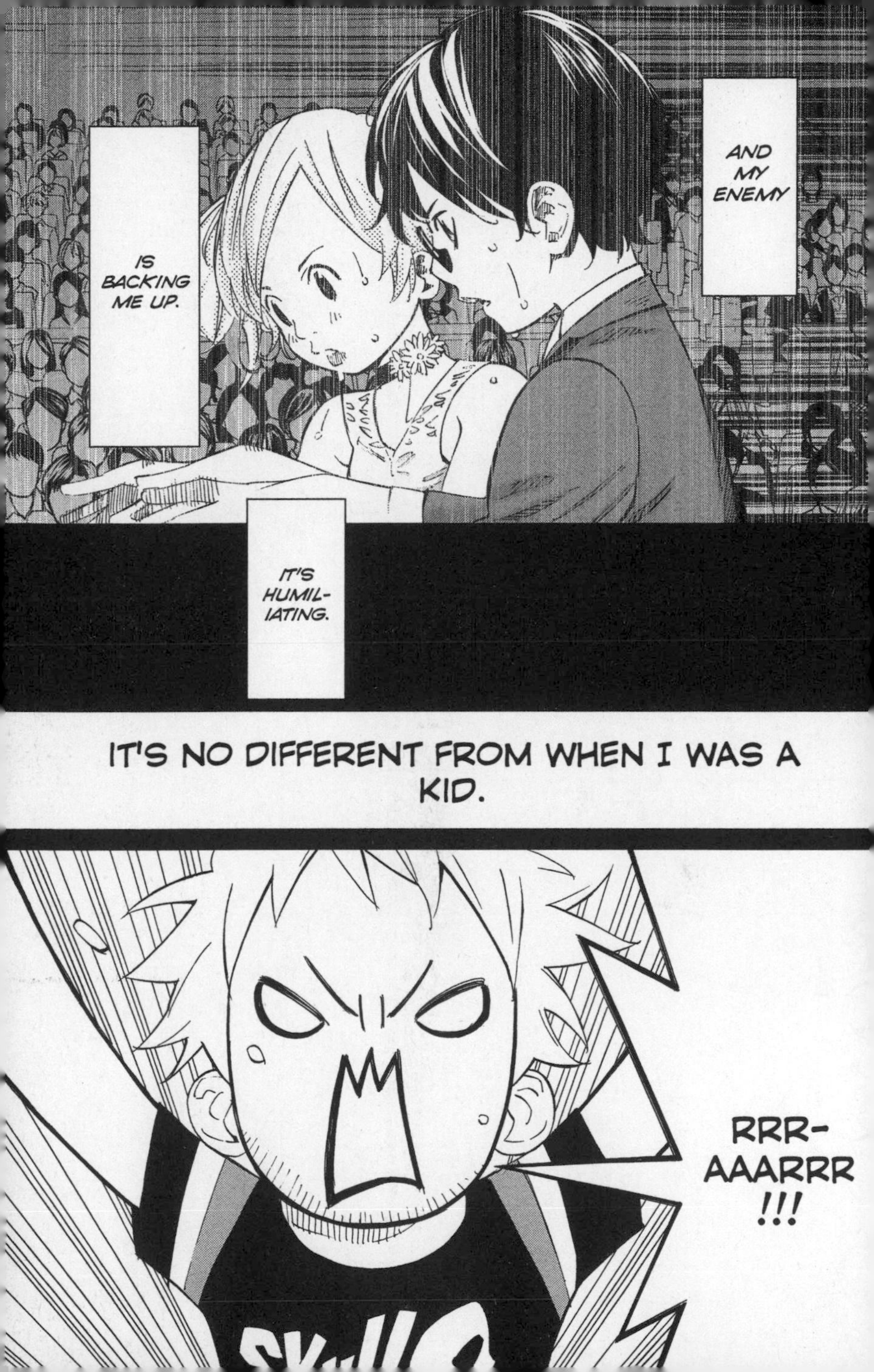
AND MY ENEMY
IS BACKING ME UP.
IT'S HUMIL-IATING.
IT'S NO DIFFERENT FROM WHEN I WAS A KID.
RRR-AAARRR!!!

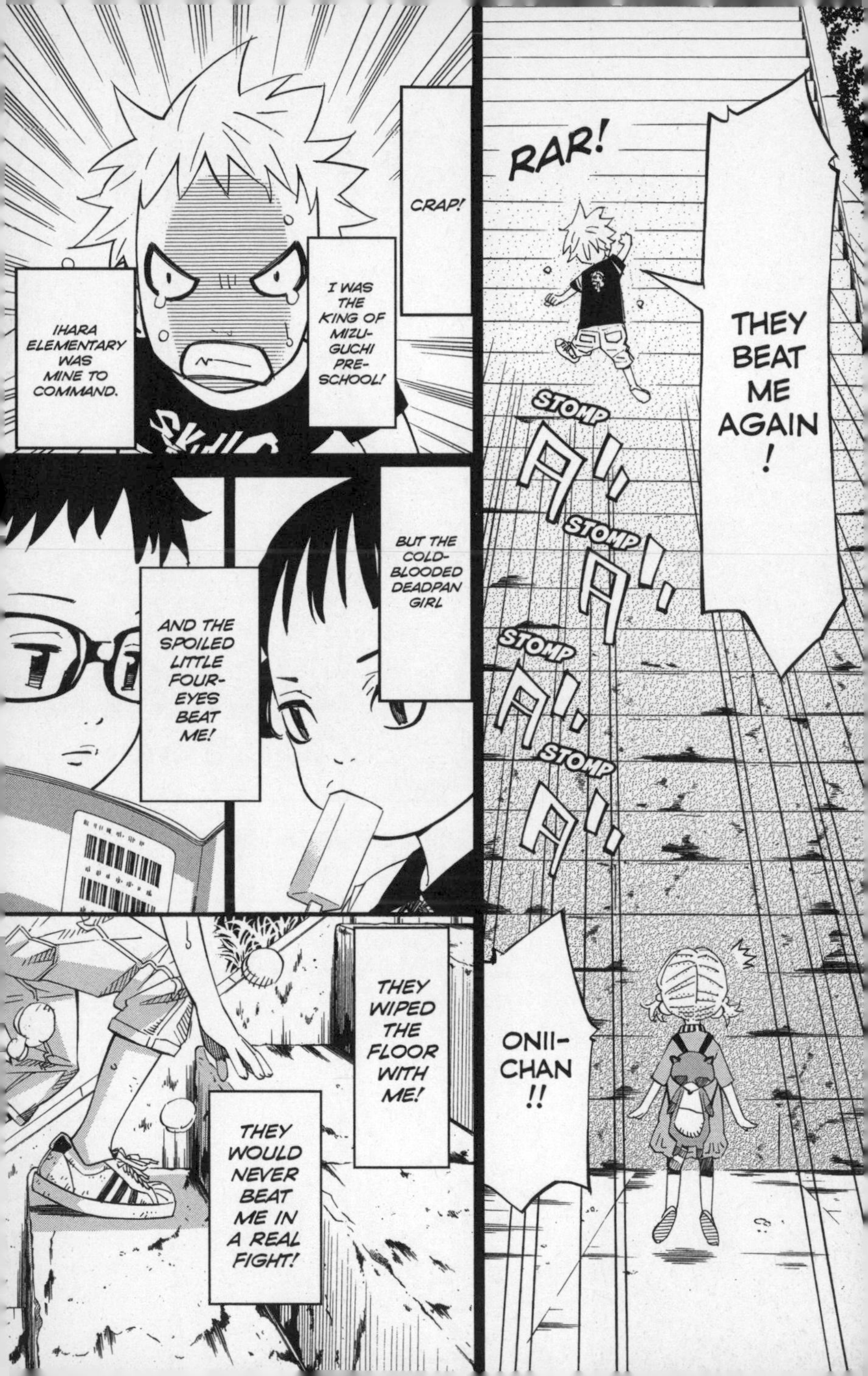

THEY BEAT ME AGAIN!
RAR!
STOMP
STOMP
STOMP
STOMP
CRAP!
I WAS THE KING OF MIZUGUCHI PRE-SCHOOL!
IHARA ELEMENTARY WAS MINE TO COMMAND.
BUT THE COLD-BLOODED DEADPAN GIRL
AND THE SPOILED LITTLE FOUR-EYES BEAT ME!
ONII-CHAN!!
THEY WIPED THE FLOOR WITH ME!
THEY WOULD NEVER BEAT ME IN A REAL FIGHT!

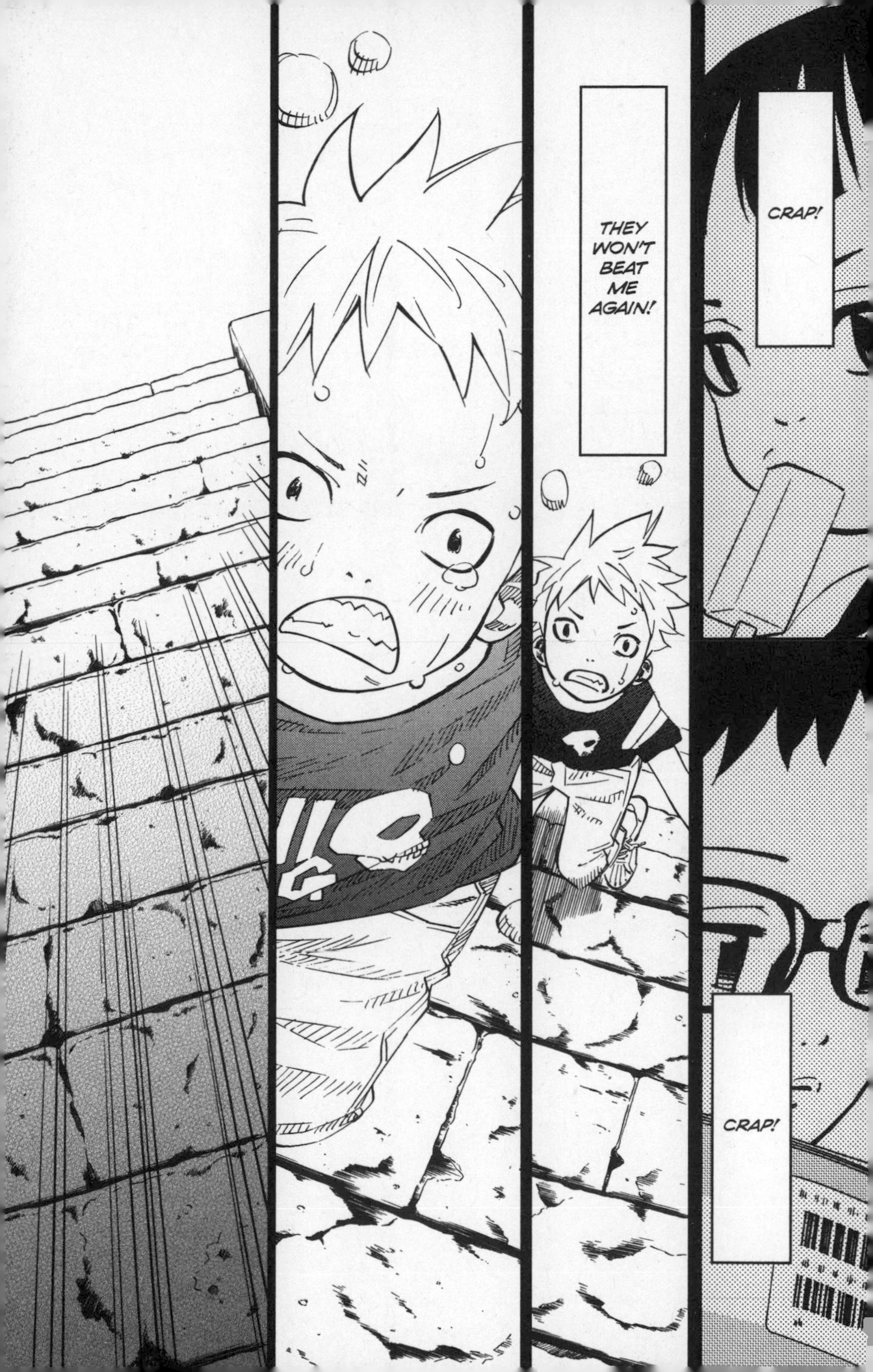
CRAP!
CRAP!
THEY WON'T BEAT ME AGAIN!

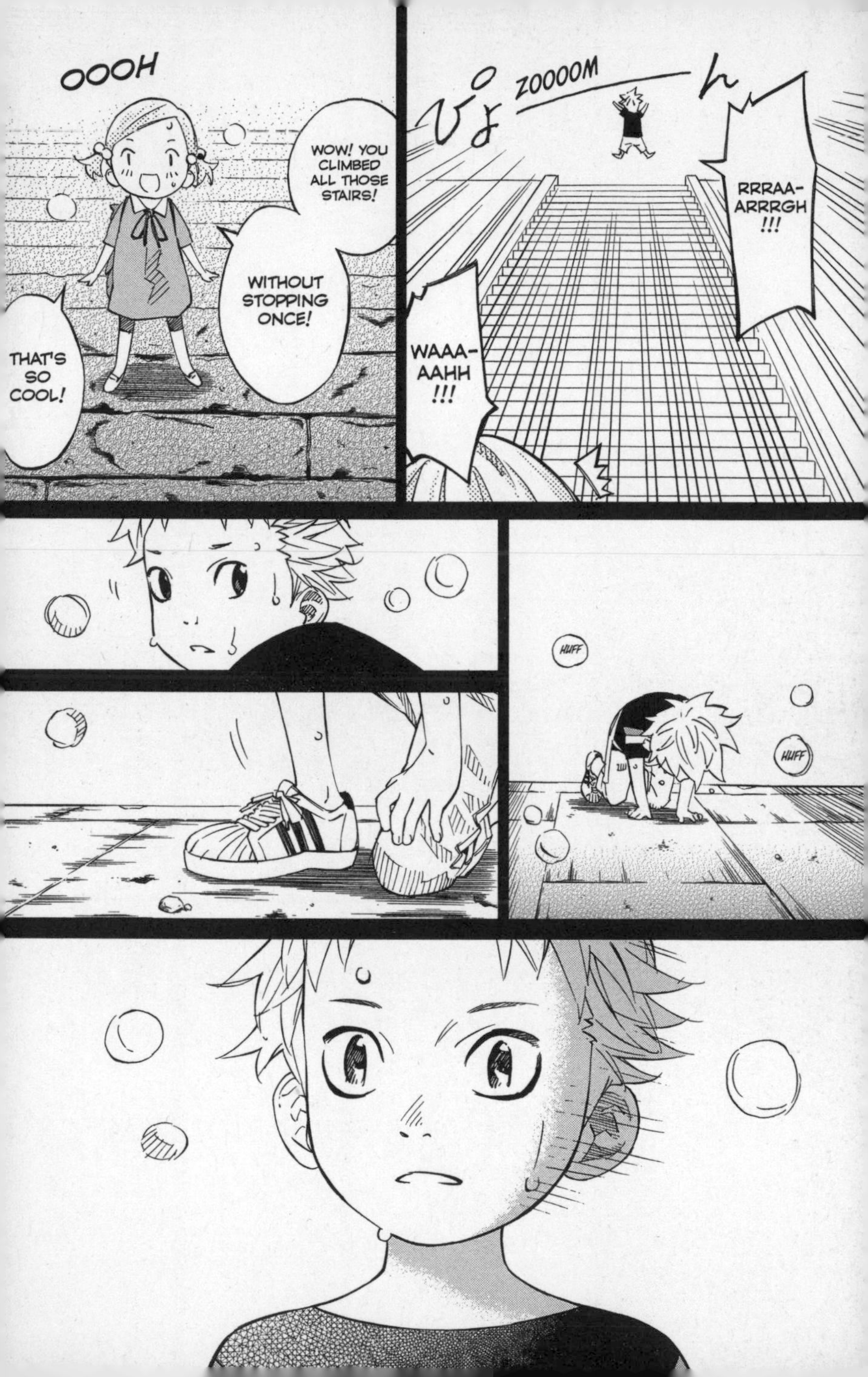
ぴょ
ZOOOOM
ん
RRRAA-ARRRGH!!!
WAAA-AAHH!!!
OOOH
WOW! YOU CLIMBED ALL THOSE STAIRS!
WITHOUT STOPPING ONCE!
THAT'S SO COOL!
HUFF
HUFF

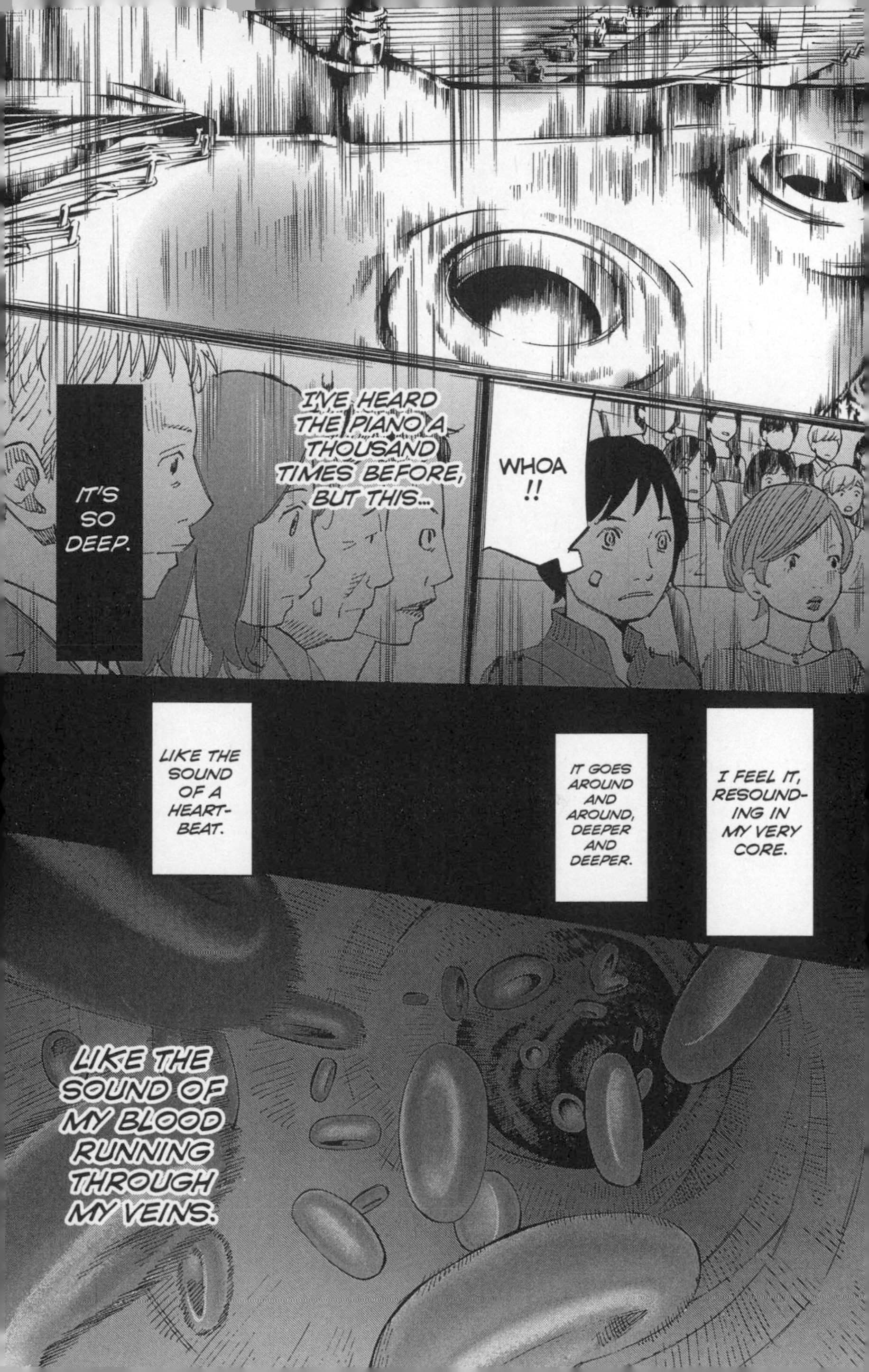
WHOA !!
I'VE HEARD THE PIANO A THOUSAND TIMES BEFORE, BUT THIS...
IT'S SO DEEP.
I FEEL IT, RESOUND-ING IN MY VERY CORE.
IT GOES AROUND AND AROUND, DEEPER AND DEEPER.
LIKE THE SOUND OF A HEART-BEAT.
LIKE THE SOUND OF MY BLOOD RUNNING THROUGH MY VEINS.

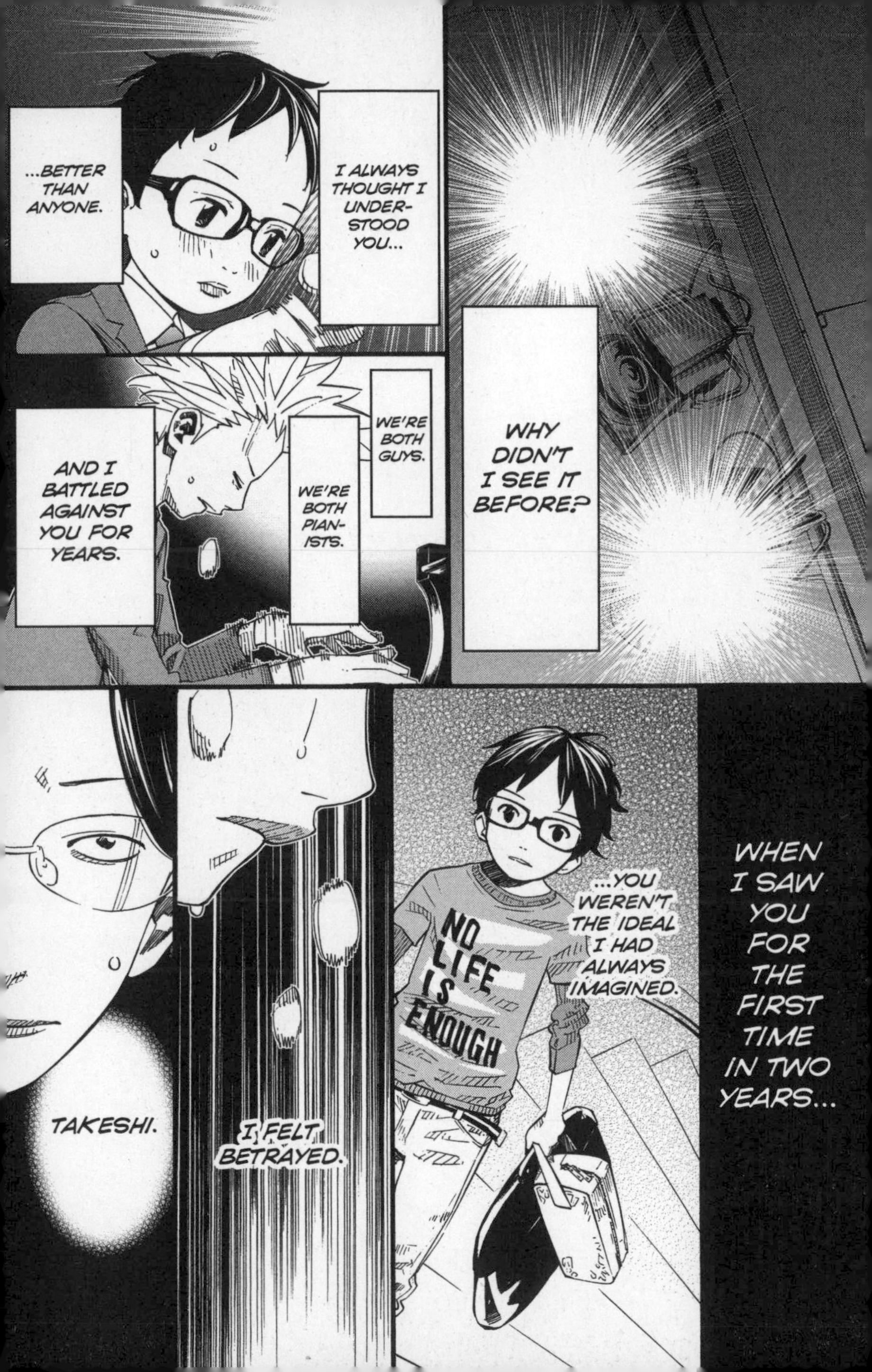
WHY DIDN'T I SEE IT BEFORE?
I ALWAYS THOUGHT I UNDER-STOOD YOU...
...BETTER THAN ANYONE.
WE'RE BOTH GUYS.
WE'RE BOTH PIAN-ISTS.
AND I BATTLED AGAINST YOU FOR YEARS.
WHEN I SAW YOU FOR THE FIRST TIME IN TWO YEARS...
...YOU WEREN'T THE IDEAL I HAD ALWAYS IMAGINED.
NO LIFE IS ENOUGH
I FELT BETRAYED.
TAKESHI.

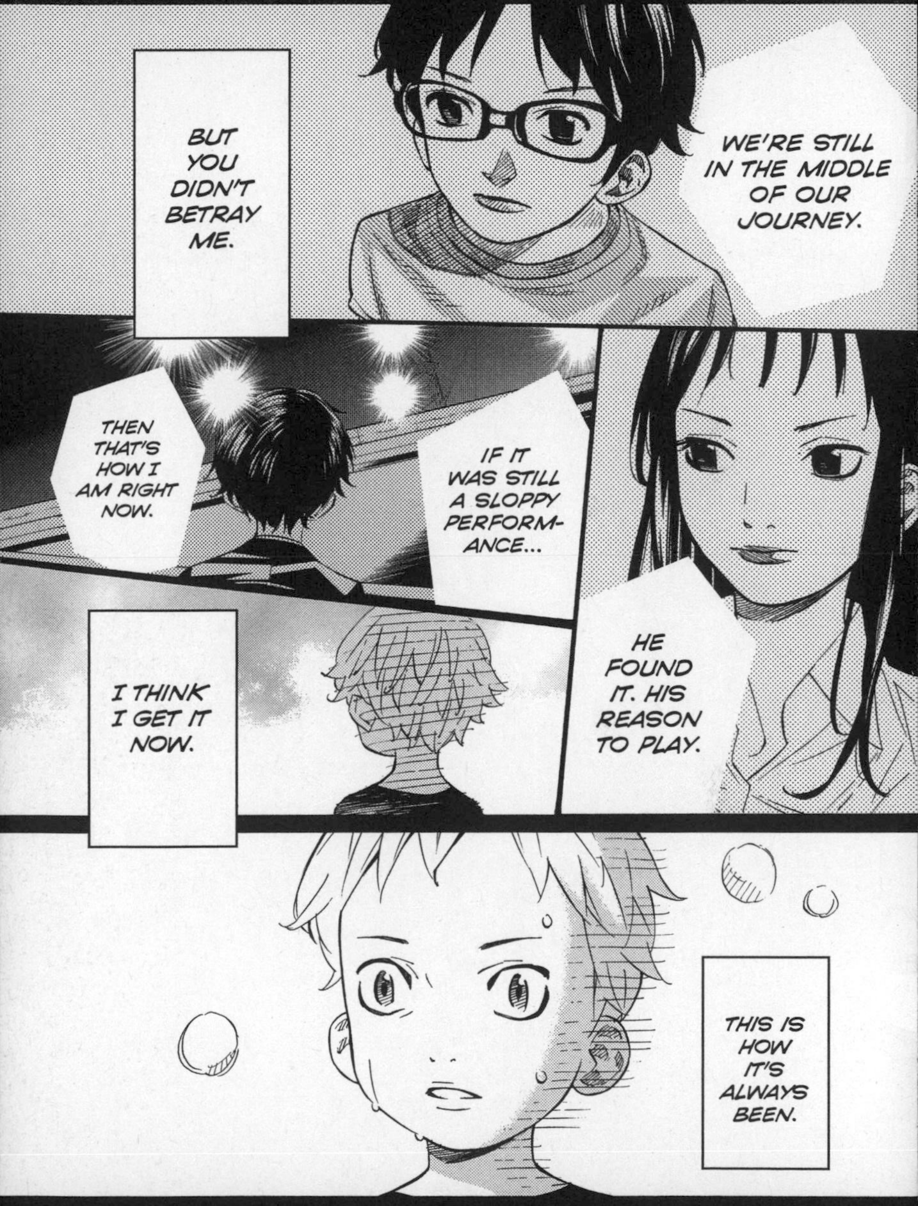
WE'RE STILL IN THE MIDDLE OF OUR JOURNEY.
BUT YOU DIDN'T BETRAY ME.
HE FOUND IT. HIS REASON TO PLAY.
IF IT WAS STILL A SLOPPY PERFORM-ANCE...
THEN THAT'S HOW I AM RIGHT NOW.
I THINK I GET IT NOW.
THIS IS HOW IT'S ALWAYS BEEN.

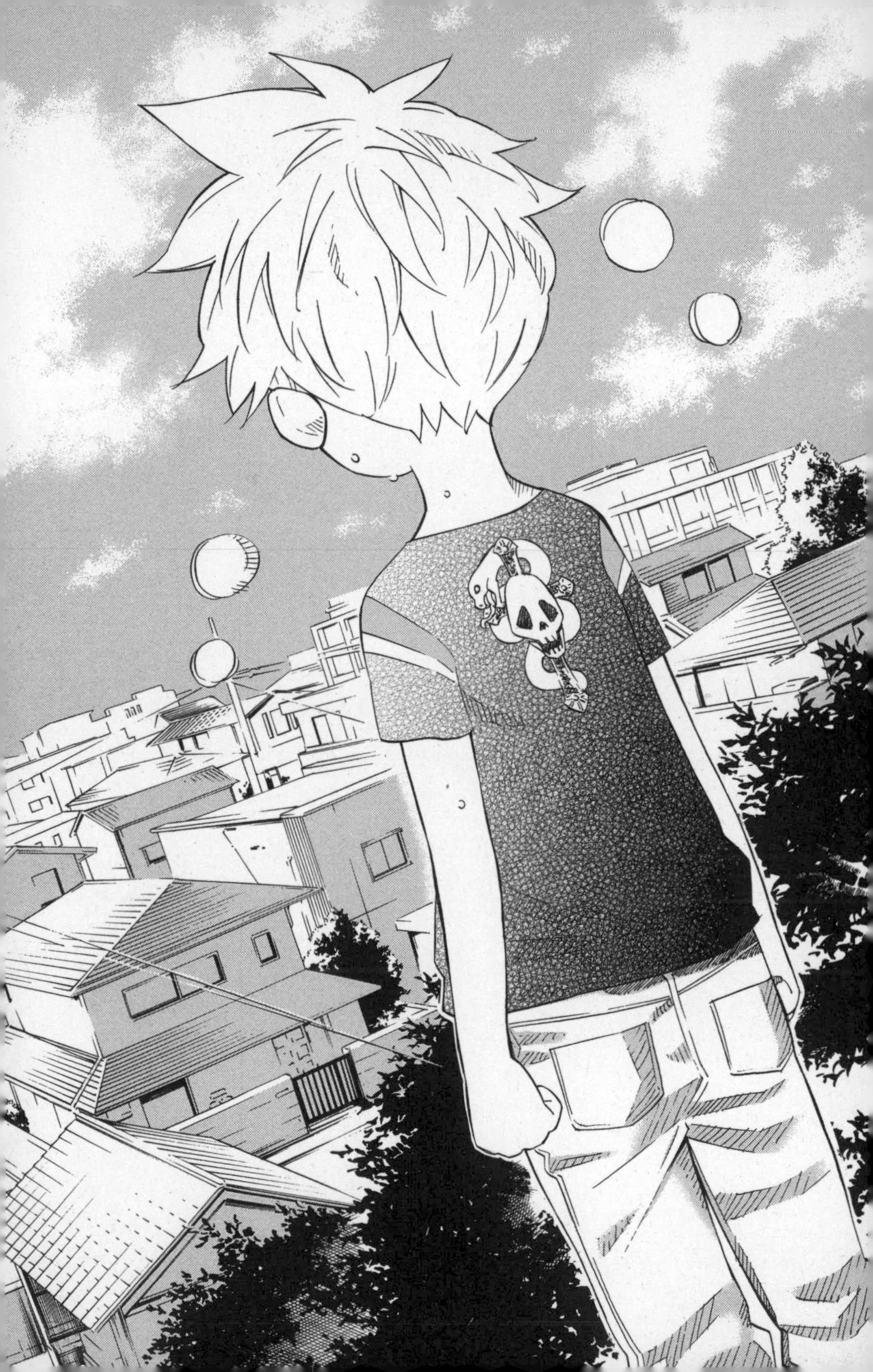

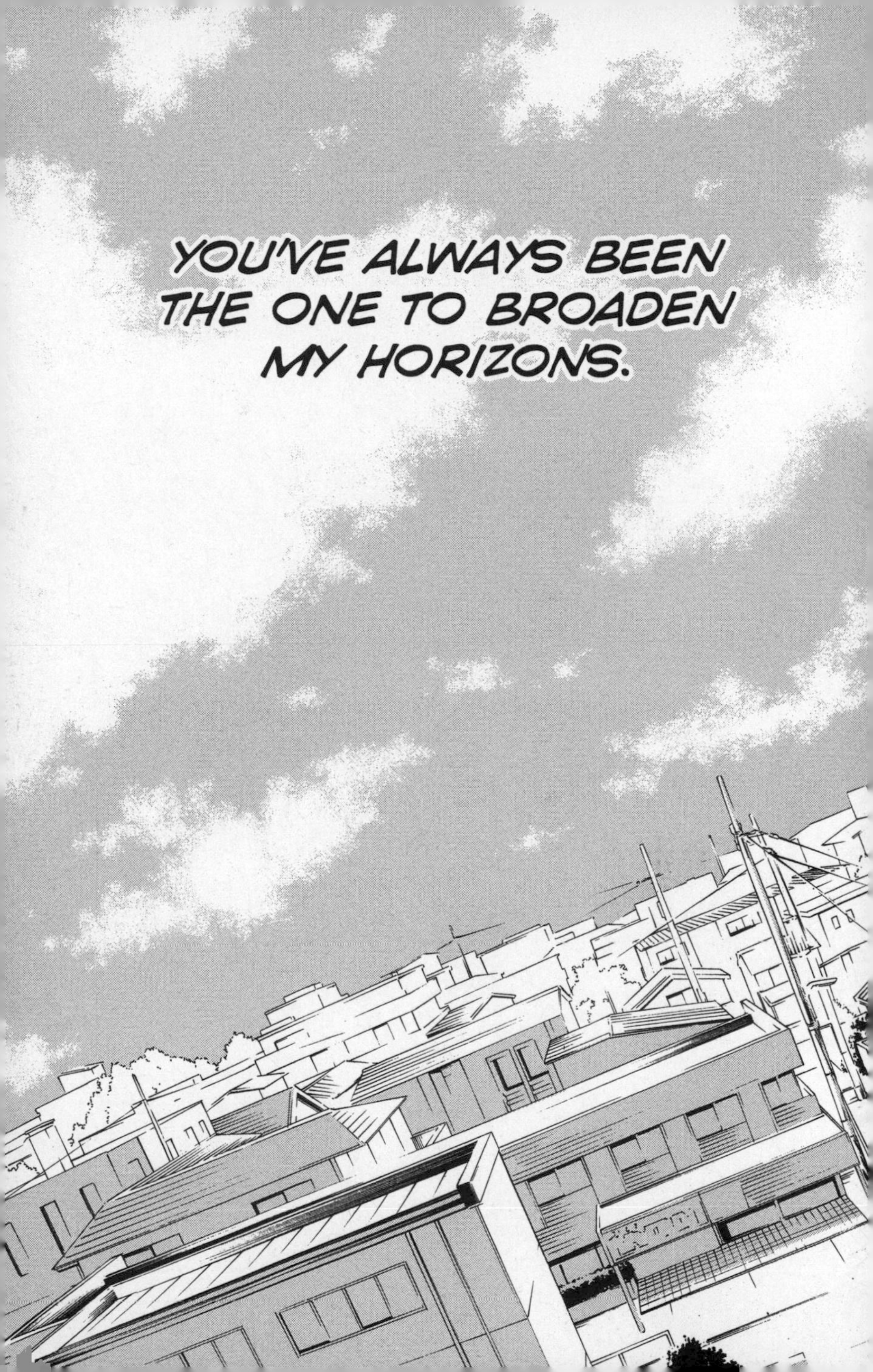
YOU'VE ALWAYS BEEN THE ONE TO BROADEN MY HORIZONS.

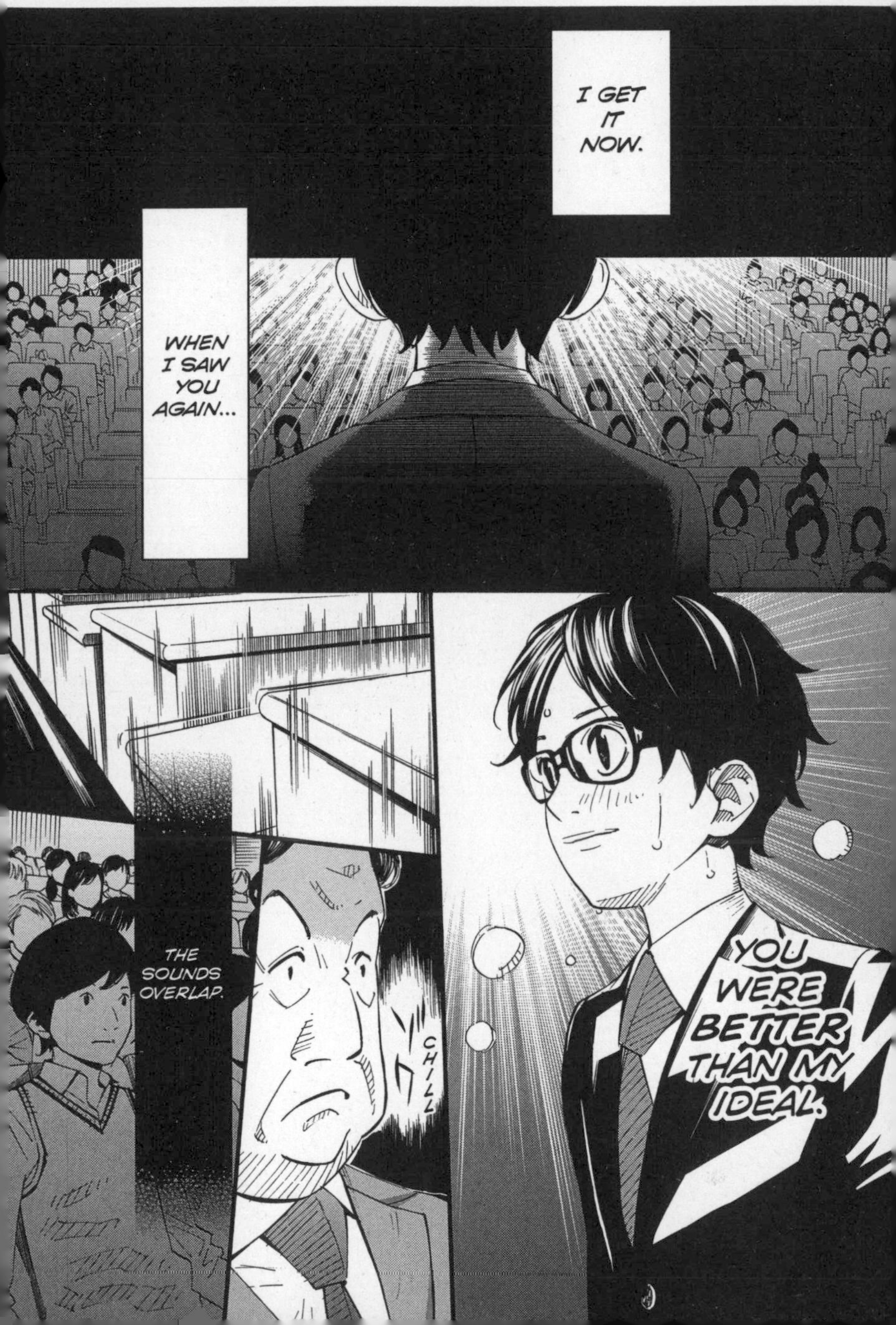
I GET IT NOW.
WHEN I SAW YOU AGAIN...
YOU WERE BETTER THAN MY IDEAL.
CHILL
THE SOUNDS OVERLAP.

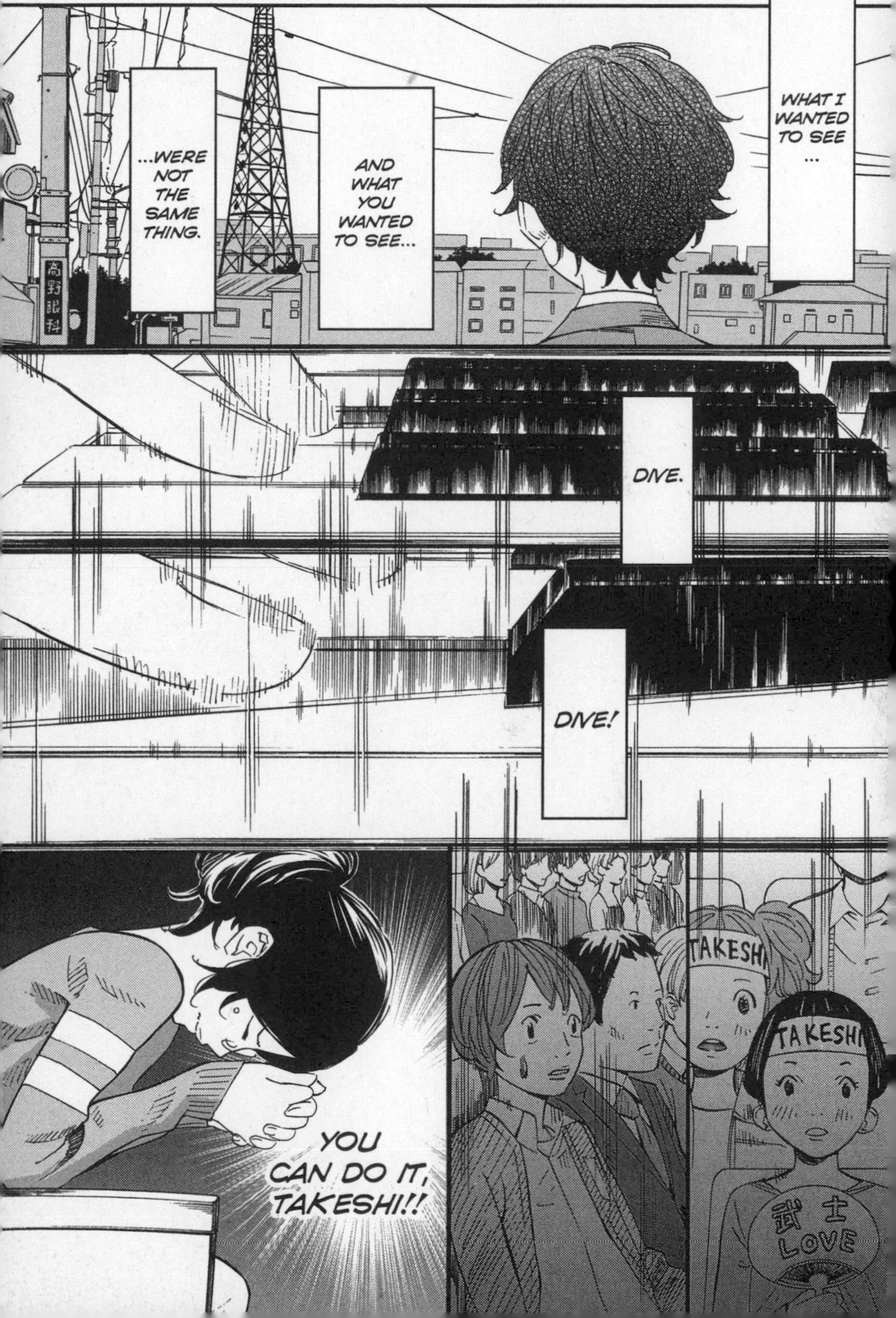
WHAT I WANTED TO SEE ...
AND WHAT YOU WANTED TO SEE...
...WERE NOT THE SAME THING.
高野眼科
DIVE.
DIVE!
TAKESHI
TAKESHI
武士 LOVE
YOU CAN DO IT, TAKESHI!!

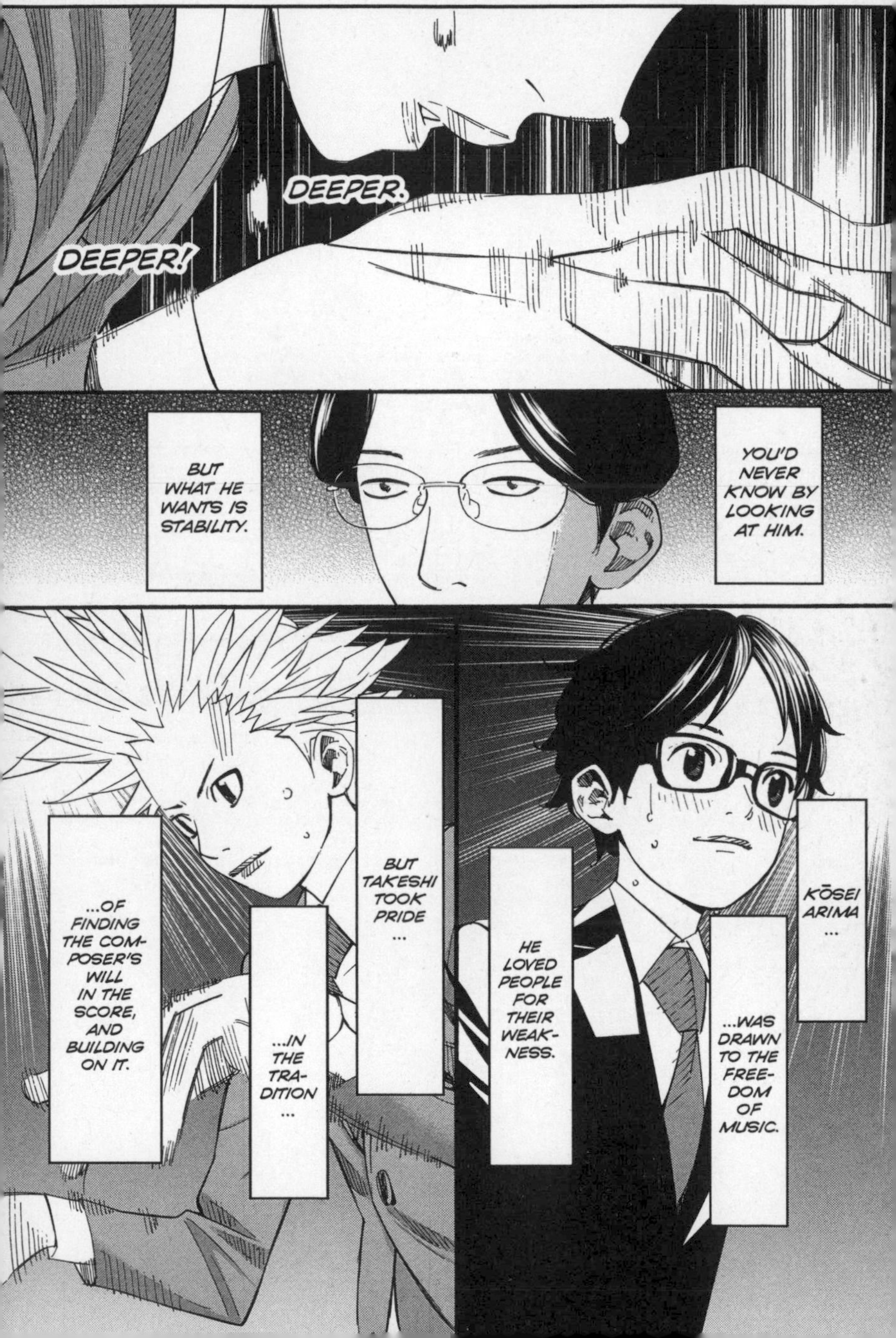
DEEPER.
DEEPER!
YOU'D NEVER KNOW BY LOOKING AT HIM.
BUT WHAT HE WANTS IS STABILITY.
KŌSEI ARIMA ...
...WAS DRAWN TO THE FREE-DOM OF MUSIC.
HE LOVED PEOPLE FOR THEIR WEAK-NESS.
BUT TAKESHI TOOK PRIDE ...
...IN THE TRA-DITION ...
...OF FINDING THE COM-POSER'S WILL IN THE SCORE, AND BUILDING ON IT.

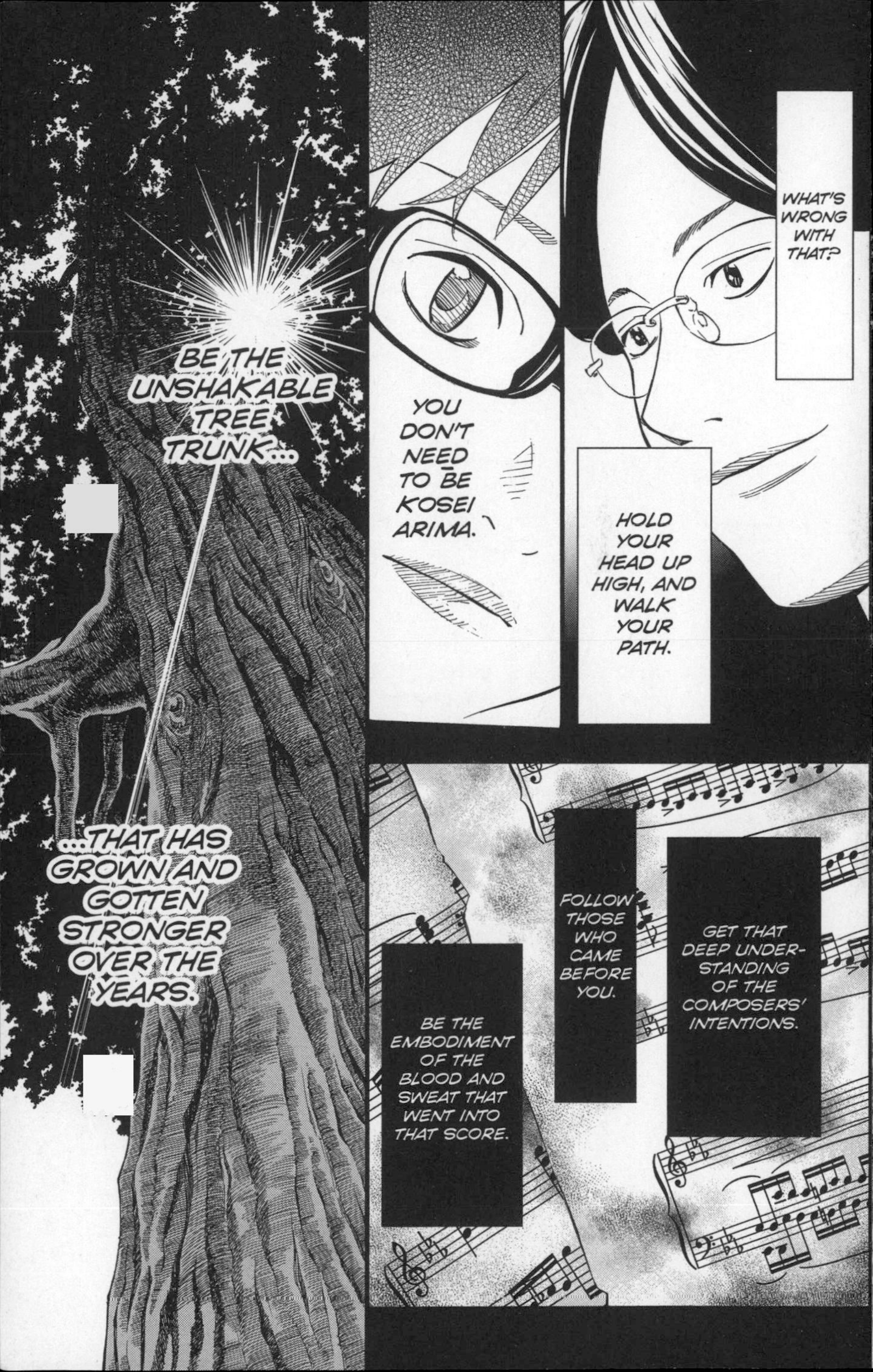

WHAT'S WRONG WITH THAT?
HOLD YOUR HEAD UP HIGH, AND WALK YOUR PATH.
YOU DON'T NEED TO BE KOSEI ARIMA.
GET THAT DEEP UNDER-STANDING OF THE COMPOSERS' INTENTIONS.
FOLLOW THOSE WHO CAME BEFORE YOU.
BE THE EMBODIMENT OF THE BLOOD AND SWEAT THAT WENT INTO THAT SCORE.
BE THE UNSHAKABLE TREE TRUNK...
...THAT HAS GROWN AND GOTTEN STRONGER OVER THE YEARS.

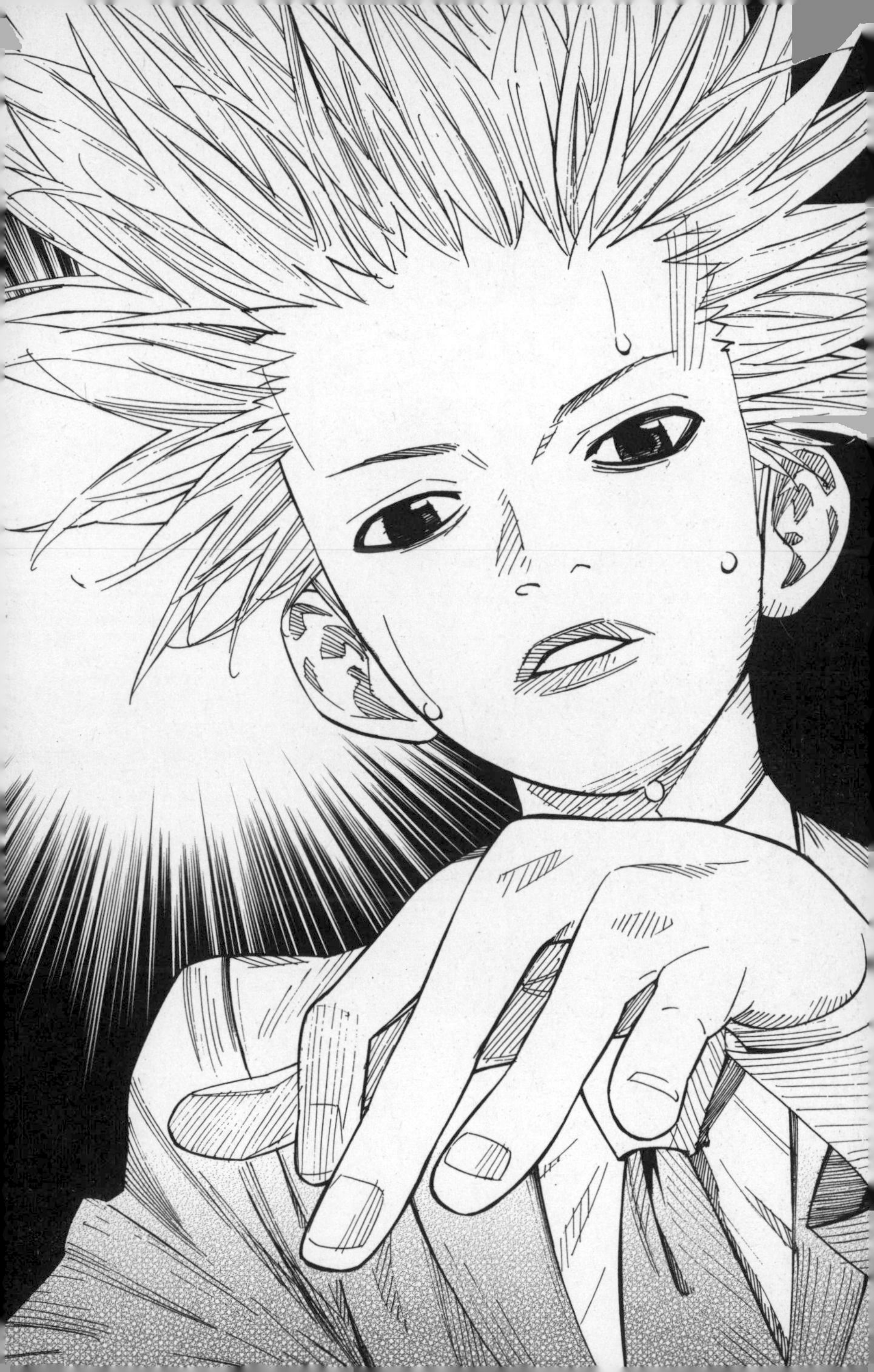

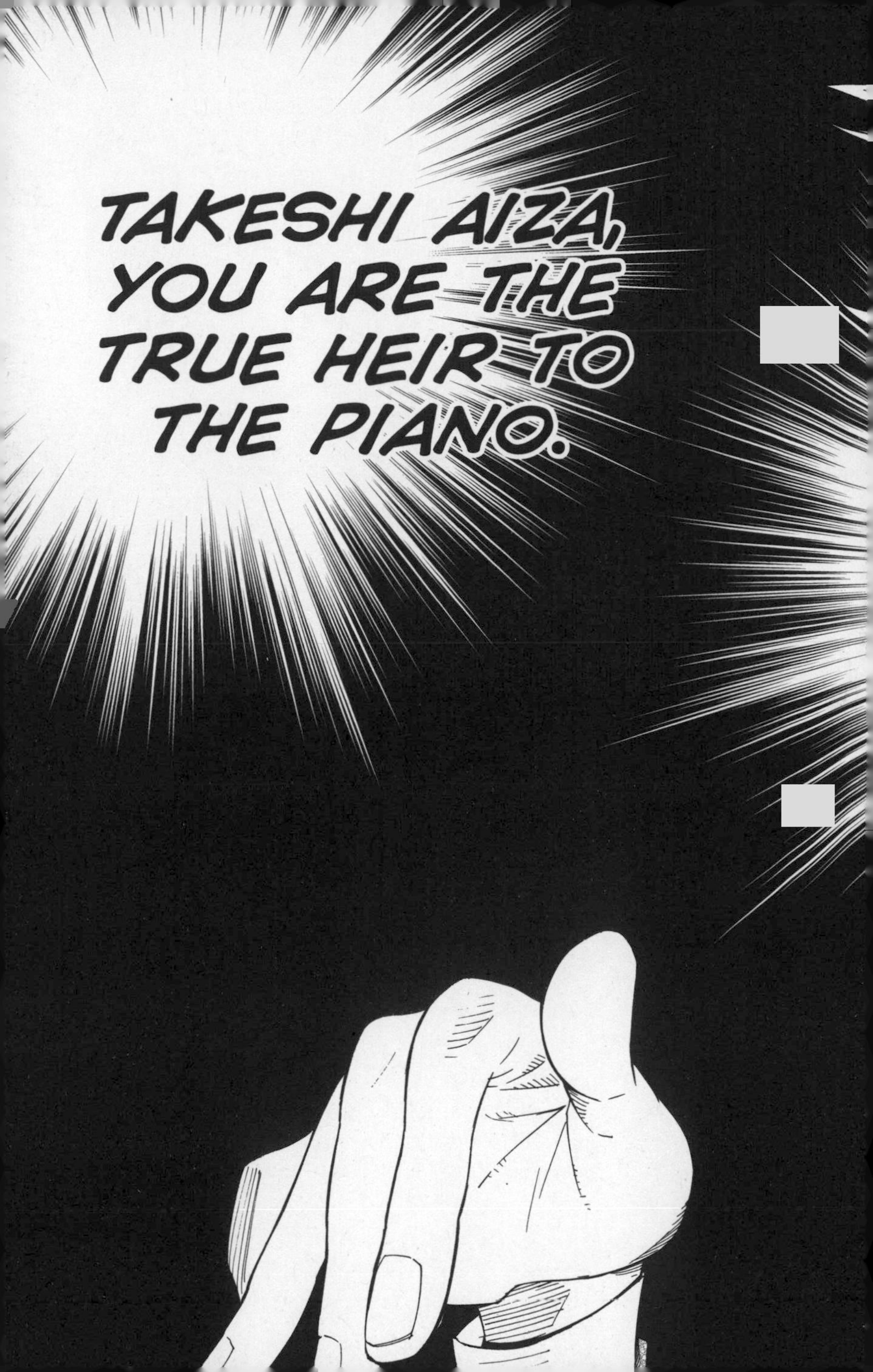
TAKESHI AIZA, YOU ARE THE TRUE HEIR TO THE PIANO.

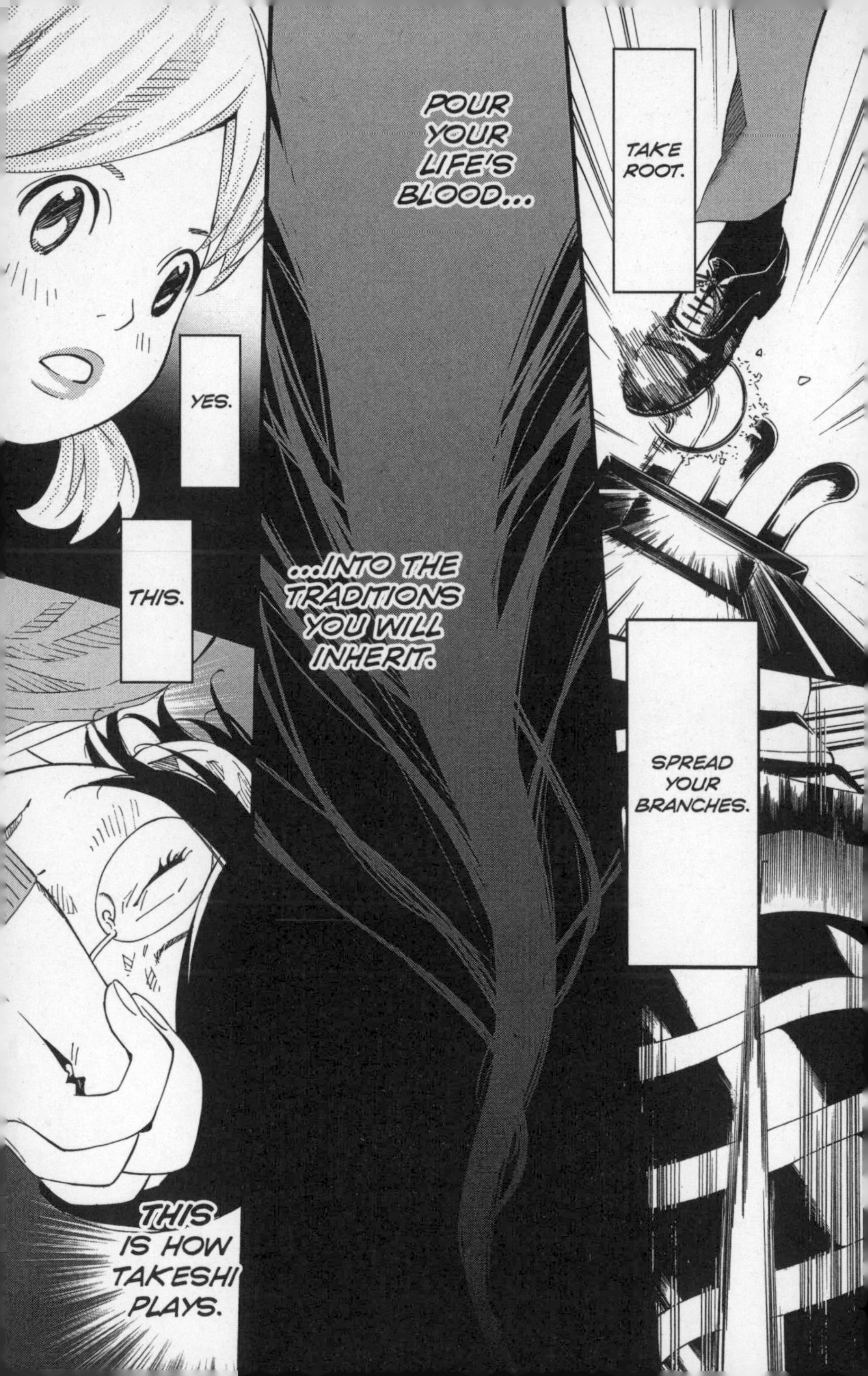
TAKE ROOT.
SPREAD YOUR BRANCHES.
POUR YOUR LIFE'S BLOOD...
...INTO THE TRADITIONS YOU WILL INHERIT.
YES.
THIS.
THIS IS HOW TAKESHI PLAYS.

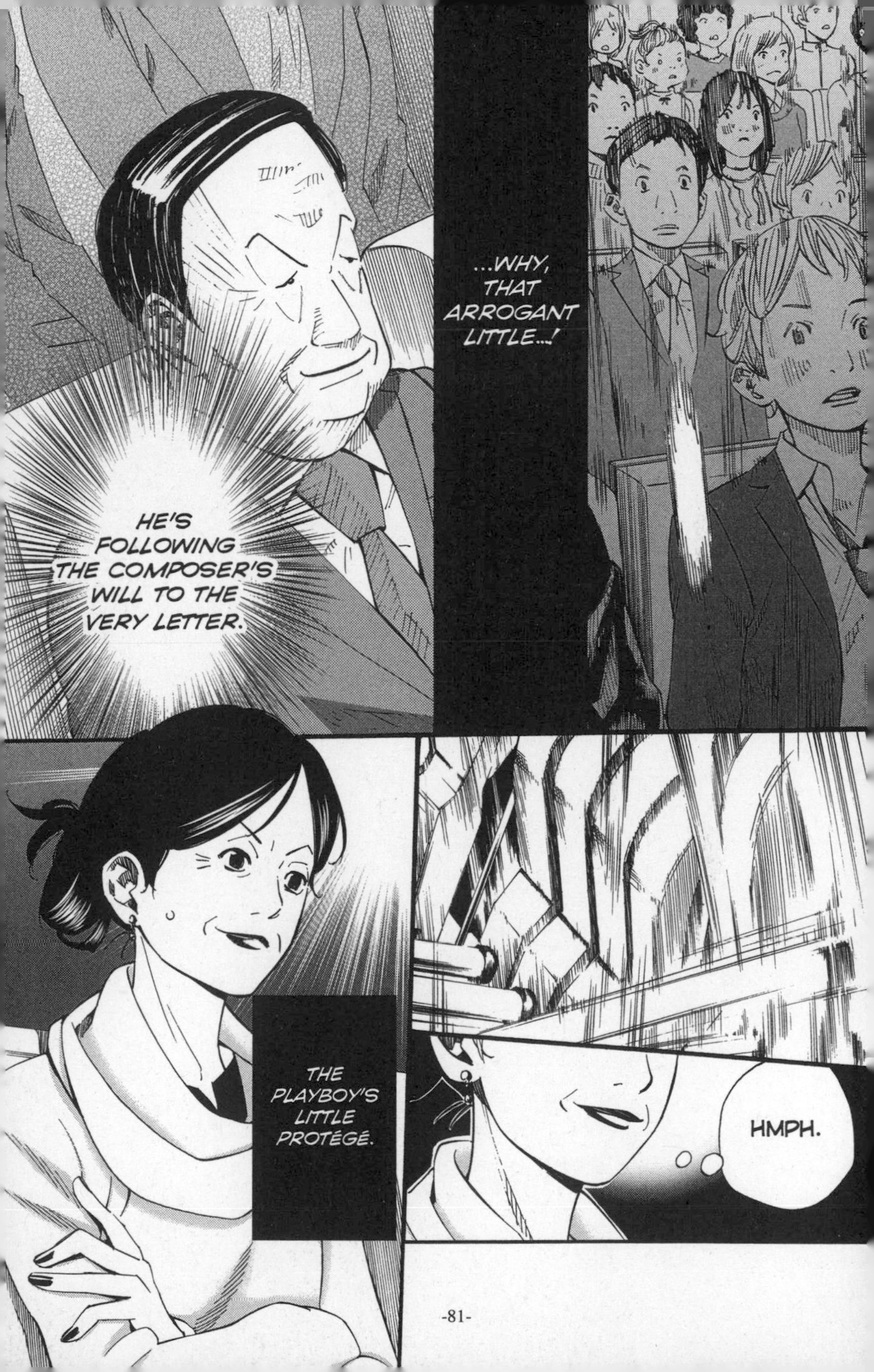
...WHY, THAT ARROGANT LITTLE...!
HE'S FOLLOWING THE COMPOSER'S WILL TO THE VERY LETTER.
HMPH.
THE PLAYBOY'S LITTLE PROTÉGÉ.

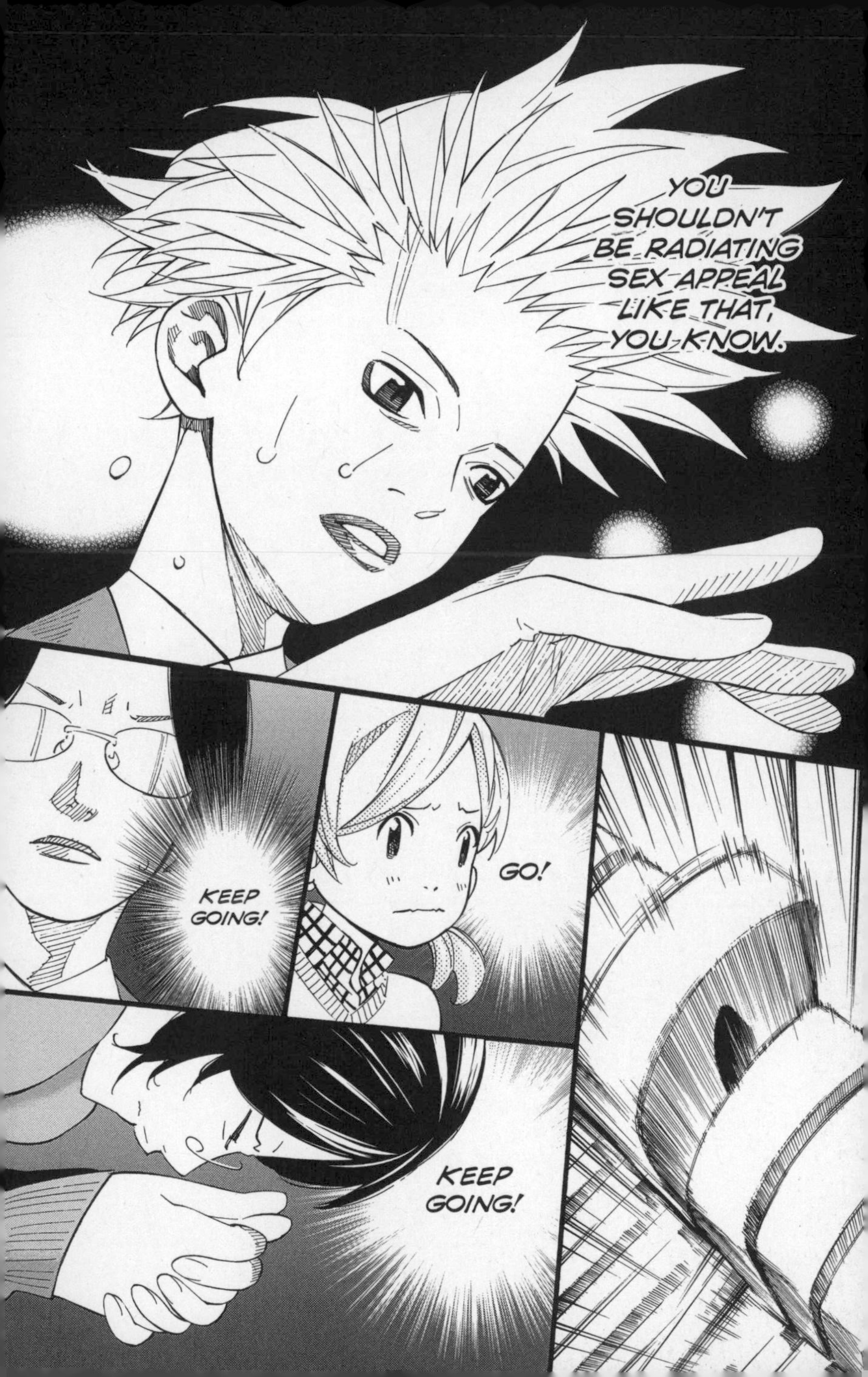
YOU SHOULDN'T BE RADIATING SEX APPEAL LIKE THAT, YOU KNOW.
GO!
KEEP GOING!
KEEP GOING!

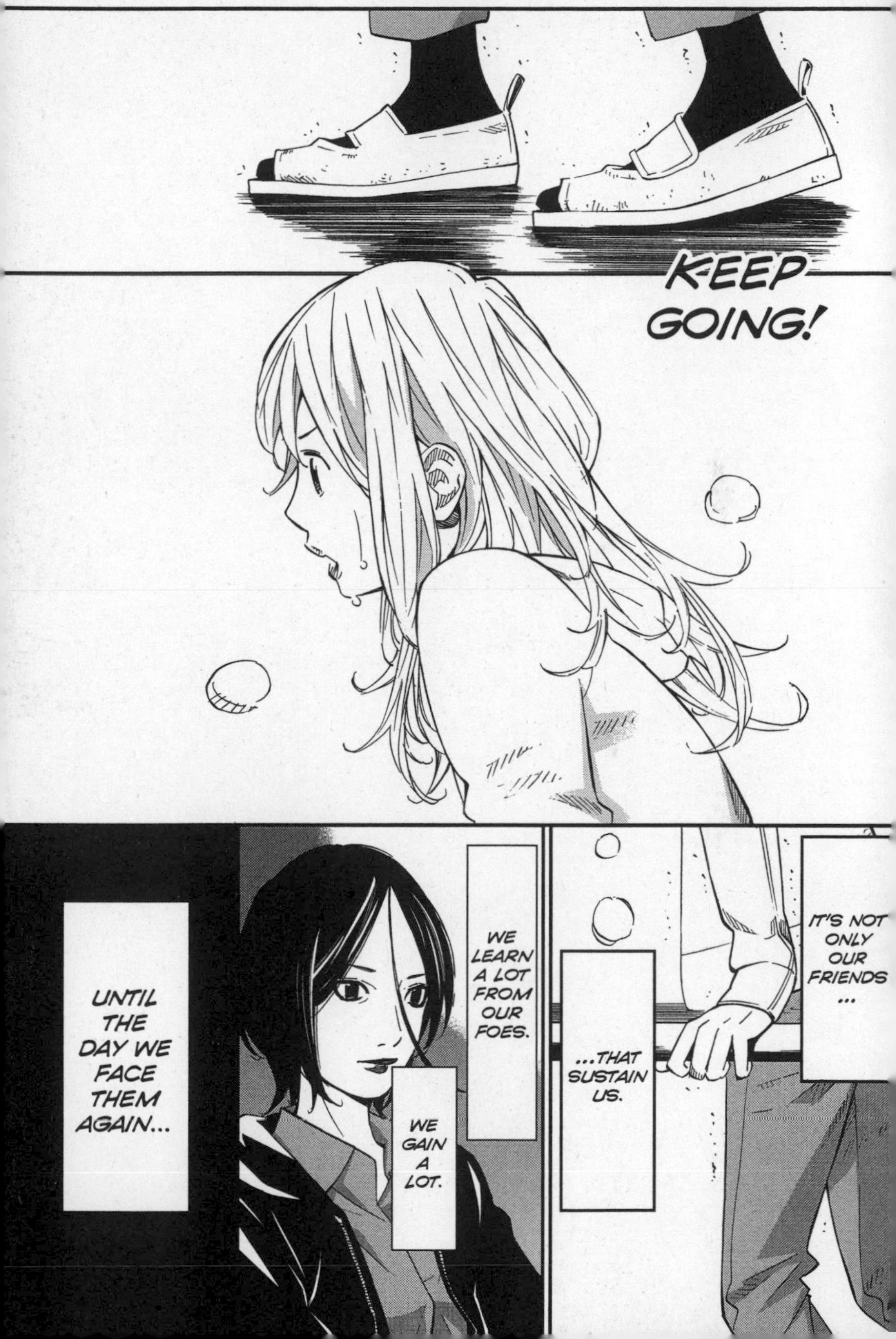
KEEP GOING!
IT'S NOT ONLY OUR FRIENDS ...
...THAT SUSTAIN US.
WE LEARN A LOT FROM OUR FOES.
WE GAIN A LOT.
UNTIL THE DAY WE FACE THEM AGAIN...

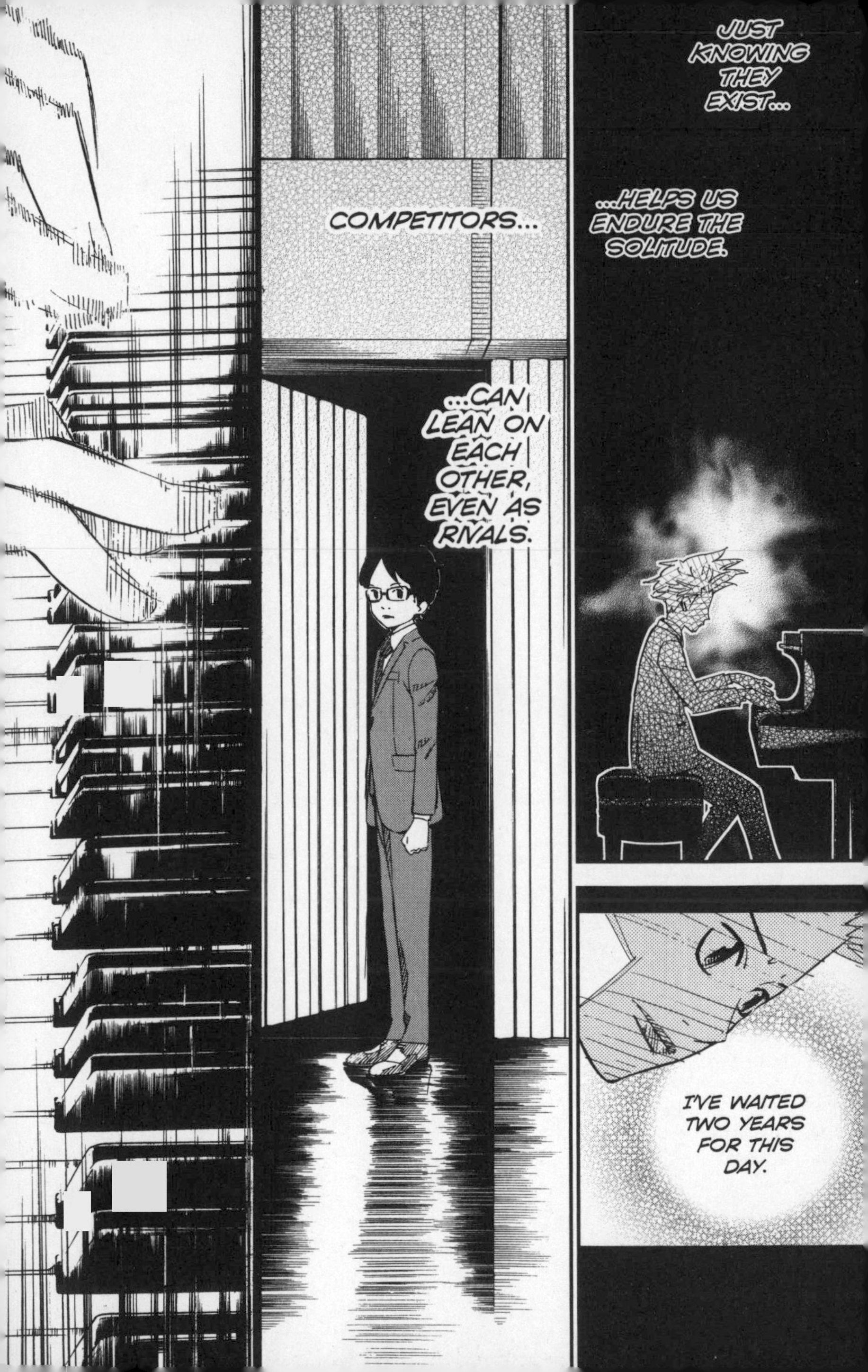
JUST KNOWING THEY EXIST...
...HELPS US ENDURE THE SOLITUDE.
I'VE WAITED TWO YEARS FOR THIS DAY.
COMPETITORS...
...CAN LEAN ON EACH OTHER, EVEN AS RIVALS.

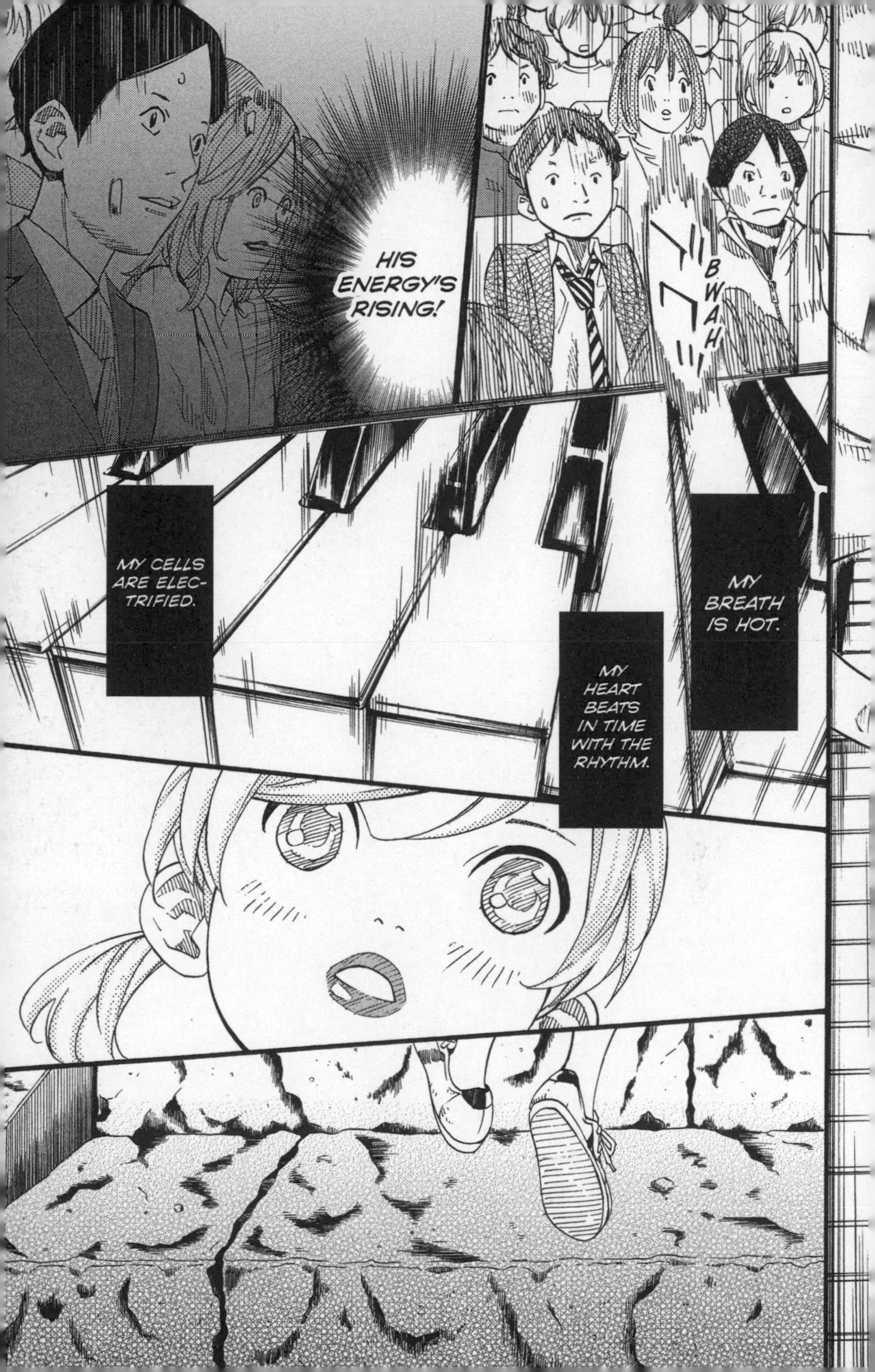
BWAH
HIS ENERGY'S RISING!
MY BREATH IS HOT.
MY HEART BEATS IN TIME WITH THE RHYTHM.
MY CELLS ARE ELECTRIFIED.

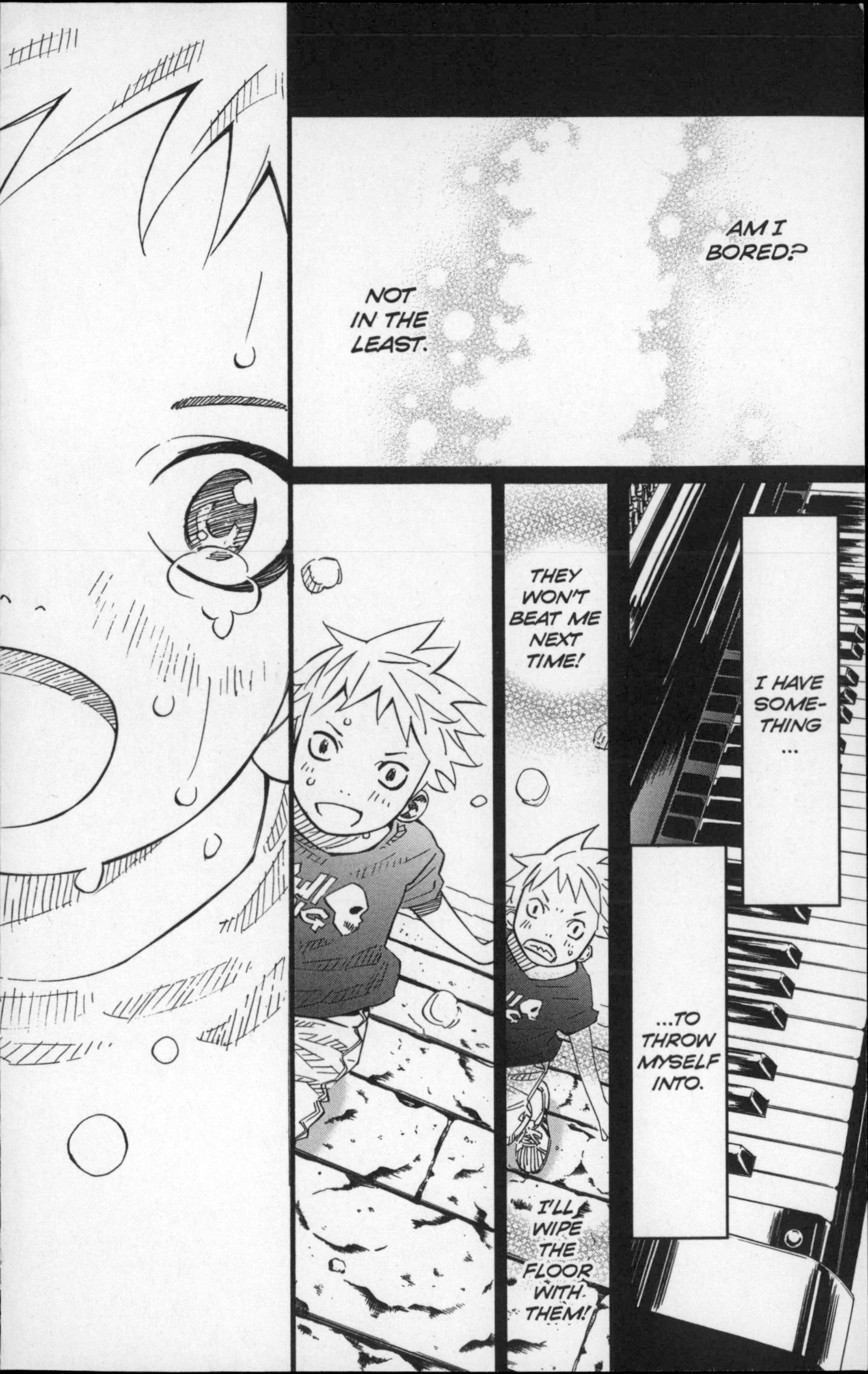
AM I BORED?
NOT IN THE LEAST.
I HAVE SOMETHING...
...TO THROW MYSELF INTO.
THEY WON'T BEAT ME NEXT TIME!
I'LL WIPE THE FLOOR WITH THEM!

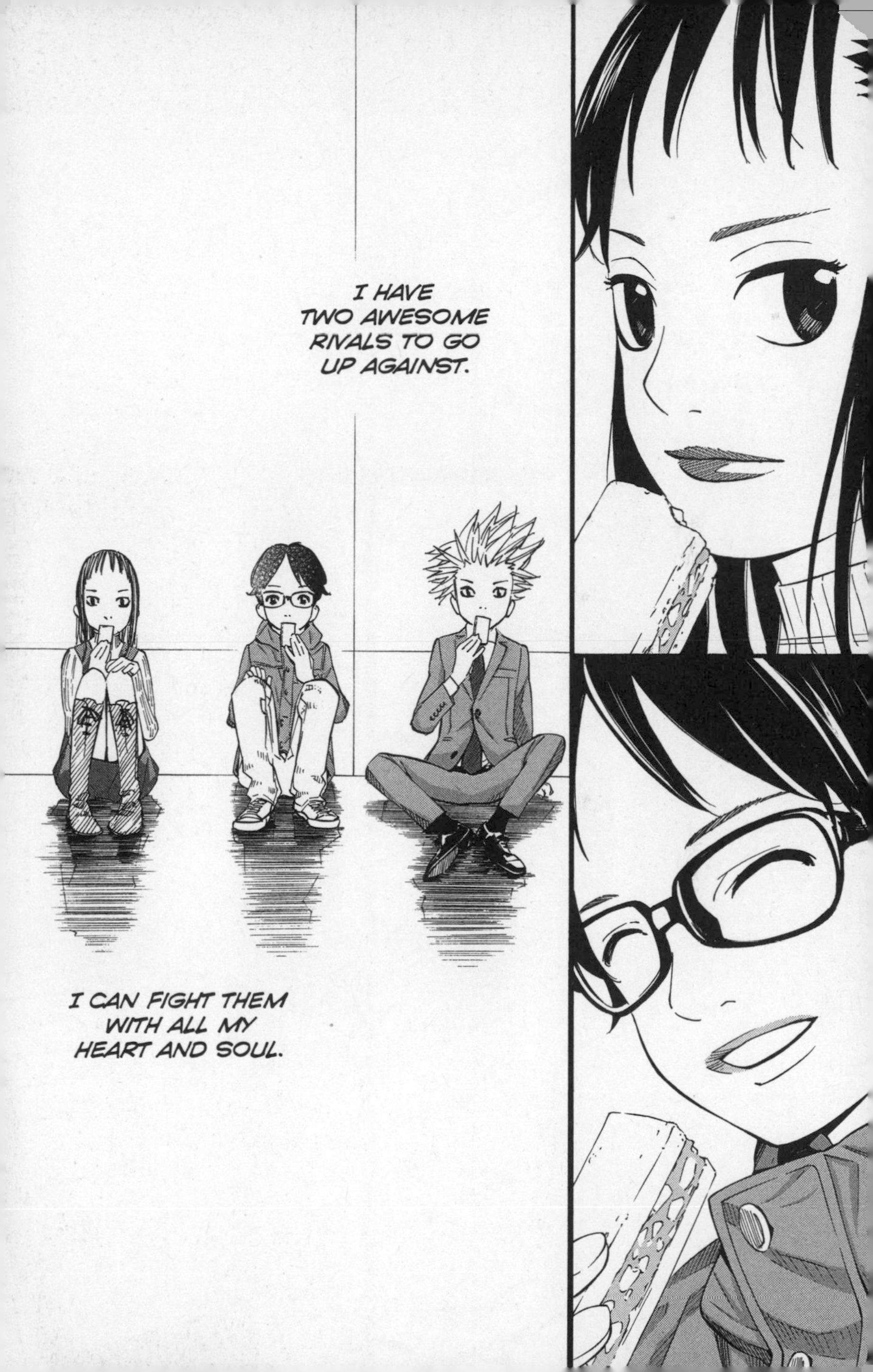
I HAVE TWO AWESOME RIVALS TO GO UP AGAINST.
I CAN FIGHT THEM WITH ALL MY HEART AND SOUL.

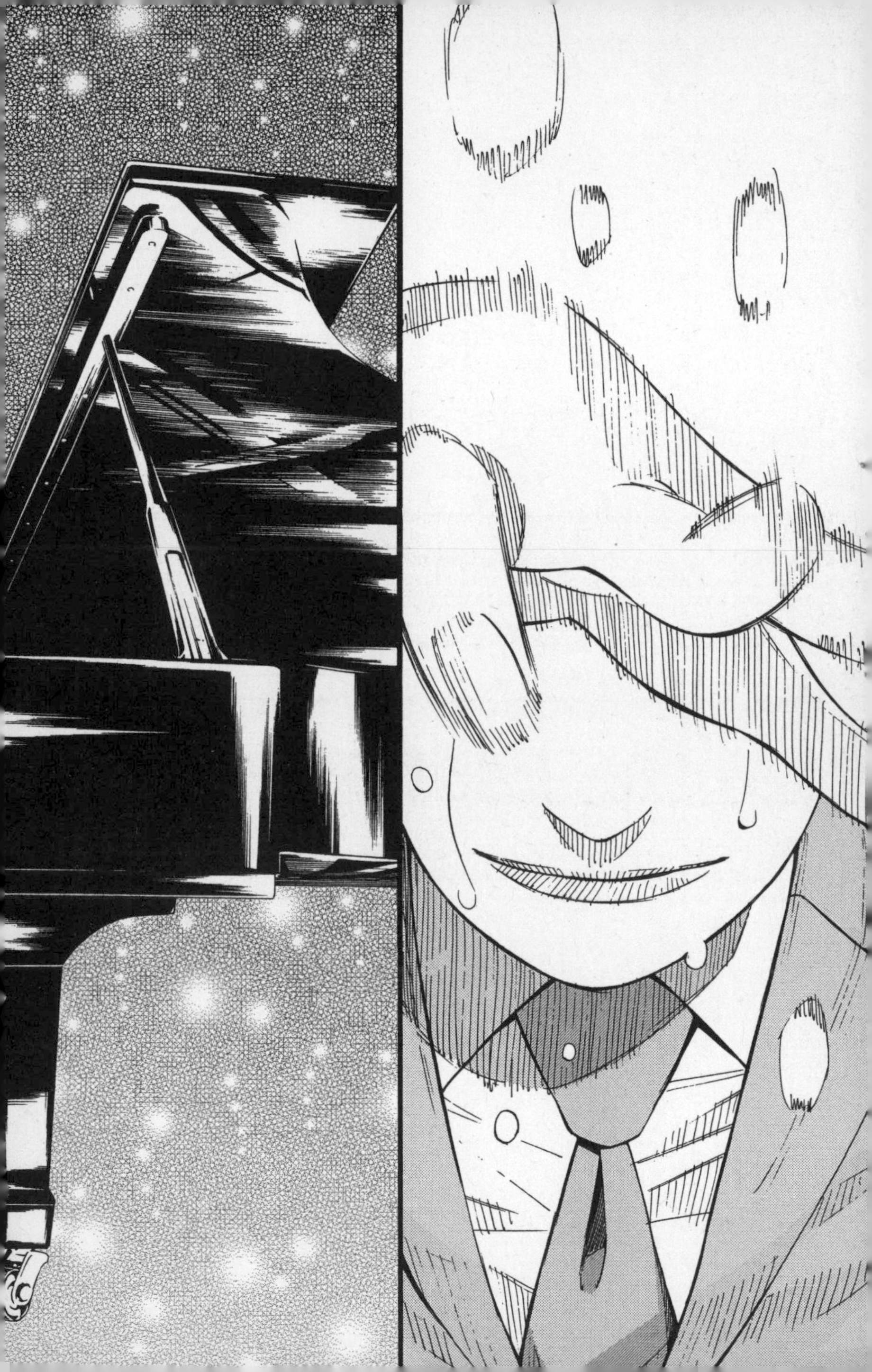

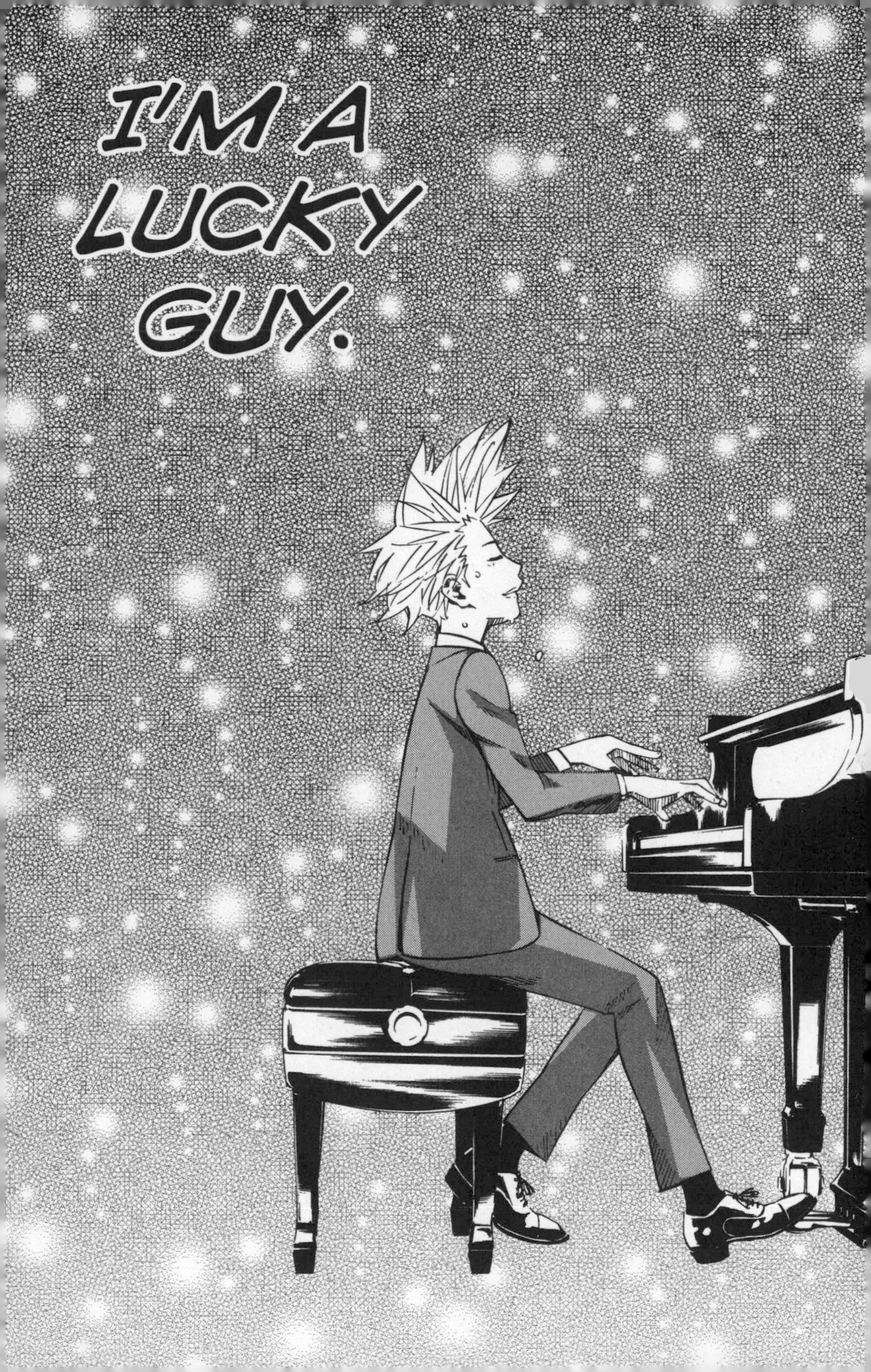
I'M A LUCKY GUY.

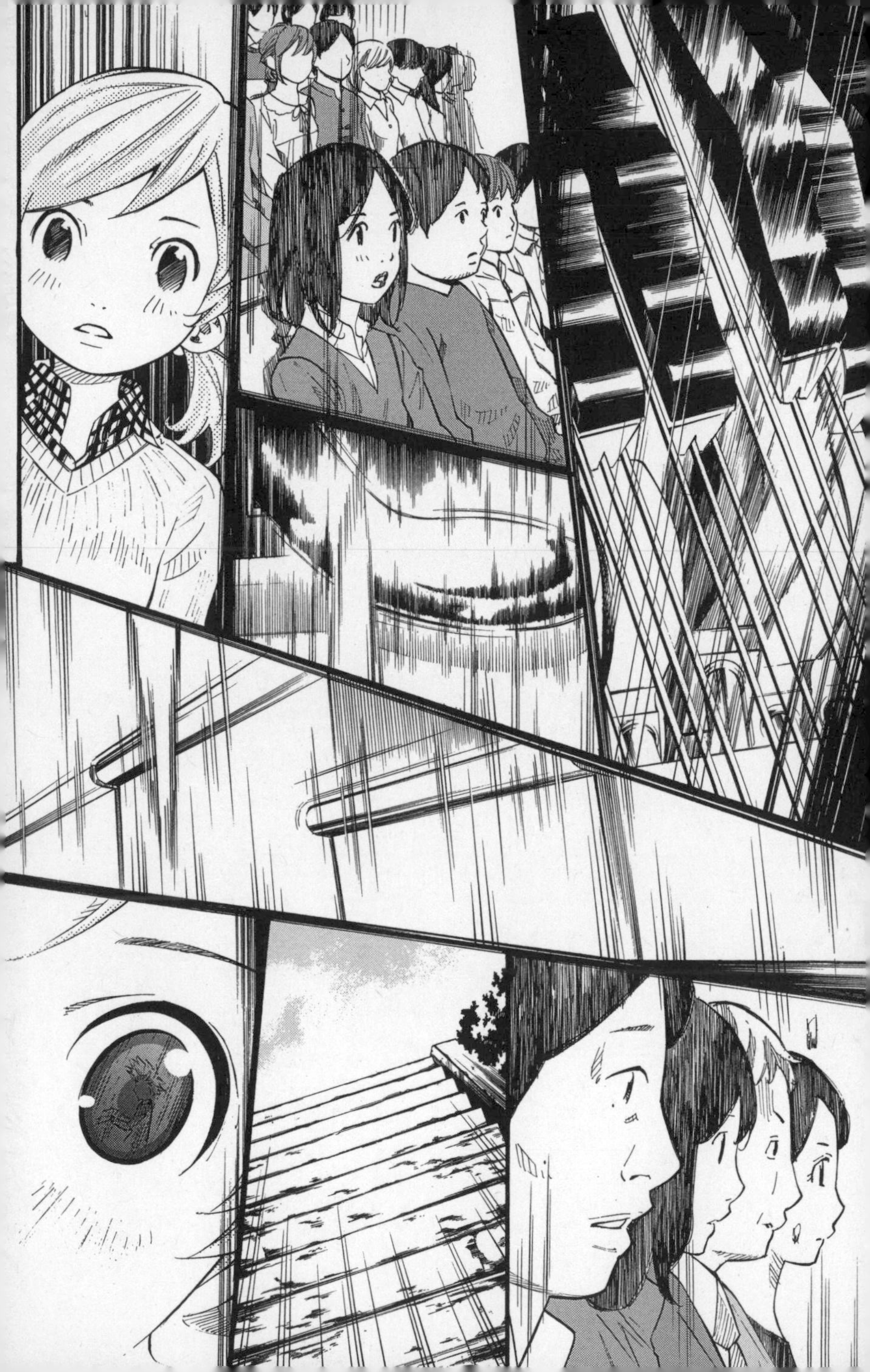

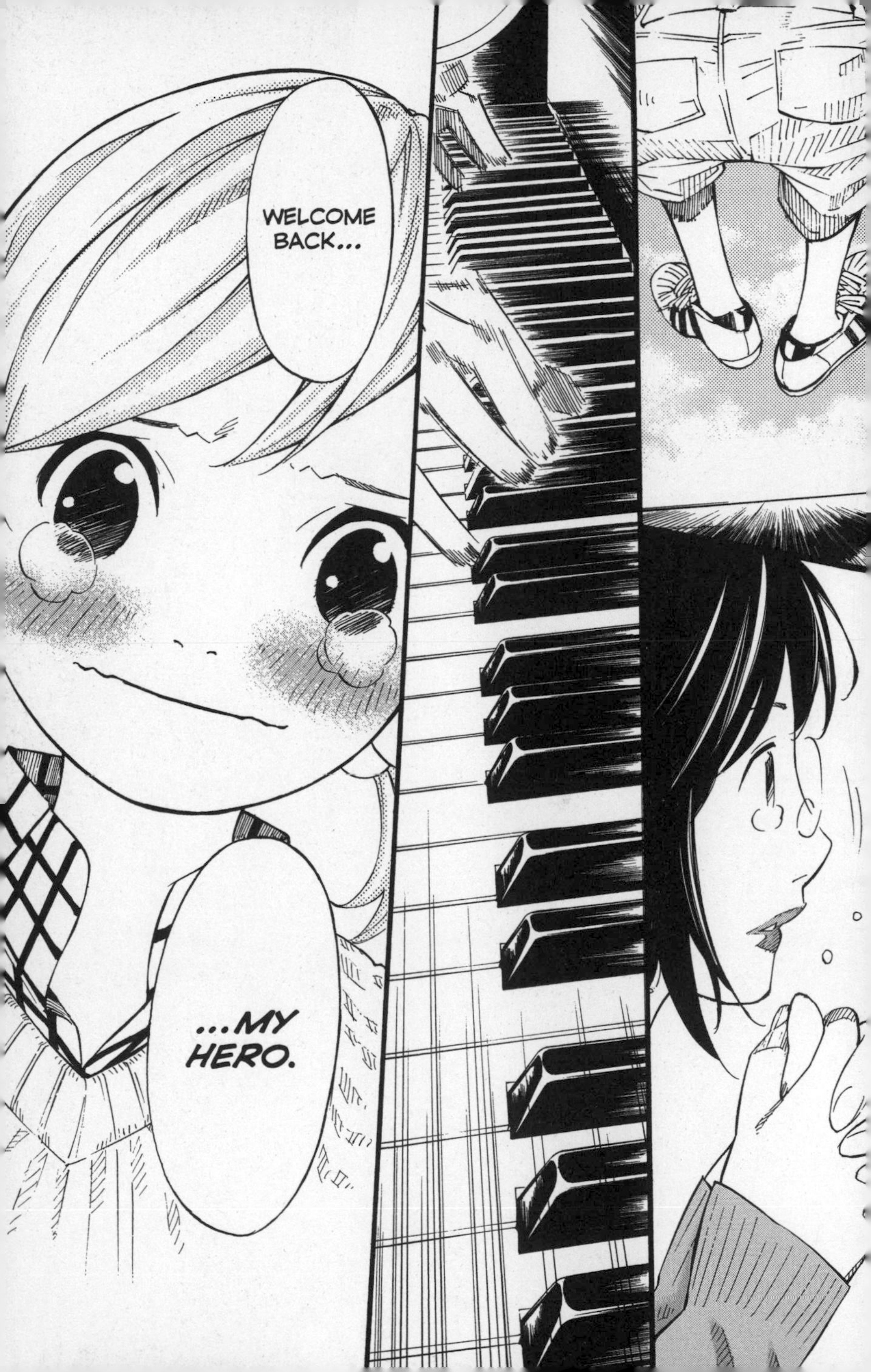
WELCOME BACK...
...MY HERO.

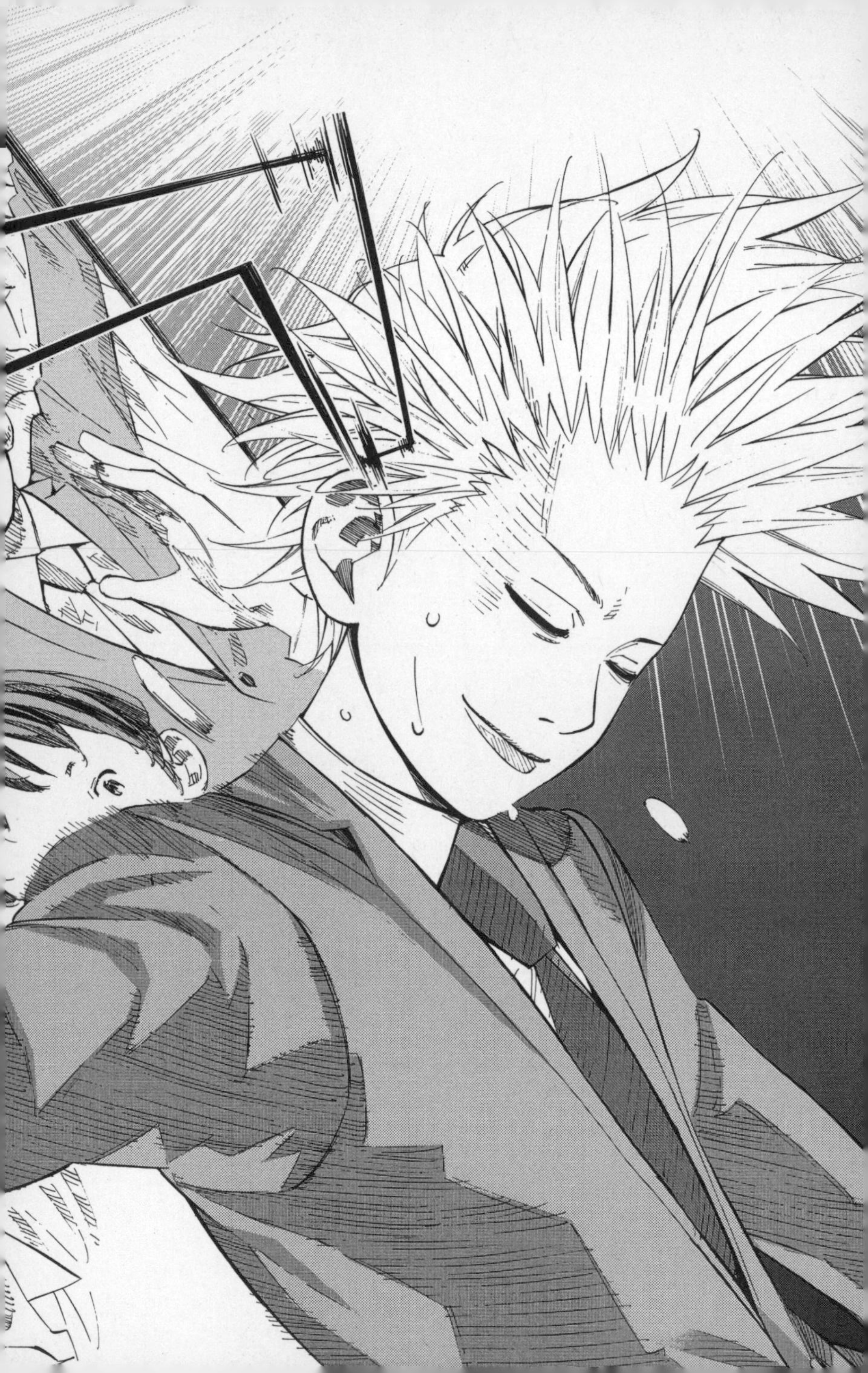

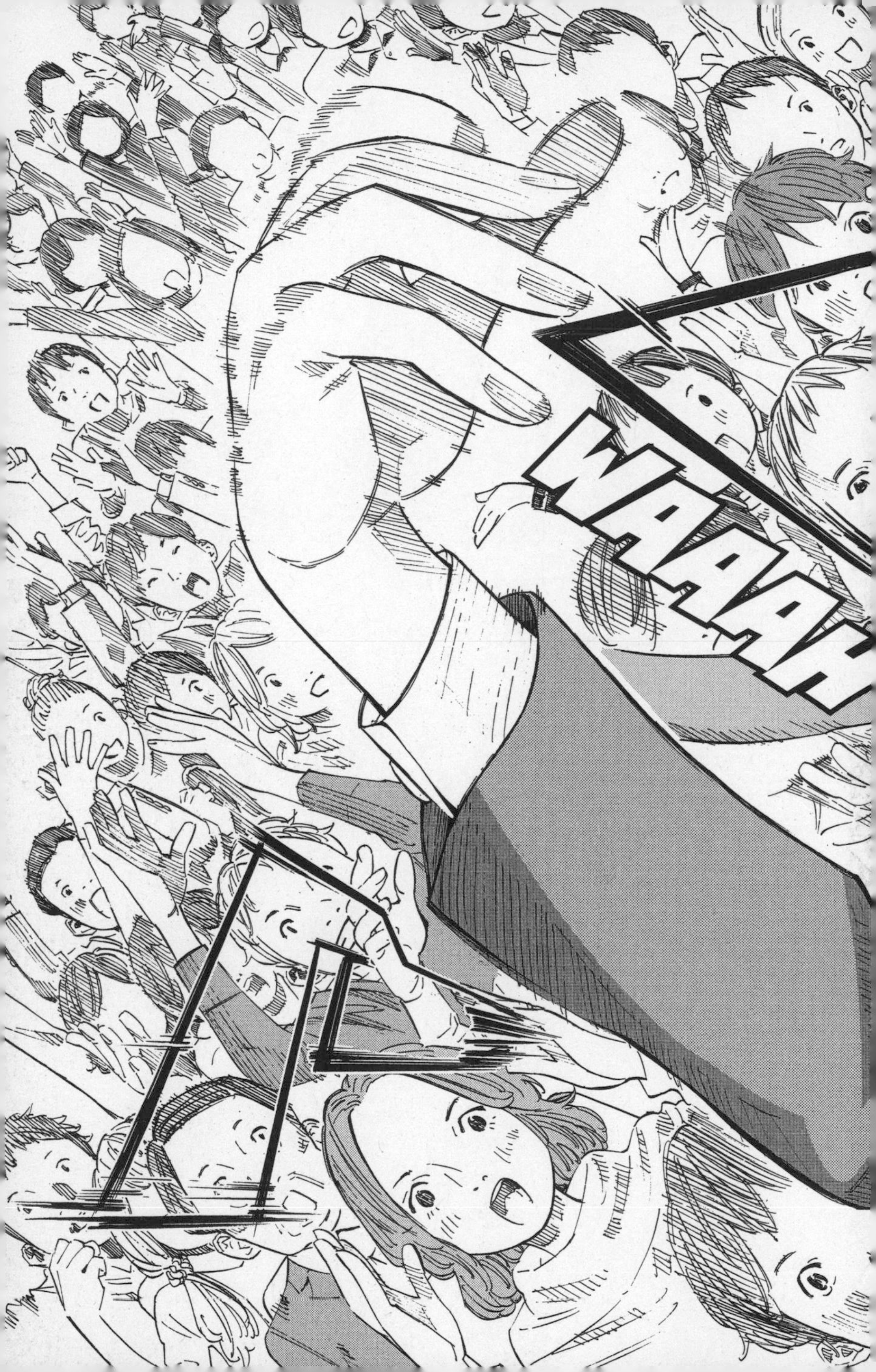
WAAAH

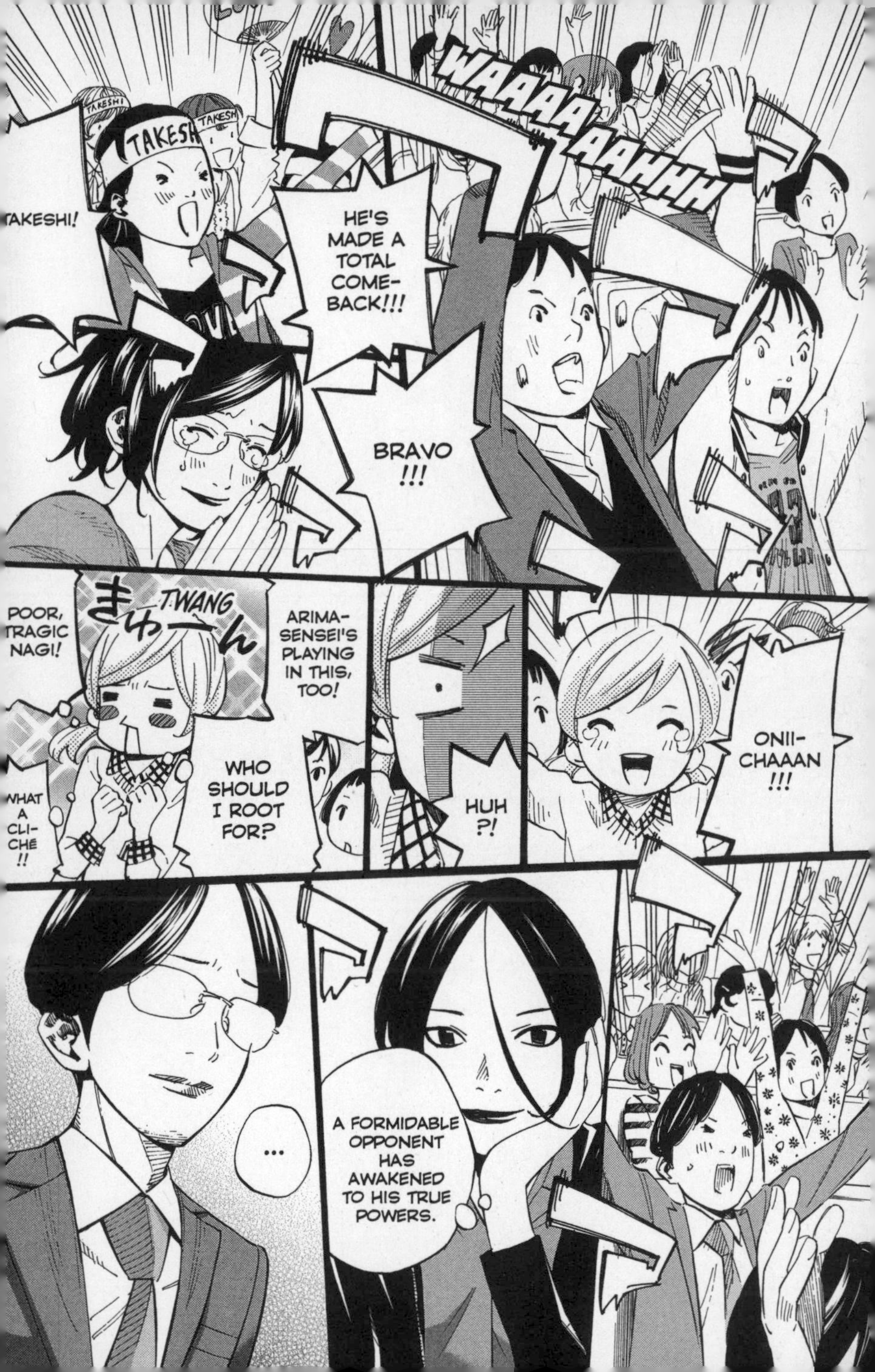
WAAAAAAHHHH
HE'S MADE A TOTAL COME-BACK!!!
BRAVO!!!
TAKESHI
TAKESHI
TAKESHI
TAKESHI!
ONII-CHAAAN!!!
HUH?!
ARIMA-SENSEI'S PLAYING IN THIS, TOO!
きゅーん
TWANG
POOR, TRAGIC NAGI!
WHO SHOULD I ROOT FOR?
WHAT A CLICHÉ!!
A FORMIDABLE OPPONENT HAS AWAKENED TO HIS TRUE POWERS.
...

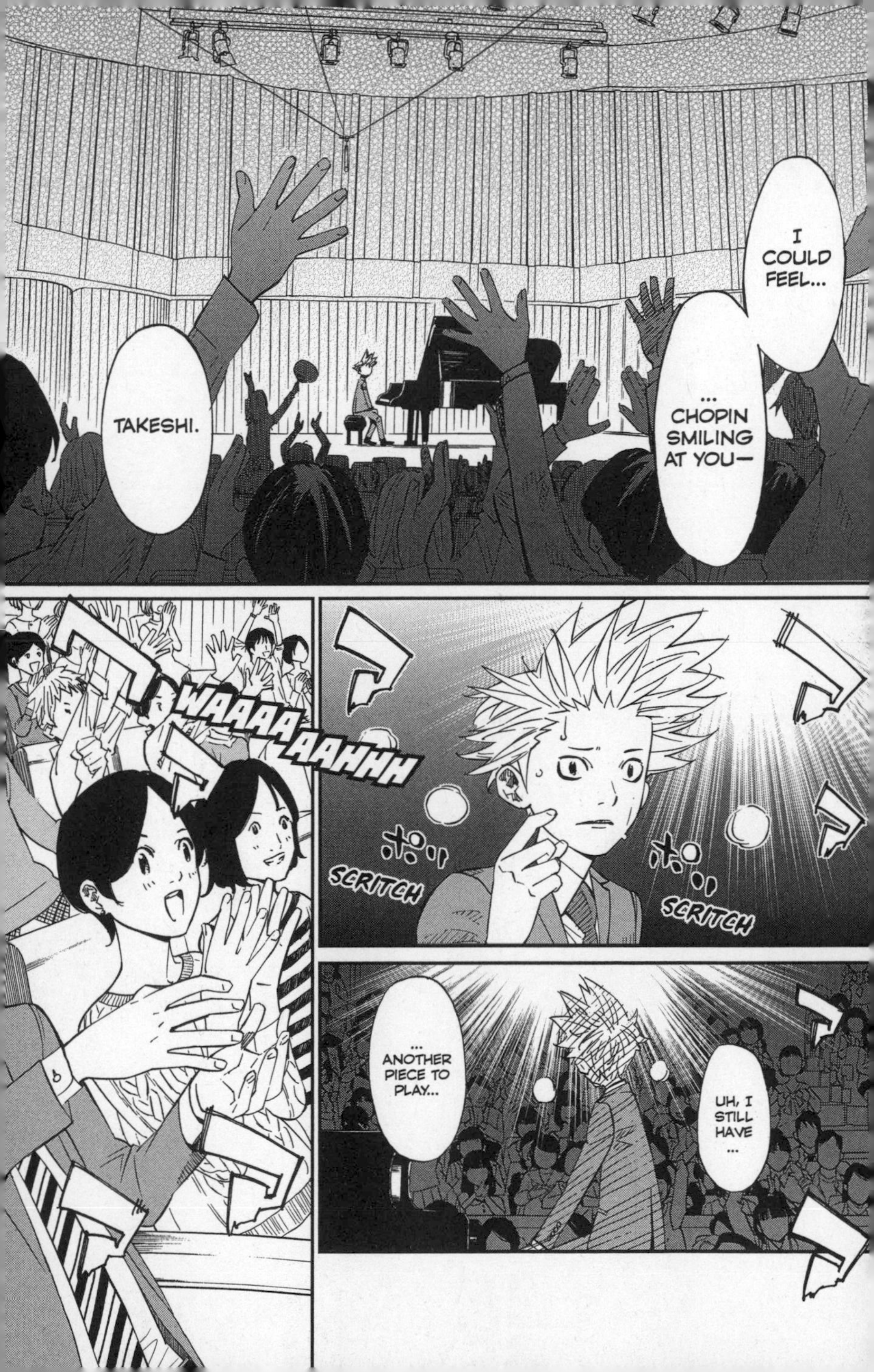
I COULD FEEL...
... CHOPIN SMILING AT YOU—
TAKESHI.
SCRITCH
SCRITCH
UH, I STILL HAVE ...
... ANOTHER PIECE TO PLAY...
WAAAAAAAHHHH

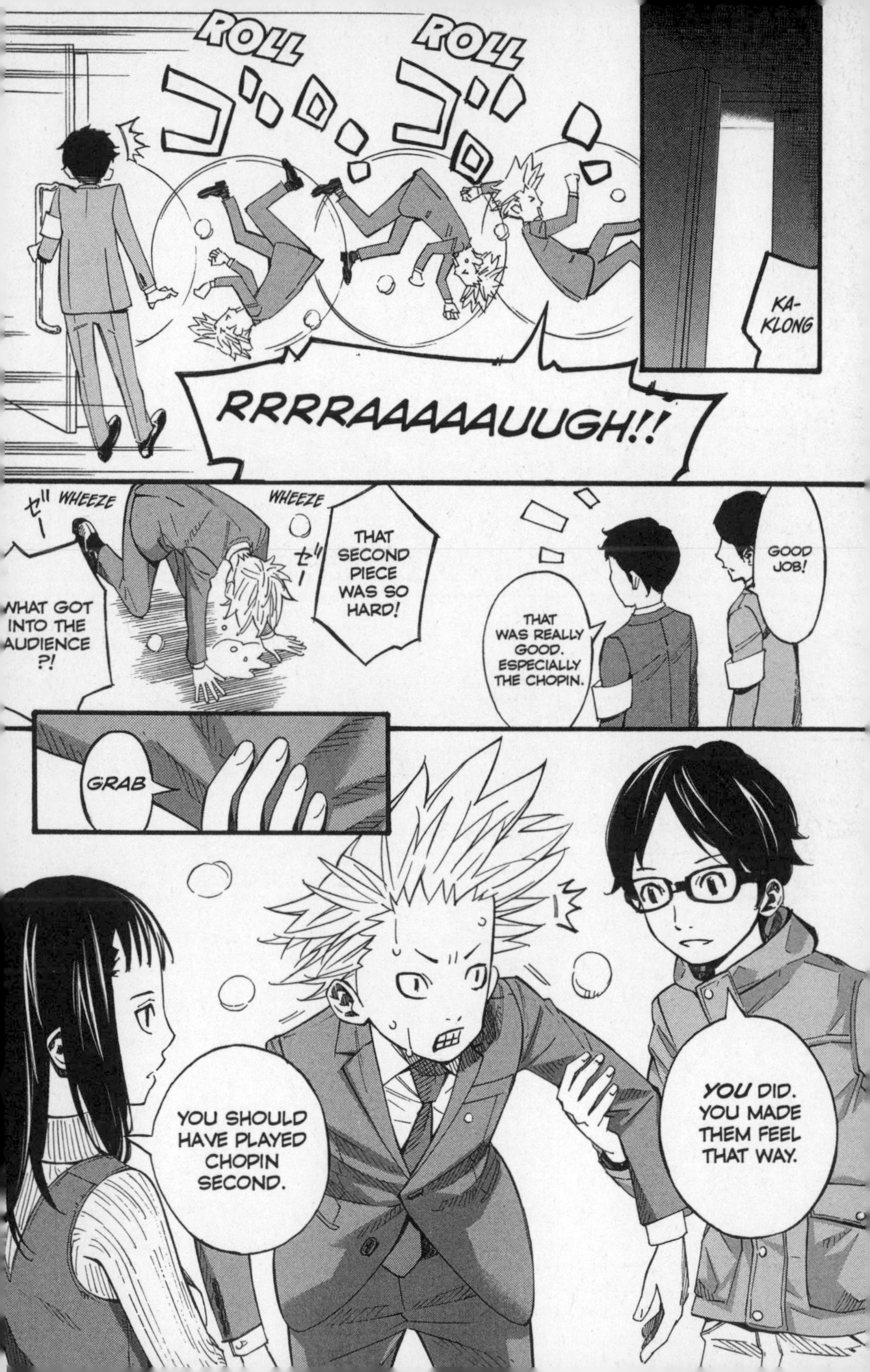
KA-
KLONG
ROLL
ROLL
RRRRAAAAAAUUGH!!
GOOD JOB!
THAT WAS REALLY GOOD. ESPECIALLY THE CHOPIN.
WHEEZE
THAT SECOND PIECE WAS SO HARD!
WHEEZE
WHAT GOT INTO THE AUDIENCE ?!
GRAB
YOU DID. YOU MADE THEM FEEL THAT WAY.
YOU SHOULD HAVE PLAYED CHOPIN SECOND.

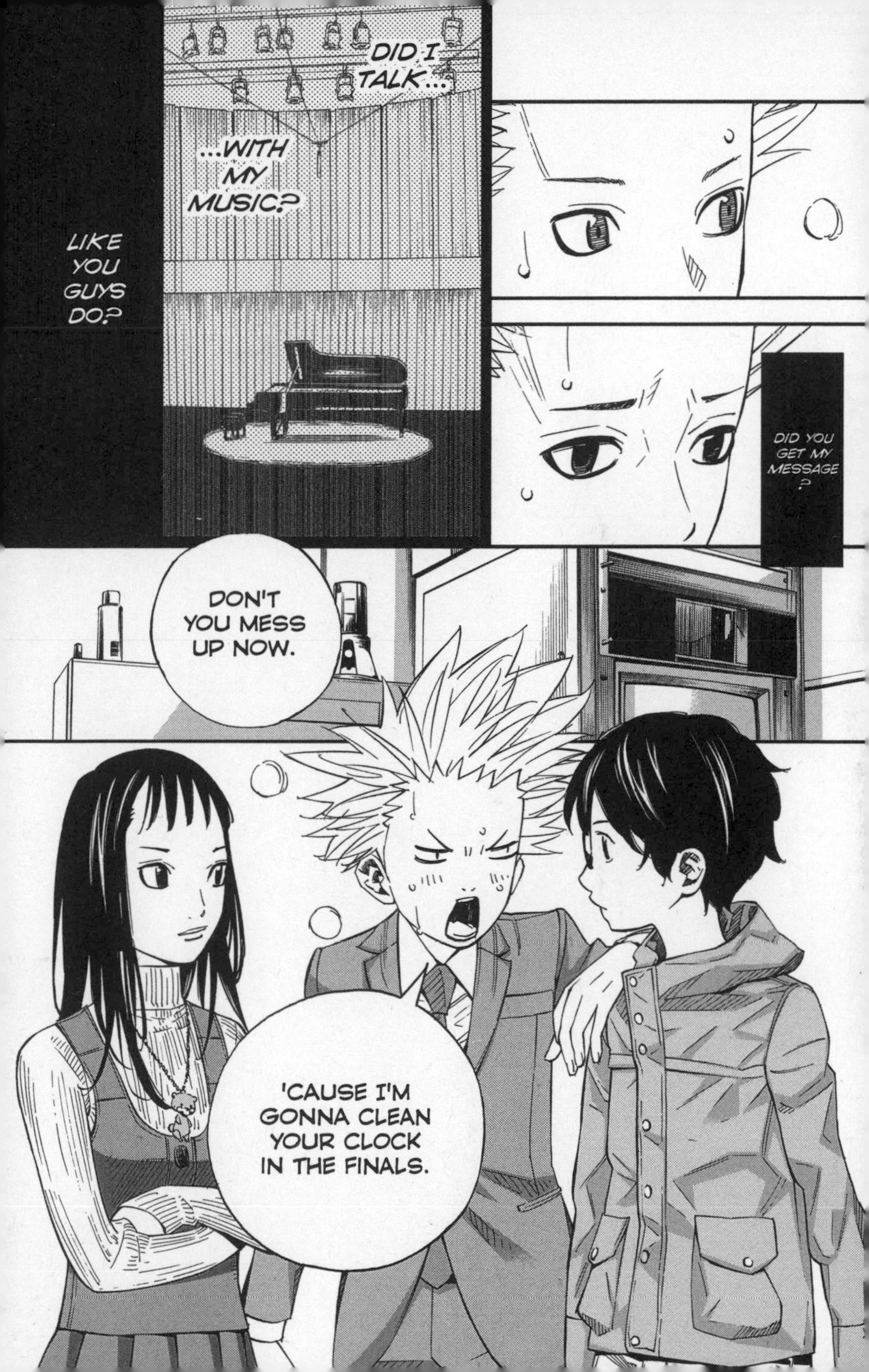
DID YOU GET MY MESSAGE?
DID I TALK...
...WITH MY MUSIC?
LIKE YOU GUYS DO?
DON'T YOU MESS UP NOW.
'CAUSE I'M GONNA CLEAN YOUR CLOCK IN THE FINALS.

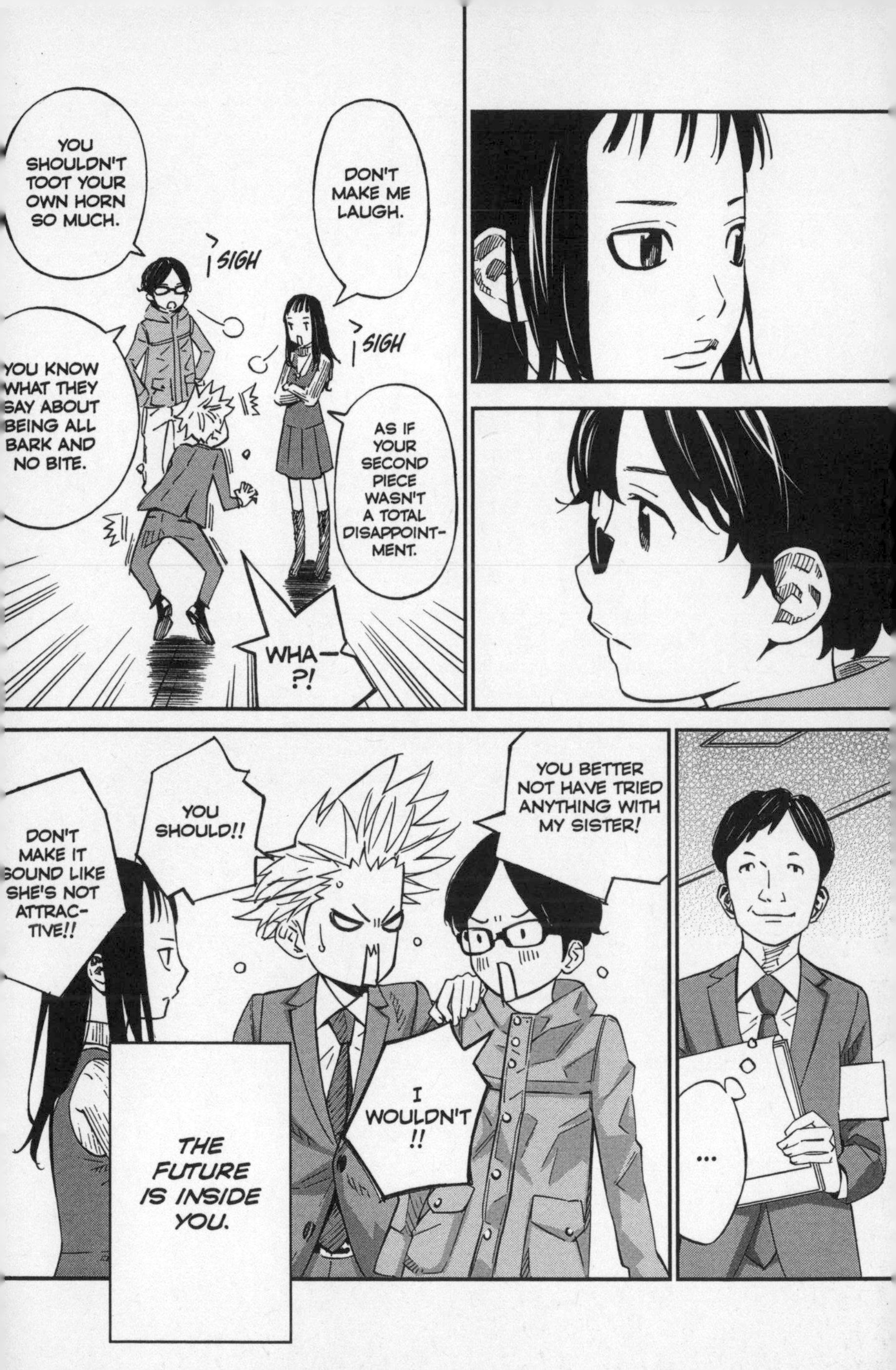
DON'T MAKE ME LAUGH.
SIGH
YOU SHOULDN'T TOOT YOUR OWN HORN SO MUCH.
SIGH
AS IF YOUR SECOND PIECE WASN'T A TOTAL DISAPPOINT-MENT.
YOU KNOW WHAT THEY SAY ABOUT BEING ALL BARK AND NO BITE.
WHA—?!
...
YOU BETTER NOT HAVE TRIED ANYTHING WITH MY SISTER!
YOU SHOULD!!
DON'T MAKE IT SOUND LIKE SHE'S NOT ATTRAC-TIVE!!
I WOULDN'T!!
THE FUTURE IS INSIDE YOU.

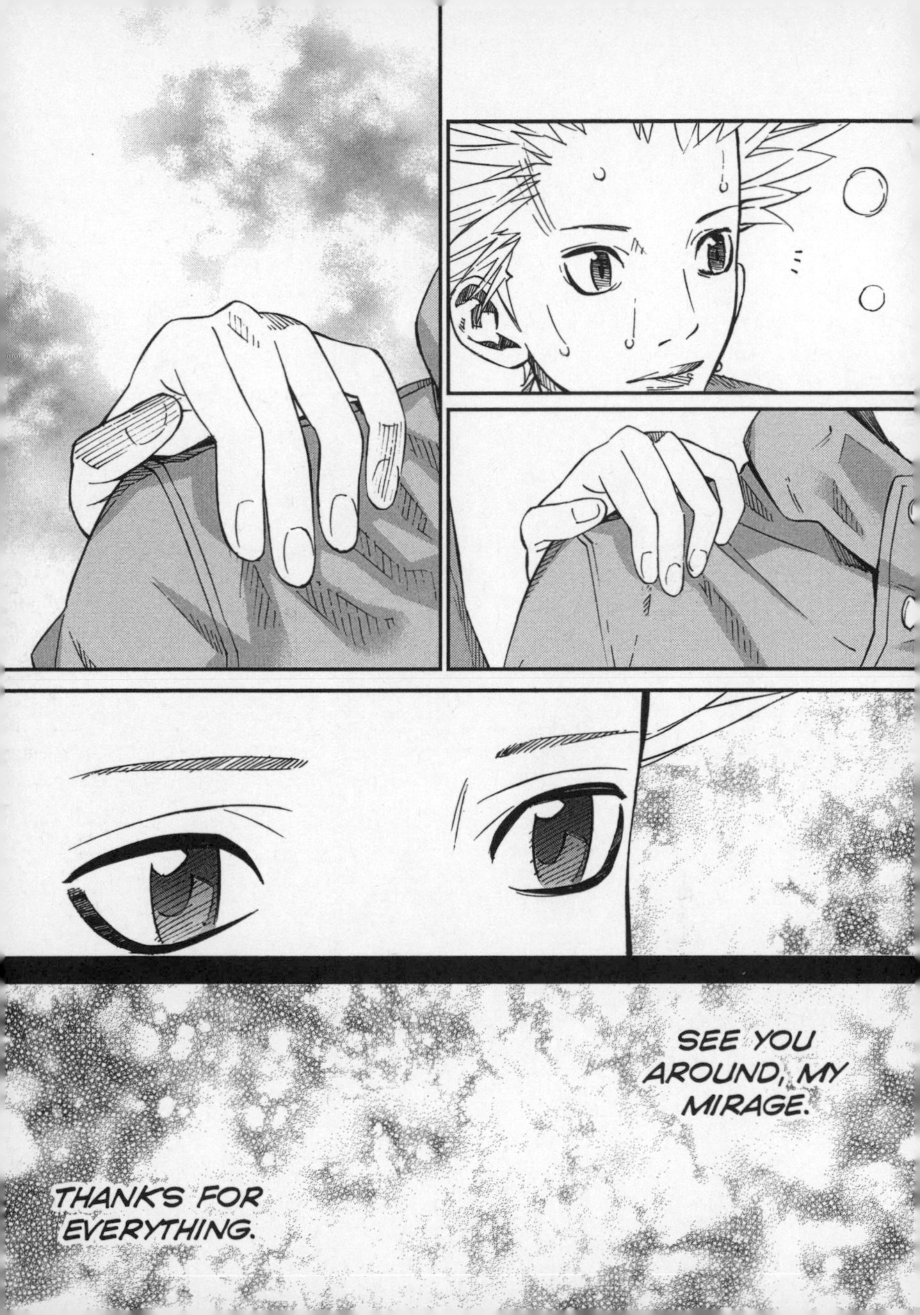
SEE YOU AROUND, MY MIRAGE.
THANKS FOR EVERYTHING.

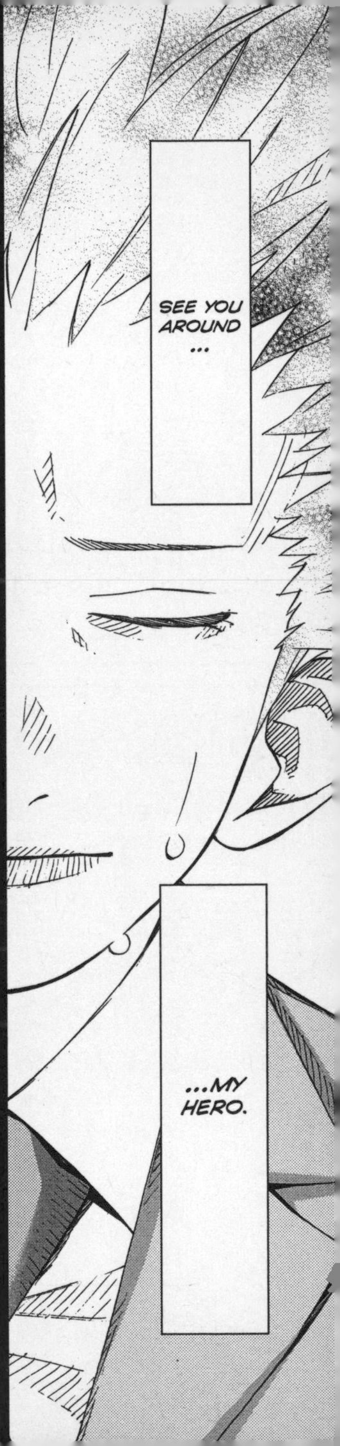
SEE YOU AROUND...
...MY HERO.
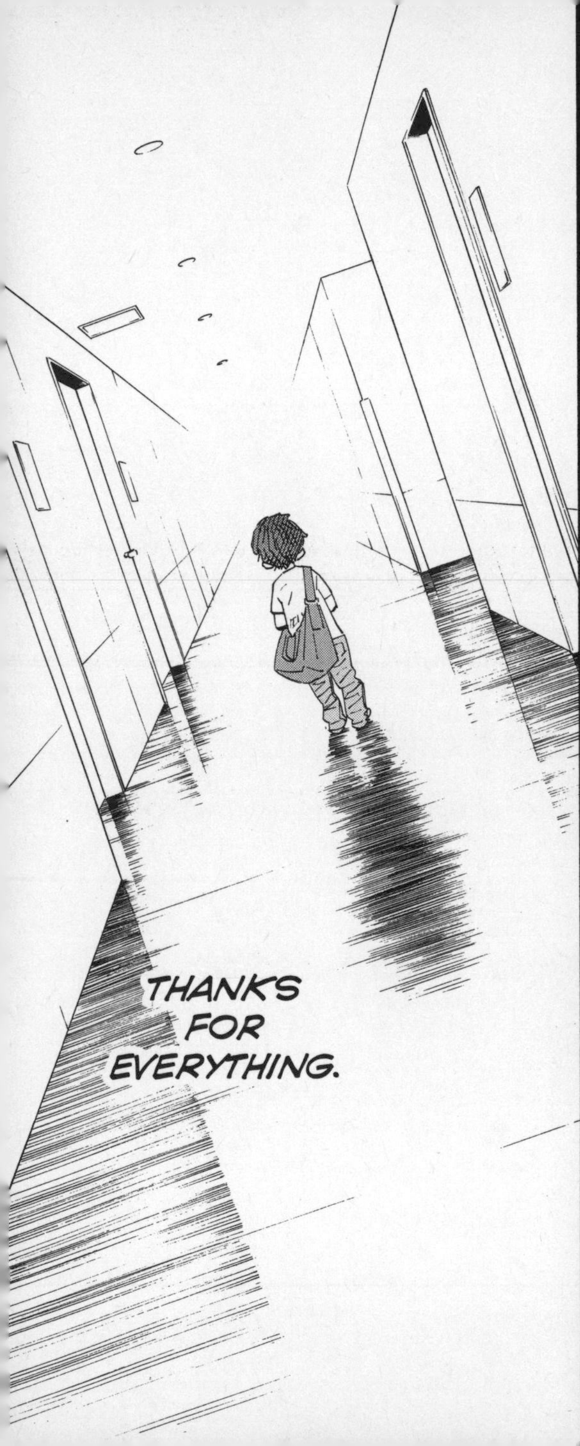
THANKS FOR EVERYTHING.

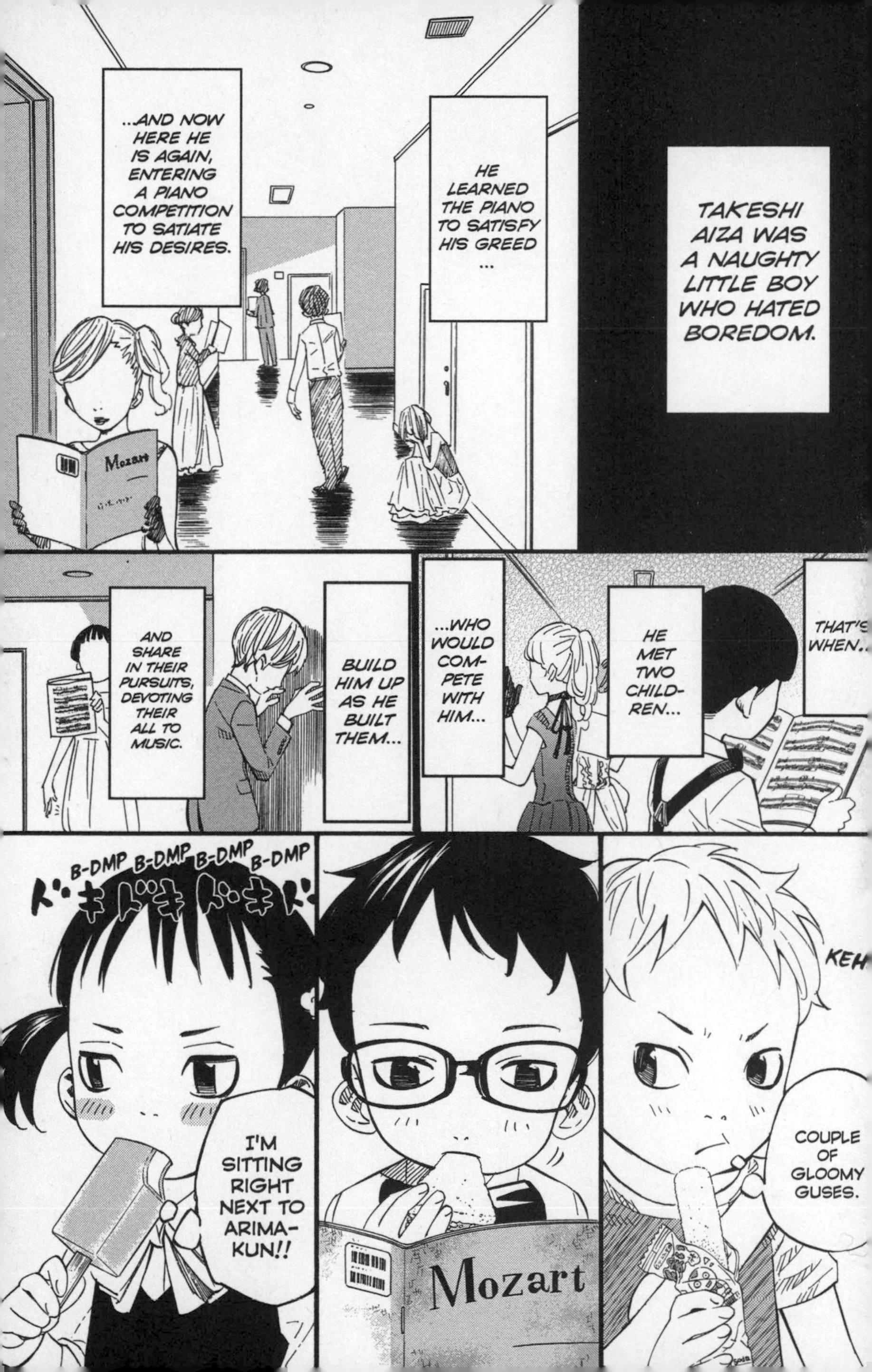
TAKESHI AIZA WAS A NAUGHTY LITTLE BOY WHO HATED BOREDOM.
HE LEARNED THE PIANO TO SATISFY HIS GREED ...
...AND NOW HERE HE IS AGAIN, ENTERING A PIANO COMPETITION TO SATIATE HIS DESIRES.
Mozart
THAT'S WHEN...
HE MET TWO CHILD-REN...
...WHO WOULD COM-PETE WITH HIM...
BUILD HIM UP AS HE BUILT THEM...
AND SHARE IN THEIR PURSUITS, DEVOTING THEIR ALL TO MUSIC.
KEH
COUPLE OF GLOOMY GUSES.
Mozart
B-DMP B-DMP B-DMP B-DMP
I'M SITTING RIGHT NEXT TO ARIMA-KUN!!

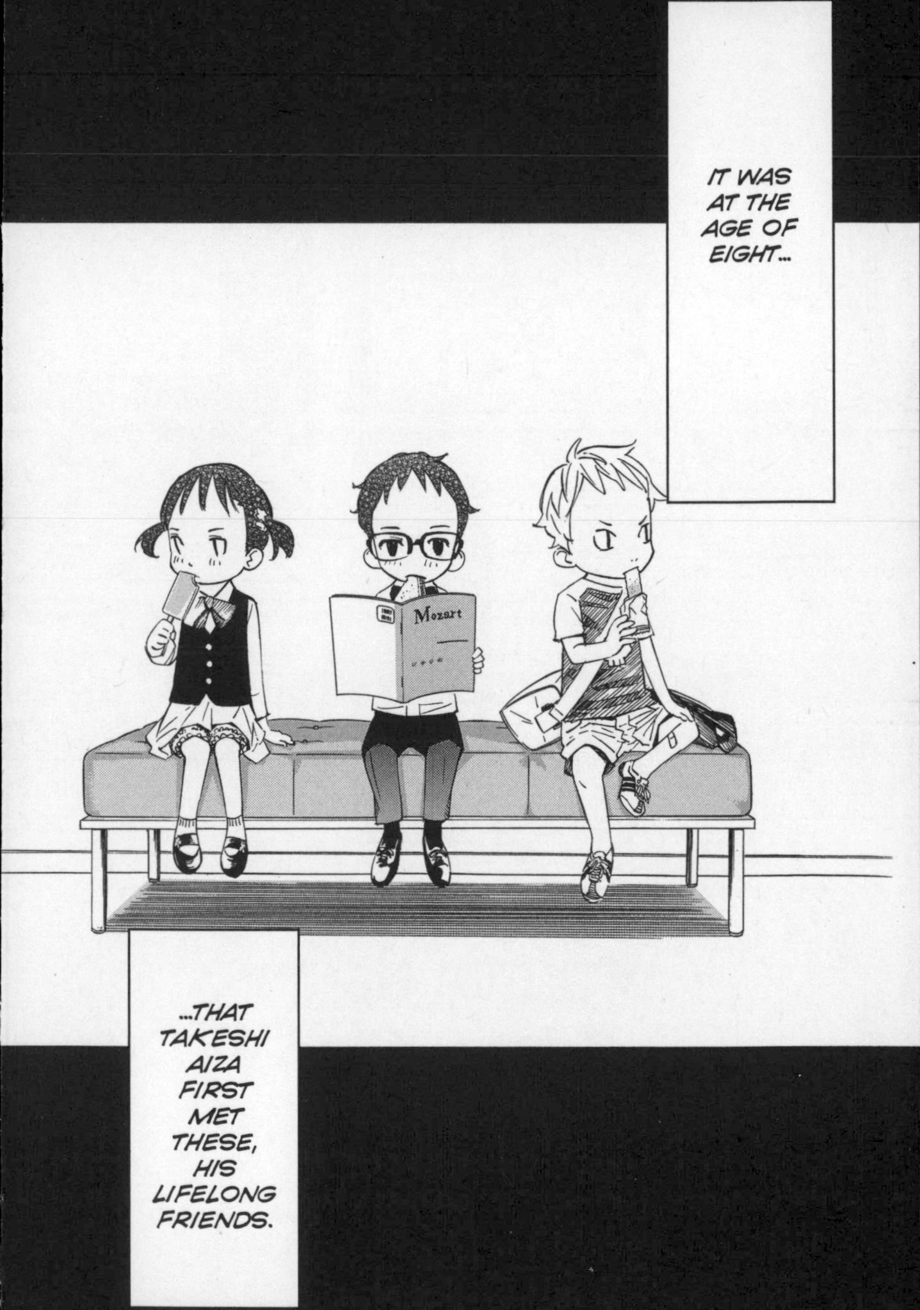
IT WAS AT THE AGE OF EIGHT...
Mozart
...THAT TAKESHI AIZA FIRST MET THESE, HIS LIFELONG FRIENDS.

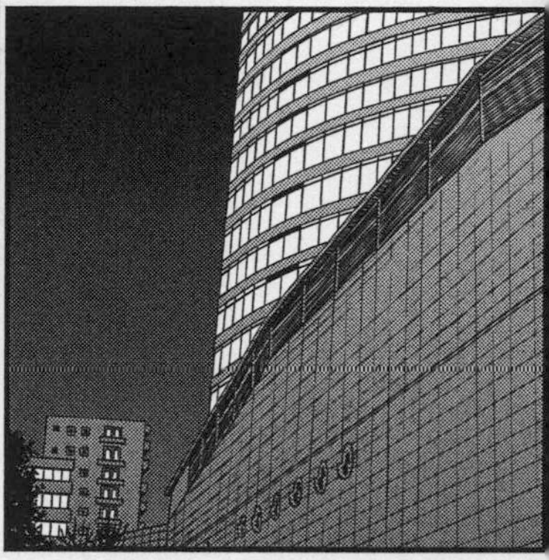

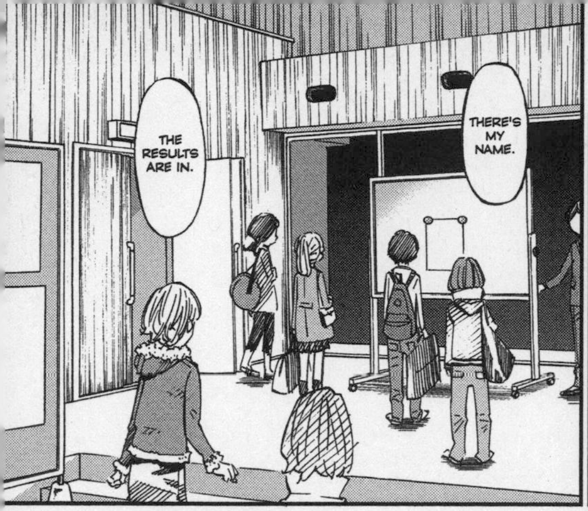
THERE'S MY NAME.
THE RESULTS ARE IN.

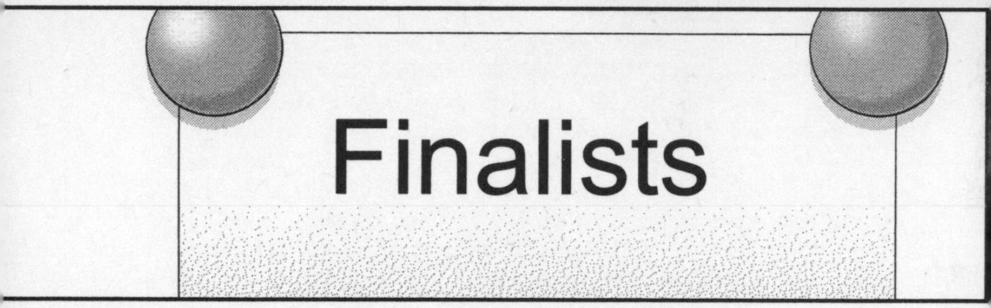
Finalists

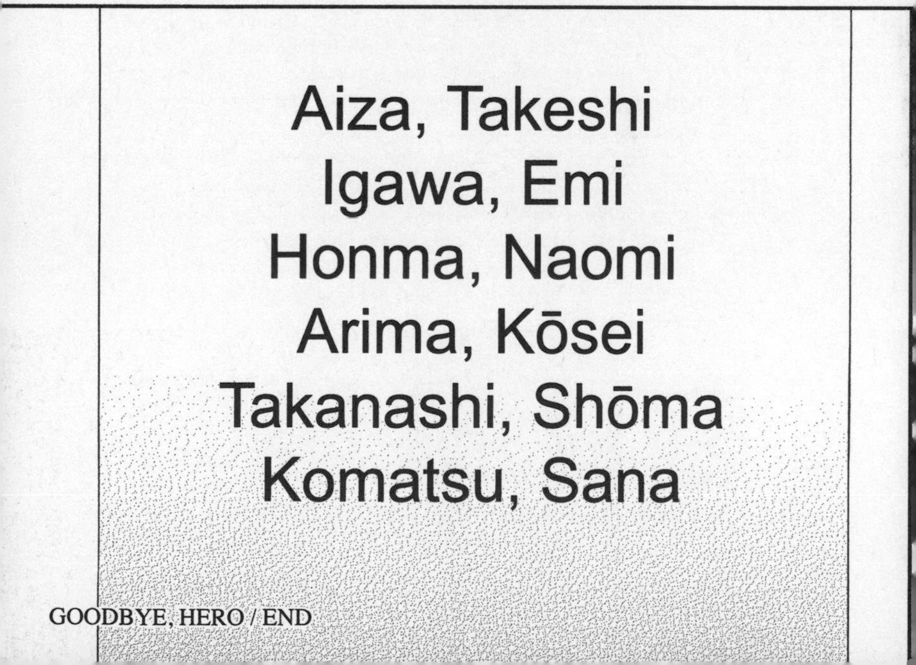
Aiza, Takeshi
Igawa, Emi
Honma, Naomi
Arima, Kōsei
Takanashi, Shōma
Komatsu, Sana

GOODBYE, HERO / END

Your Lie in April Featured Music

Chopin's *Études Op.10, No.12: The Revolutionary Étude*

Chopin is called the "Poet of the Piano," thanks to his lilting waltzes and charming nocturnes with romantic, colorful melodies and harmonies. *The Revolutionary Étude*, one of his most famous pieces, is an unusual one, with swelling left hand passages and a melody full of octaves and chords that convey a frenzied bloodlust to the listener. Behind this intense musical piece, one will find Chopin's feelings for his family and homeland.

Because his home country of Poland is surrounded by Austria, Germany, and Russia, it has been invaded time and again by its neighbors. When Chopin was born, Poland belonged to Russia. In November of 1830, at 20 years old, Chopin set out for Vienna, the "City of Music", in search of a place to perform. Soon after he left, there was an uprising as Poland fought for independence. Knowing that his family and friends were fighting against Russia back home, it was only with terrible reluctance that Chopin went to Paris. On the road there he learned that the fight for independence had ended in defeat, with his homeland assimilated into Russia.

"And here I am, traveling!" he wrote. "...Sometimes I can only groan and suffer and pour out my despair at the piano— I'm going to lose my mind!"

He wrote the *Études* around this time dedicating them to piano virtuoso Franz Liszt, who named this piece *The Revolutionary*. Perhaps he sensed in it the maddening sadness and love that Chopin felt for his home and family.

—Pianist Masanori Sugano
lecturer, Tokyo University of the Arts
and Musashino Academia Musicae

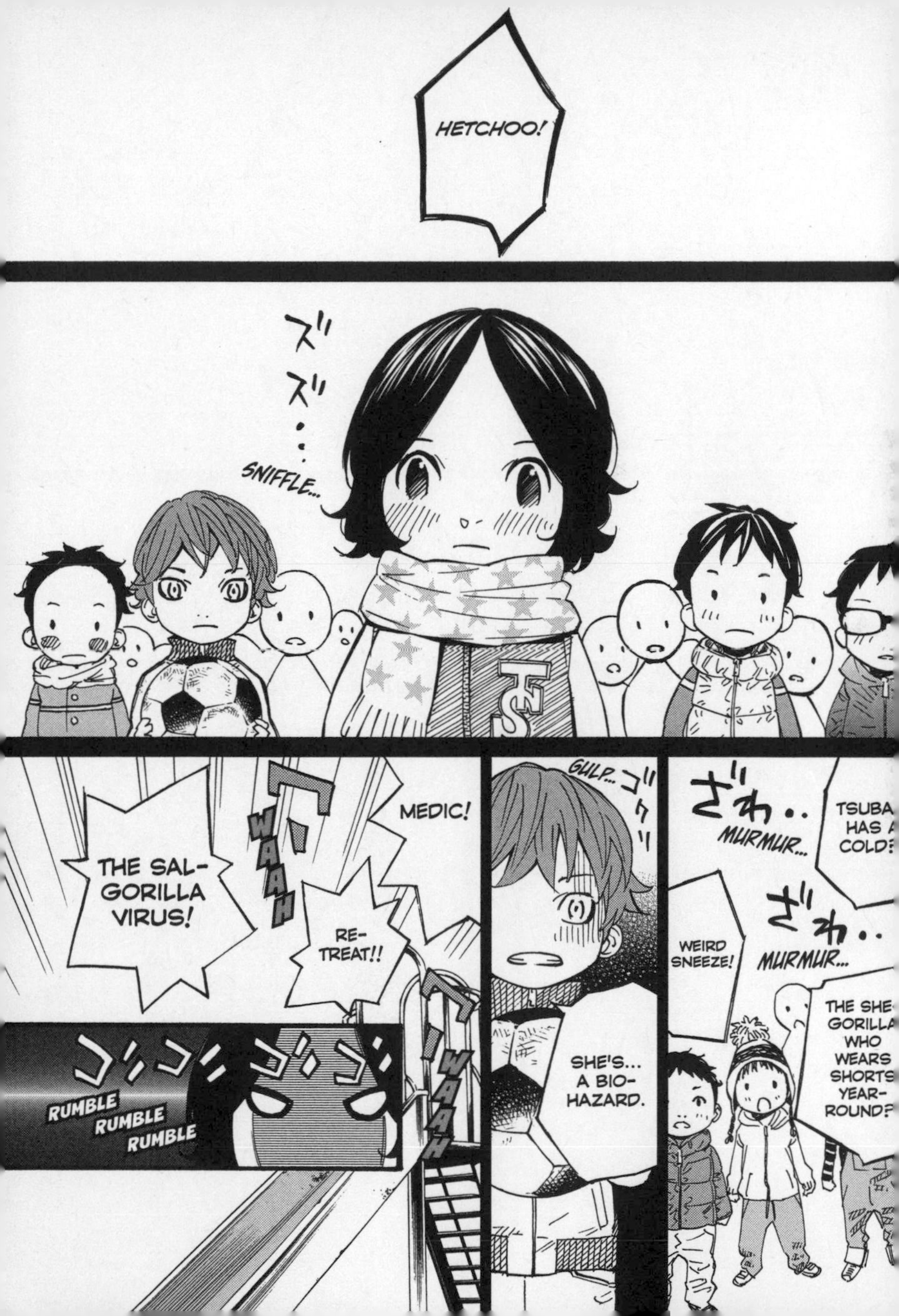
HETCHOO!
ズズ…
SNIFFLE...
ざわ..
MURMUR...
TSUBA HAS A COLD?
ざわ..
MURMUR...
WEIRD SNEEZE!
THE SHE-GORILLA WHO WEARS SHORTS YEAR-ROUND?
GULP...
SHE'S... A BIO-HAZARD.
MEDIC!
WAAAH
THE SAL-GORILLA VIRUS!
RE-TREAT!!
WAAAH
RUMBLE
RUMBLE
RUMBLE

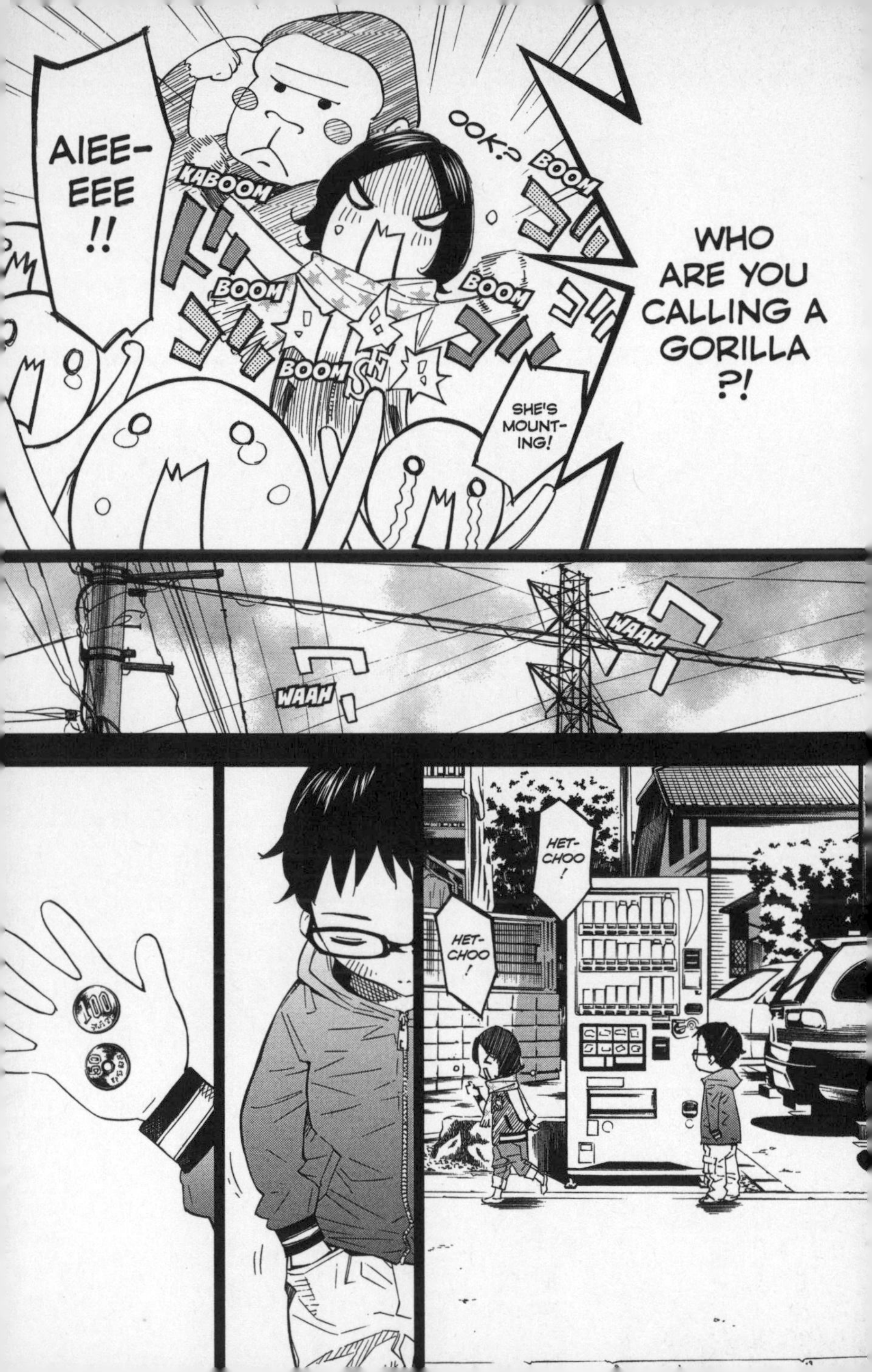
WHO ARE YOU CALLING A GORILLA ?!
OOK?
BOOM
BOOM
KABOOM
BOOM
BOOM
SHE'S MOUNTING!
AIEEE-EEE !!
WAAH
WAAH
HET-CHOO!
HET-CHOO!

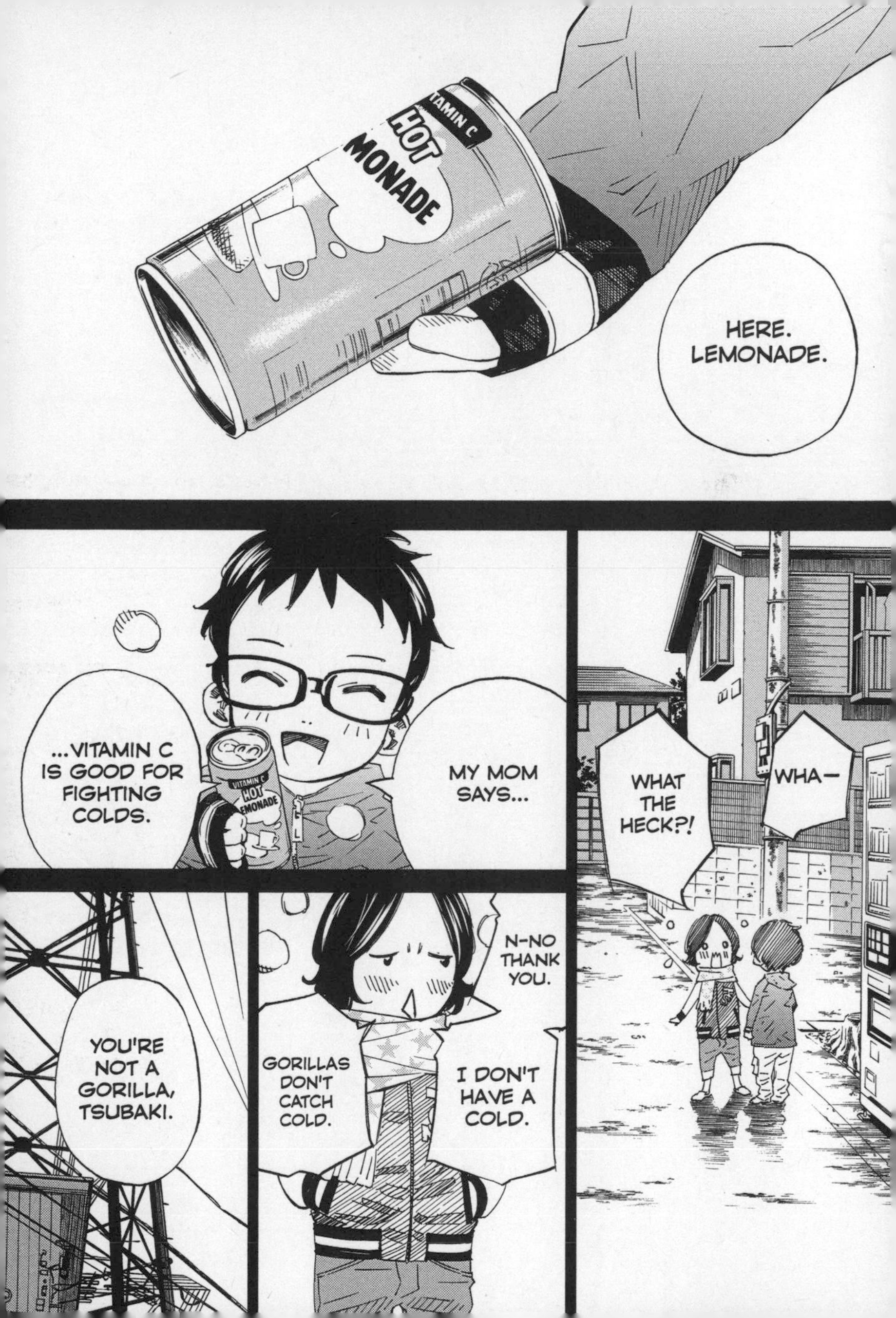
TAMIN C
HOT
MONADE
HERE. LEMONADE.
WHA—
WHAT THE HECK?!
MY MOM SAYS...
...VITAMIN C IS GOOD FOR FIGHTING COLDS.
VITAMIN C HOT LEMONADE
N-NO THANK YOU.
I DON'T HAVE A COLD.
GORILLAS DON'T CATCH COLD.
YOU'RE NOT A GORILLA, TSUBAKI.

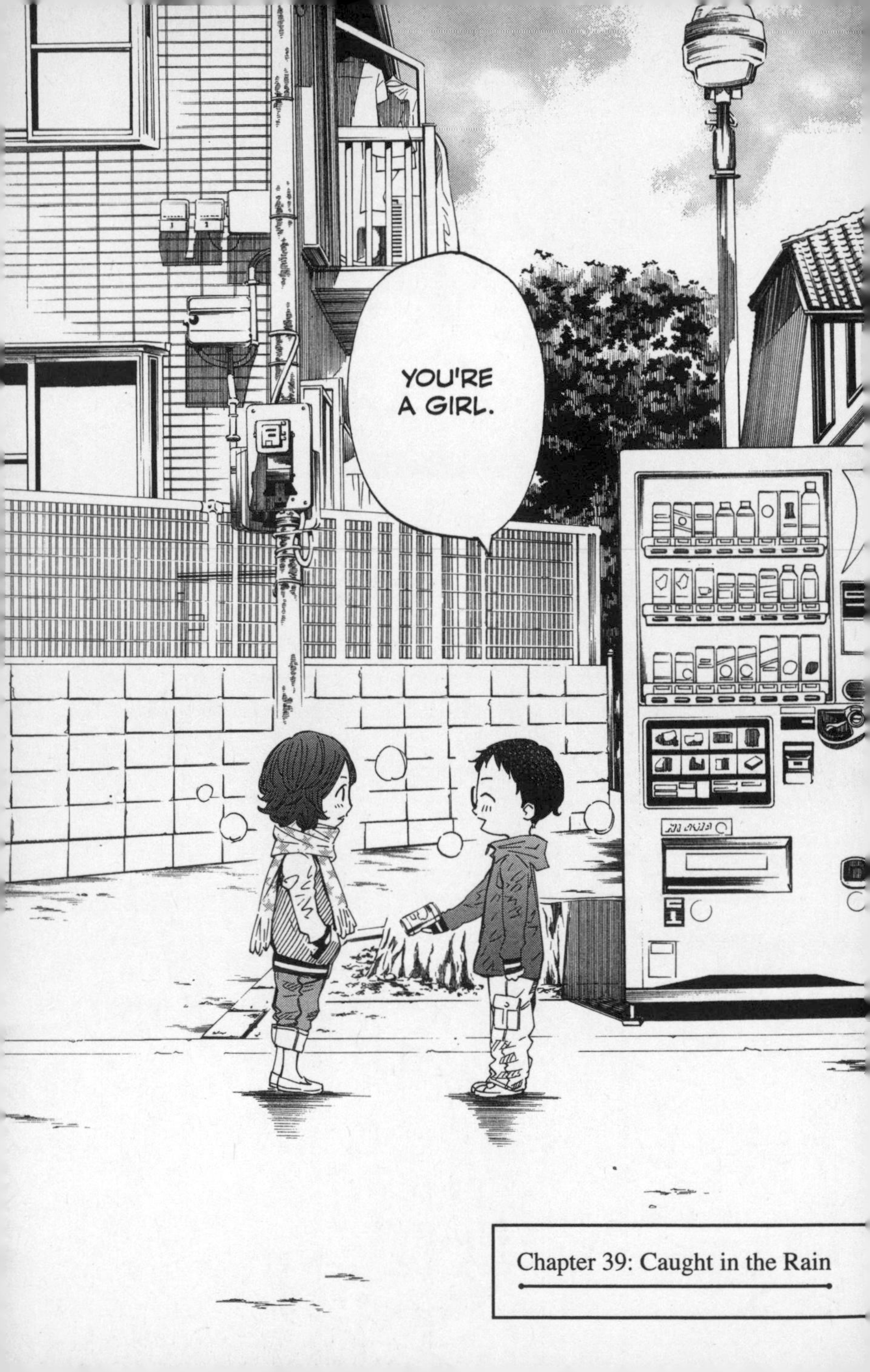
YOU'RE A GIRL.

Chapter 39: Caught in the Rain

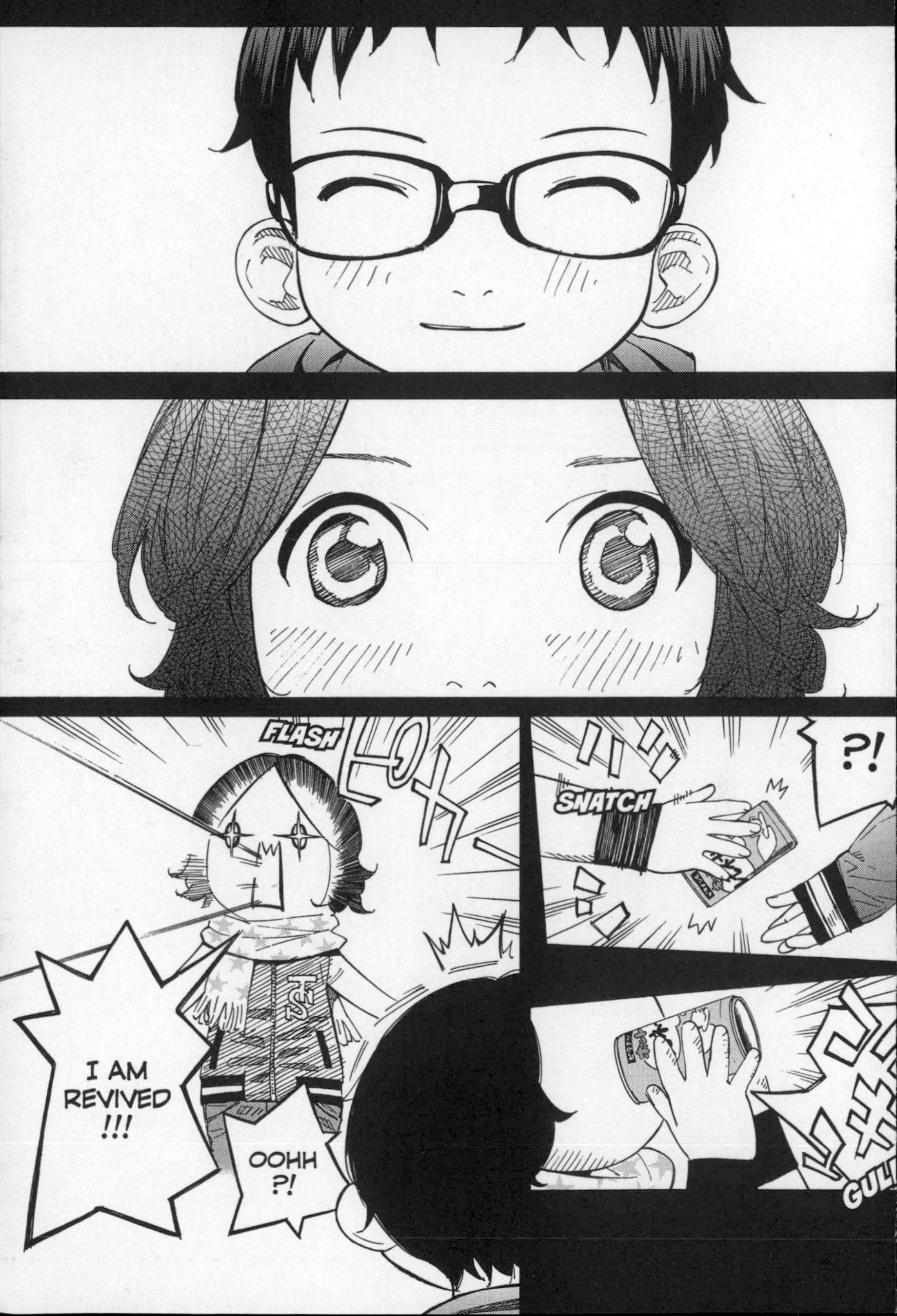
?!
SNATCH
GUL
FLASH
I AM REVIVED !!!
OOHH ?!

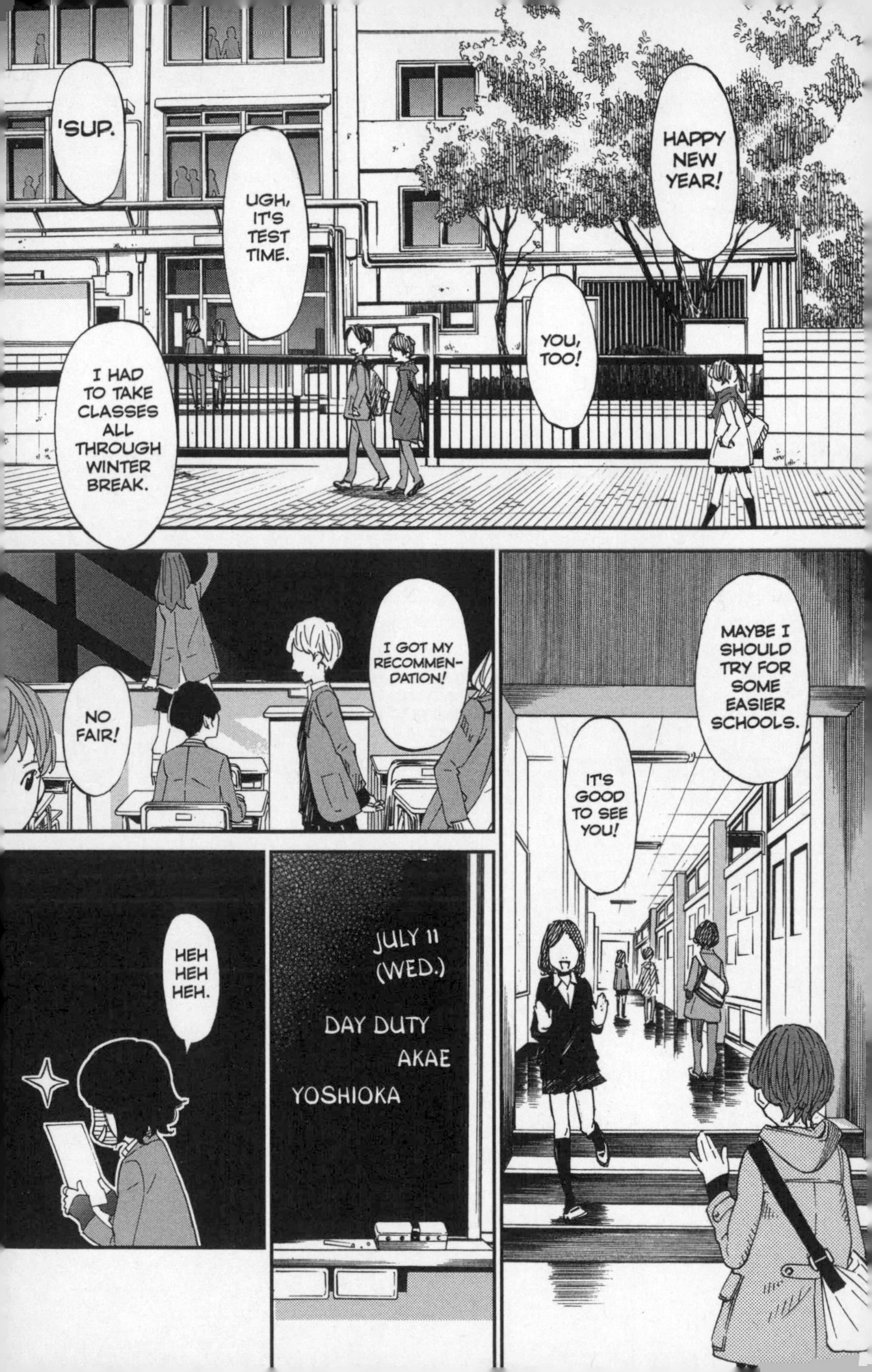
HAPPY NEW YEAR!
YOU, TOO!
UGH, IT'S TEST TIME.
'SUP.
I HAD TO TAKE CLASSES ALL THROUGH WINTER BREAK.
MAYBE I SHOULD TRY FOR SOME EASIER SCHOOLS.
IT'S GOOD TO SEE YOU!
I GOT MY RECOMMEN-DATION!
NO FAIR!
JULY 11 (WED.)
DAY DUTY
AKAE
YOSHIOKA
HEH HEH HEH.

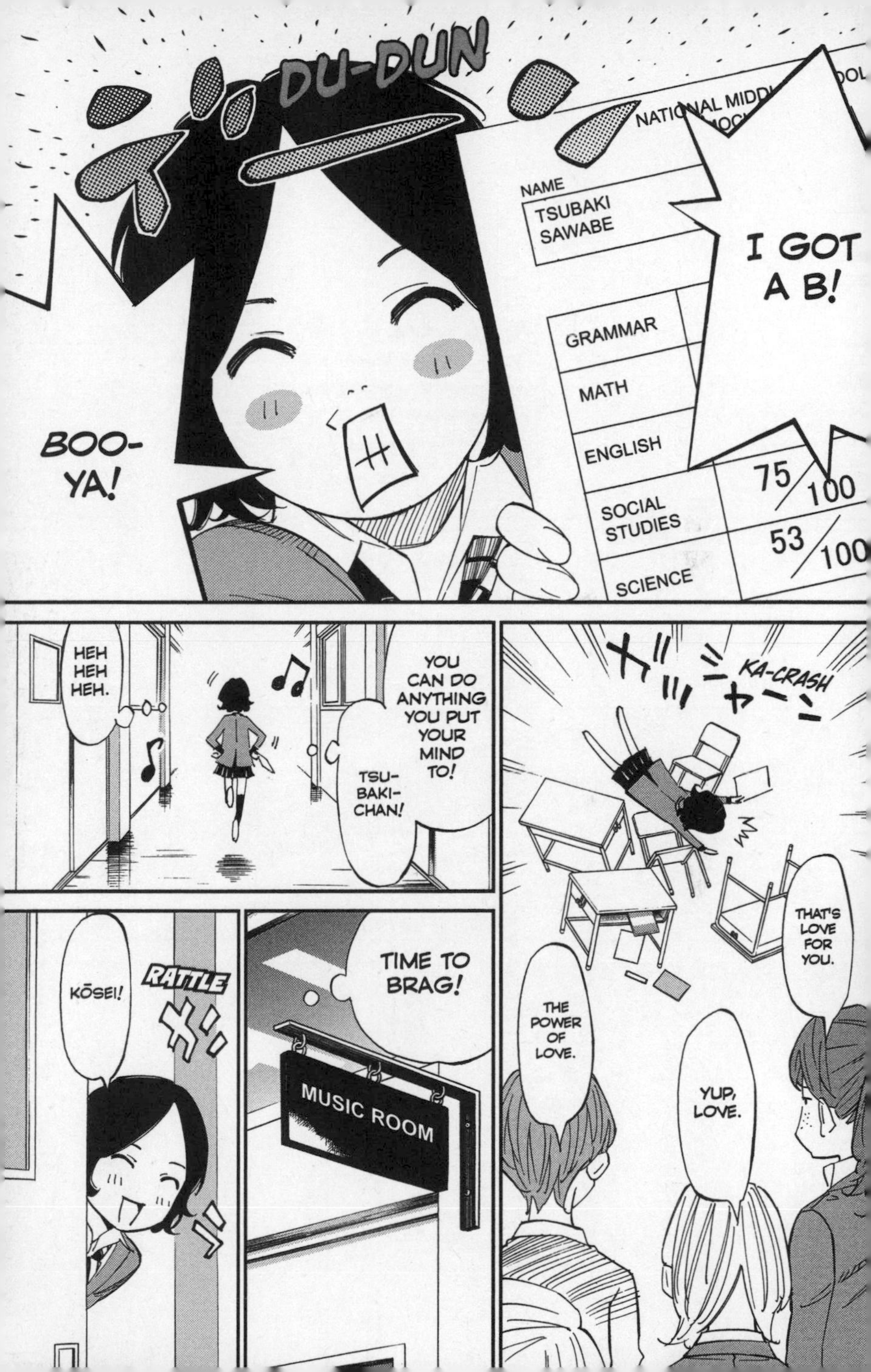
DU-DUN
NAME
TSUBAKI SAWABE
GRAMMAR
MATH
ENGLISH
SOCIAL STUDIES
SCIENCE
75/100
53/100
I GOT A B!
BOO-YA!
KA-CRASH
THAT'S LOVE FOR YOU.
THE POWER OF LOVE.
YUP, LOVE.
YOU CAN DO ANYTHING YOU PUT YOUR MIND TO!
TSU-BAKI-CHAN!
HEH HEH HEH.
TIME TO BRAG!
MUSIC ROOM
RATTLE
KŌSEI!

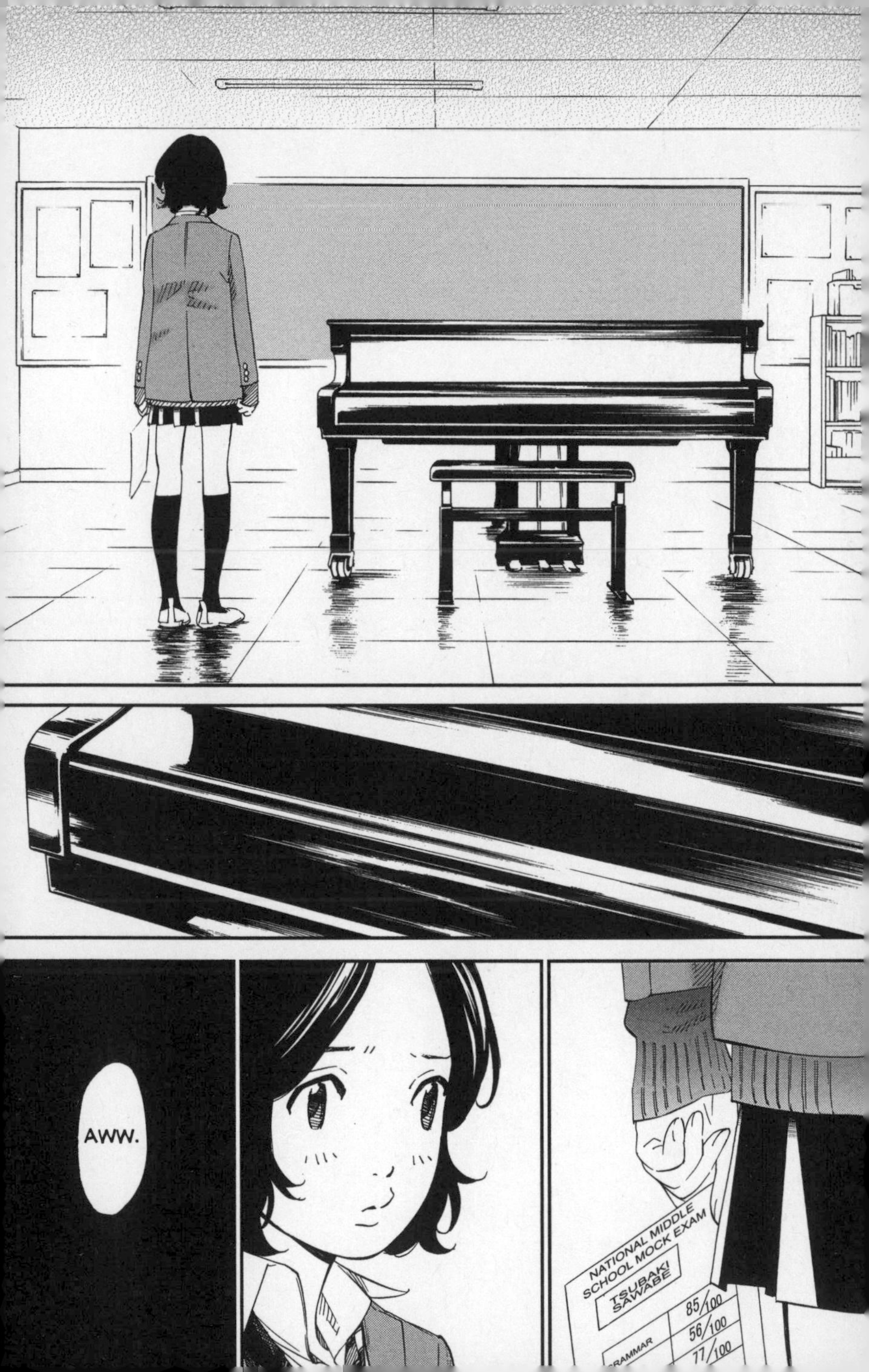
NATIONAL MIDDLE SCHOOL MOCK EXAM
TSUBAKI SAWABE
85/100
56/100
77/100
AWW.

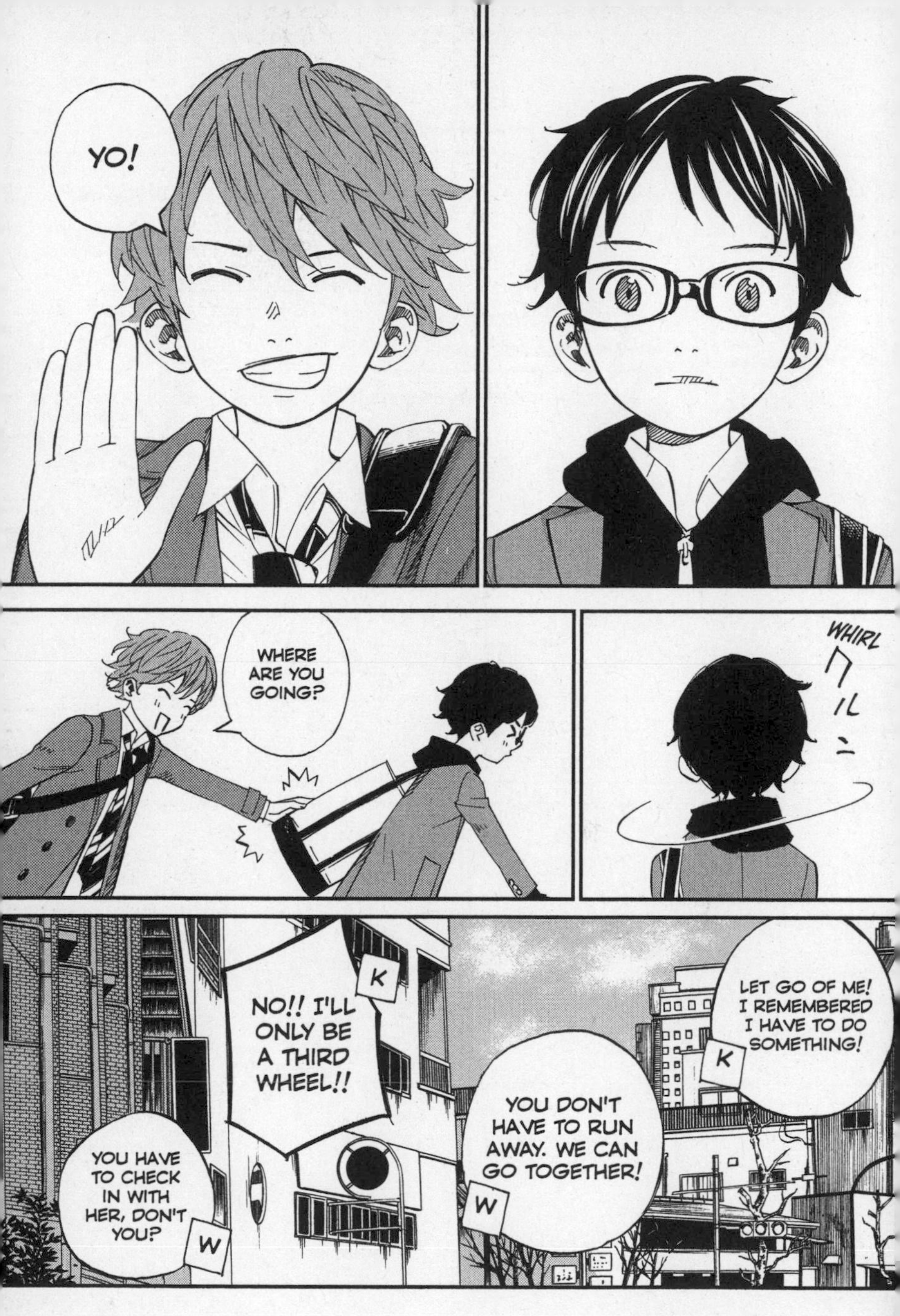
YO!
WHIRL
WHERE ARE YOU GOING?
LET GO OF ME! I REMEMBERED I HAVE TO DO SOMETHING!
K
NO!! I'LL ONLY BE A THIRD WHEEL!!
K
YOU DON'T HAVE TO RUN AWAY. WE CAN GO TOGETHER!
W
YOU HAVE TO CHECK IN WITH HER, DON'T YOU?
W

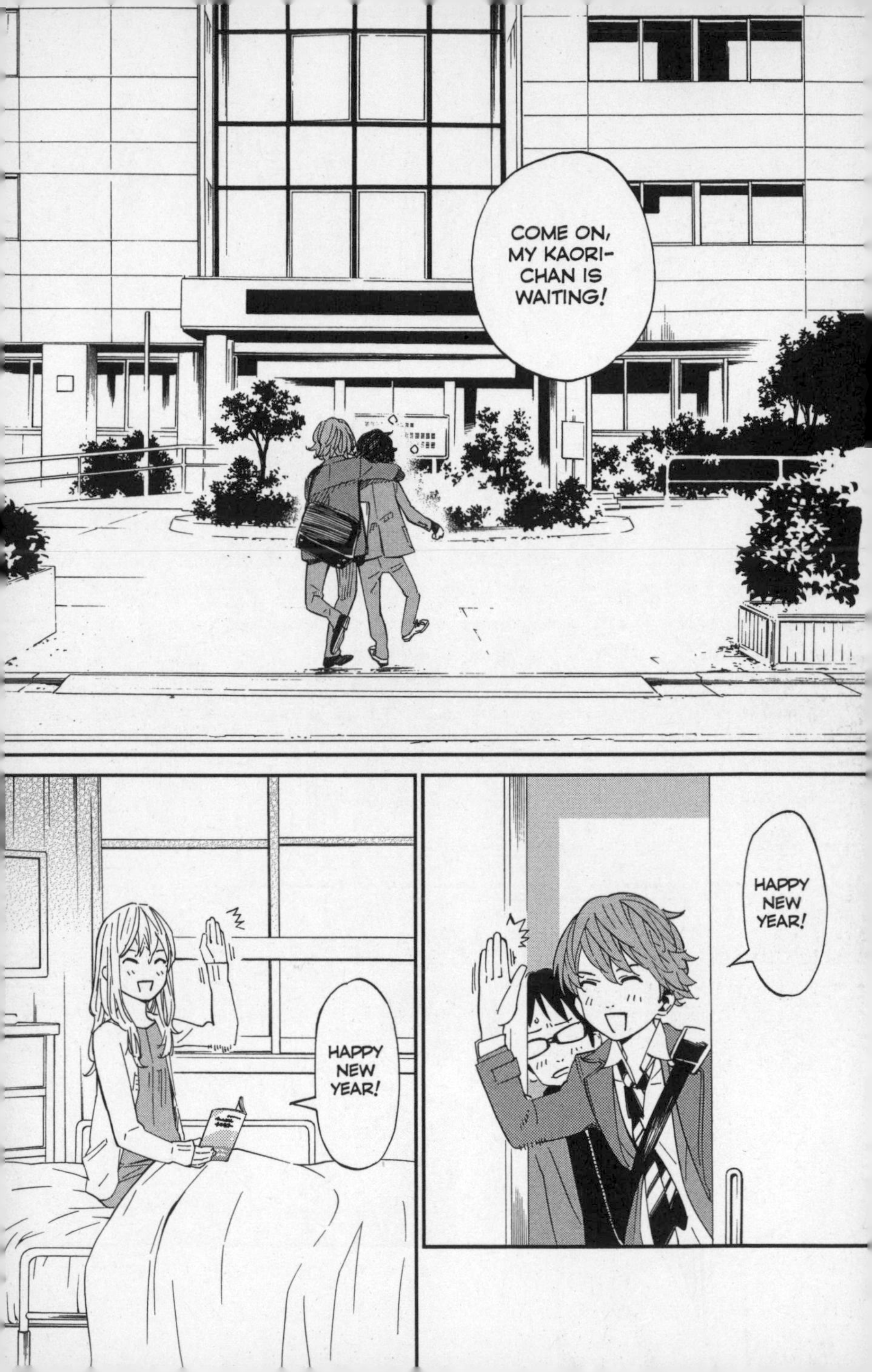
COME ON, MY KAORI-CHAN IS WAITING!
HAPPY NEW YEAR!
HAPPY NEW YEAR!

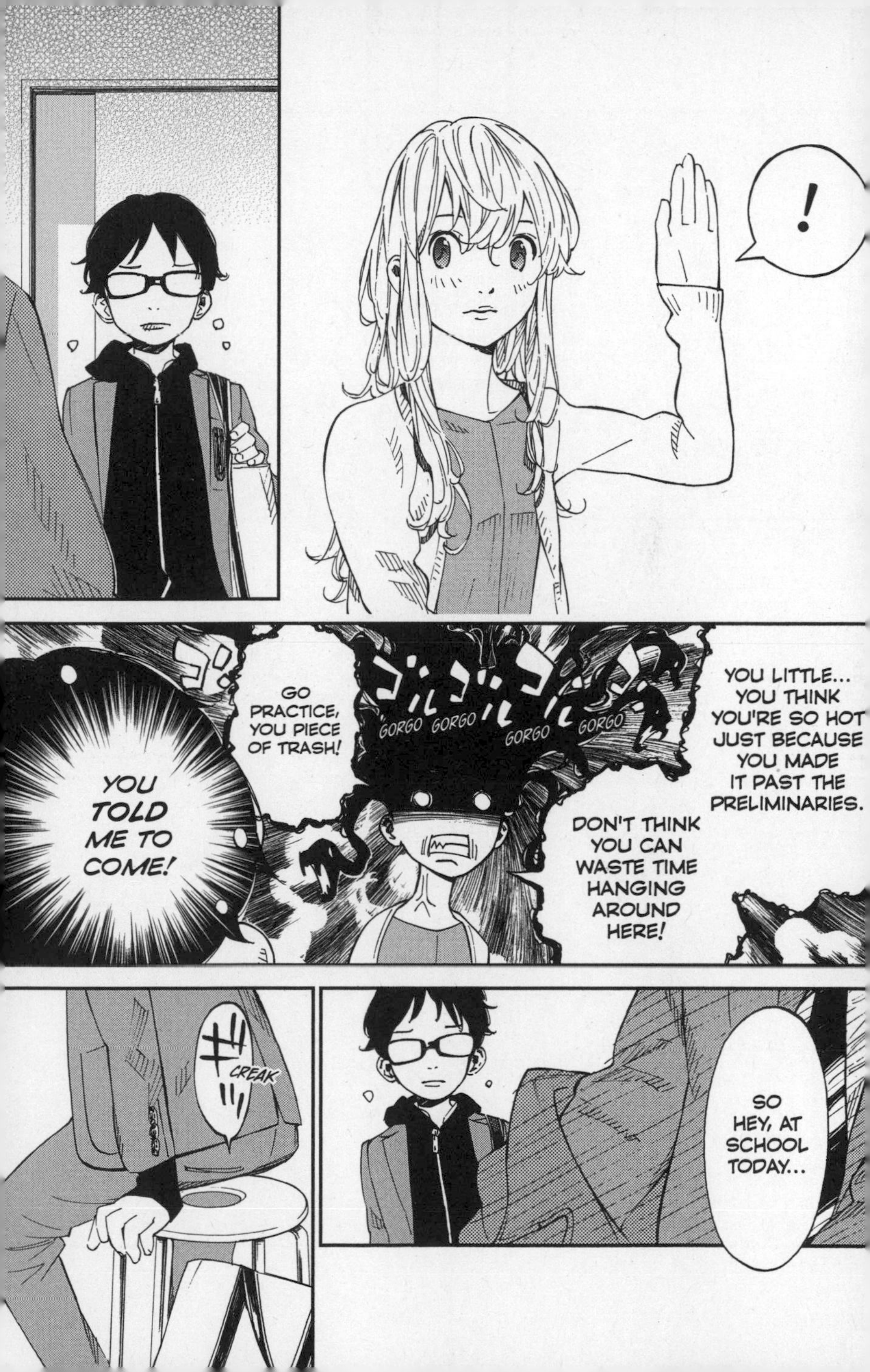
!
YOU LITTLE... YOU THINK YOU'RE SO HOT JUST BECAUSE YOU MADE IT PAST THE PRELIMINARIES.
DON'T THINK YOU CAN WASTE TIME HANGING AROUND HERE!
GORGO GORGO GORGO GORGO
GO PRACTICE, YOU PIECE OF TRASH!
YOU TOLD ME TO COME!
SO HEY, AT SCHOOL TODAY...
CREAK

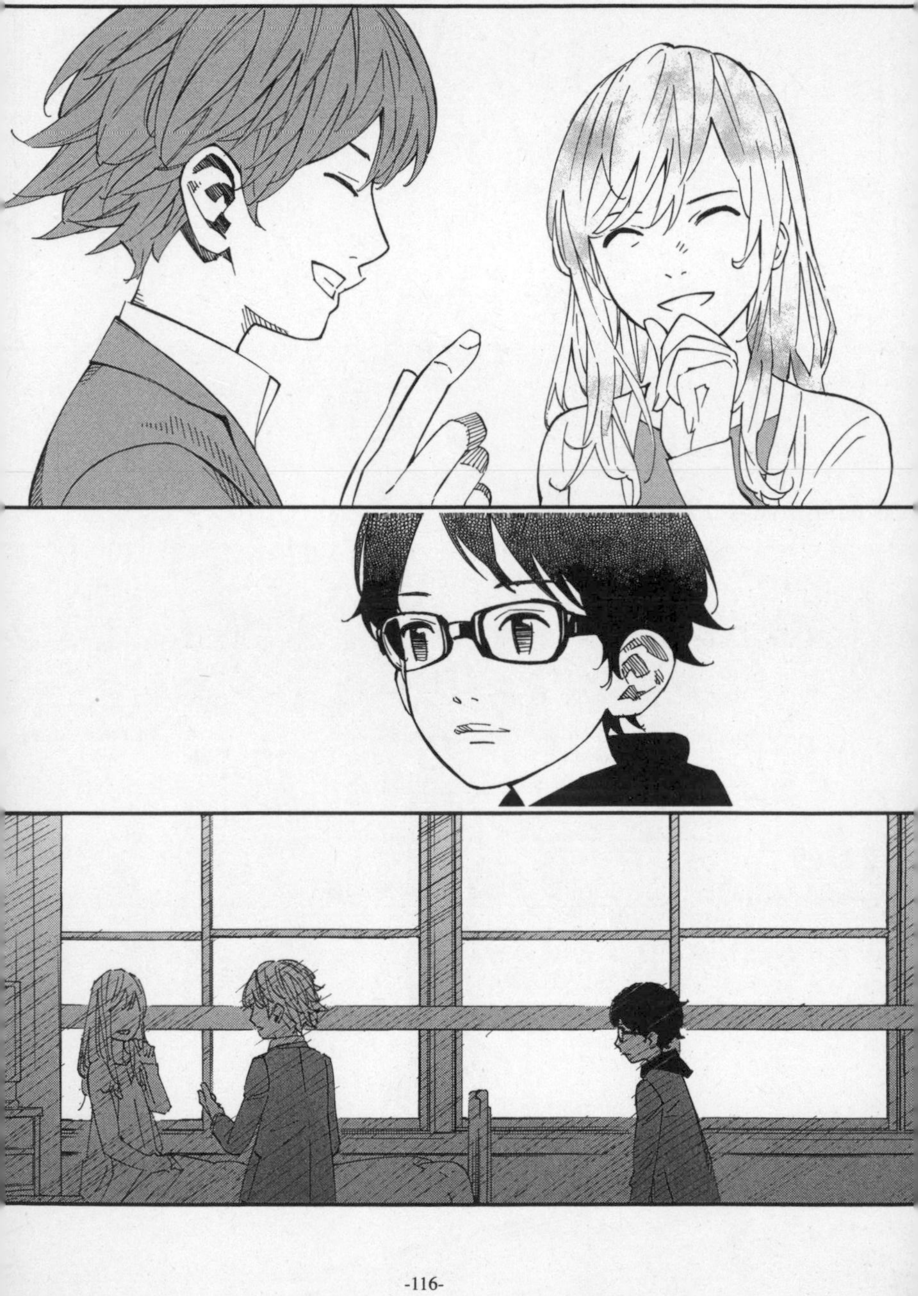

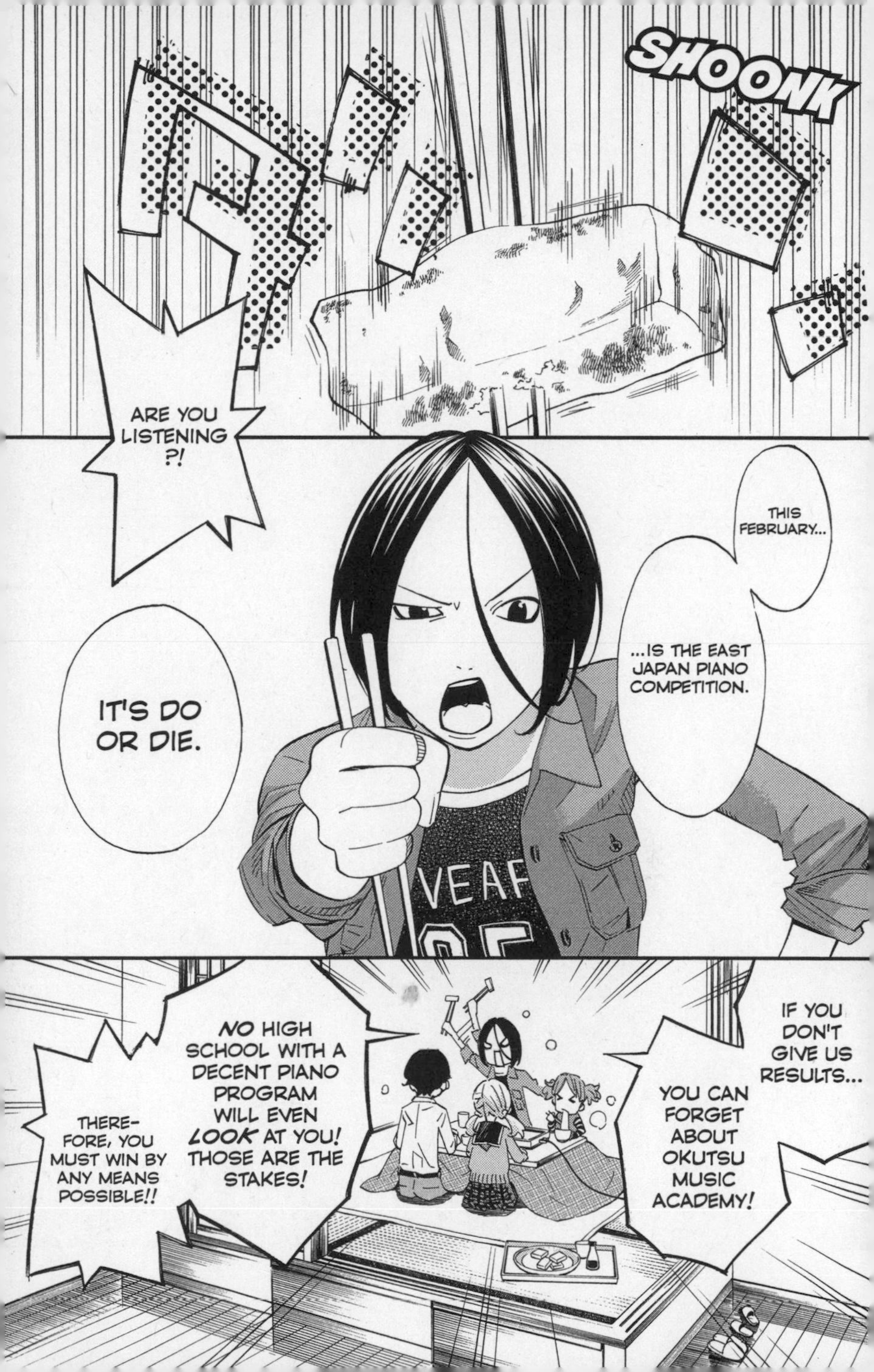
SHOONK
ARE YOU LISTENING ?!
THIS FEBRUARY...
...IS THE EAST JAPAN PIANO COMPETITION.
IT'S DO OR DIE.
IF YOU DON'T GIVE US RESULTS...
YOU CAN FORGET ABOUT OKUTSU MUSIC ACADEMY!
NO HIGH SCHOOL WITH A DECENT PIANO PROGRAM WILL EVEN LOOK AT YOU! THOSE ARE THE STAKES!
THERE-FORE, YOU MUST WIN BY ANY MEANS POSSIBLE!!

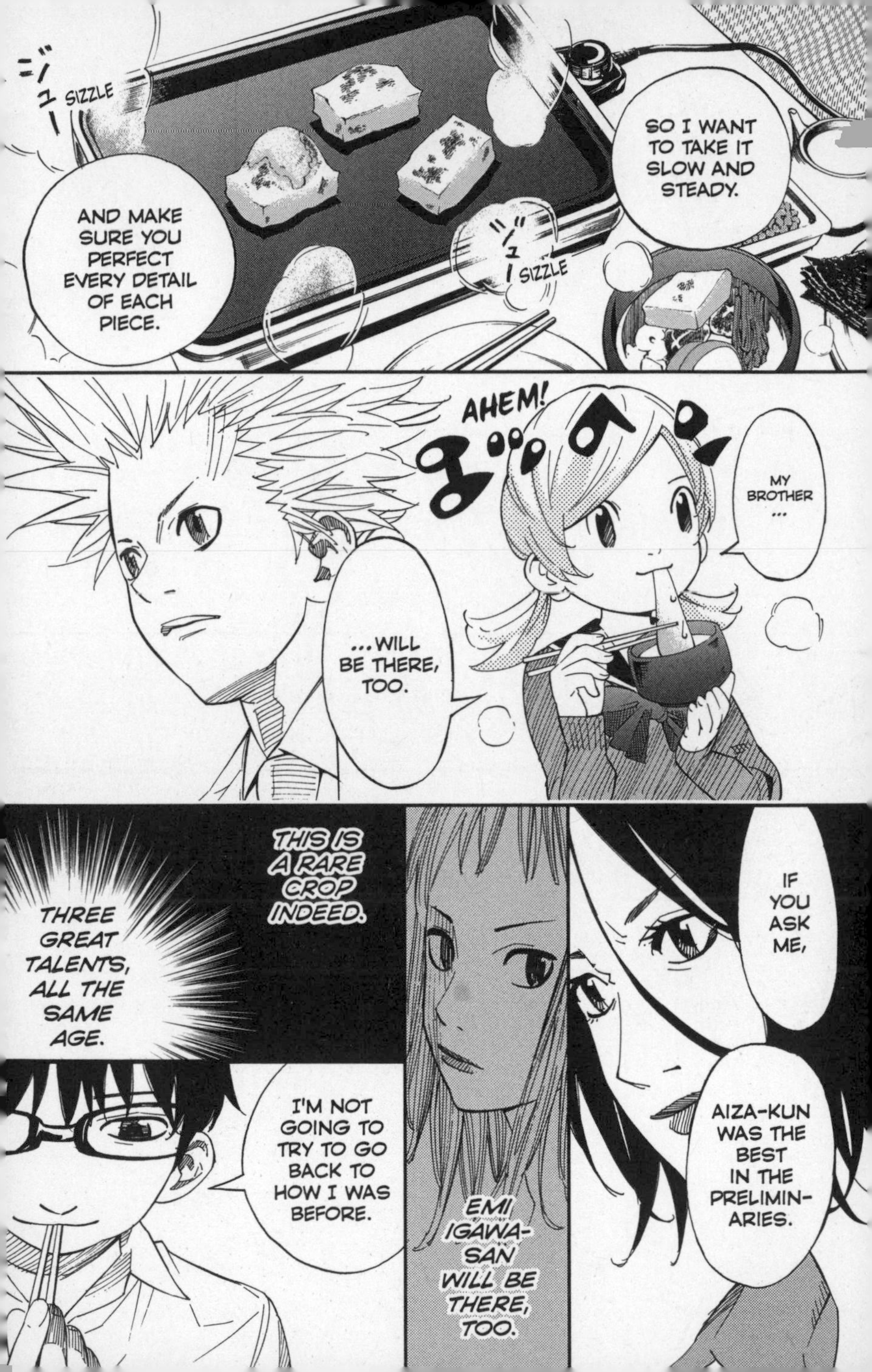
SO I WANT TO TAKE IT SLOW AND STEADY.
SIZZLE
SIZZLE
AND MAKE SURE YOU PERFECT EVERY DETAIL OF EACH PIECE.
MY BROTHER ...
AHEM!
...WILL BE THERE, TOO.
IF YOU ASK ME,
AIZA-KUN WAS THE BEST IN THE PRELIMIN-ARIES.
EMI IGAWA-SAN WILL BE THERE, TOO.
THIS IS A RARE CROP INDEED.
THREE GREAT TALENTS, ALL THE SAME AGE.
I'M NOT GOING TO TRY TO GO BACK TO HOW I WAS BEFORE.

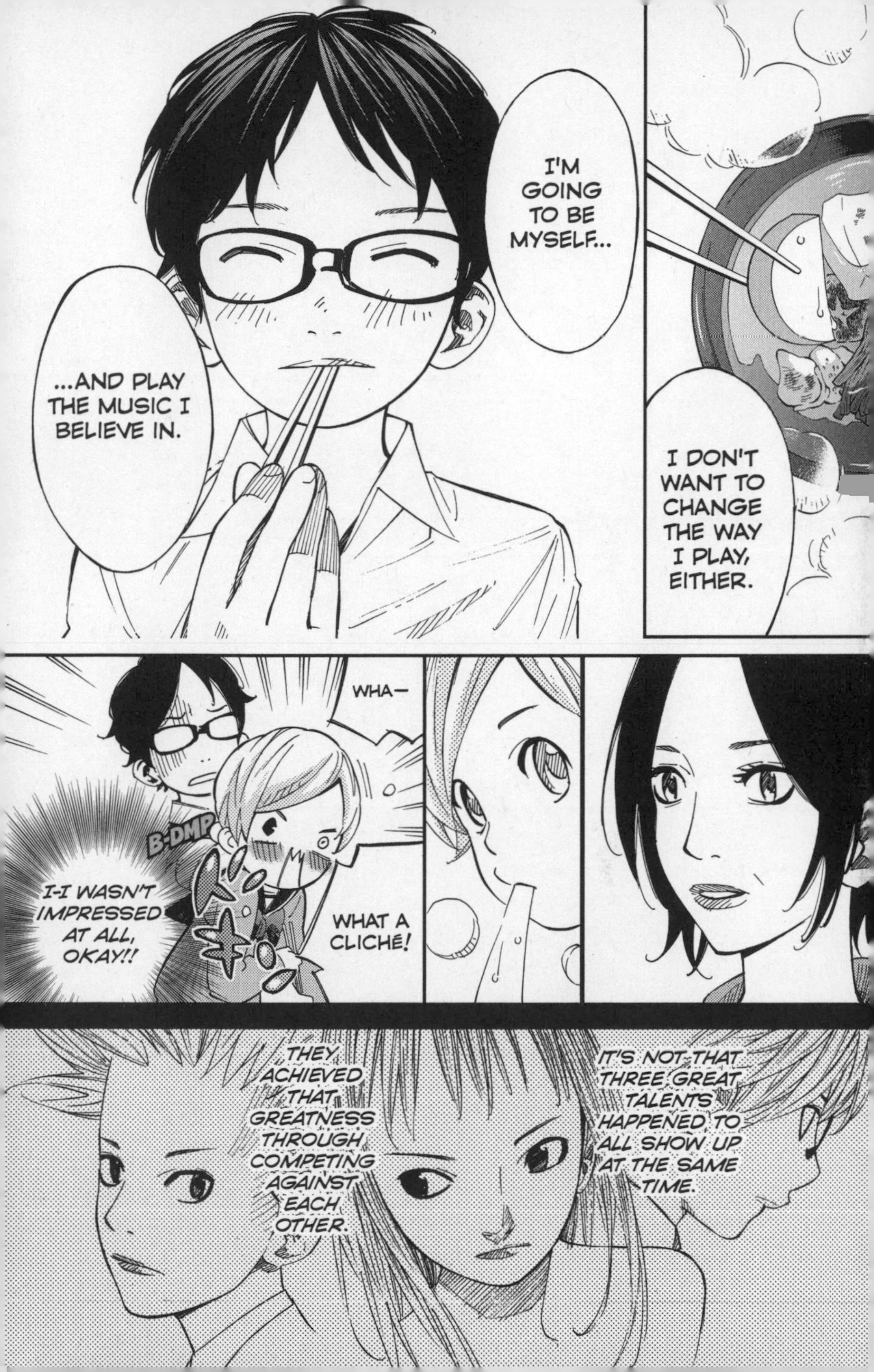
I DON'T WANT TO CHANGE THE WAY I PLAY, EITHER.
I'M GOING TO BE MYSELF...
...AND PLAY THE MUSIC I BELIEVE IN.
WHA—
WHAT A CLICHÉ!
B-DMP
I-I WASN'T IMPRESSED AT ALL, OKAY!!
IT'S NOT THAT THREE GREAT TALENTS HAPPENED TO ALL SHOW UP AT THE SAME TIME.
THEY ACHIEVED THAT GREATNESS THROUGH COMPETING AGAINST EACH OTHER.

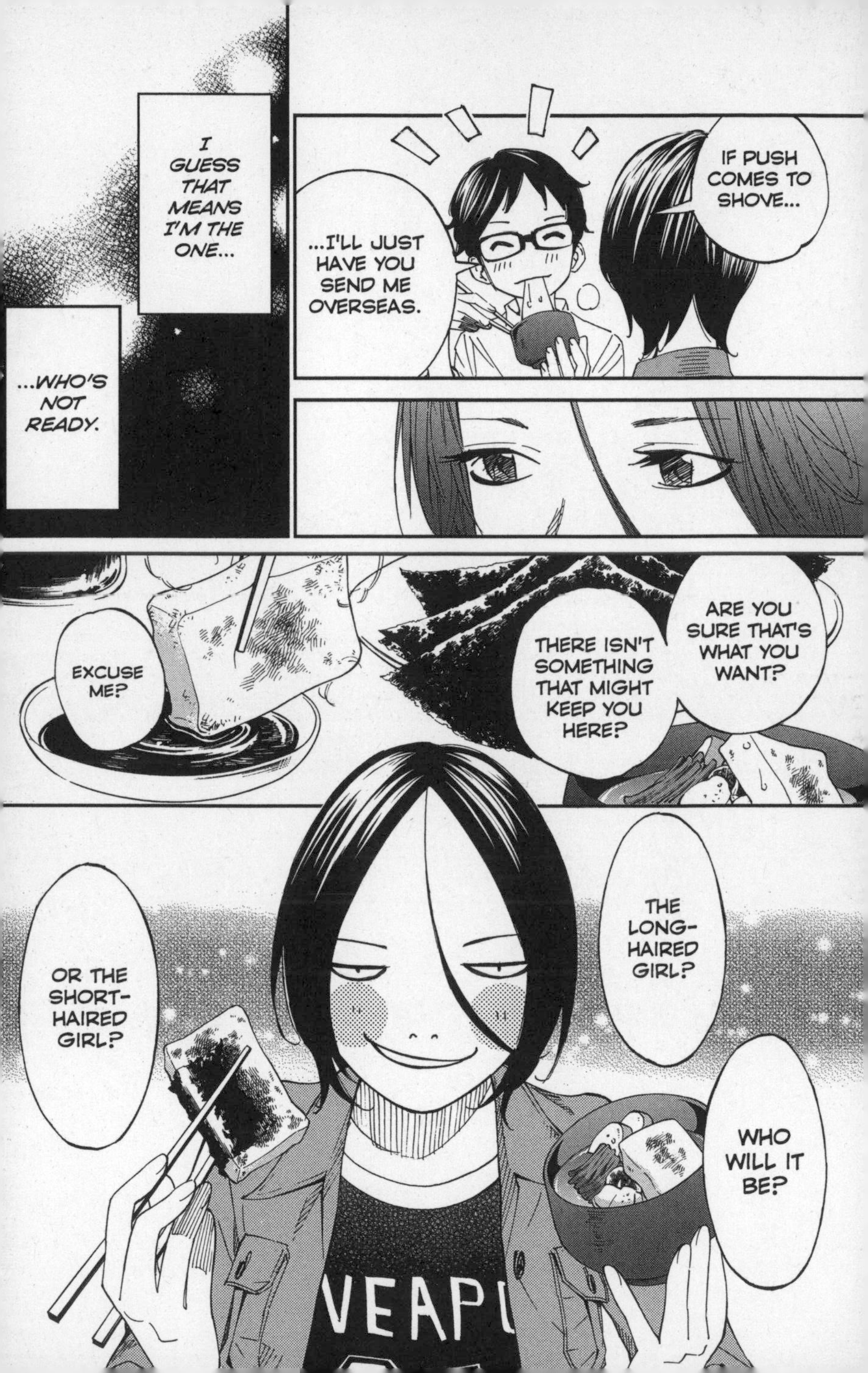
IF PUSH COMES TO SHOVE...
...I'LL JUST HAVE YOU SEND ME OVERSEAS.
I GUESS THAT MEANS I'M THE ONE...
...WHO'S NOT READY.
ARE YOU SURE THAT'S WHAT YOU WANT?
THERE ISN'T SOMETHING THAT MIGHT KEEP YOU HERE?
EXCUSE ME?
THE LONG-HAIRED GIRL?
OR THE SHORT-HAIRED GIRL?
WHO WILL IT BE?

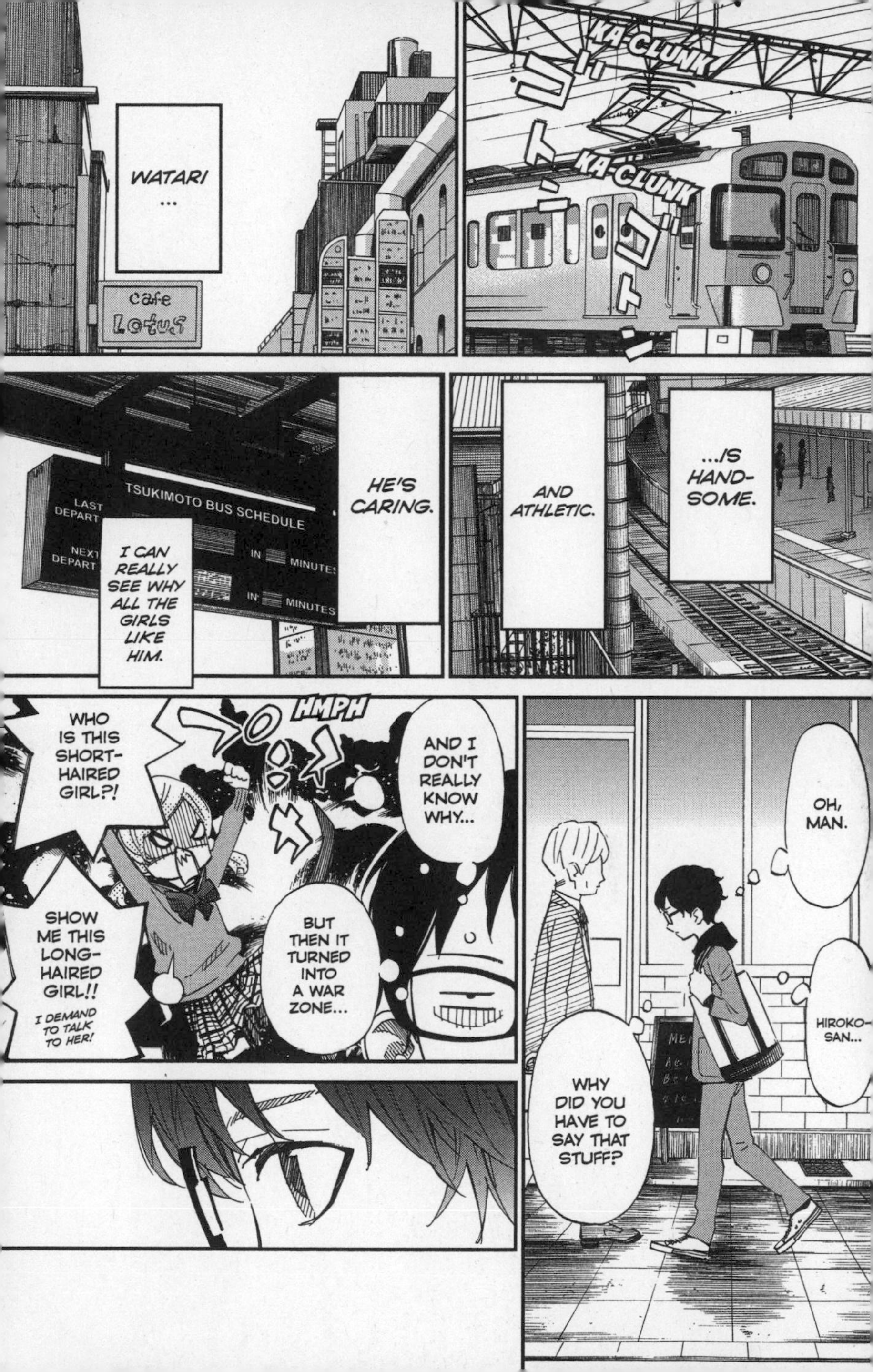
KA-CLUNK
KA-CLUNK
WATARI ...
cafe Lotus
...IS HANDSOME.
AND ATHLETIC.
HE'S CARING.
TSUKIMOTO BUS SCHEDULE
LAST DEPART
NEXT DEPART
IN MINUTES
IN MINUTES
I CAN REALLY SEE WHY ALL THE GIRLS LIKE HIM.
OH, MAN.
HIROKO-SAN...
WHY DID YOU HAVE TO SAY THAT STUFF?
AND I DON'T REALLY KNOW WHY...
HMPH
BUT THEN IT TURNED INTO A WAR ZONE...
WHO IS THIS SHORT-HAIRED GIRL?!
SHOW ME THIS LONG-HAIRED GIRL!!
I DEMAND TO TALK TO HER!

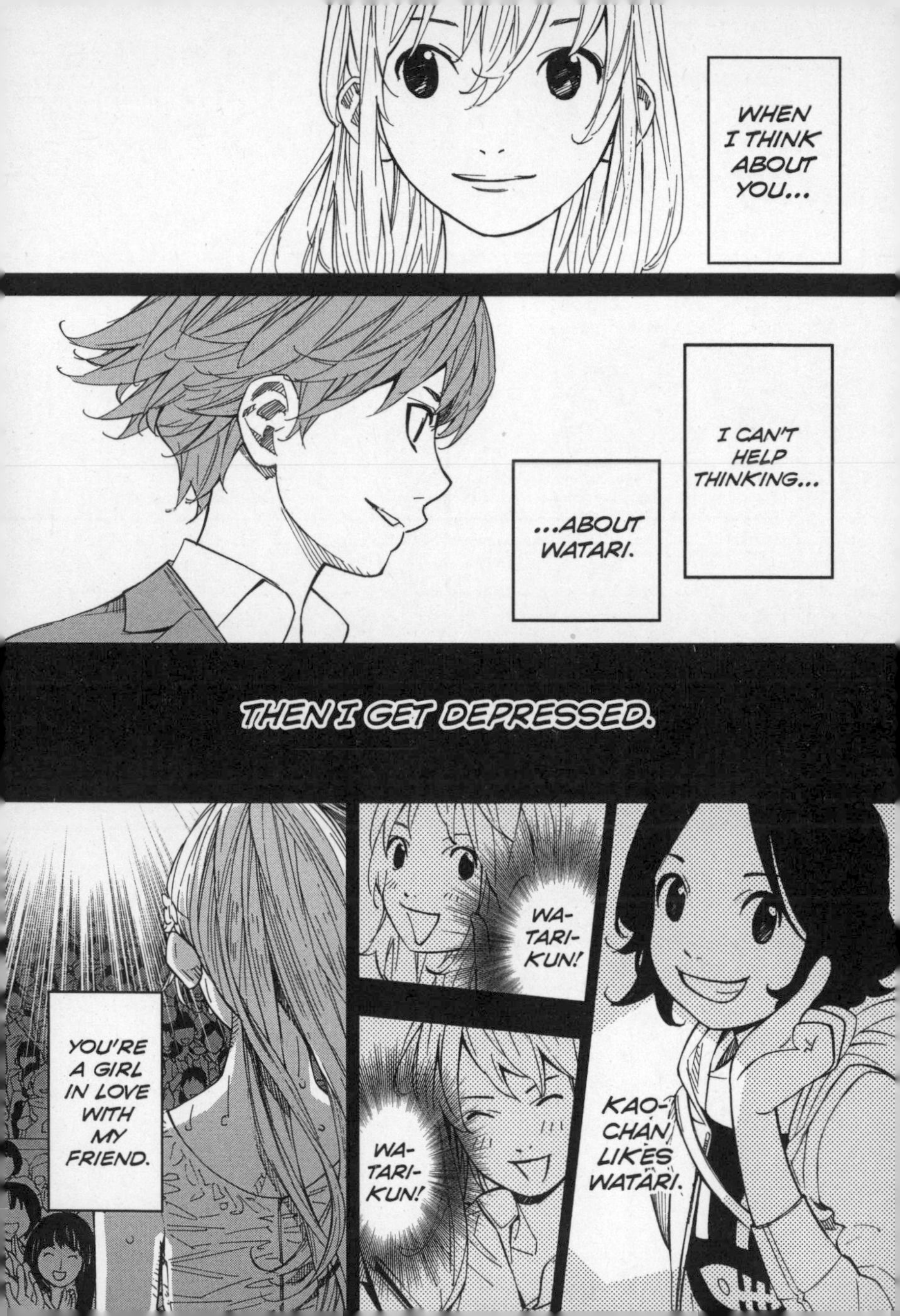
WHEN I THINK ABOUT YOU...
I CAN'T HELP THINKING...
...ABOUT WATARI.
THEN I GET DEPRESSED.
KAO-CHAN LIKES WATARI.
WA-TARI-KUN!
WA-TARI-KUN!
YOU'RE A GIRL IN LOVE WITH MY FRIEND.

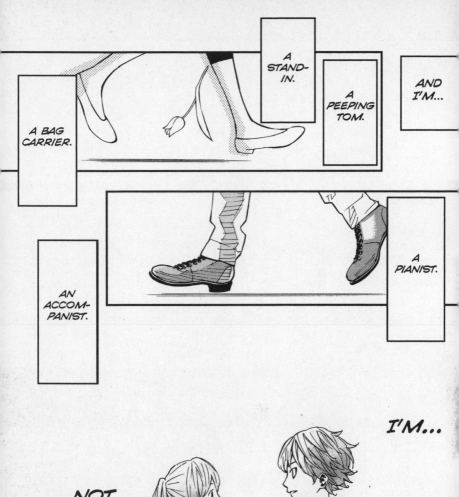

A BAG CARRIER.

A STAND-IN.

A PEEPING TOM.

AND I'M...

AN ACCOM-PANIST.

A PIANIST.

I'M...

...NOT WATARI.

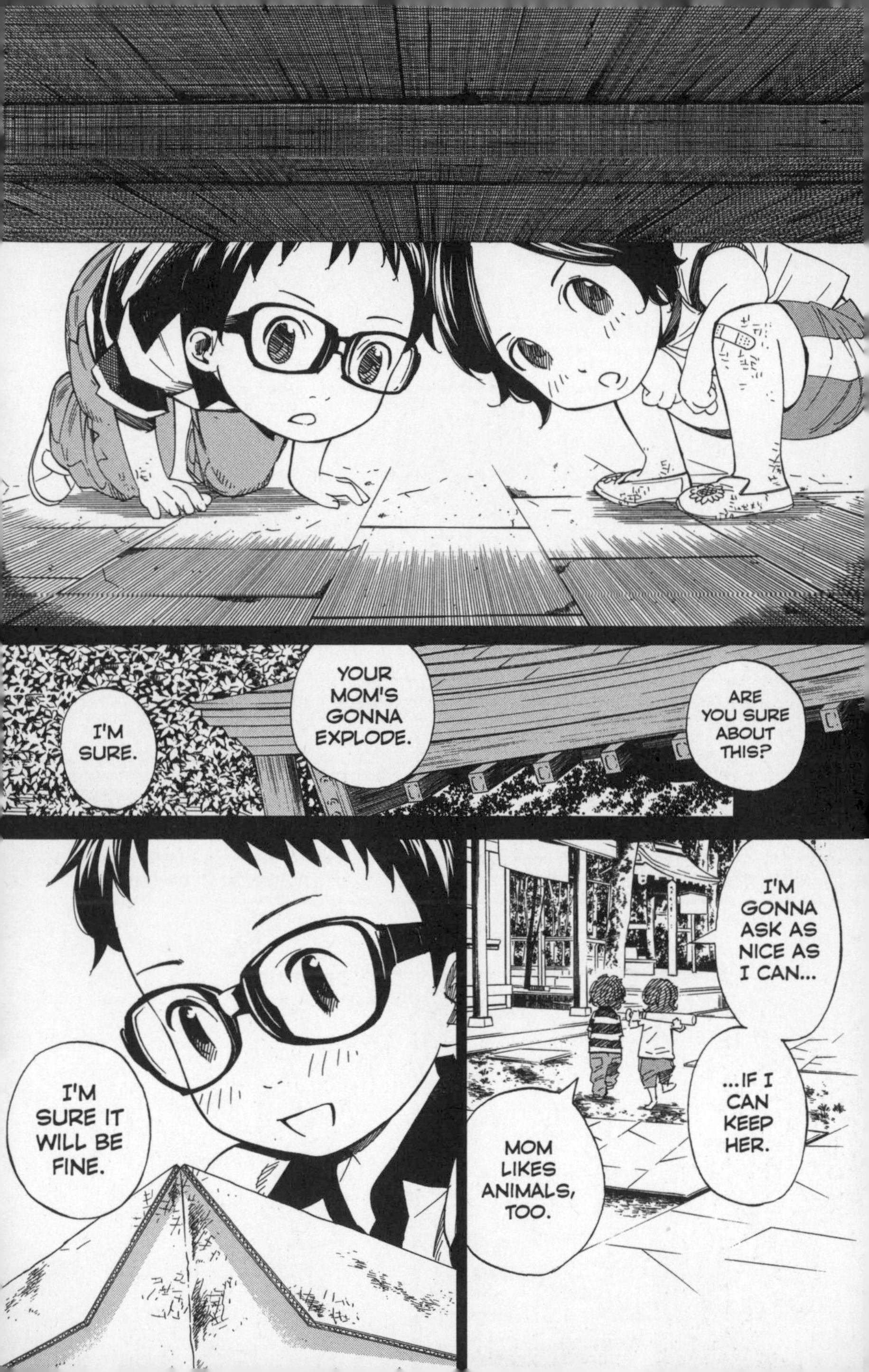
ARE YOU SURE ABOUT THIS?
YOUR MOM'S GONNA EXPLODE.
I'M SURE.
I'M GONNA ASK AS NICE AS I CAN...
...IF I CAN KEEP HER.
MOM LIKES ANIMALS, TOO.
I'M SURE IT WILL BE FINE.

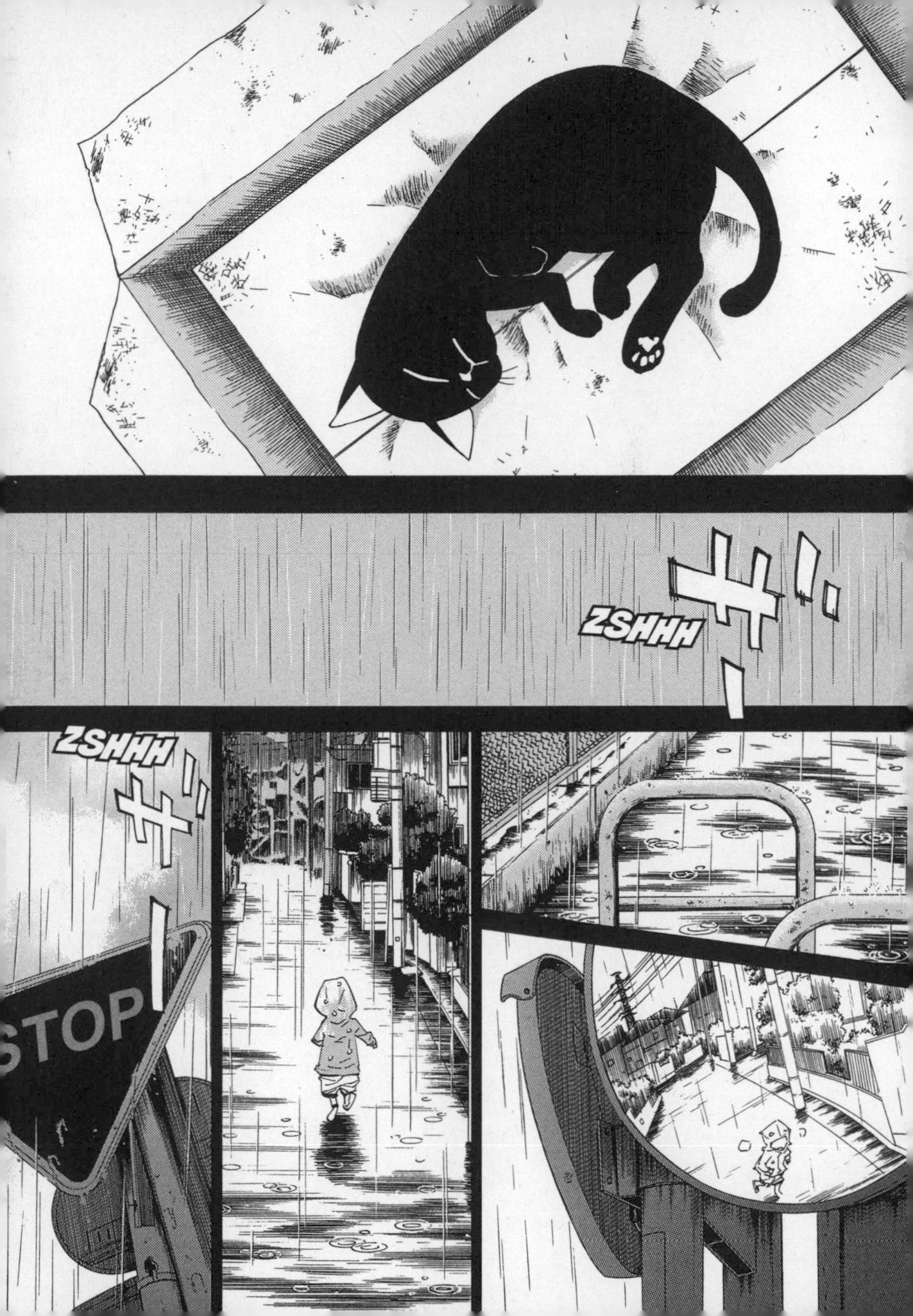
ザー
ZSHHH
ザー
ZSHHH
STOP

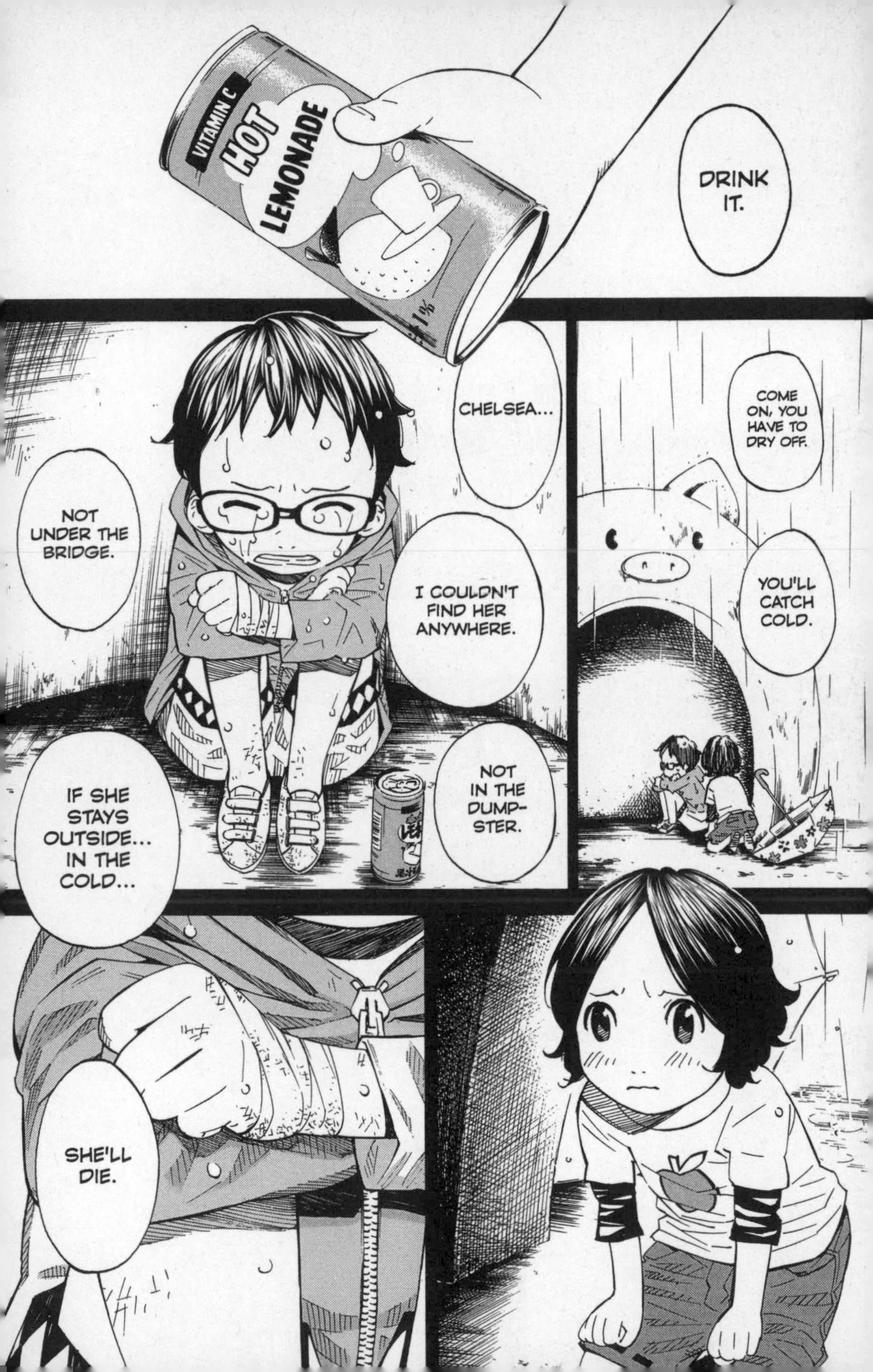
VITAMIN C
HOT
LEMONADE
DRINK IT.
COME ON, YOU HAVE TO DRY OFF.
YOU'LL CATCH COLD.
CHELSEA...
I COULDN'T FIND HER ANYWHERE.
NOT UNDER THE BRIDGE.
NOT IN THE DUMP-STER.
IF SHE STAYS OUTSIDE... IN THE COLD...
SHE'LL DIE.

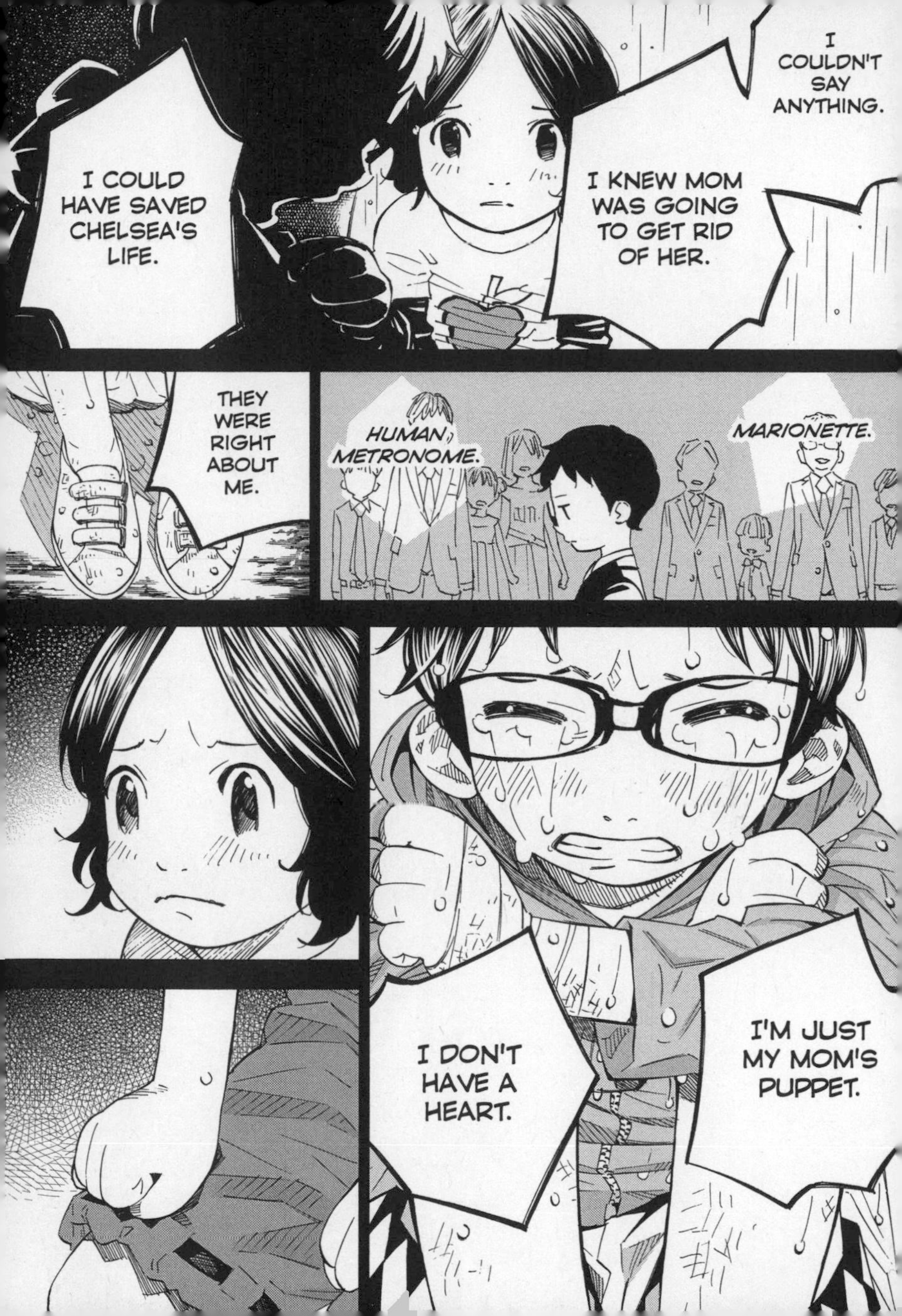

I COULDN'T SAY ANYTHING.
I KNEW MOM WAS GOING TO GET RID OF HER.
I COULD HAVE SAVED CHELSEA'S LIFE.
MARIONETTE.
HUMAN METRONOME.
THEY WERE RIGHT ABOUT ME.
I'M JUST MY MOM'S PUPPET.
I DON'T HAVE A HEART.

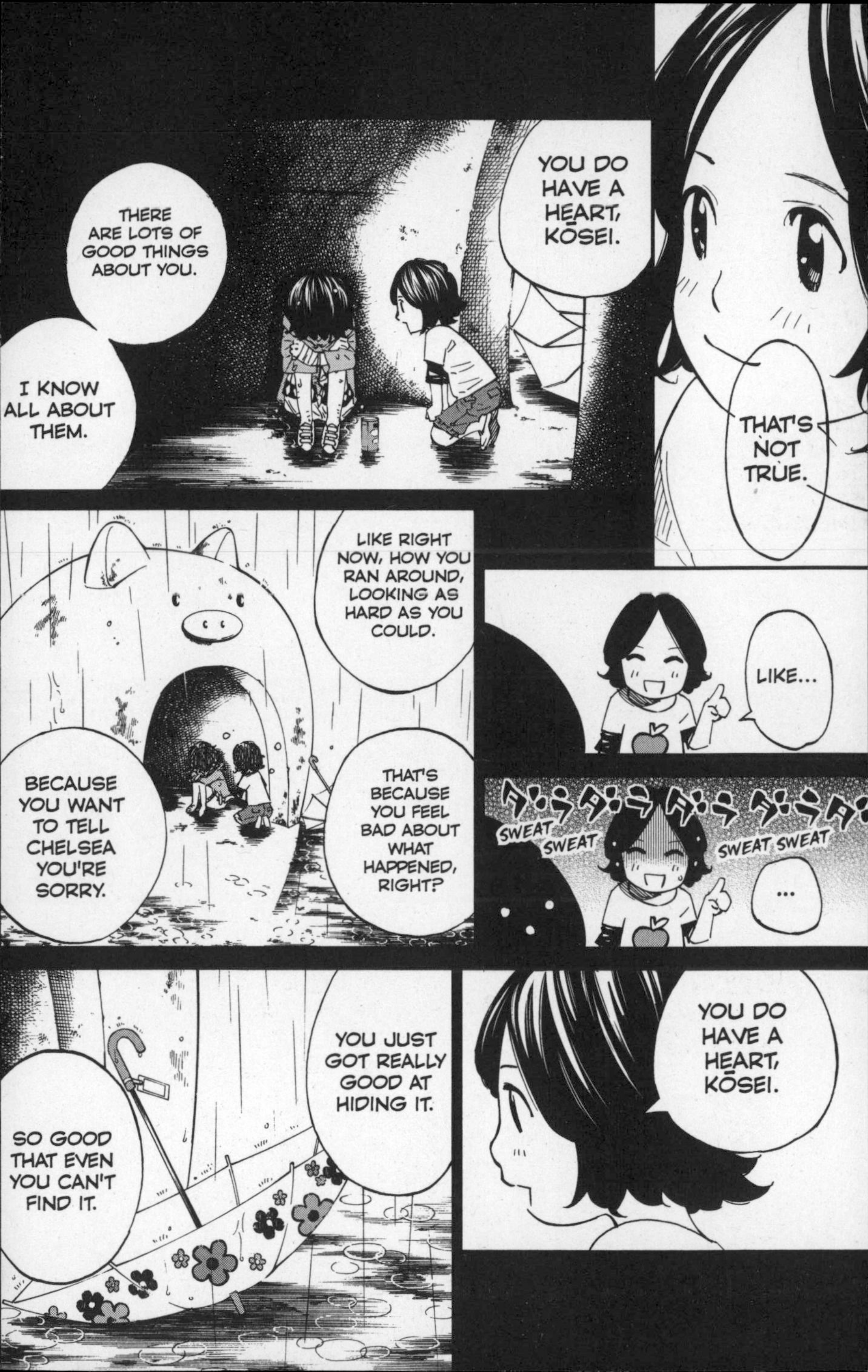
YOU DO HAVE A HEART, KŌSEI.
THAT'S NOT TRUE.
THERE ARE LOTS OF GOOD THINGS ABOUT YOU.
I KNOW ALL ABOUT THEM.
LIKE...
ダラダラ ダラダラ
SWEAT SWEAT SWEAT SWEAT
...
LIKE RIGHT NOW, HOW YOU RAN AROUND, LOOKING AS HARD AS YOU COULD.
THAT'S BECAUSE YOU FEEL BAD ABOUT WHAT HAPPENED, RIGHT?
BECAUSE YOU WANT TO TELL CHELSEA YOU'RE SORRY.
YOU DO HAVE A HEART, KŌSEI.
YOU JUST GOT REALLY GOOD AT HIDING IT.
SO GOOD THAT EVEN YOU CAN'T FIND IT.

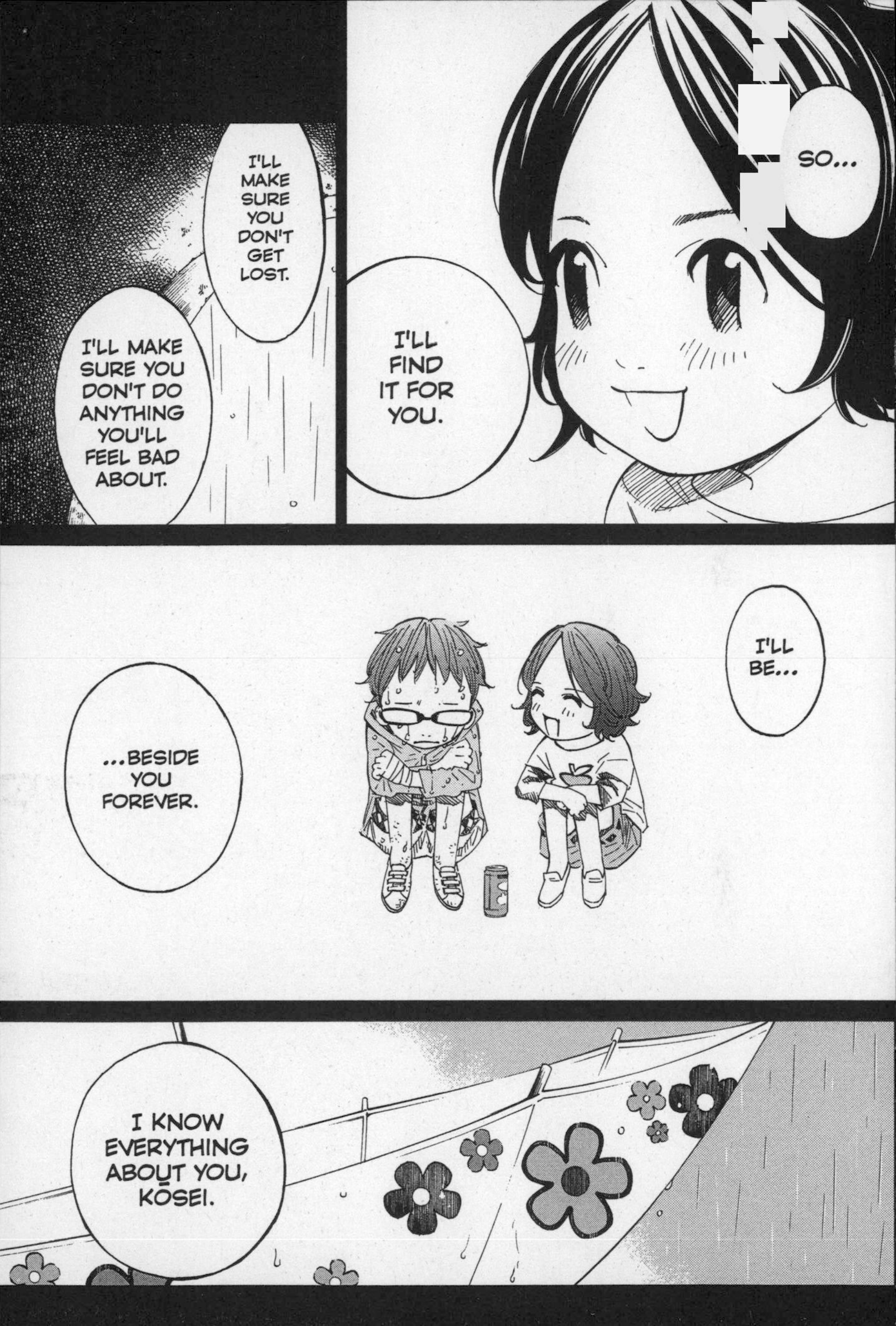
SO...
I'LL FIND IT FOR YOU.
I'LL MAKE SURE YOU DON'T GET LOST.
I'LL MAKE SURE YOU DON'T DO ANYTHING YOU'LL FEEL BAD ABOUT.
I'LL BE...
...BESIDE YOU FOREVER.
I KNOW EVERYTHING ABOUT YOU, KŌSEI.

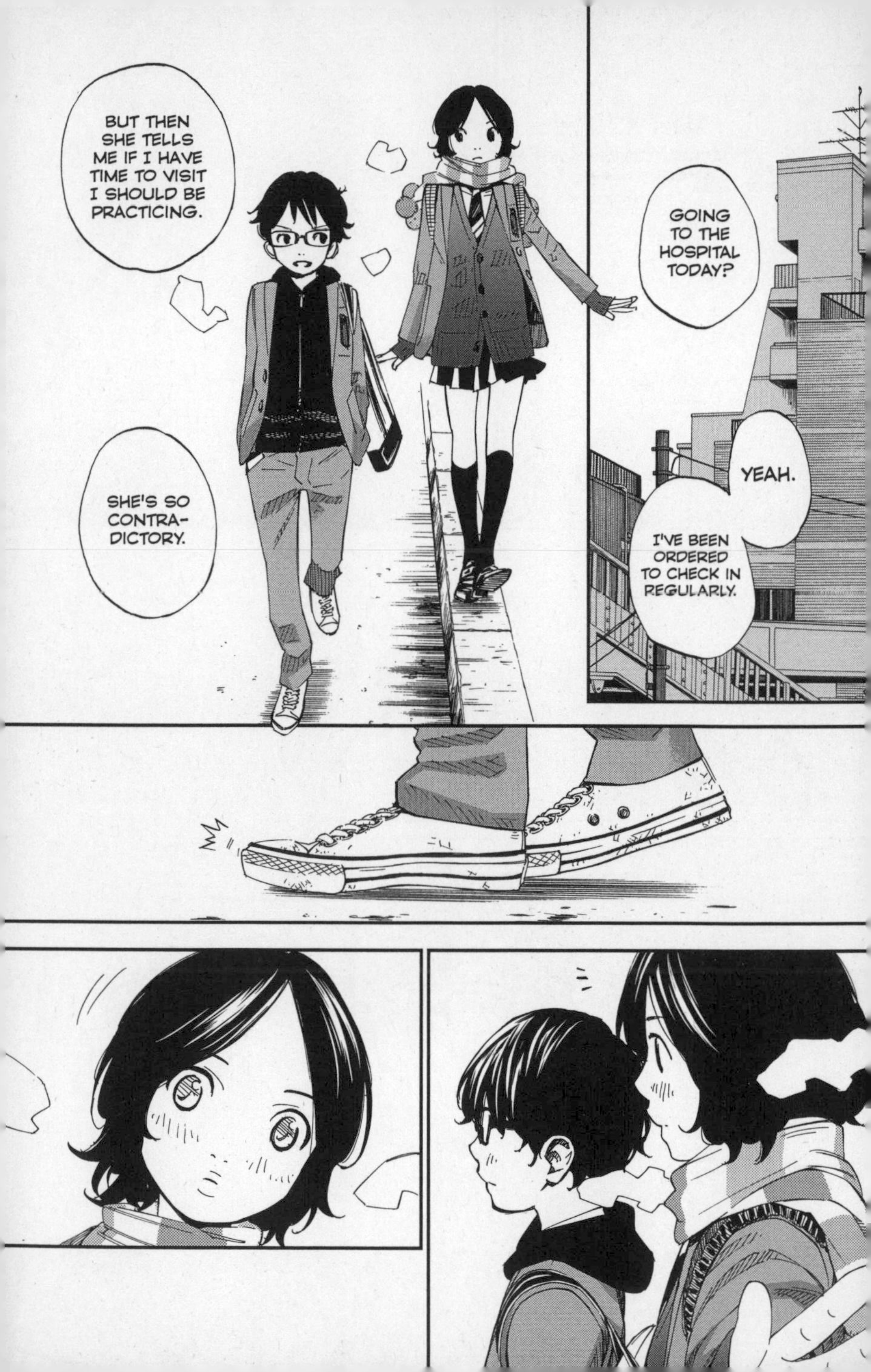
GOING TO THE HOSPITAL TODAY?
YEAH.
I'VE BEEN ORDERED TO CHECK IN REGULARLY.
BUT THEN SHE TELLS ME IF I HAVE TIME TO VISIT I SHOULD BE PRACTICING.
SHE'S SO CONTRA-DICTORY.

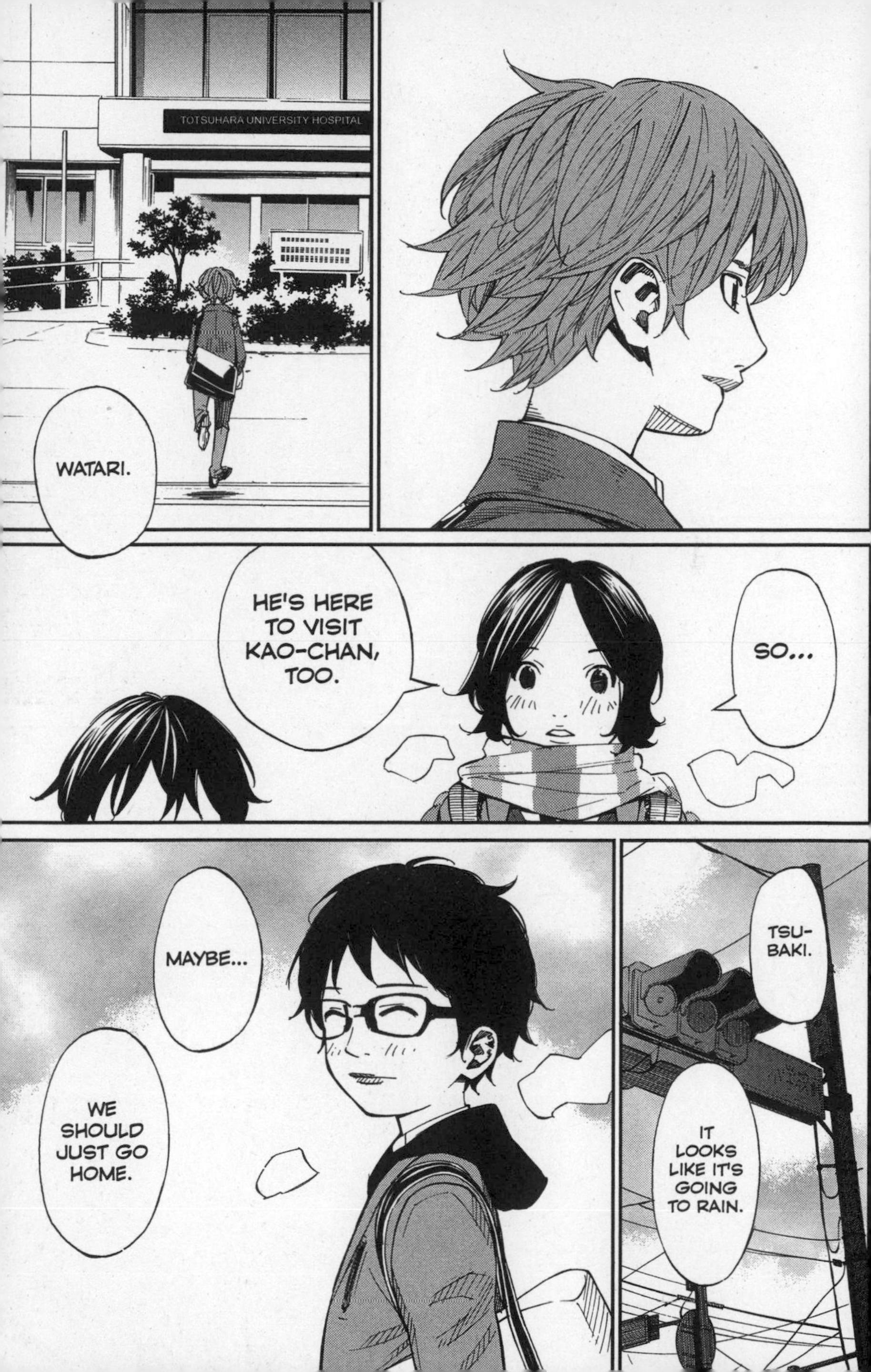
TOTSUHARA UNIVERSITY HOSPITAL
WATARI.
SO...
HE'S HERE TO VISIT KAO-CHAN, TOO.
TSU-BAKI.
IT LOOKS LIKE IT'S GOING TO RAIN.
MAYBE...
WE SHOULD JUST GO HOME.

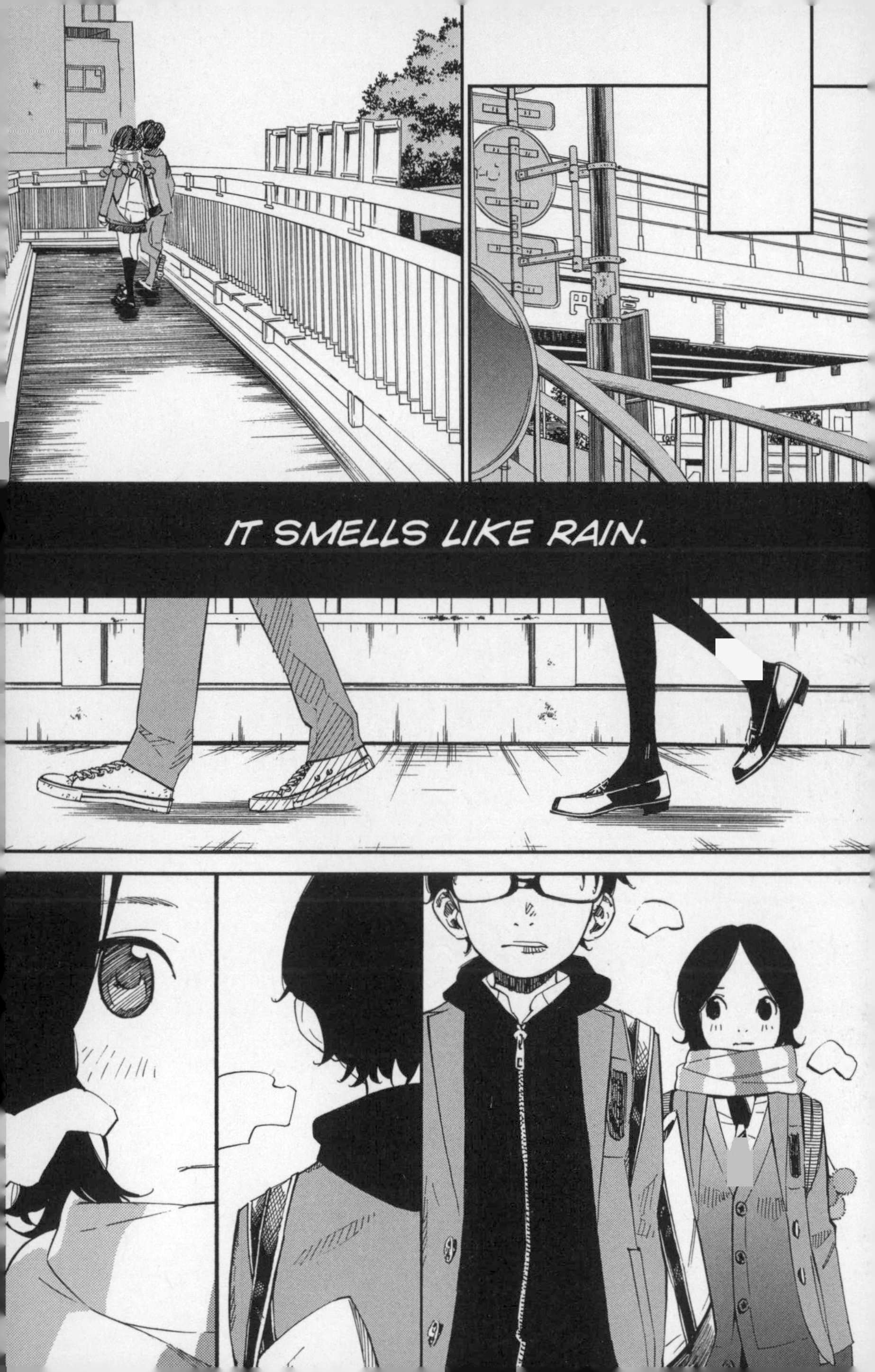
IT SMELLS LIKE RAIN.

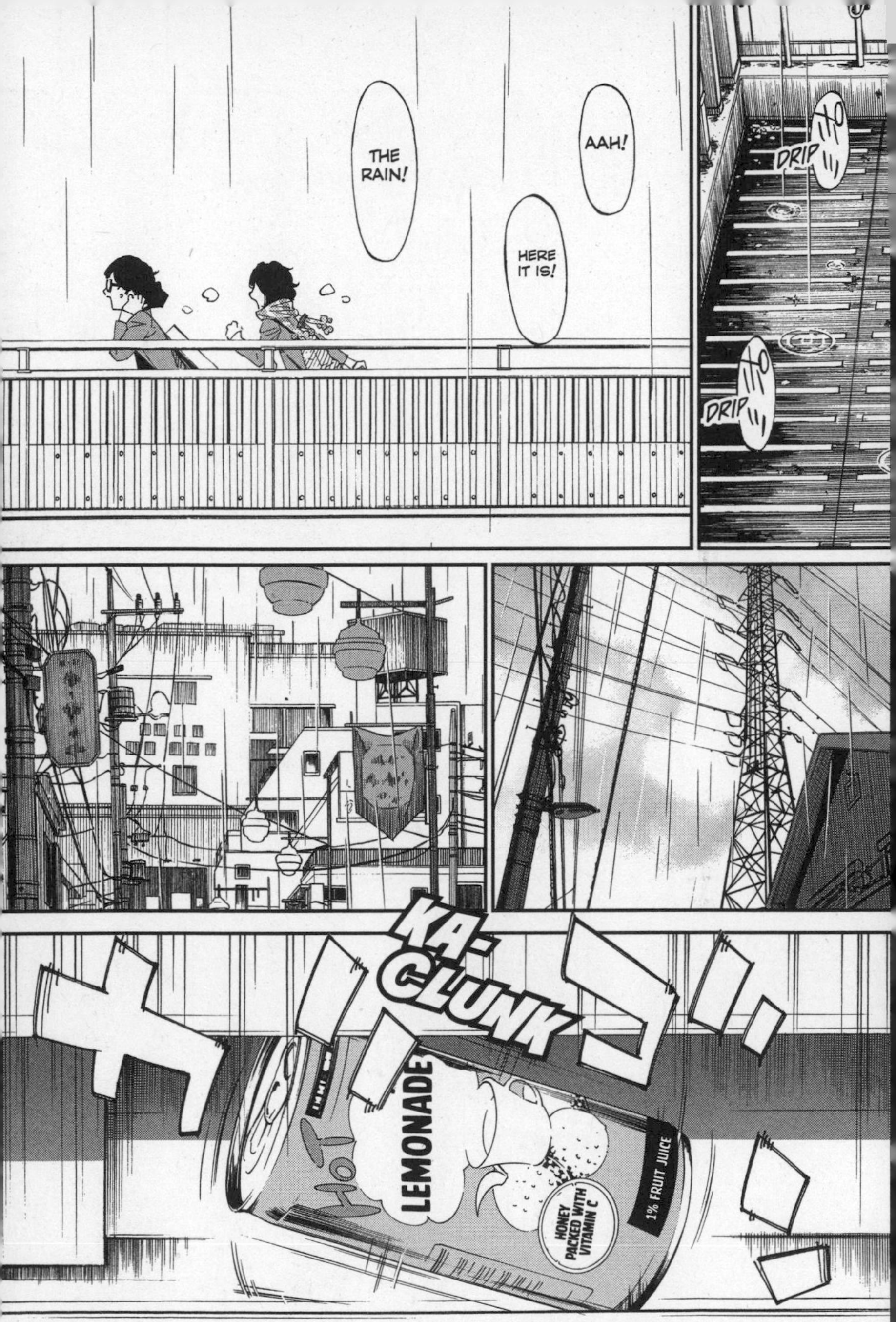
DRIP
DRIP
AAH!
HERE IT IS!
THE RAIN!
KA-CLUNK
LEMONADE
1% FRUIT JUICE
HONEY
PACKED WITH VITAMIN C

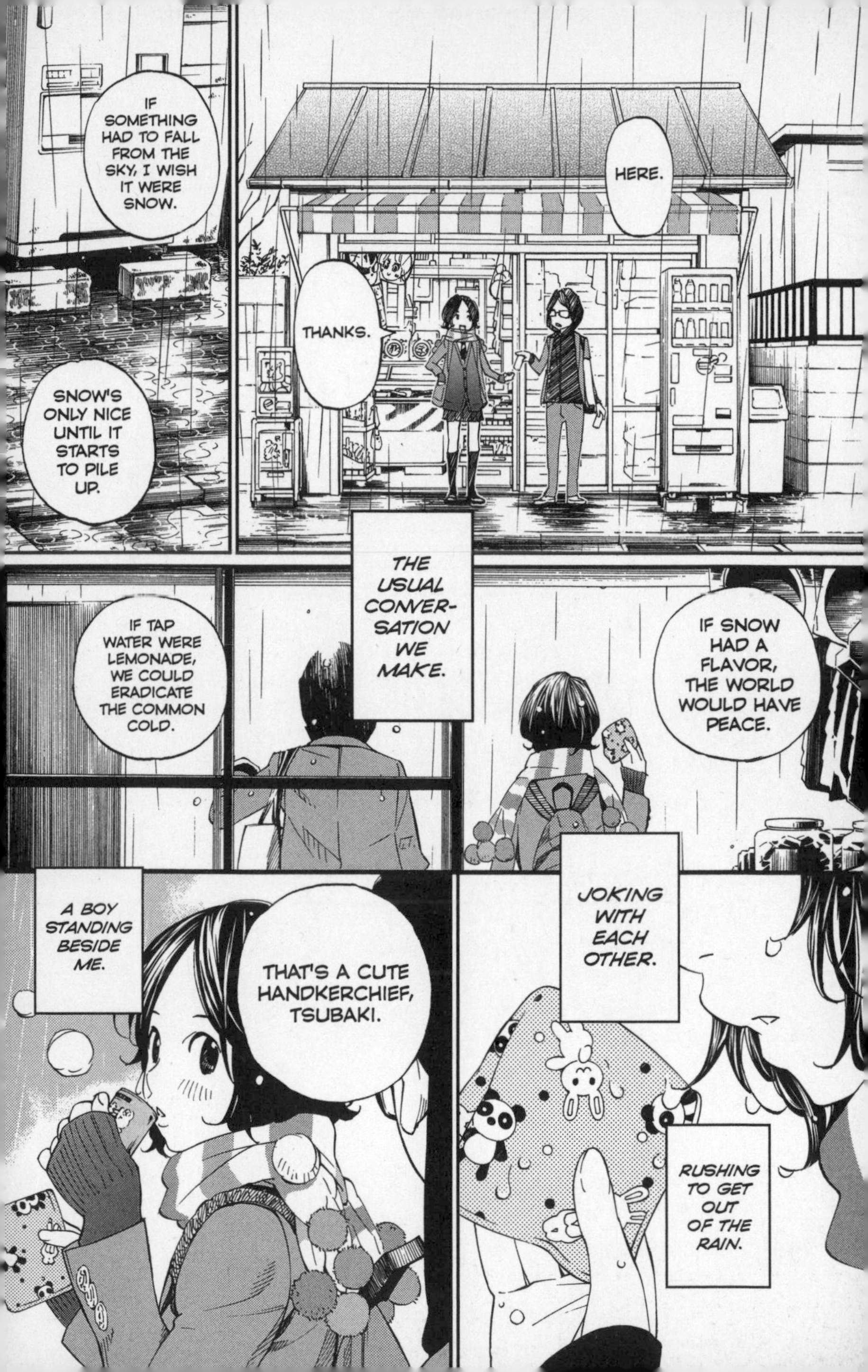
HERE.
THANKS.
IF SOMETHING HAD TO FALL FROM THE SKY, I WISH IT WERE SNOW.
SNOW'S ONLY NICE UNTIL IT STARTS TO PILE UP.
THE USUAL CONVER-SATION WE MAKE.
IF SNOW HAD A FLAVOR, THE WORLD WOULD HAVE PEACE.
IF TAP WATER WERE LEMONADE, WE COULD ERADICATE THE COMMON COLD.
JOKING WITH EACH OTHER.
RUSHING TO GET OUT OF THE RAIN.
THAT'S A CUTE HANDKERCHIEF, TSUBAKI.
A BOY STANDING BESIDE ME.

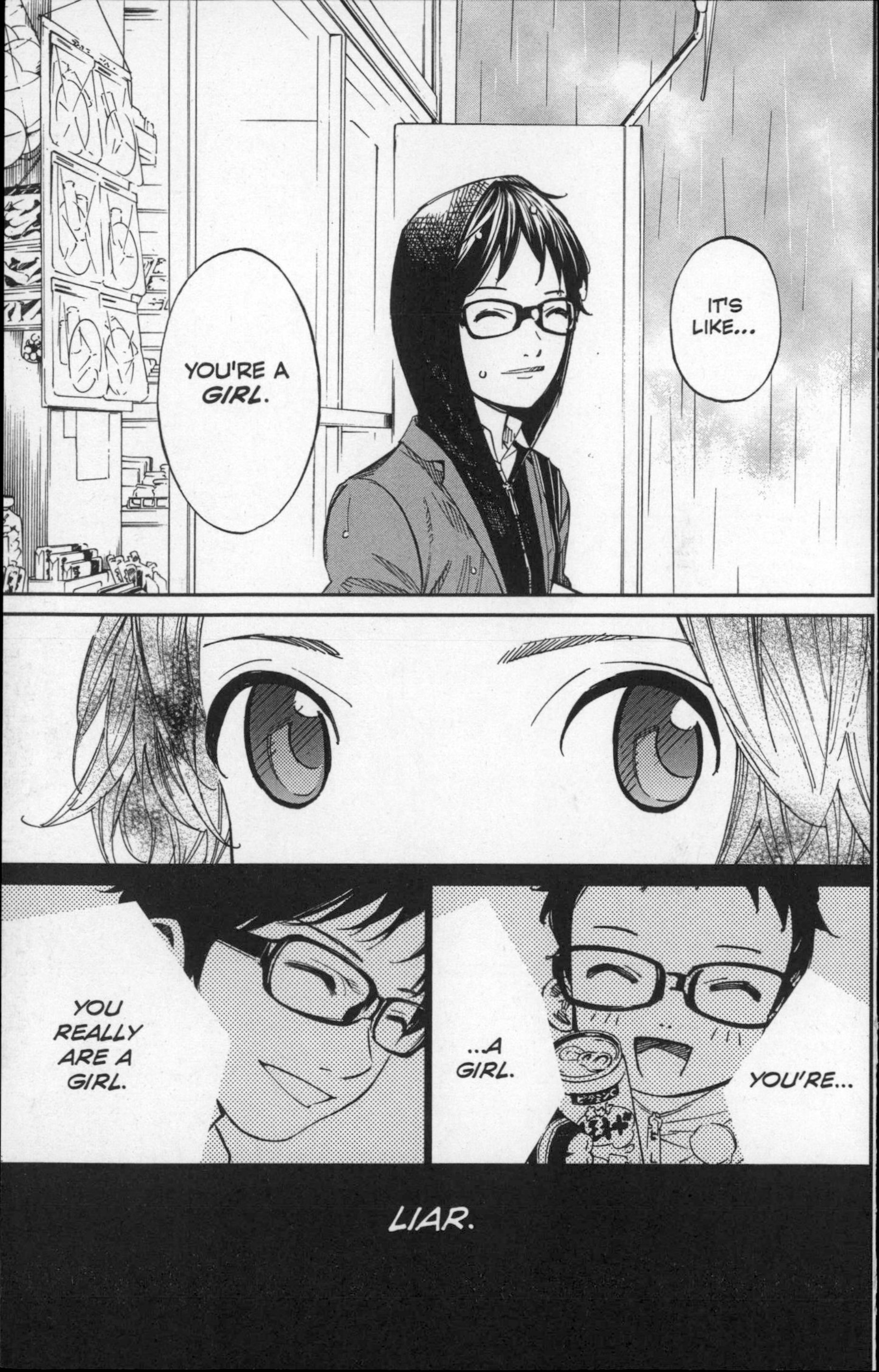

IT'S LIKE...
YOU'RE A GIRL.
YOU'RE...
...A GIRL.
YOU REALLY ARE A GIRL.
LIAR.

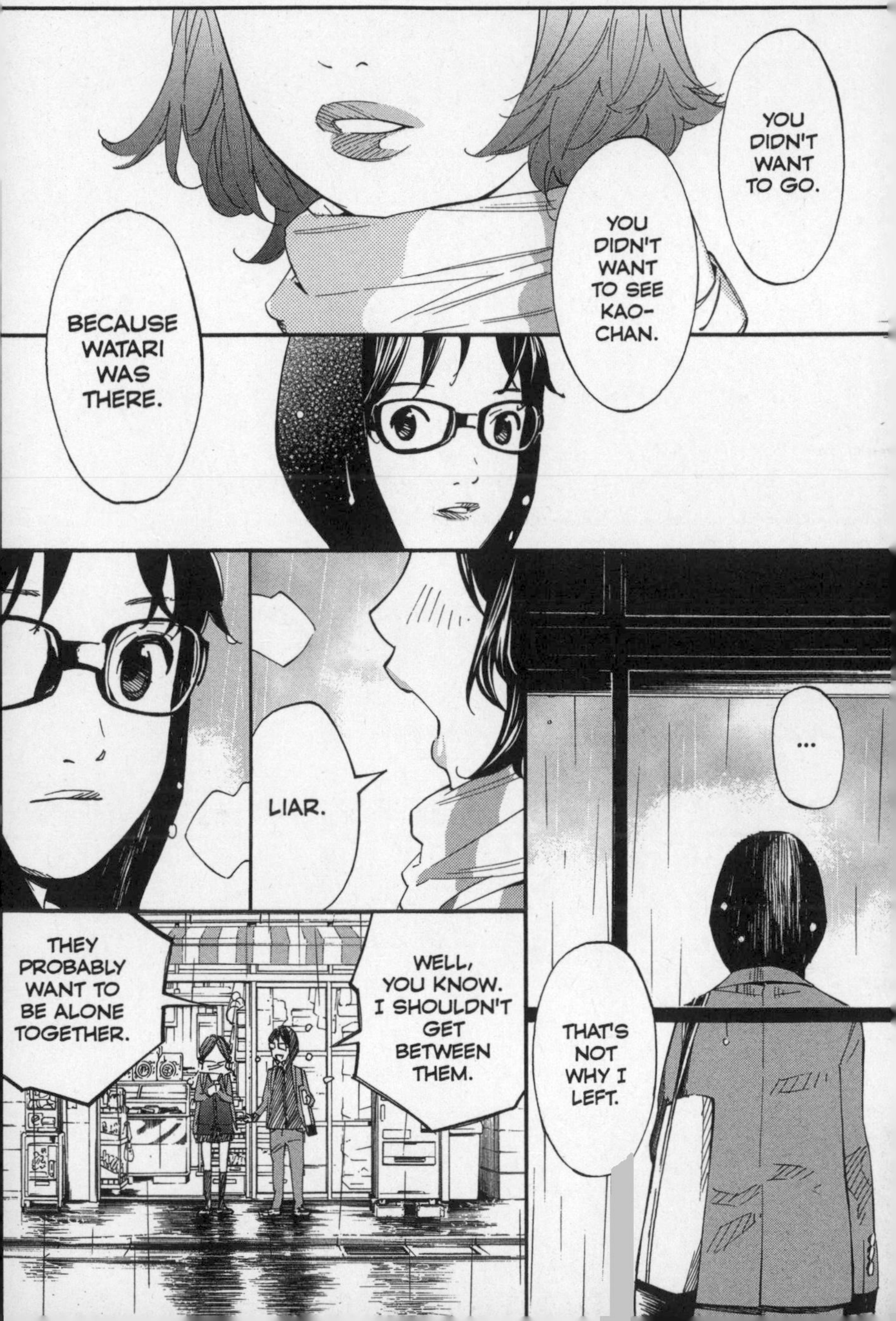
YOU DIDN'T WANT TO GO.
YOU DIDN'T WANT TO SEE KAO-CHAN.
BECAUSE WATARI WAS THERE.
...
THAT'S NOT WHY I LEFT.
LIAR.
WELL, YOU KNOW. I SHOULDN'T GET BETWEEN THEM.
THEY PROBABLY WANT TO BE ALONE TOGETHER.

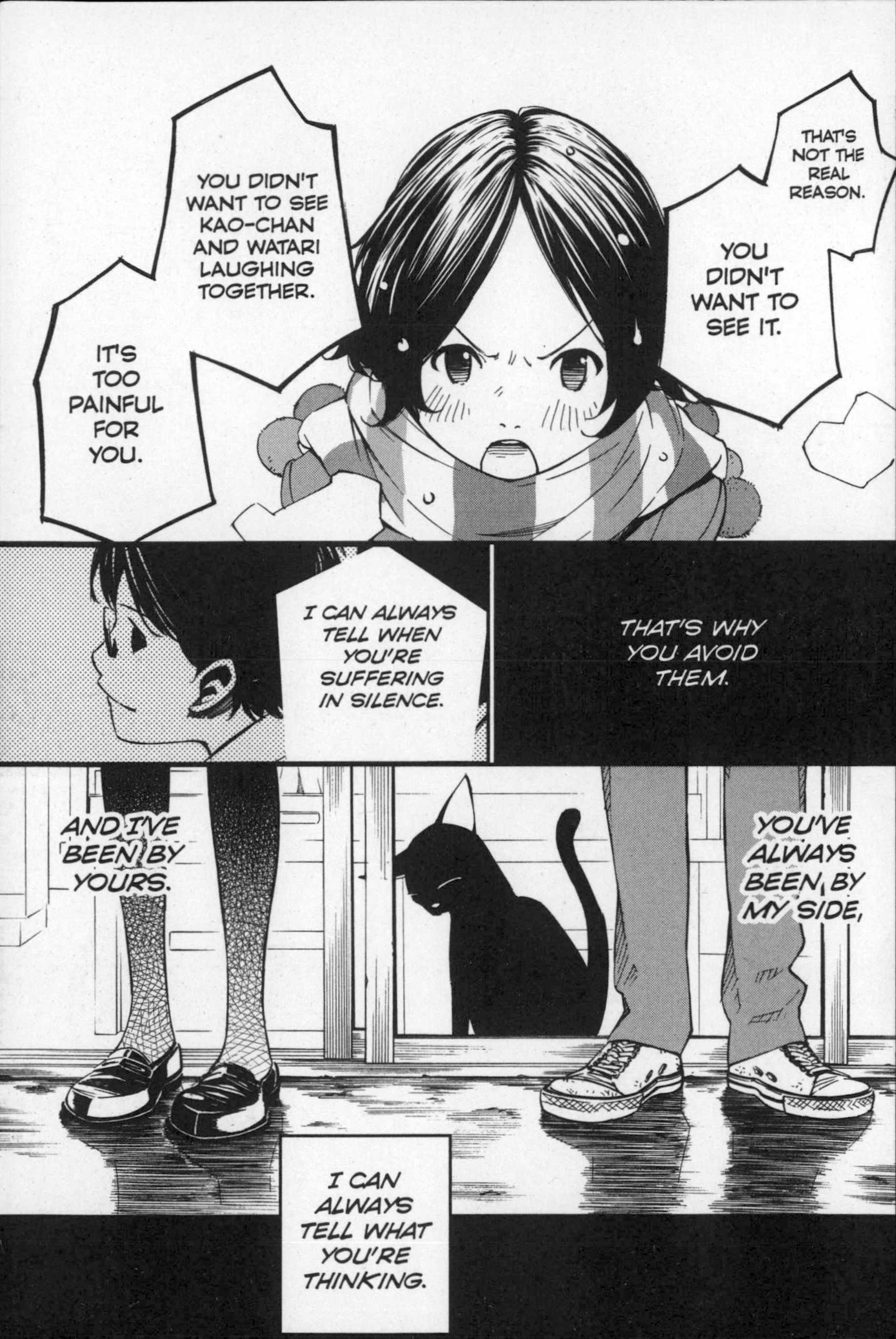
THAT'S NOT THE REAL REASON.
YOU DIDN'T WANT TO SEE IT.
YOU DIDN'T WANT TO SEE KAO-CHAN AND WATARI LAUGHING TOGETHER.
IT'S TOO PAINFUL FOR YOU.
THAT'S WHY YOU AVOID THEM.
I CAN ALWAYS TELL WHEN YOU'RE SUFFERING IN SILENCE.
YOU'VE ALWAYS BEEN BY MY SIDE,
AND I'VE BEEN BY YOURS.
I CAN ALWAYS TELL WHAT YOU'RE THINKING.

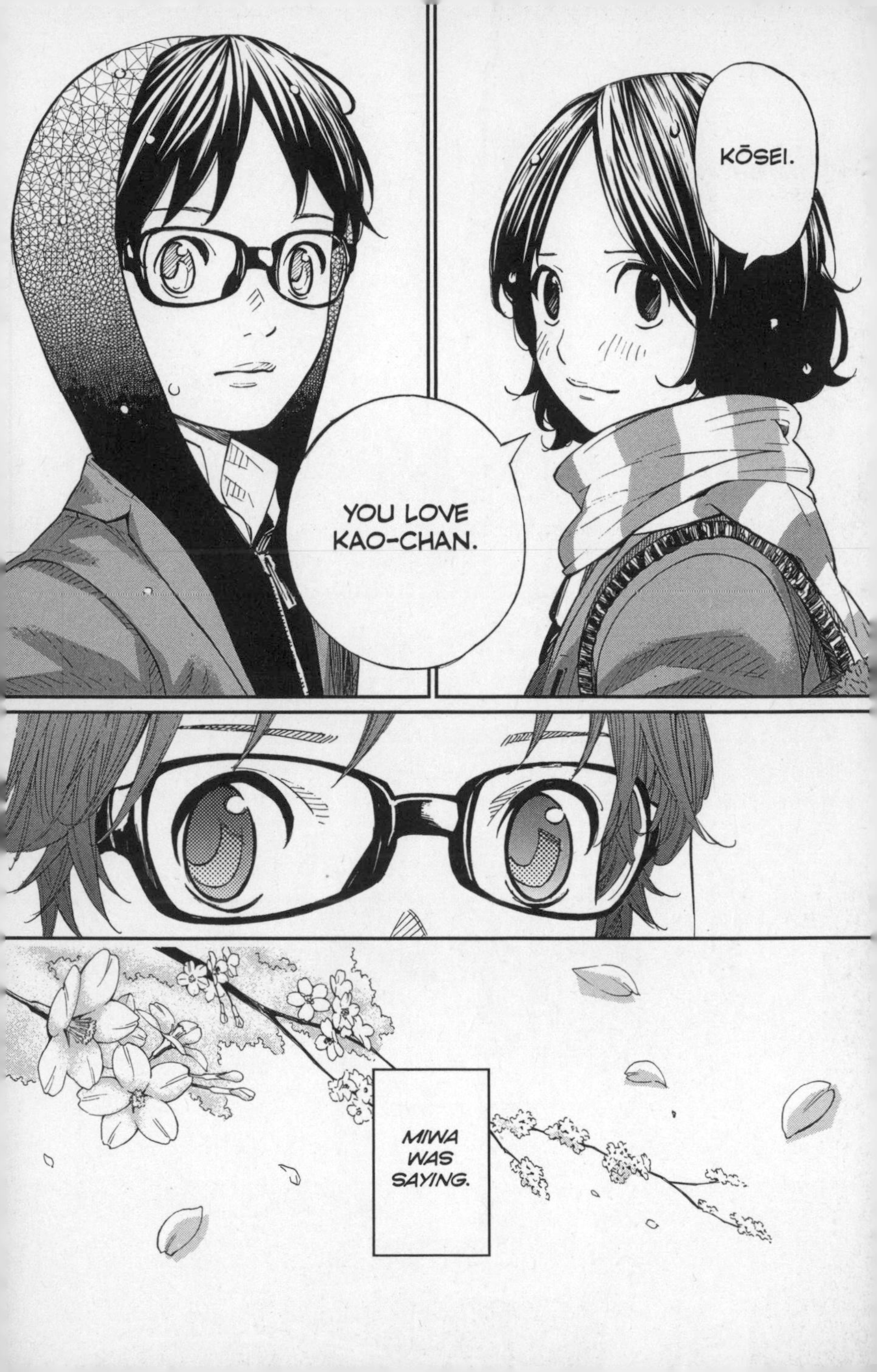
KŌSEI.
YOU LOVE KAO-CHAN.
MIWA WAS SAYING.

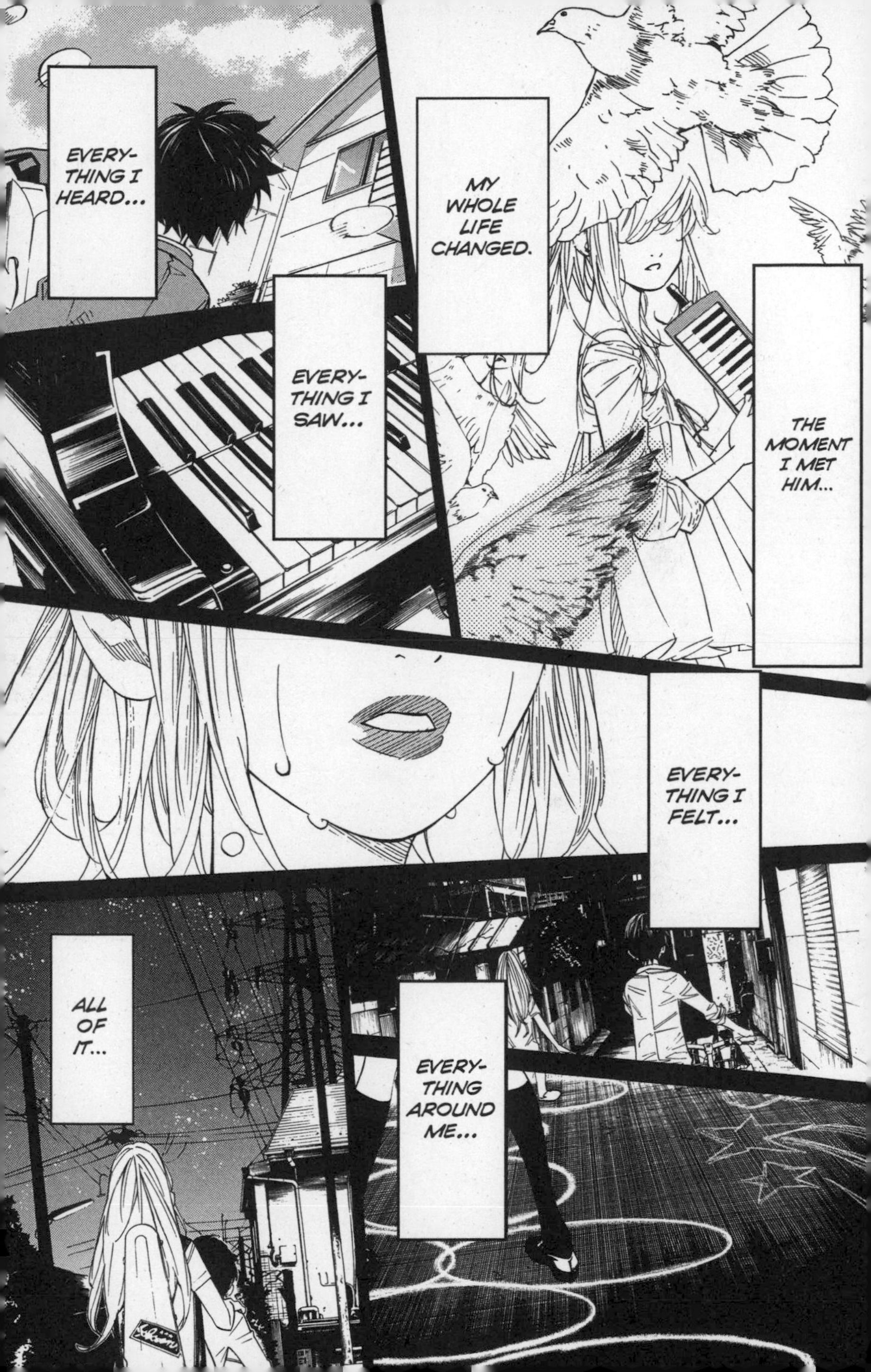
THE MOMENT I MET HIM...
MY WHOLE LIFE CHANGED.
EVERY-THING I HEARD...
EVERY-THING I SAW...
EVERY-THING I FELT...
EVERY-THING AROUND ME...
ALL OF IT...

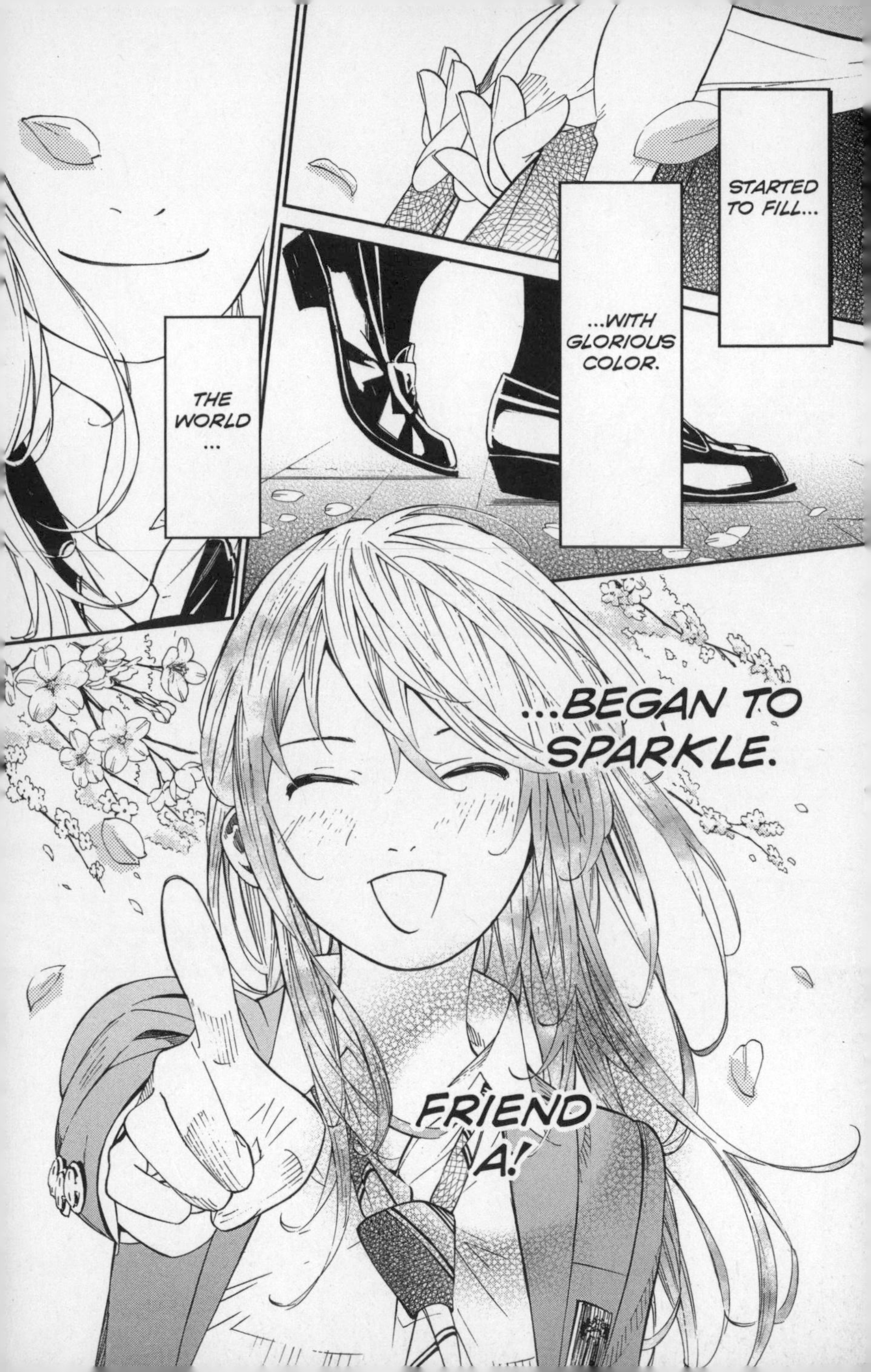
STARTED TO FILL...
...WITH GLORIOUS COLOR.
THE WORLD ...
...BEGAN TO SPARKLE.
FRIEND A!

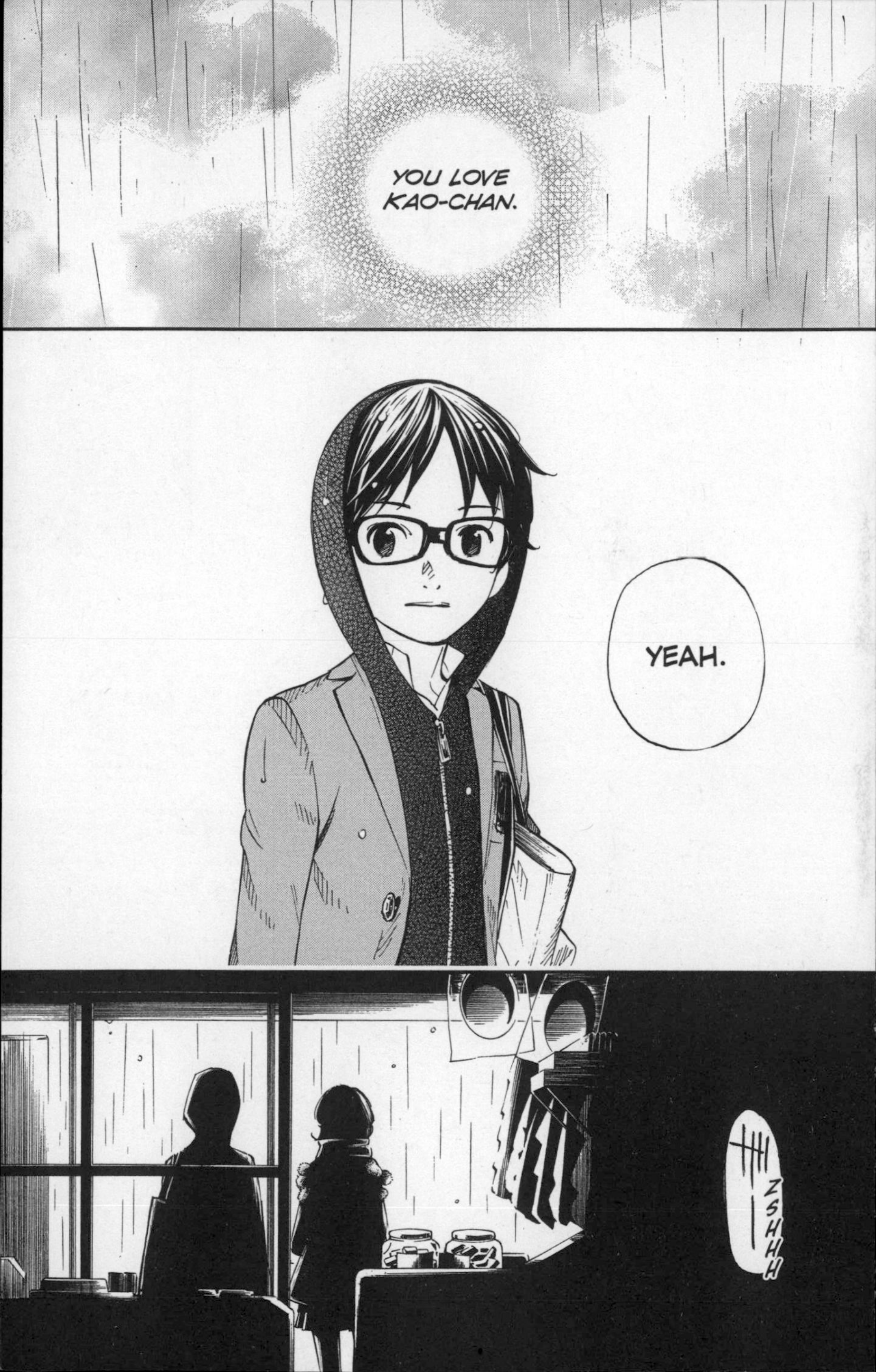
YOU LOVE KAO-CHAN.
YEAH.
ZSHHH

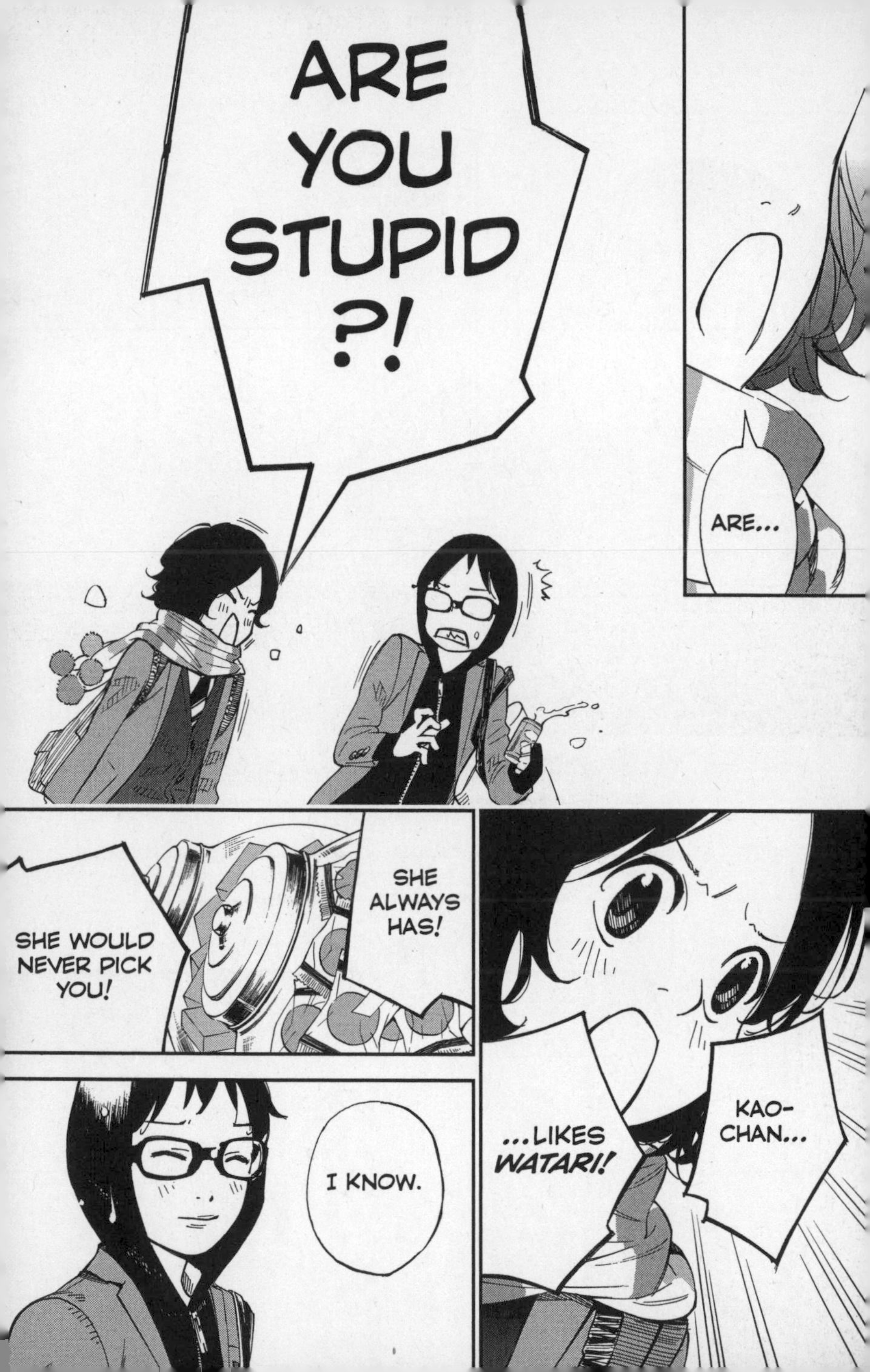
ARE...
ARE YOU STUPID ?!
KAO-CHAN...
...LIKES *WATARI!*
SHE ALWAYS HAS!
SHE WOULD NEVER PICK YOU!
I KNOW.

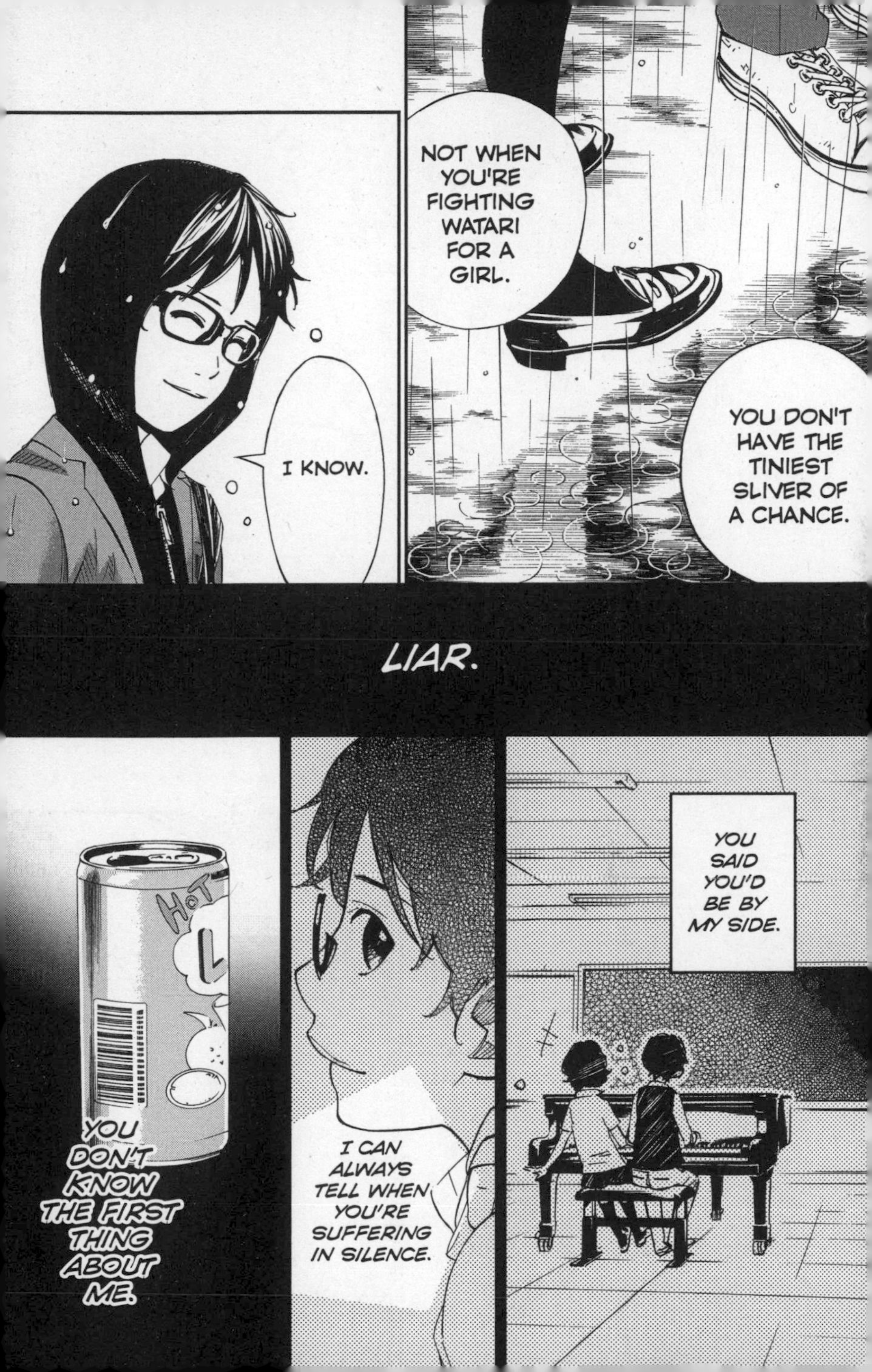
NOT WHEN YOU'RE FIGHTING WATARI FOR A GIRL.
YOU DON'T HAVE THE TINIEST SLIVER OF A CHANCE.
I KNOW.
LIAR.
YOU SAID YOU'D BE BY MY SIDE.
I CAN ALWAYS TELL WHEN YOU'RE SUFFERING IN SILENCE.
YOU DON'T KNOW THE FIRST THING ABOUT ME.

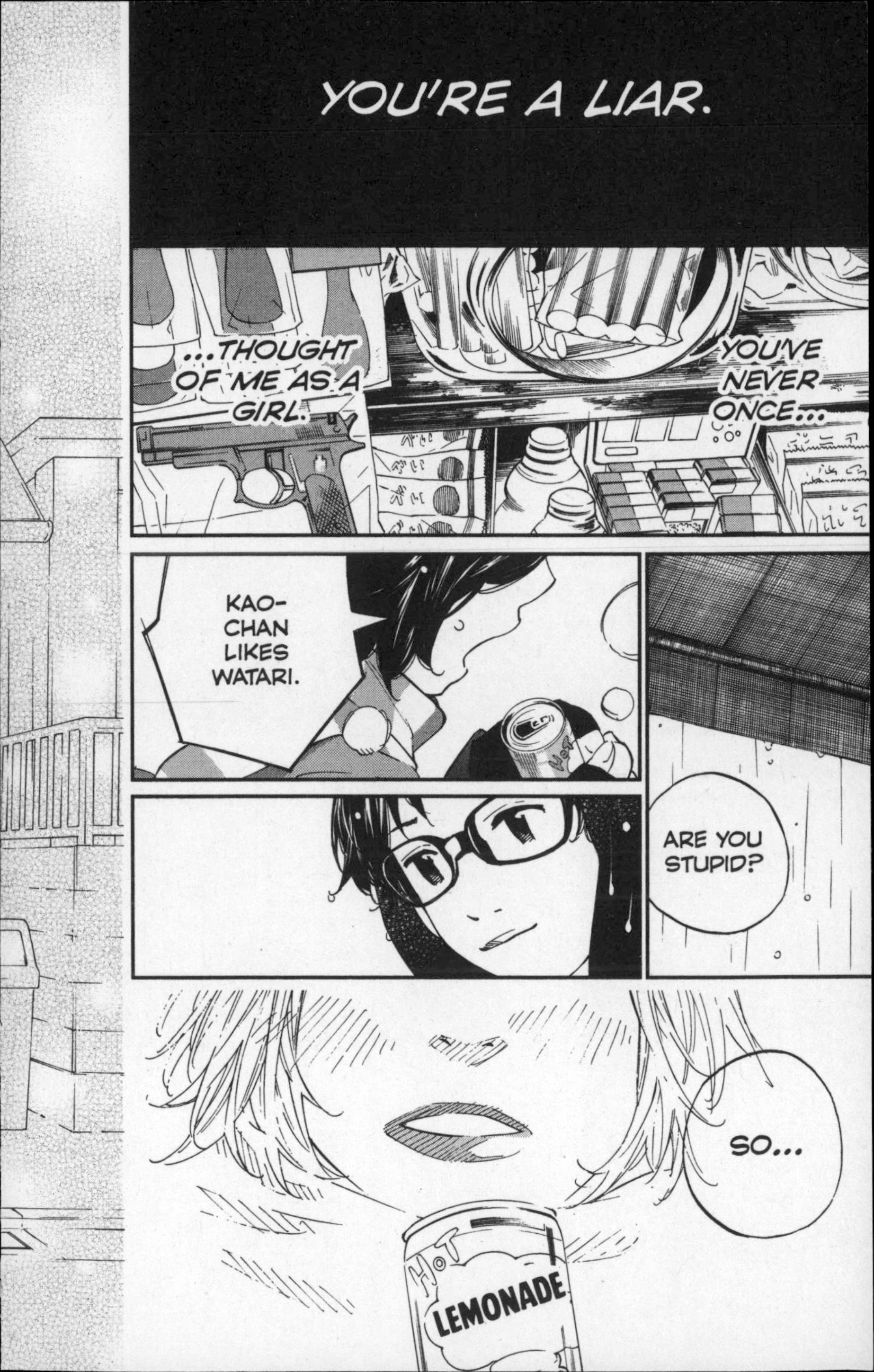
YOU'RE A LIAR.
YOU'VE NEVER ONCE...
...THOUGHT OF ME AS A GIRL.
ARE YOU STUPID?
KAO-CHAN LIKES WATARI.
SO...
HOT
LEMONADE

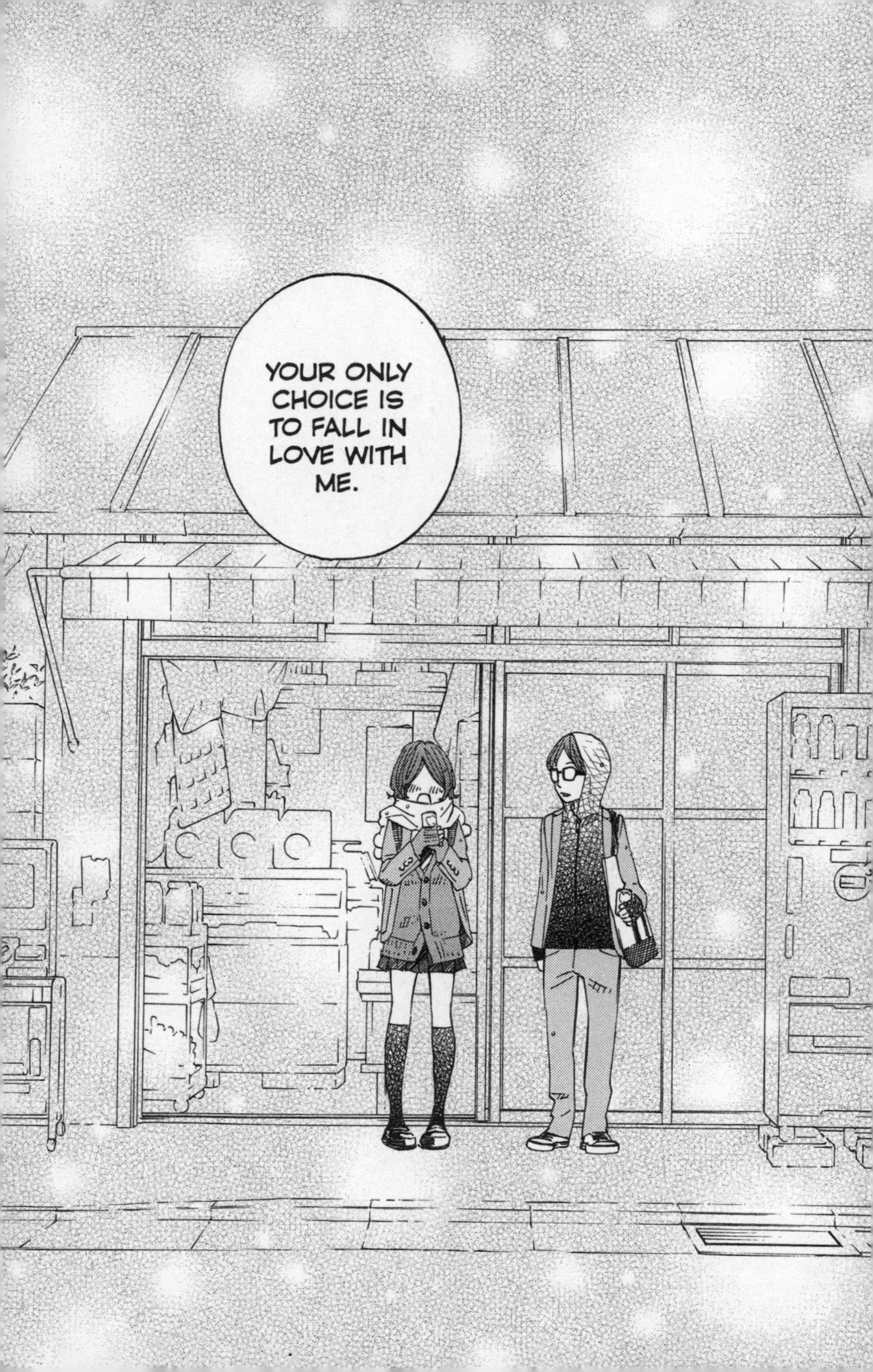
YOUR ONLY CHOICE IS TO FALL IN LOVE WITH ME.

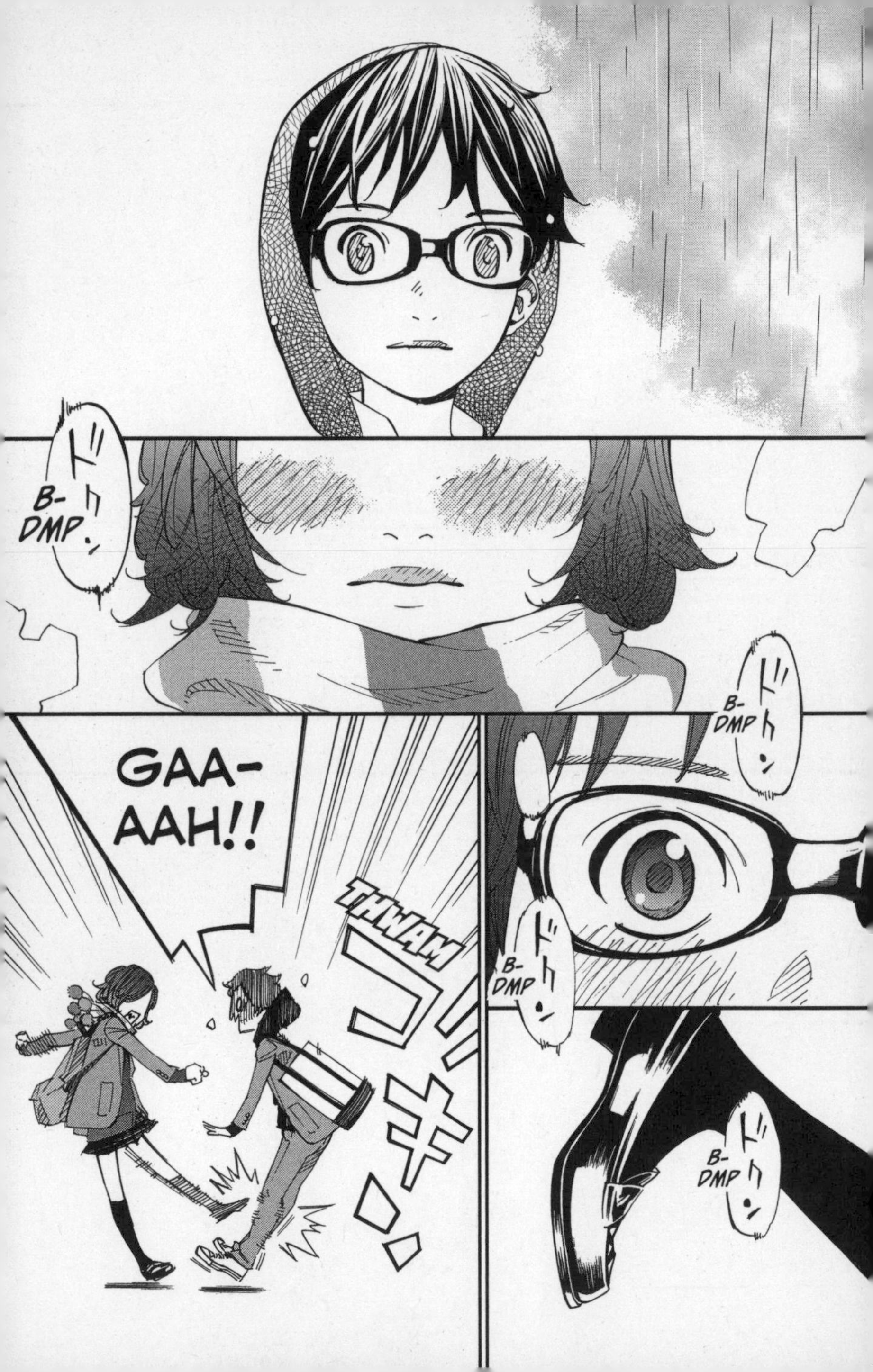
B-DMP
B-DMP
B-DMP
B-DMP
GAAAAH!!
THWAM

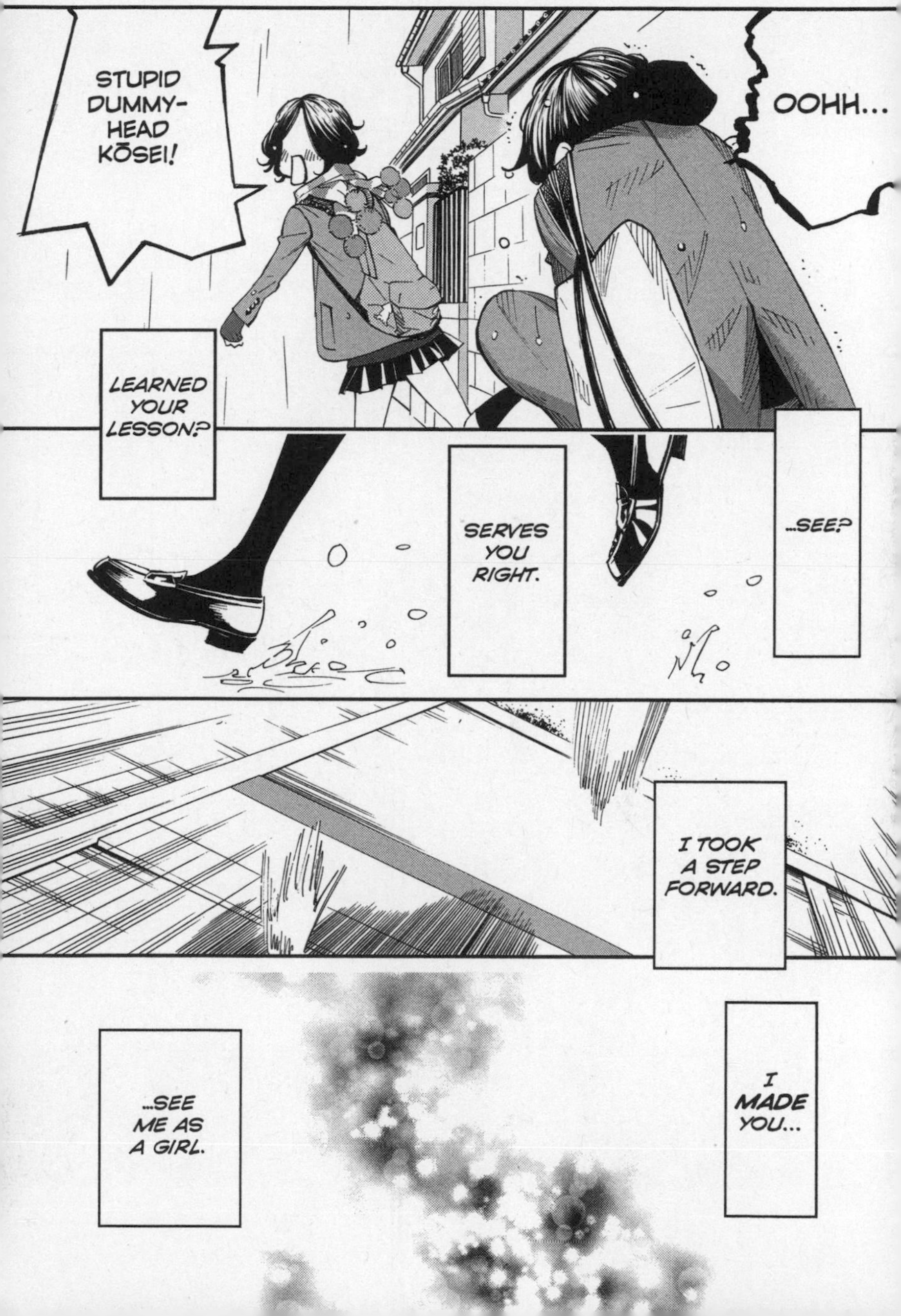
OOHH...
STUPID DUMMY-HEAD KŌSEI!
LEARNED YOUR LESSON?
...SEE?
SERVES YOU RIGHT.
I TOOK A STEP FORWARD.
I MADE YOU...
...SEE ME AS A GIRL.

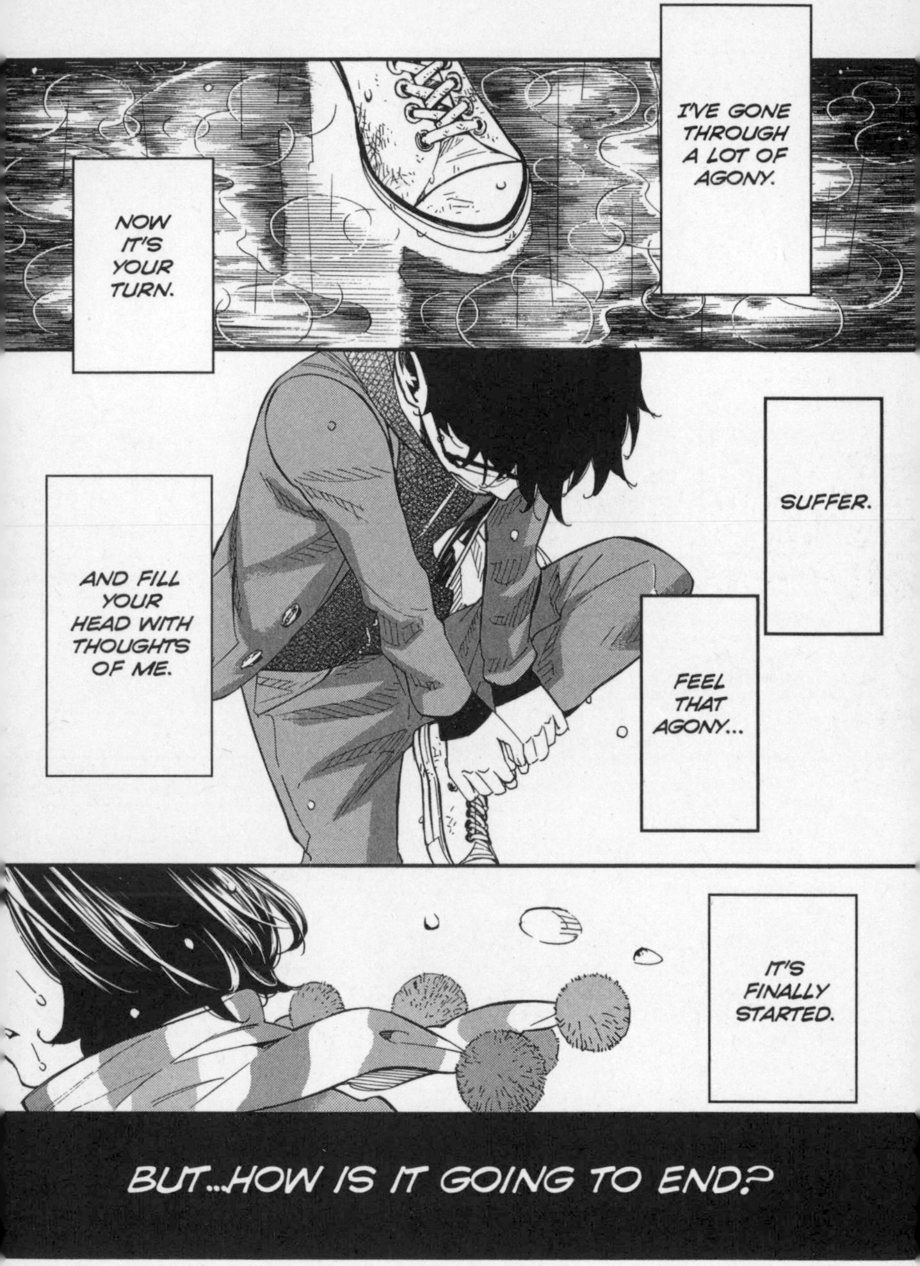
I'VE GONE THROUGH A LOT OF AGONY.
NOW IT'S YOUR TURN.
SUFFER.
FEEL THAT AGONY...
AND FILL YOUR HEAD WITH THOUGHTS OF ME.
IT'S FINALLY STARTED.
BUT...HOW IS IT GOING TO END?

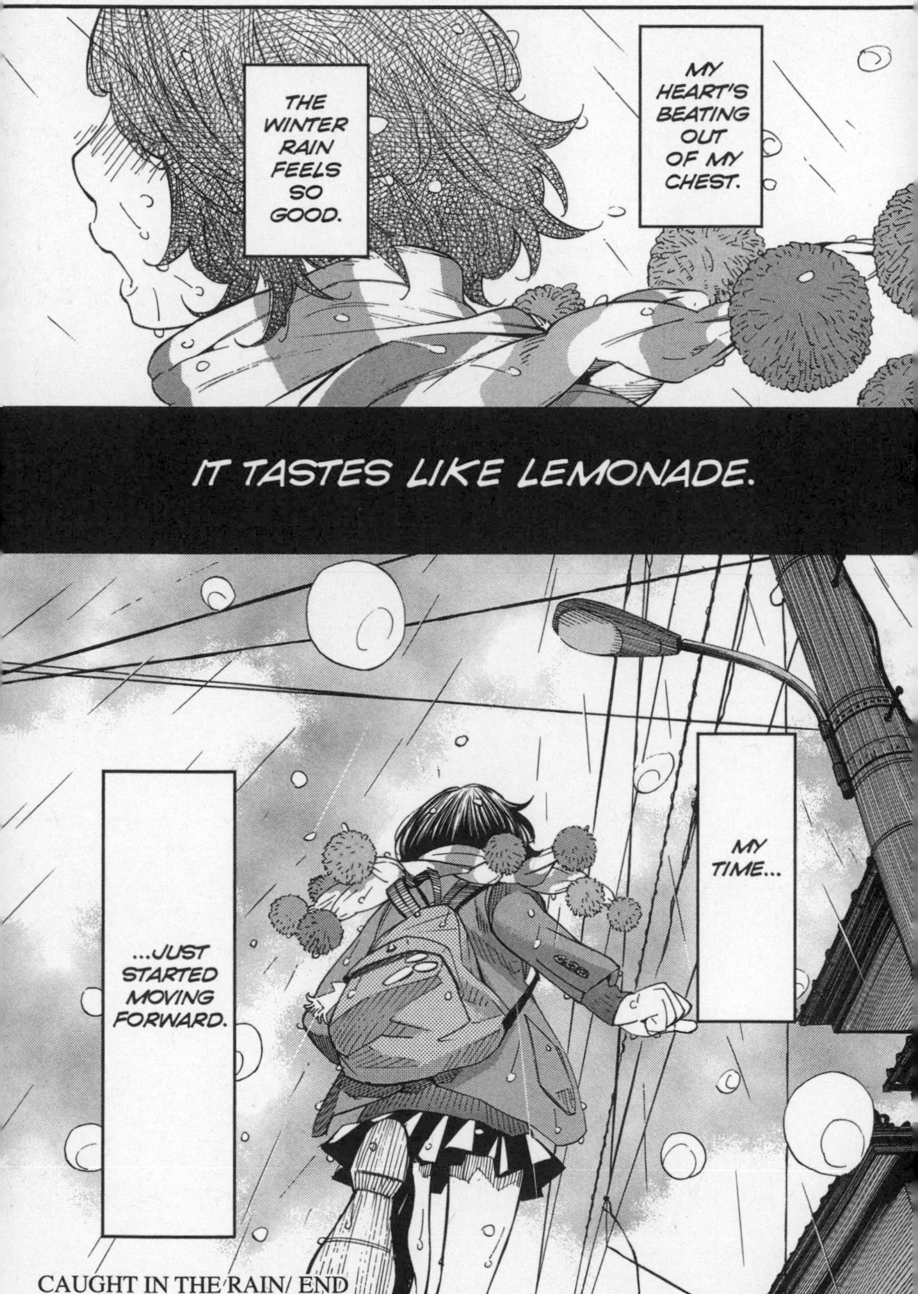
MY HEART'S BEATING OUT OF MY CHEST.
THE WINTER RAIN FEELS SO GOOD.
IT TASTES LIKE LEMONADE.
MY TIME...
...JUST STARTED MOVING FORWARD.

CAUGHT IN THE RAIN/ END

Your Lie in April

I met the girl under full-bloomed cherry blossoms, and my fate has begun to change.

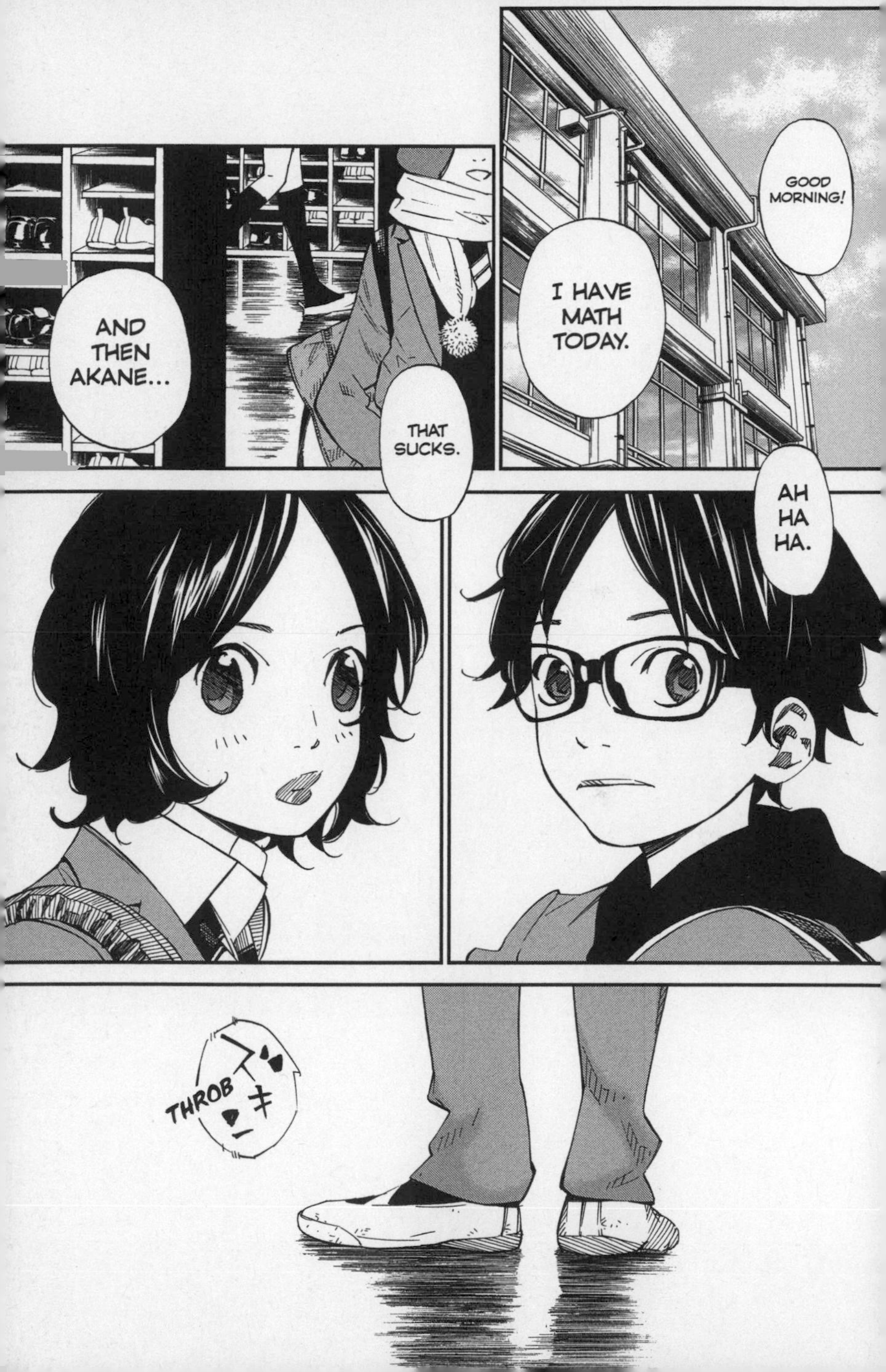
GOOD MORNING!
I HAVE MATH TODAY.
THAT SUCKS.
AND THEN AKANE...
AH HA HA.
THROB
ズキ

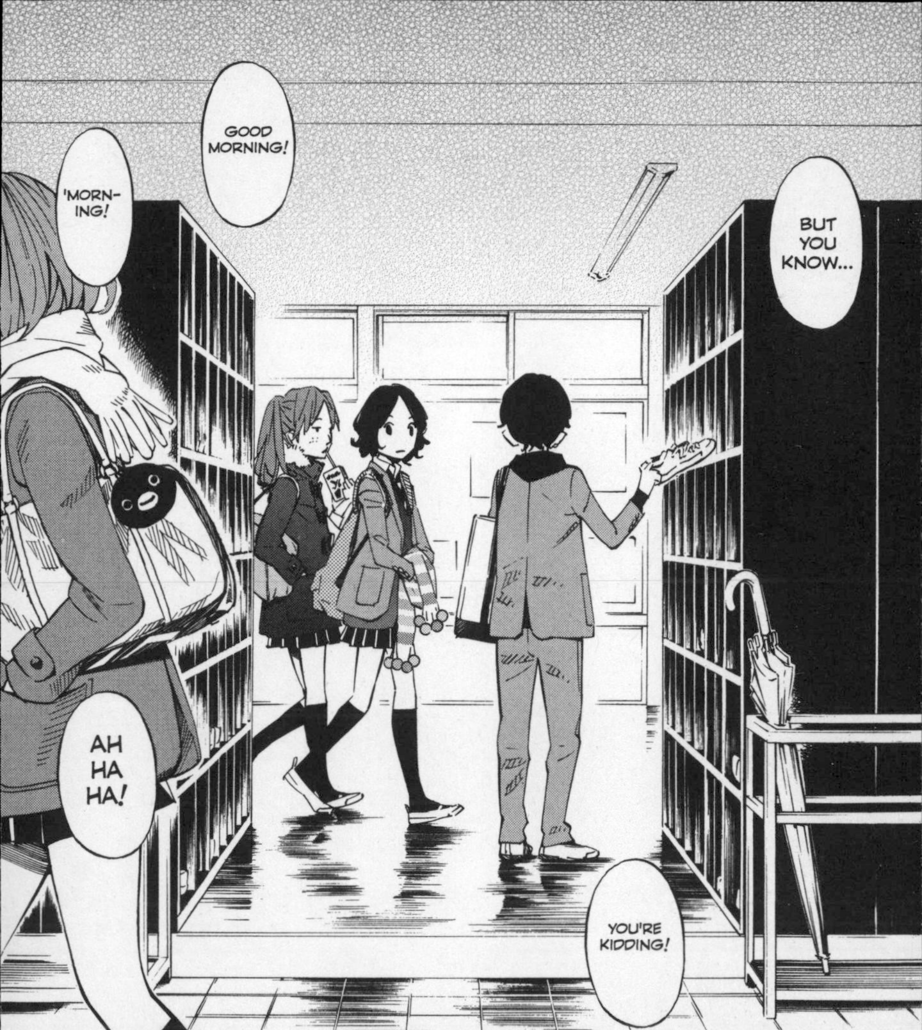
BUT YOU KNOW...
GOOD MORNING!
'MORN-ING!
YOU'RE KIDDING!
AH HA HA!
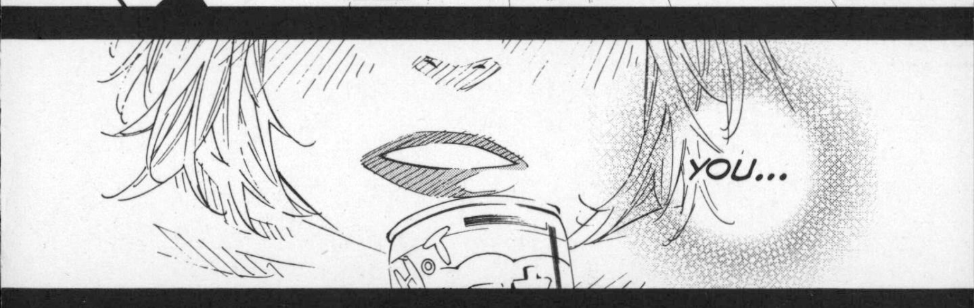
YOU...

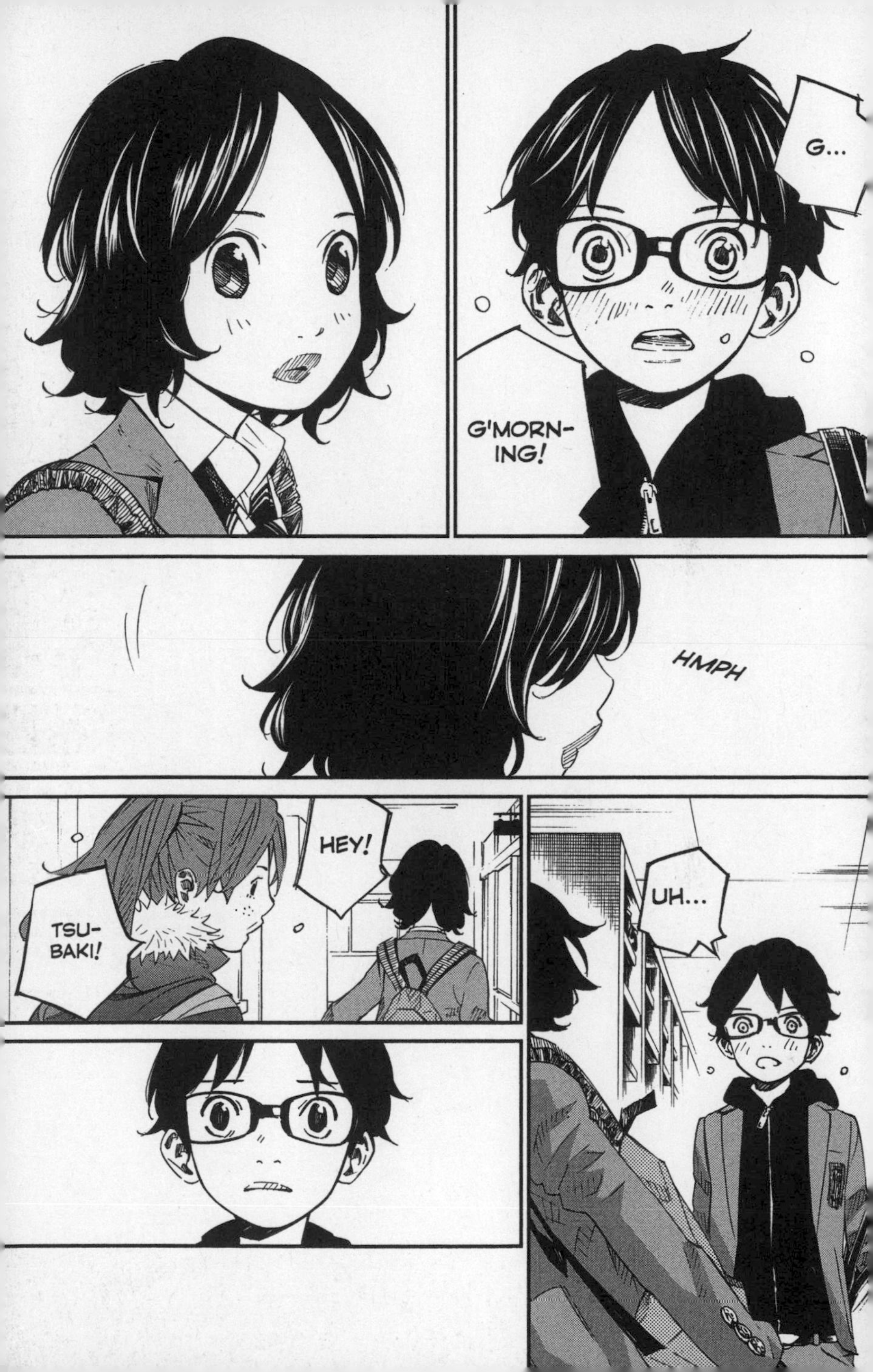
G...
G'MORN-ING!
HMPH
UH...
HEY!
TSU-BAKI!

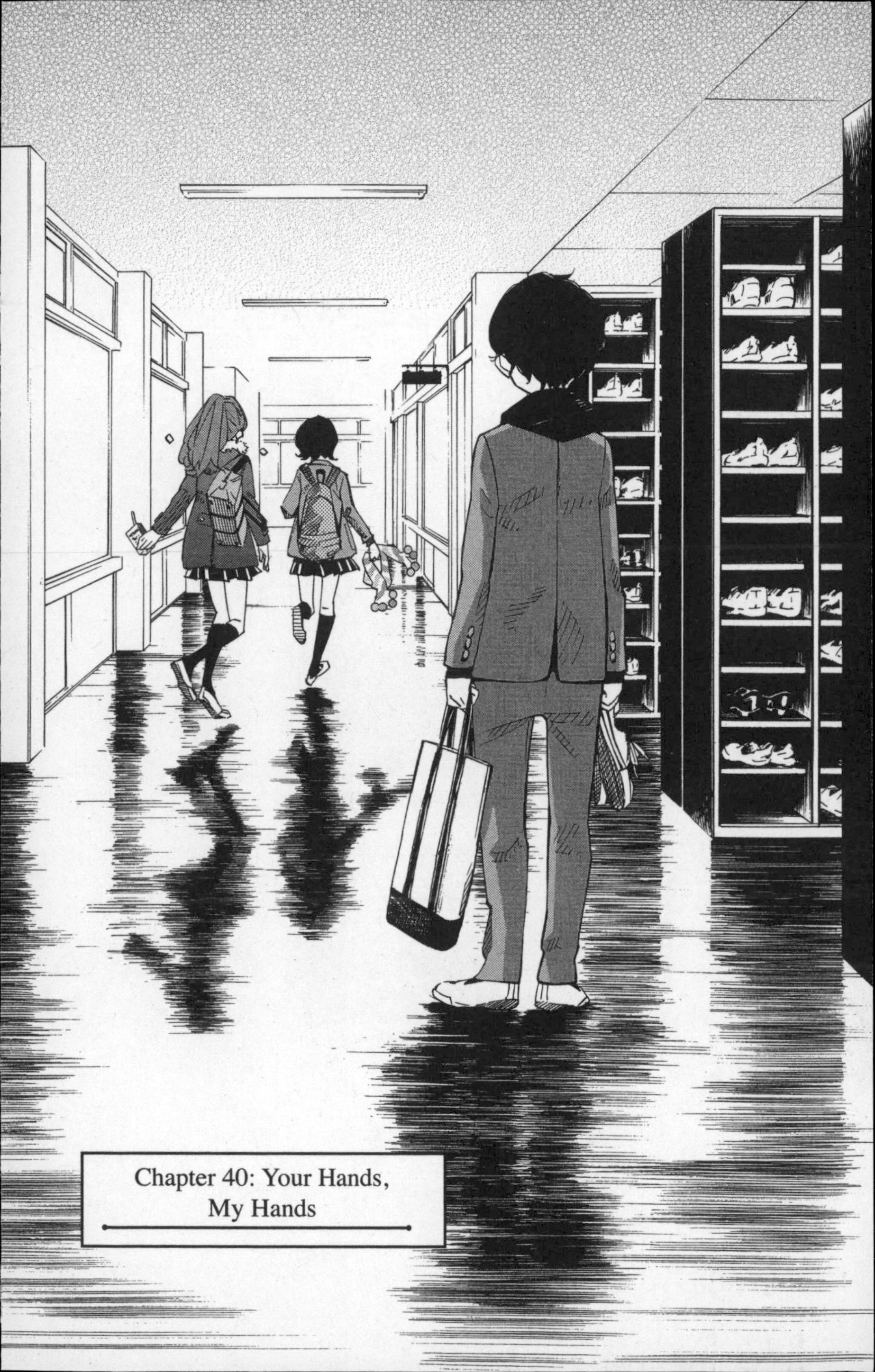
Chapter 40: Your Hands,
My Hands

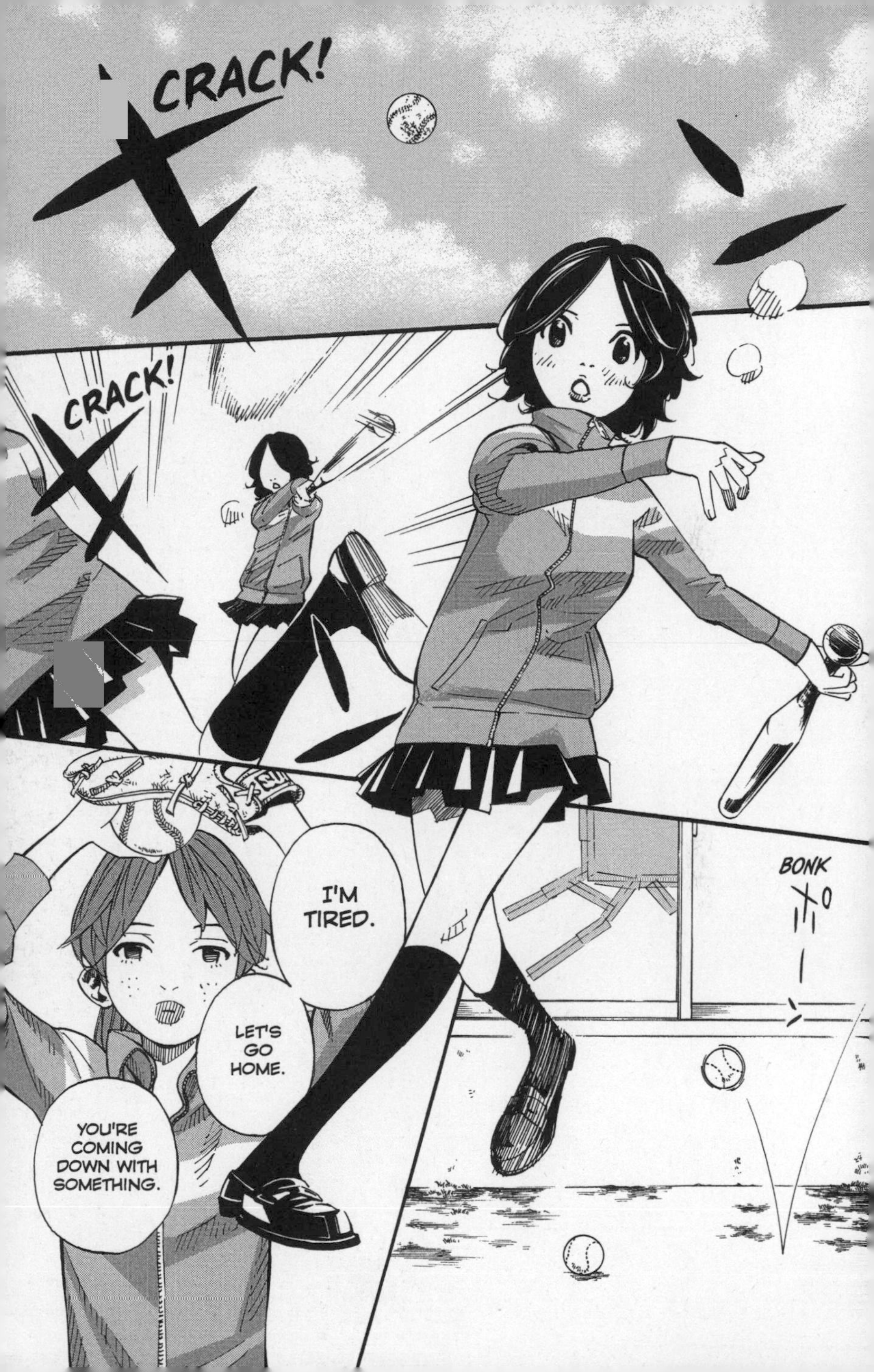
CRACK!
CRACK!
BONK
I'M TIRED.
LET'S GO HOME.
YOU'RE COMING DOWN WITH SOMETHING.

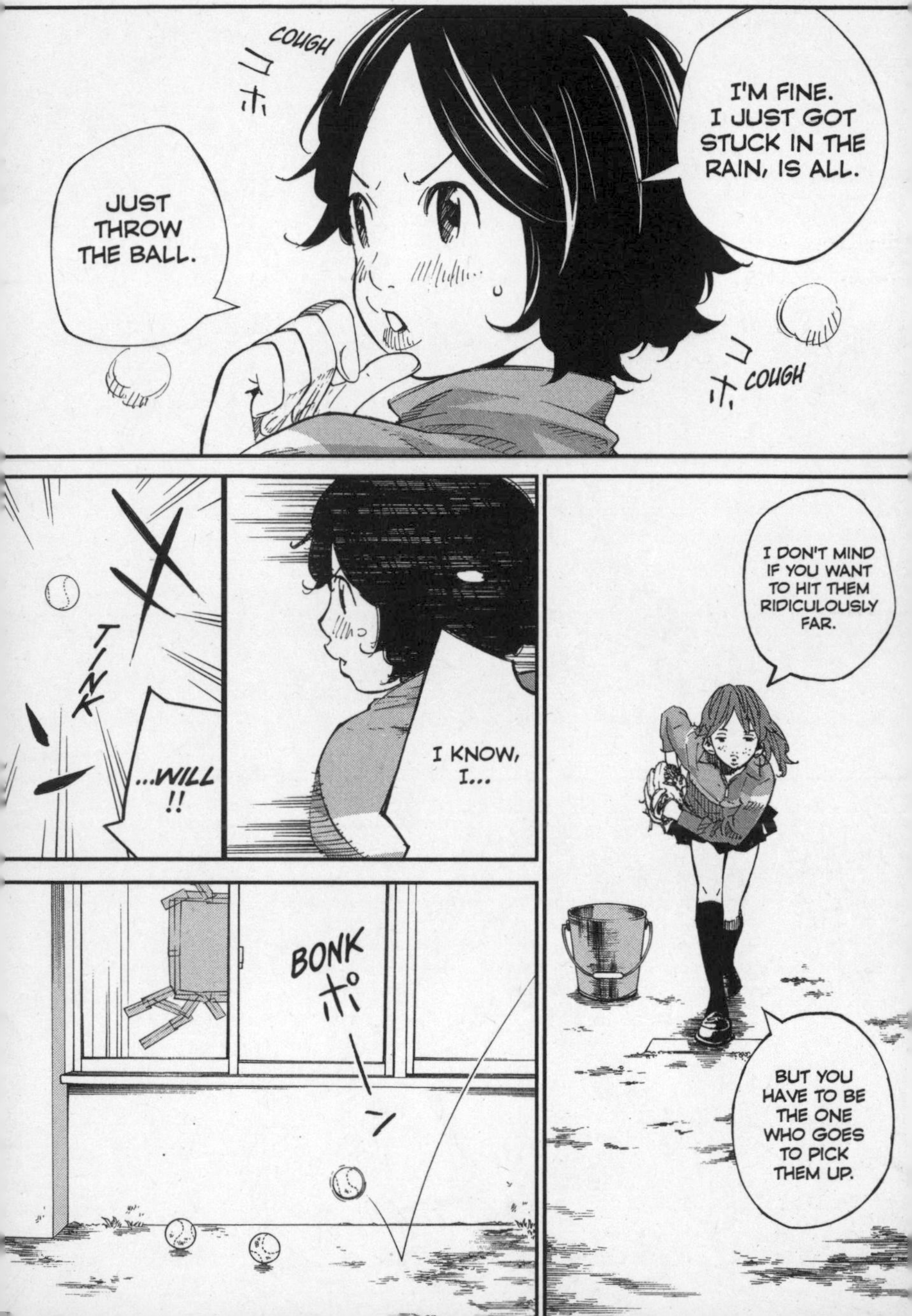
I'M FINE. I JUST GOT STUCK IN THE RAIN, IS ALL.
COUGH
コホ
JUST THROW THE BALL.
コホ
COUGH
I DON'T MIND IF YOU WANT TO HIT THEM RIDICULOUSLY FAR.
BUT YOU HAVE TO BE THE ONE WHO GOES TO PICK THEM UP.
I KNOW, I...
TINK
...WILL !!
BONK
ポーン

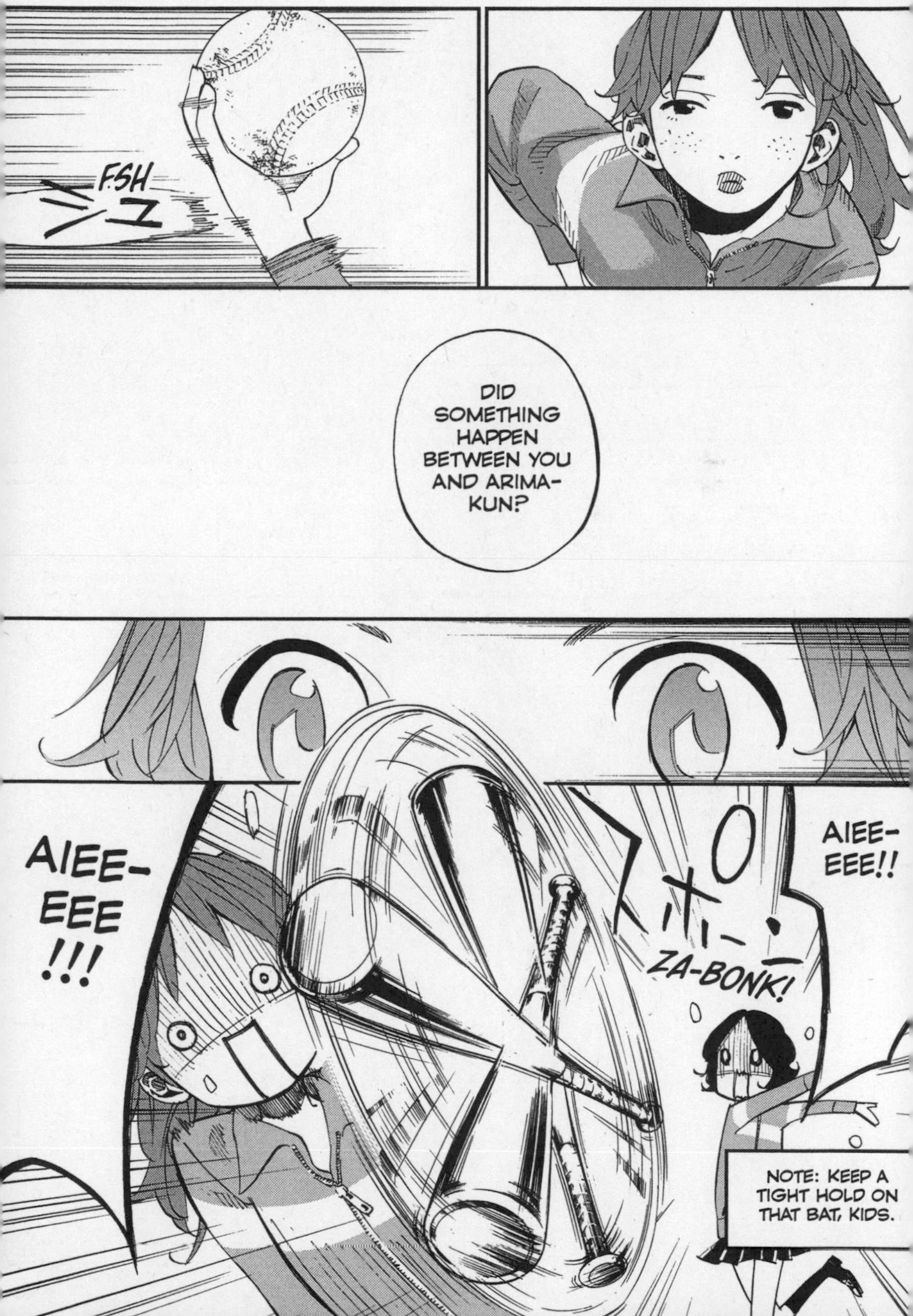
F.SH
DID SOMETHING HAPPEN BETWEEN YOU AND ARIMA-KUN?
AIEE-EEE!!
ZA-BONK!
AIEE-EEE!!!
NOTE: KEEP A TIGHT HOLD ON THAT BAT, KIDS.

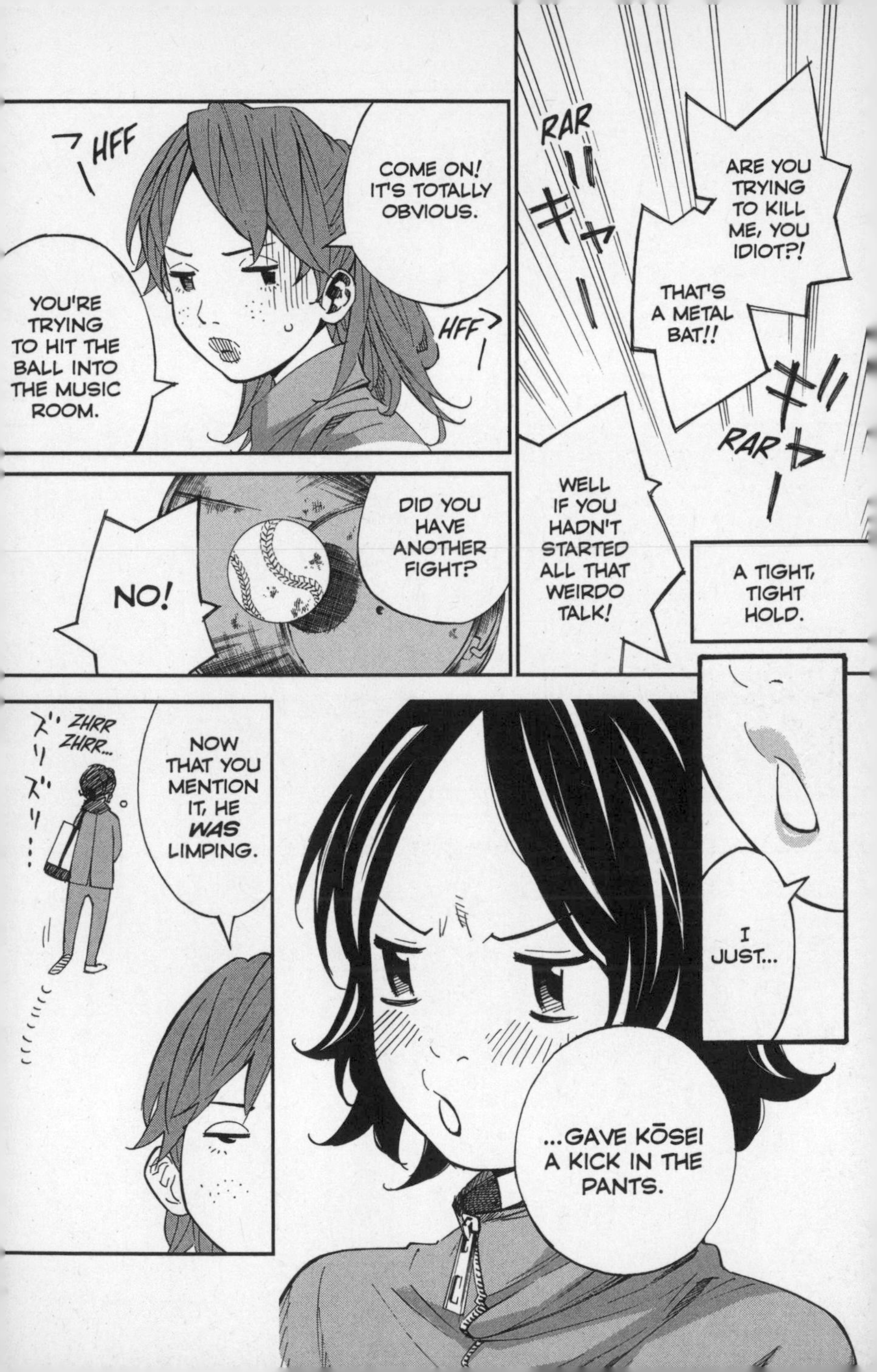
RAR
ARE YOU TRYING TO KILL ME, YOU IDIOT?!
THAT'S A METAL BAT!!
RAR
WELL IF YOU HADN'T STARTED ALL THAT WEIRDO TALK!
A TIGHT, TIGHT HOLD.
HFF
COME ON! IT'S TOTALLY OBVIOUS.
HFF
YOU'RE TRYING TO HIT THE BALL INTO THE MUSIC ROOM.
DID YOU HAVE ANOTHER FIGHT?
NO!
I JUST...
...GAVE KŌSEI A KICK IN THE PANTS.
NOW THAT YOU MENTION IT, HE *WAS* LIMPING.
ZHRR ZHRR...

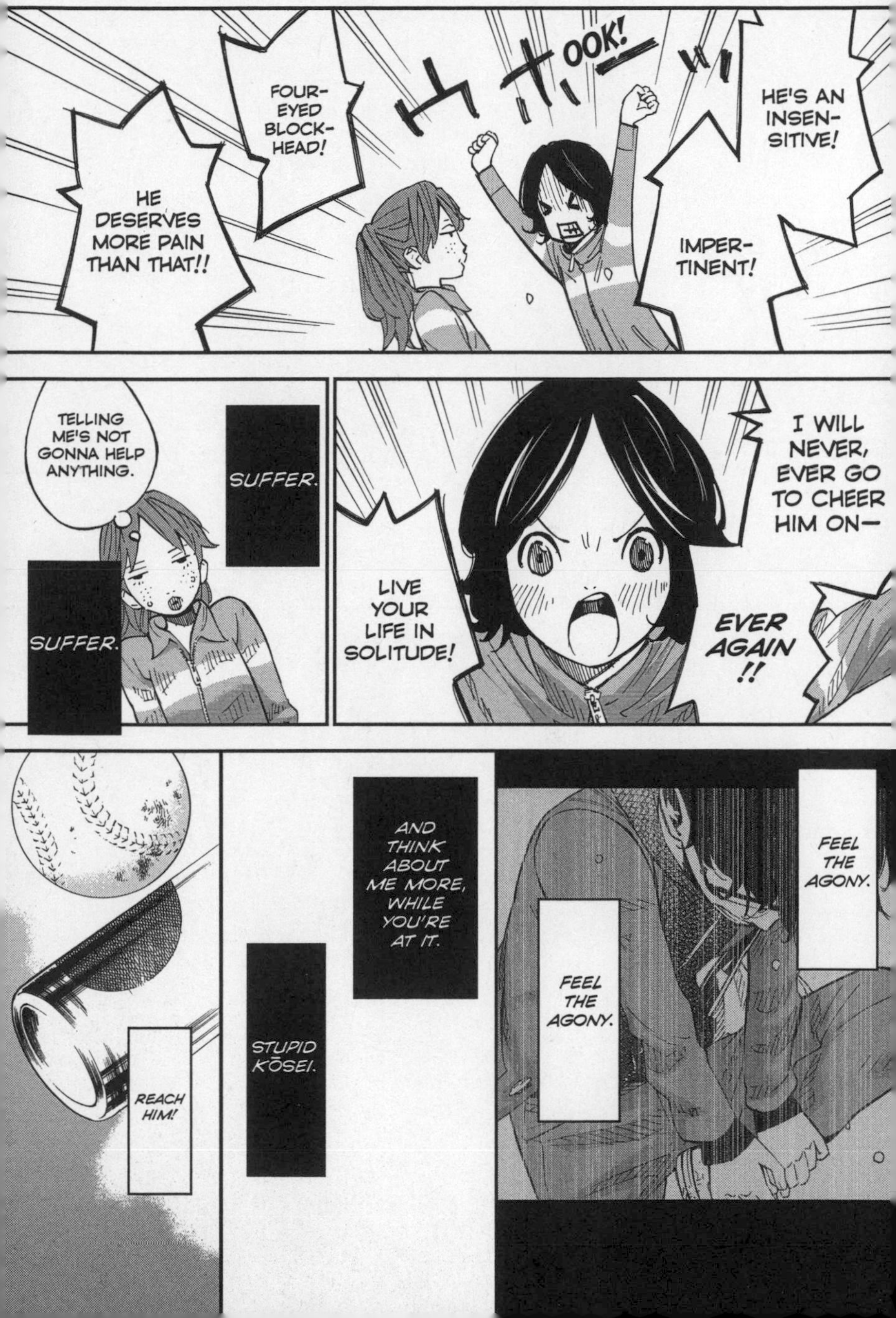

HE'S AN INSEN-SITIVE!
IMPER-TINENT!
OOK!
FOUR-EYED BLOCK-HEAD!
HE DESERVES MORE PAIN THAN THAT!!
I WILL NEVER, EVER GO TO CHEER HIM ON—
EVER AGAIN!!
LIVE YOUR LIFE IN SOLITUDE!
SUFFER.
TELLING ME'S NOT GONNA HELP ANYTHING.
SUFFER.
FEEL THE AGONY.
FEEL THE AGONY.
AND THINK ABOUT ME MORE, WHILE YOU'RE AT IT.
STUPID KŌSEI.
REACH HIM!

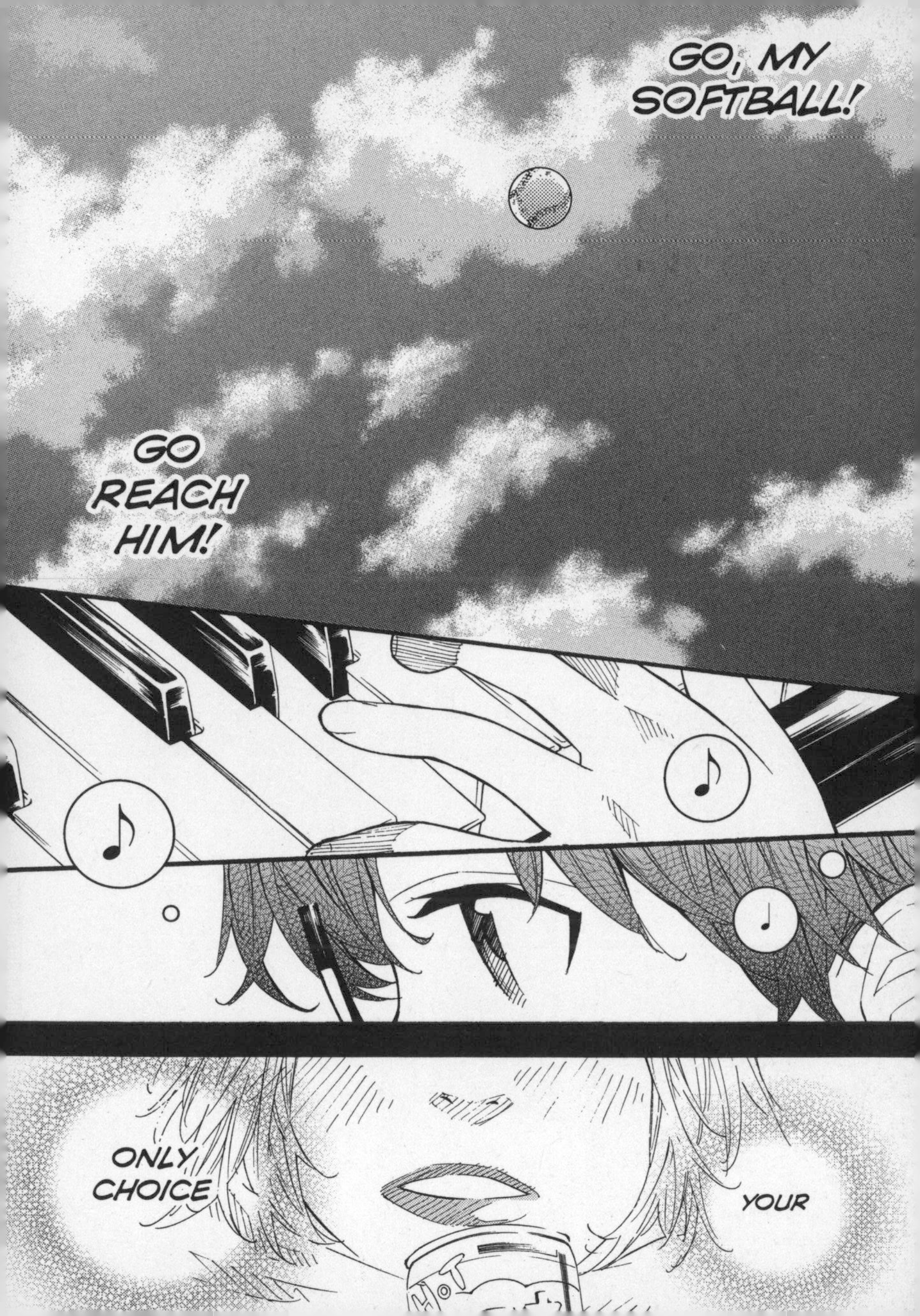
GO, MY SOFTBALL!
GO REACH HIM!
YOUR
ONLY CHOICE

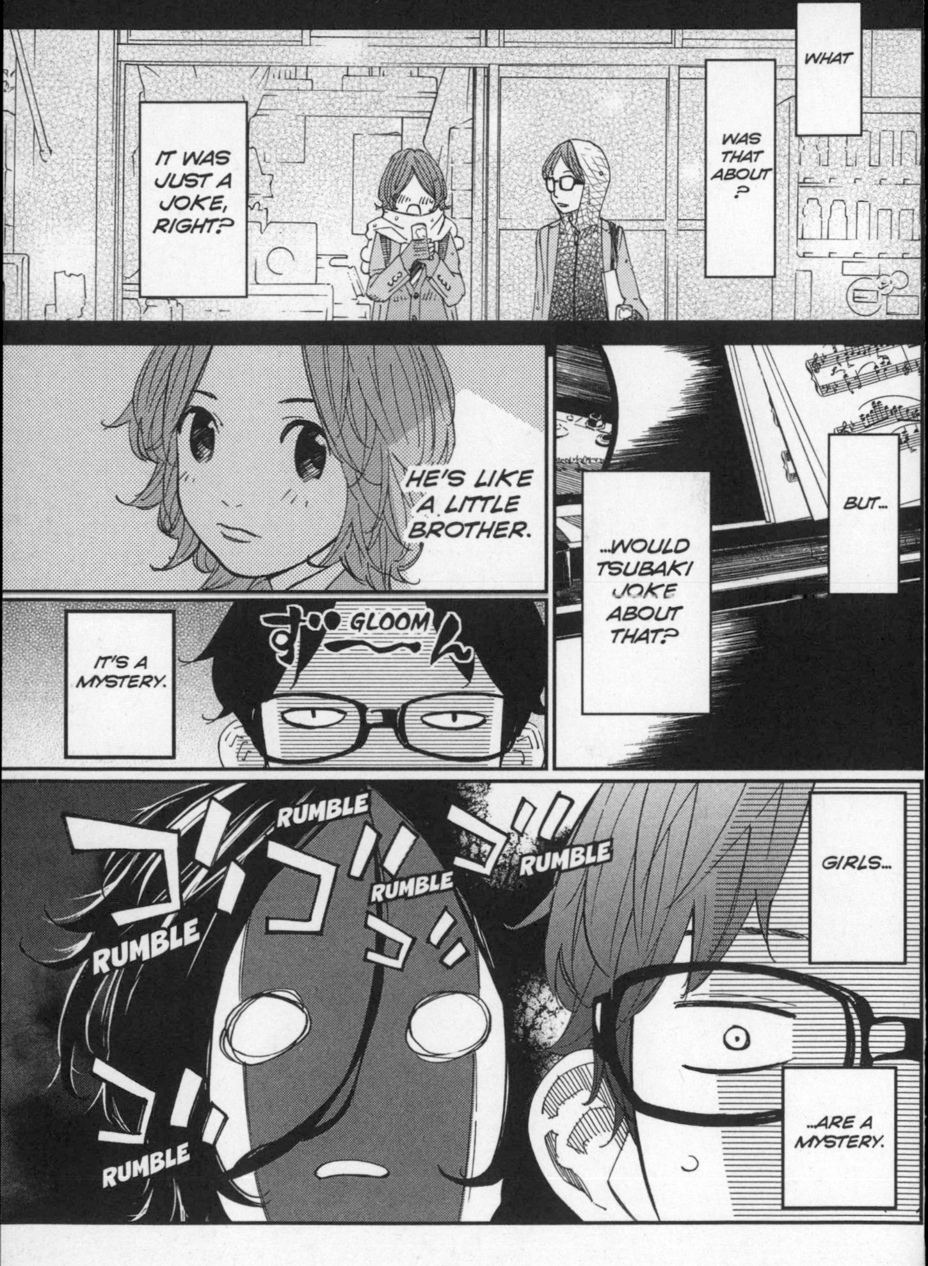
WHAT
WAS THAT ABOUT?
IT WAS JUST A JOKE, RIGHT?
BUT...
...WOULD TSUBAKI JOKE ABOUT THAT?
HE'S LIKE A LITTLE BROTHER.
GLOOM
IT'S A MYSTERY.
GIRLS...
...ARE A MYSTERY.
RUMBLE
RUMBLE
RUMBLE
RUMBLE
RUMBLE

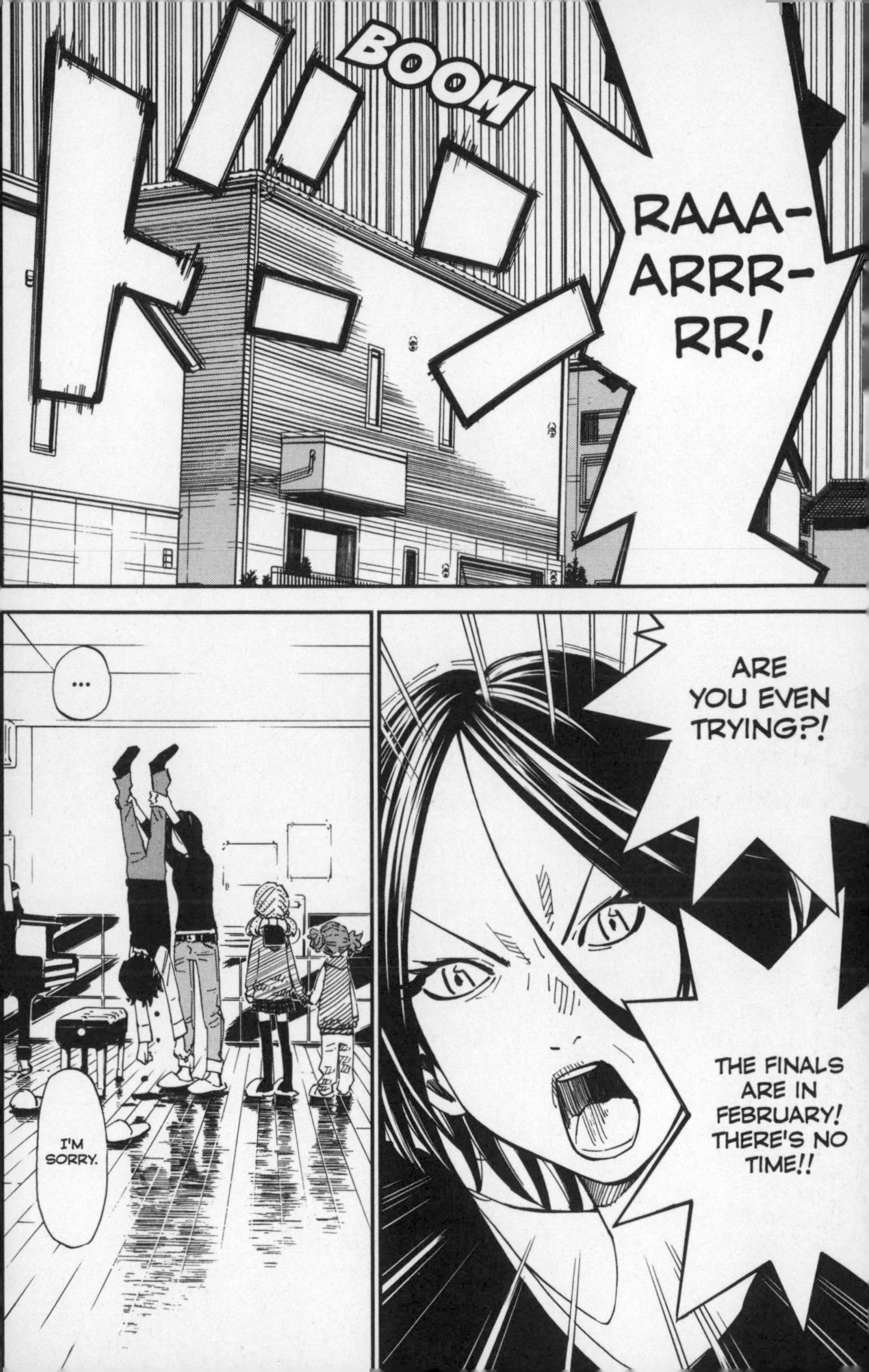
BOOM
RAAA-ARRR-RR!
ARE YOU EVEN TRYING?!
THE FINALS ARE IN FEBRUARY! THERE'S NO TIME!!
...
I'M SORRY.

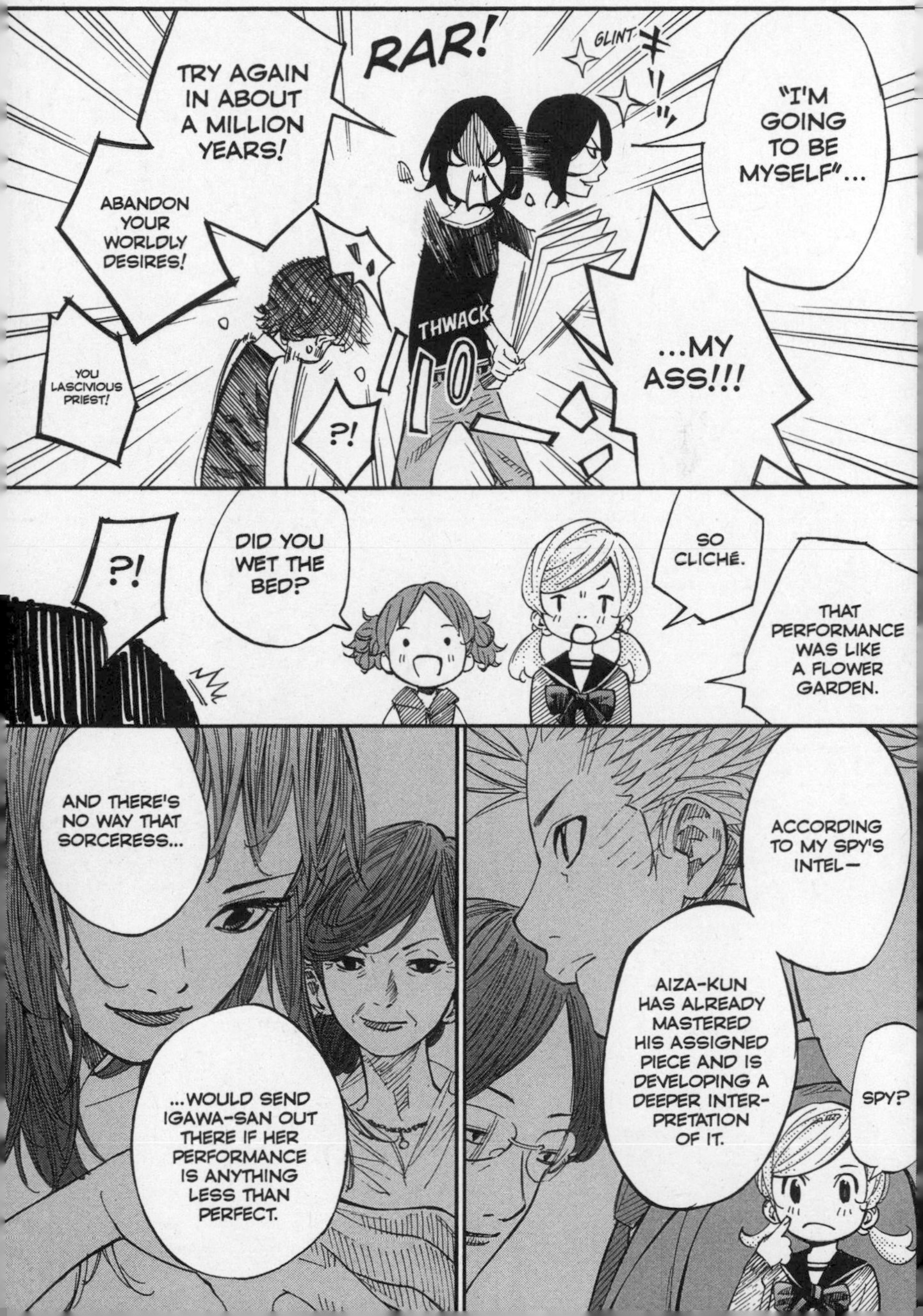
"I'M GOING TO BE MYSELF"...
GLINT
RAR!
TRY AGAIN IN ABOUT A MILLION YEARS!
ABANDON YOUR WORLDLY DESIRES!
...MY ASS!!!
THWACK
YOU LASCIVIOUS PRIEST!
?!
THAT PERFORMANCE WAS LIKE A FLOWER GARDEN.
SO CLICHÉ.
DID YOU WET THE BED?
?!
ACCORDING TO MY SPY'S INTEL—
AIZA-KUN HAS ALREADY MASTERED HIS ASSIGNED PIECE AND IS DEVELOPING A DEEPER INTERPRETATION OF IT.
SPY?
AND THERE'S NO WAY THAT SORCERESS...
...WOULD SEND IGAWA-SAN OUT THERE IF HER PERFORMANCE IS ANYTHING LESS THAN PERFECT.

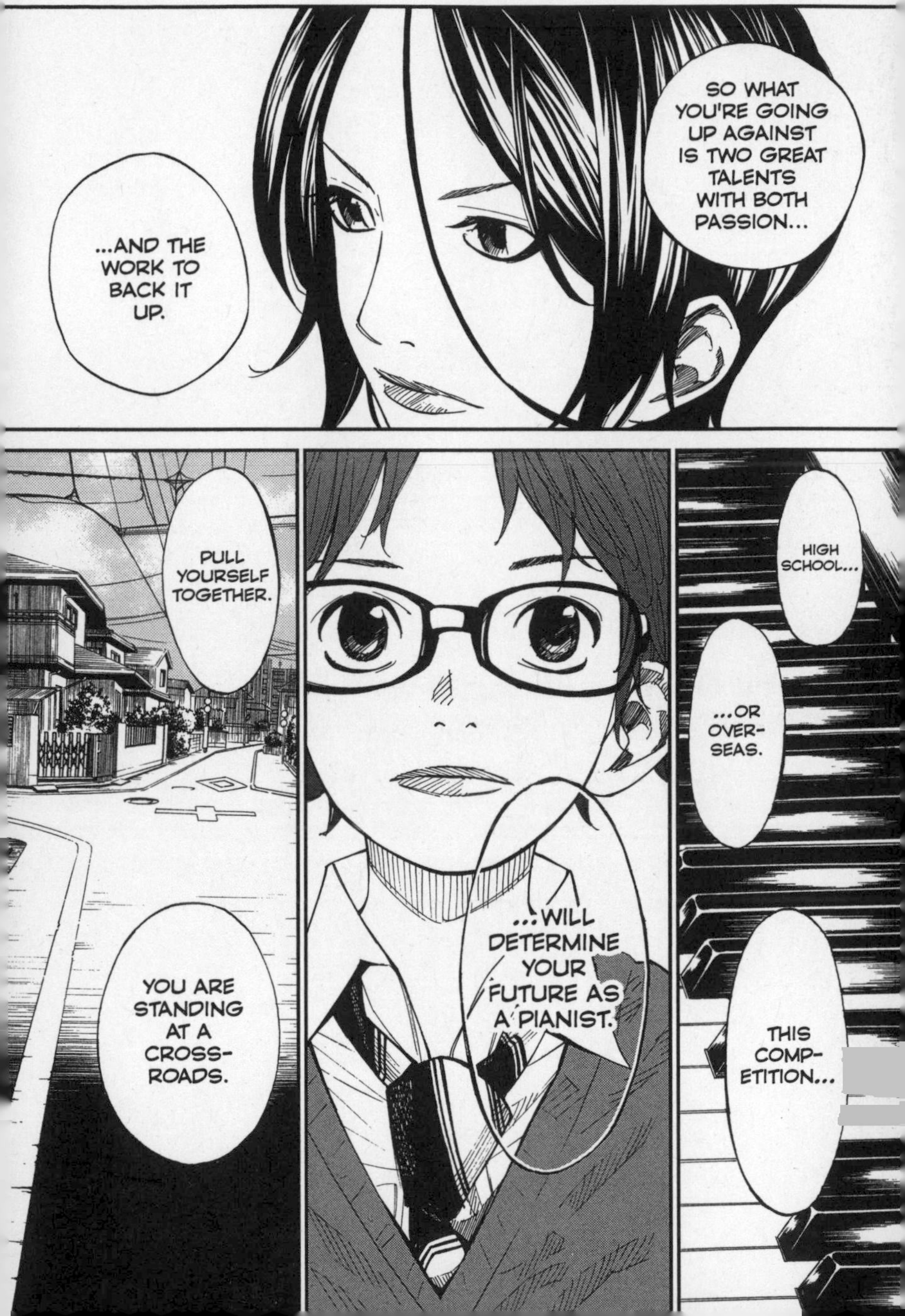
SO WHAT YOU'RE GOING UP AGAINST IS TWO GREAT TALENTS WITH BOTH PASSION...
...AND THE WORK TO BACK IT UP.
HIGH SCHOOL...
...OR OVER-SEAS.
THIS COMP-ETITION...
...WILL DETERMINE YOUR FUTURE AS A PIANIST.
PULL YOURSELF TOGETHER.
YOU ARE STANDING AT A CROSS-ROADS.

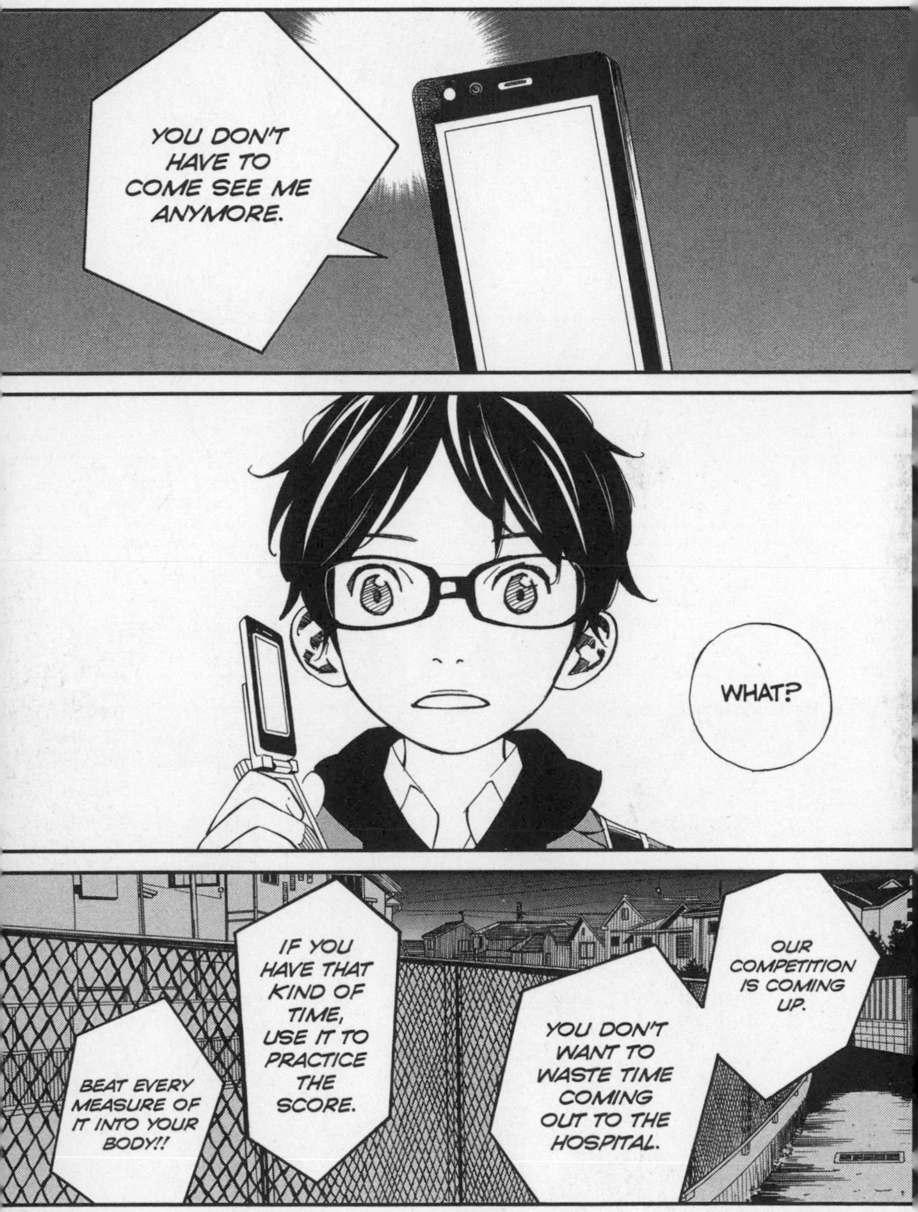
YOU DON'T HAVE TO COME SEE ME ANYMORE.
WHAT?
OUR COMPETITION IS COMING UP.
YOU DON'T WANT TO WASTE TIME COMING OUT TO THE HOSPITAL.
IF YOU HAVE THAT KIND OF TIME, USE IT TO PRACTICE THE SCORE.
BEAT EVERY MEASURE OF IT INTO YOUR BODY!!

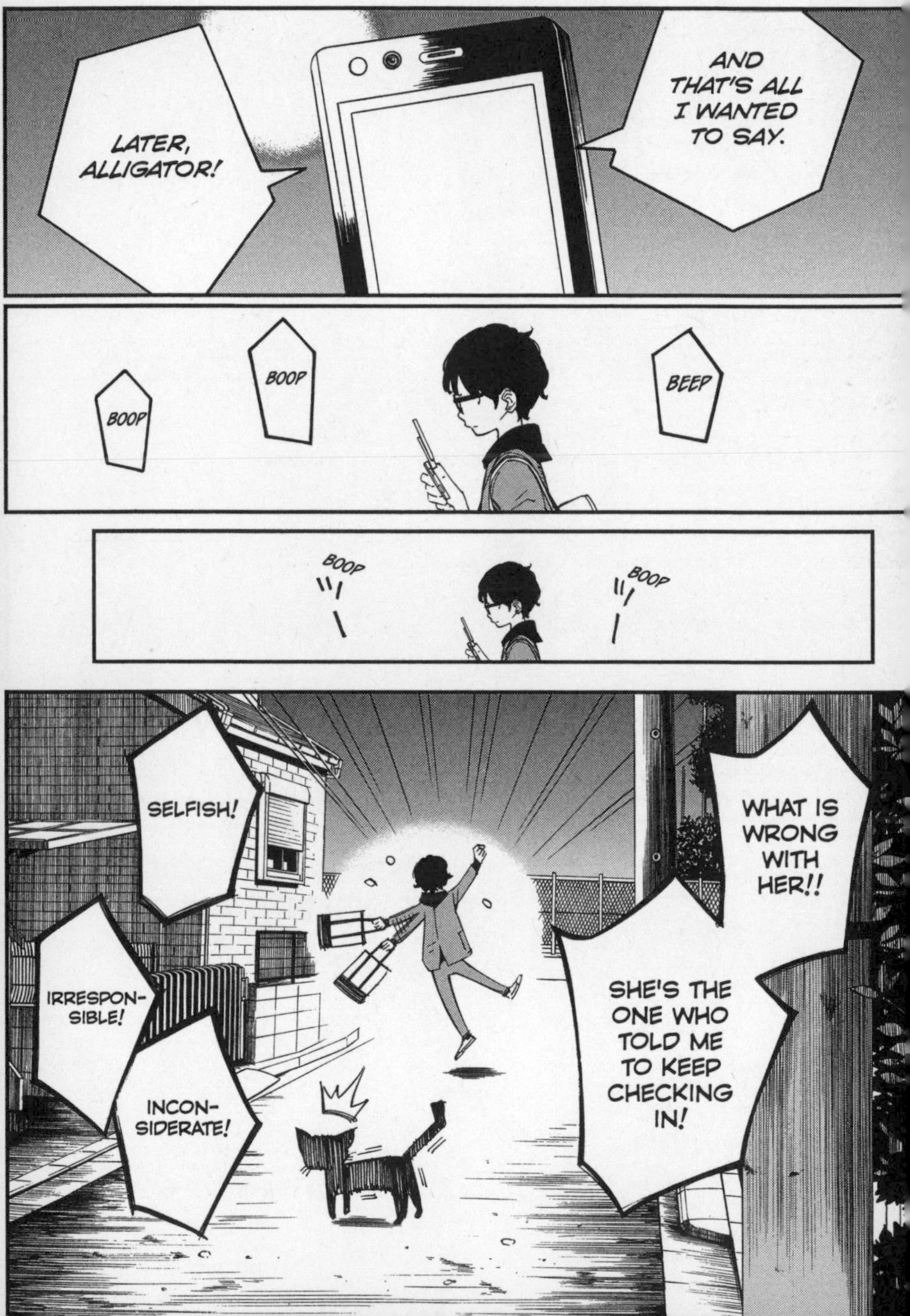
AND THAT'S ALL I WANTED TO SAY.
LATER, ALLIGATOR!
BEEP
BOOP
BOOP
BOOP
BOOP
WHAT IS WRONG WITH HER!!
SHE'S THE ONE WHO TOLD ME TO KEEP CHECKING IN!
SELFISH!
IRRESPON-SIBLE!
INCON-SIDERATE!

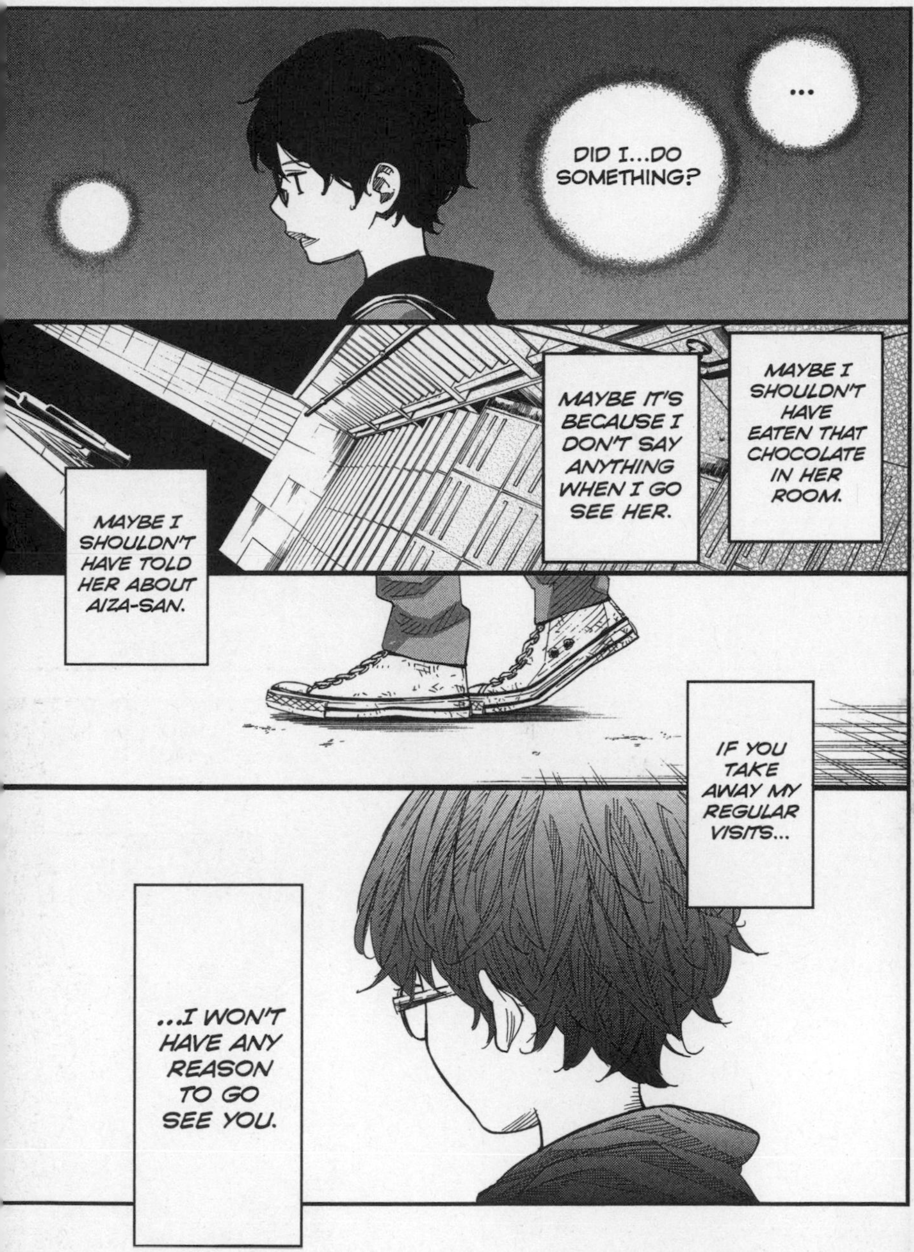
...
DID I...DO SOMETHING?
MAYBE I SHOULDN'T HAVE EATEN THAT CHOCOLATE IN HER ROOM.
MAYBE IT'S BECAUSE I DON'T SAY ANYTHING WHEN I GO SEE HER.
MAYBE I SHOULDN'T HAVE TOLD HER ABOUT AIZA-SAN.
IF YOU TAKE AWAY MY REGULAR VISITS...
...I WON'T HAVE ANY REASON TO GO SEE YOU.

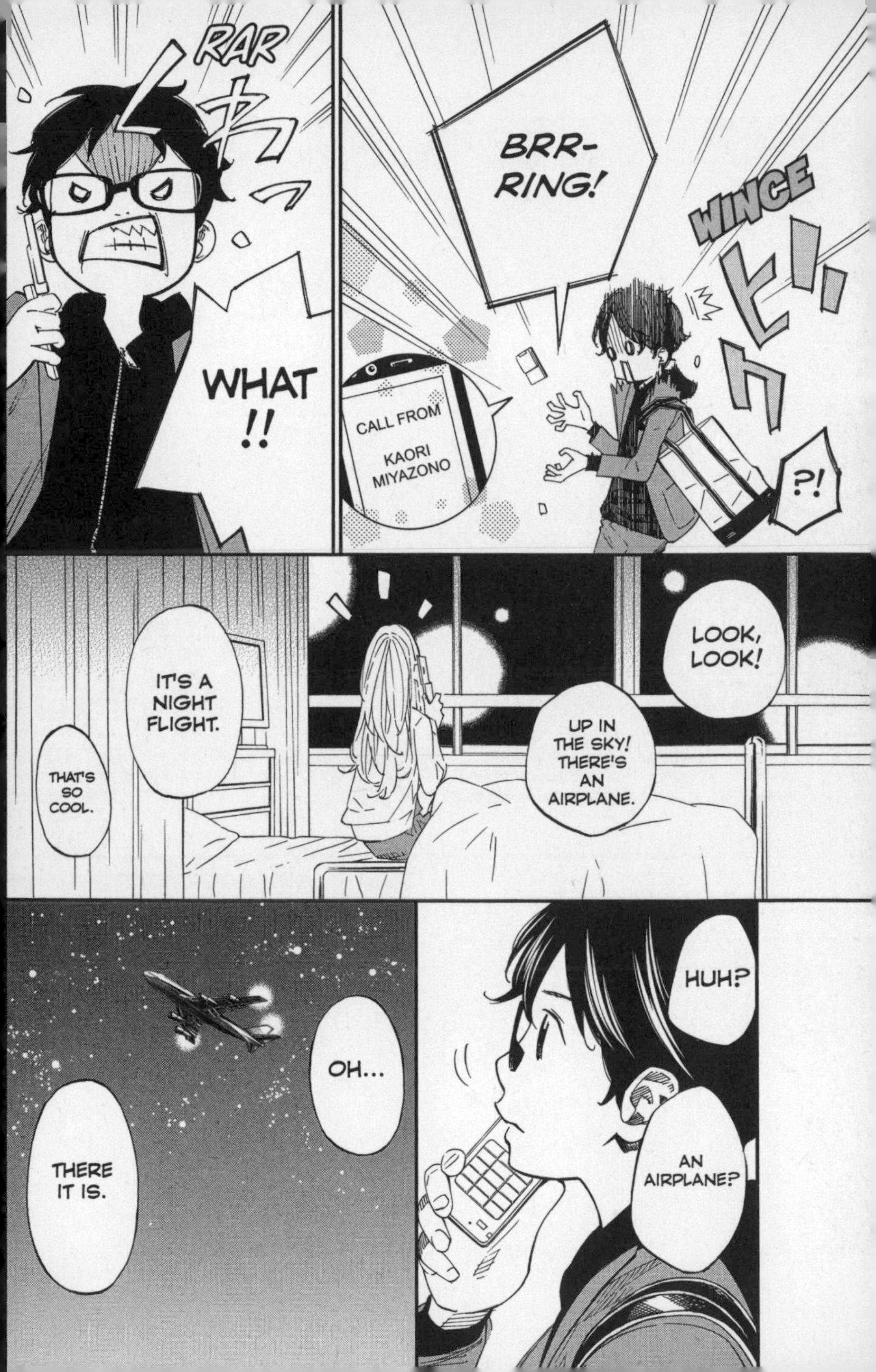
BRR-RING!
WINCE
?!
CALL FROM KAORI MIYAZONO
RAR
WHAT !!
LOOK, LOOK!
UP IN THE SKY! THERE'S AN AIRPLANE.
IT'S A NIGHT FLIGHT.
THAT'S SO COOL.
HUH?
AN AIRPLANE?
OH...
THERE IT IS.

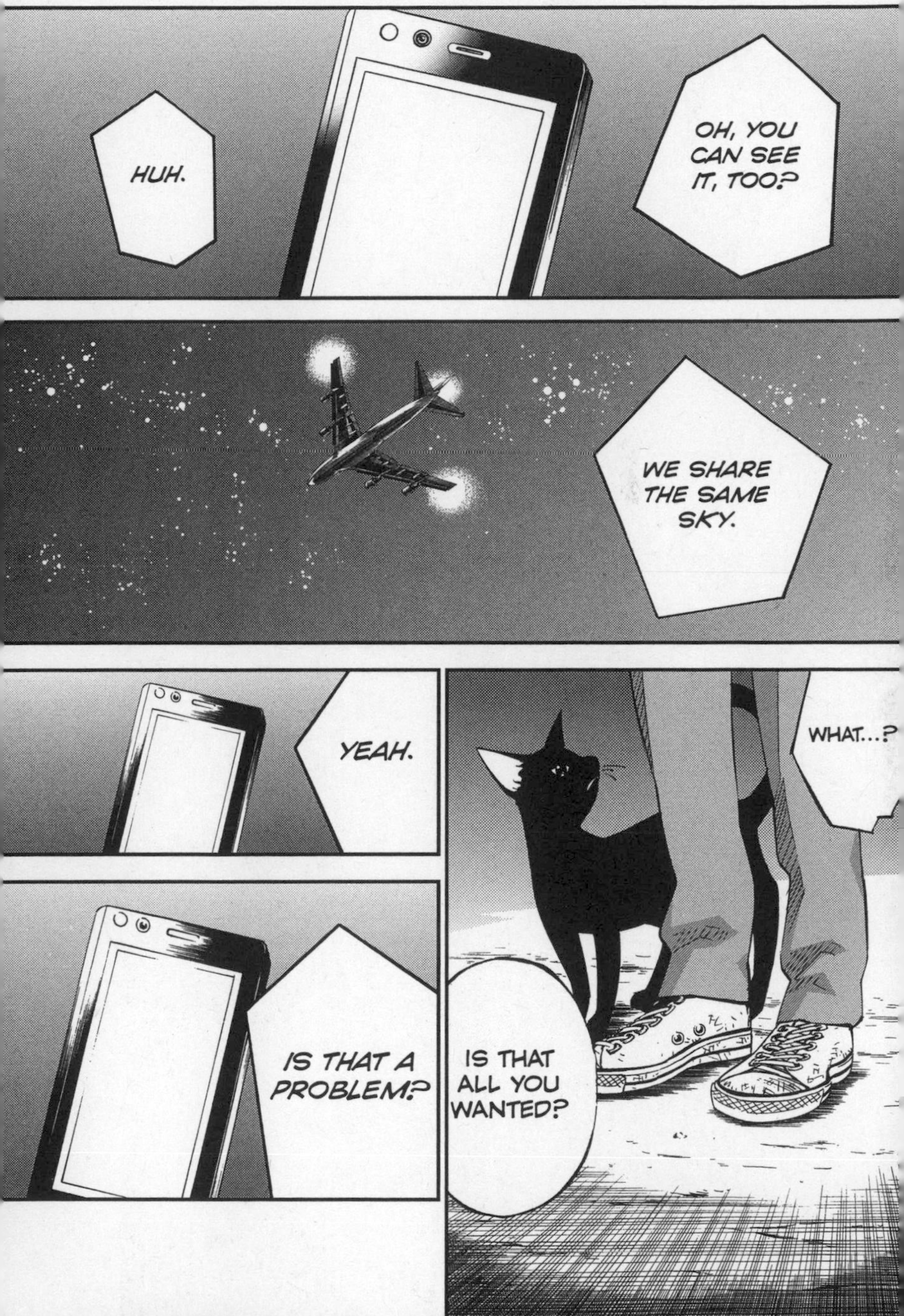
OH, YOU CAN SEE IT, TOO?
HUH.
WE SHARE THE SAME SKY.
WHAT...?
IS THAT ALL YOU WANTED?
YEAH.
IS THAT A PROBLEM?

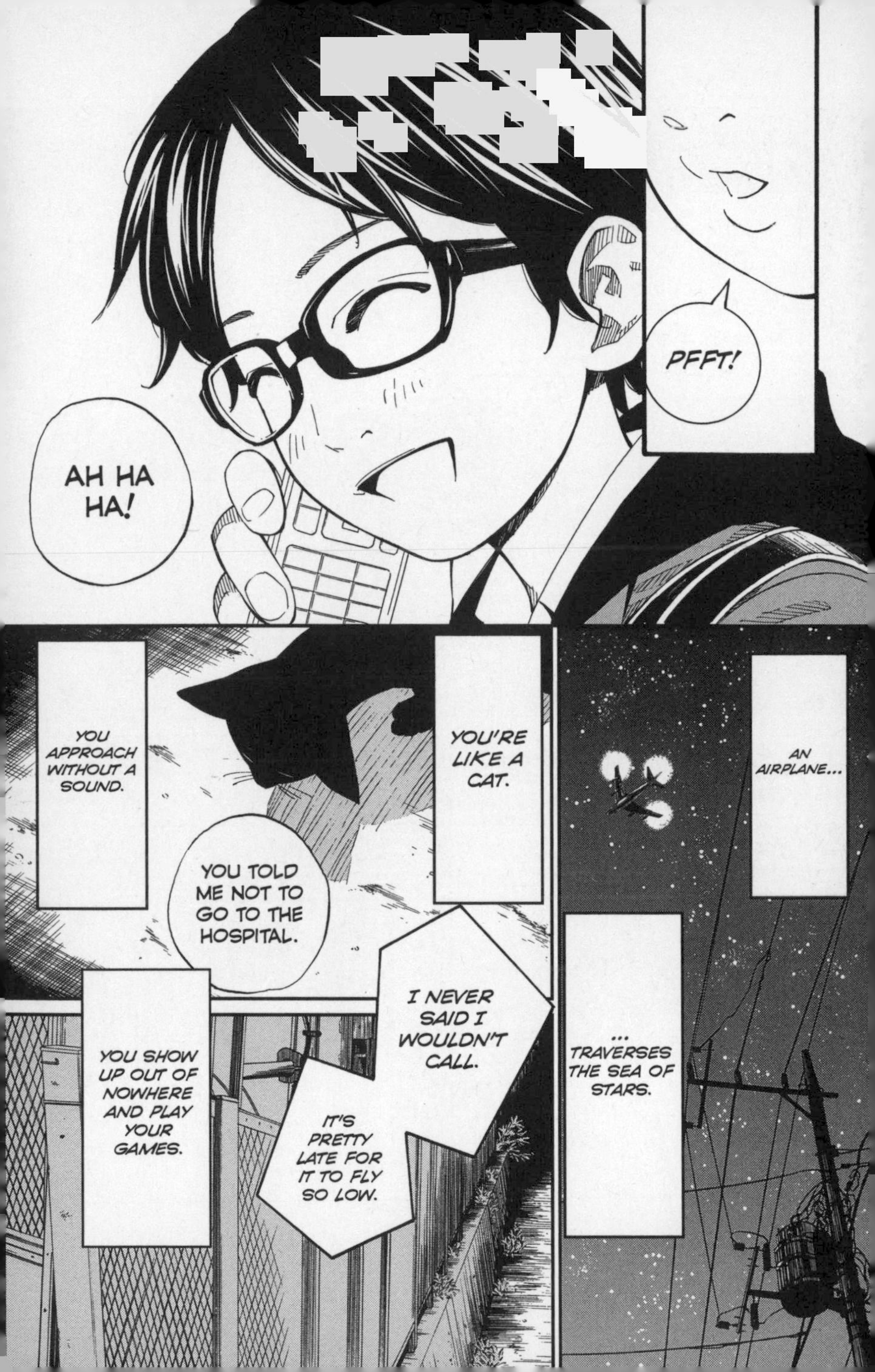
PFFT!
AH HA HA!
AN AIRPLANE...
...TRAVERSES THE SEA OF STARS.
YOU'RE LIKE A CAT.
YOU APPROACH WITHOUT A SOUND.
YOU TOLD ME NOT TO GO TO THE HOSPITAL.
I NEVER SAID I WOULDN'T CALL.
IT'S PRETTY LATE FOR IT TO FLY SO LOW.
YOU SHOW UP OUT OF NOWHERE AND PLAY YOUR GAMES.

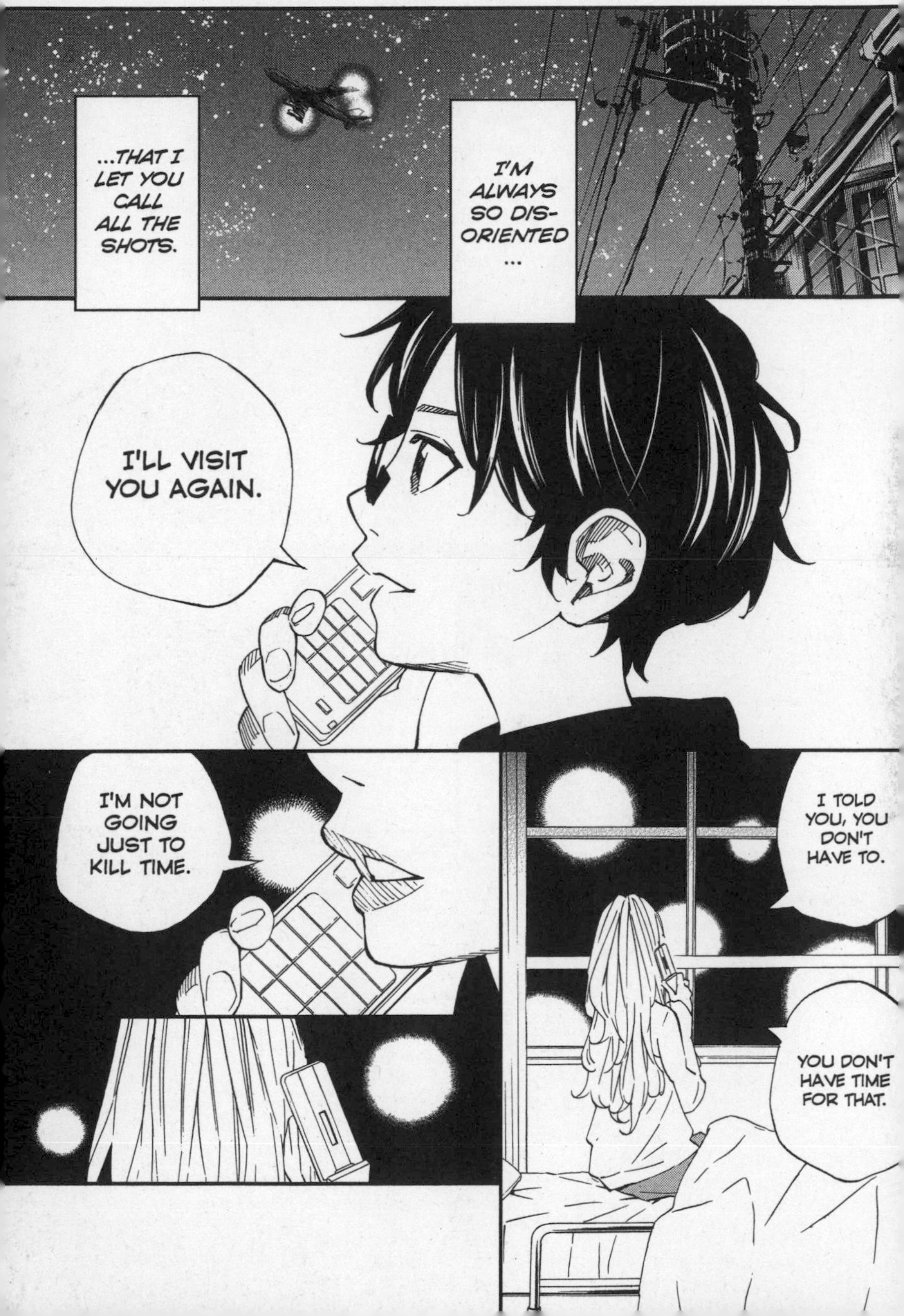
I'M ALWAYS SO DIS-ORIENTED ...
...THAT I LET YOU CALL ALL THE SHOTS.
I'LL VISIT YOU AGAIN.
I TOLD YOU, YOU DON'T HAVE TO.
YOU DON'T HAVE TIME FOR THAT.
I'M NOT GOING JUST TO KILL TIME.

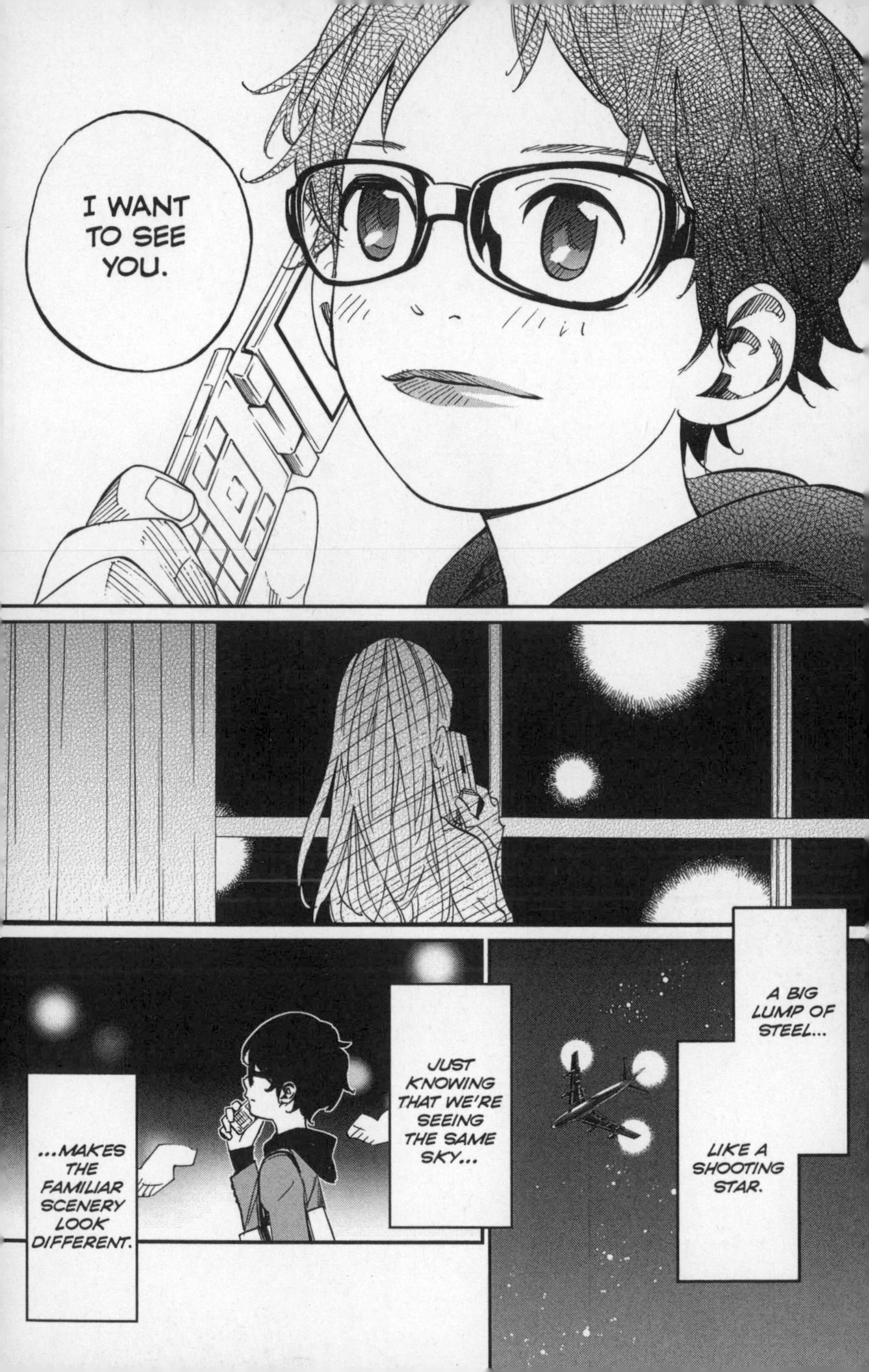
I WANT TO SEE YOU.
A BIG LUMP OF STEEL...
LIKE A SHOOTING STAR.
JUST KNOWING THAT WE'RE SEEING THE SAME SKY...
...MAKES THE FAMILIAR SCENERY LOOK DIFFERENT.

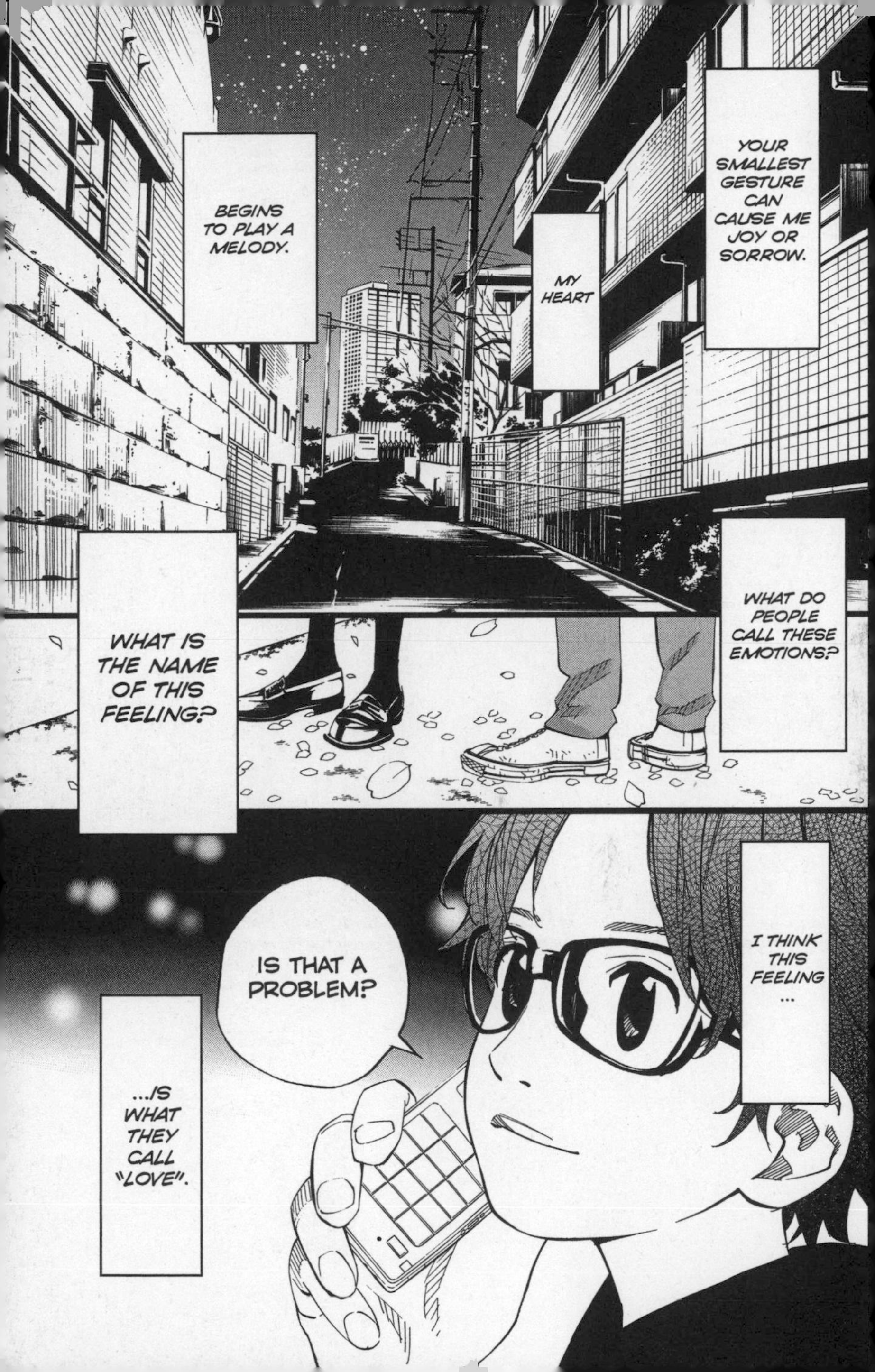
YOUR SMALLEST GESTURE CAN CAUSE ME JOY OR SORROW.
MY HEART
BEGINS TO PLAY A MELODY.
WHAT DO PEOPLE CALL THESE EMOTIONS?
WHAT IS THE NAME OF THIS FEELING?
I THINK THIS FEELING ...
IS THAT A PROBLEM?
...IS WHAT THEY CALL "LOVE".

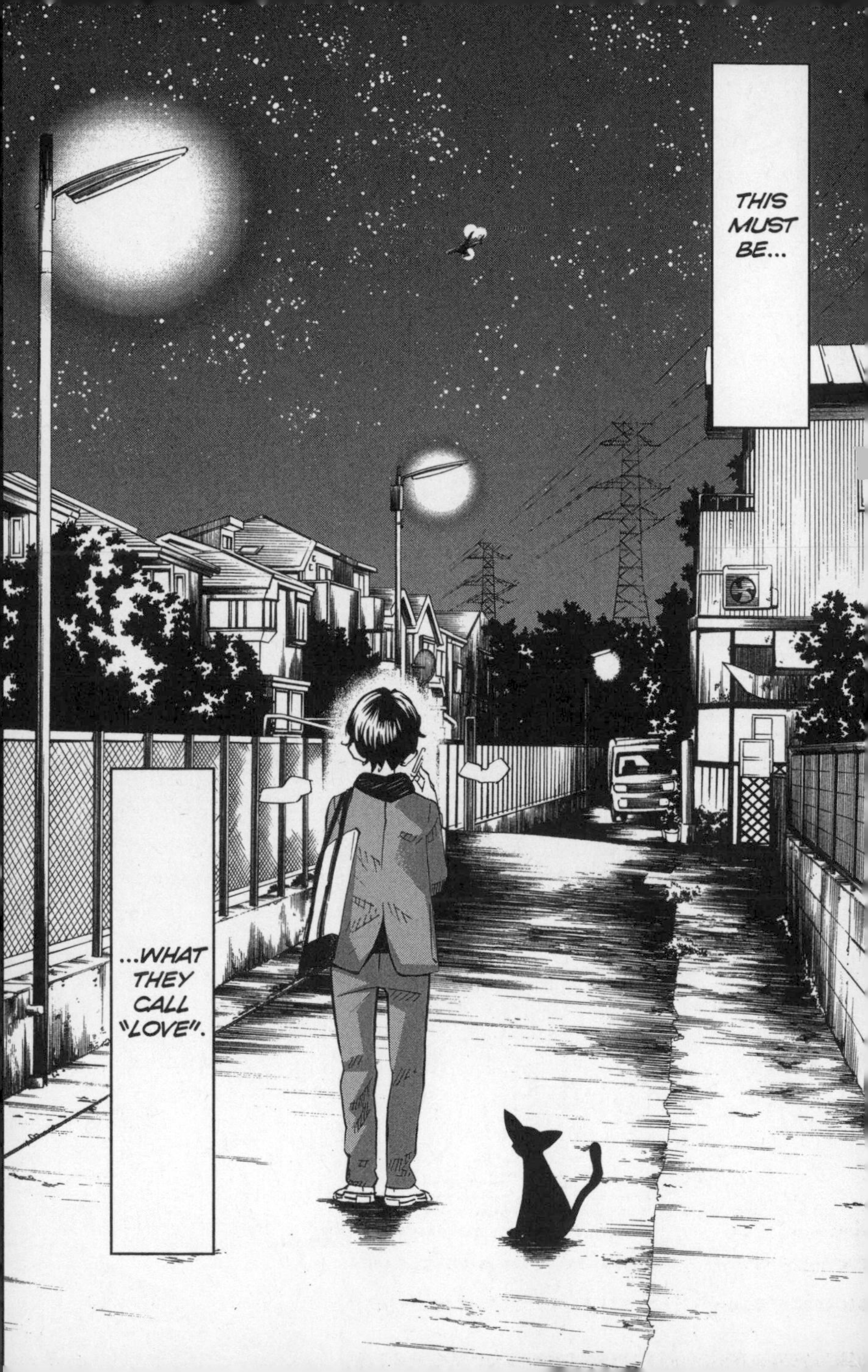
THIS MUST BE...
...WHAT THEY CALL "LOVE".

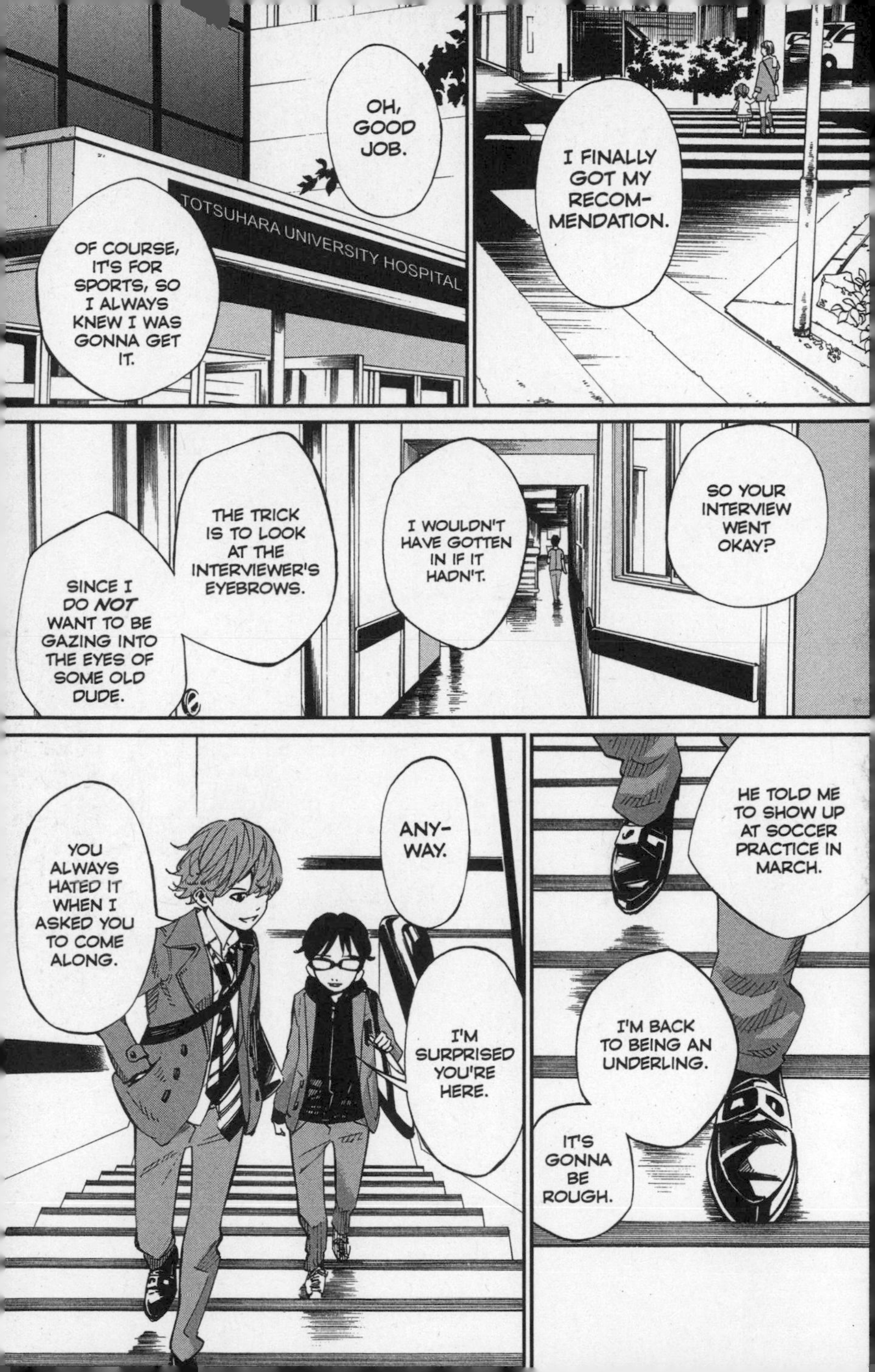
I FINALLY GOT MY RECOM-MENDATION.
OH, GOOD JOB.
TOTSUHARA UNIVERSITY HOSPITAL
OF COURSE, IT'S FOR SPORTS, SO I ALWAYS KNEW I WAS GONNA GET IT.
SO YOUR INTERVIEW WENT OKAY?
I WOULDN'T HAVE GOTTEN IN IF IT HADN'T.
THE TRICK IS TO LOOK AT THE INTERVIEWER'S EYEBROWS.
SINCE I DO *NOT* WANT TO BE GAZING INTO THE EYES OF SOME OLD DUDE.
HE TOLD ME TO SHOW UP AT SOCCER PRACTICE IN MARCH.
I'M BACK TO BEING AN UNDERLING.
IT'S GONNA BE ROUGH.
ANY-WAY.
I'M SURPRISED YOU'RE HERE.
YOU ALWAYS HATED IT WHEN I ASKED YOU TO COME ALONG.

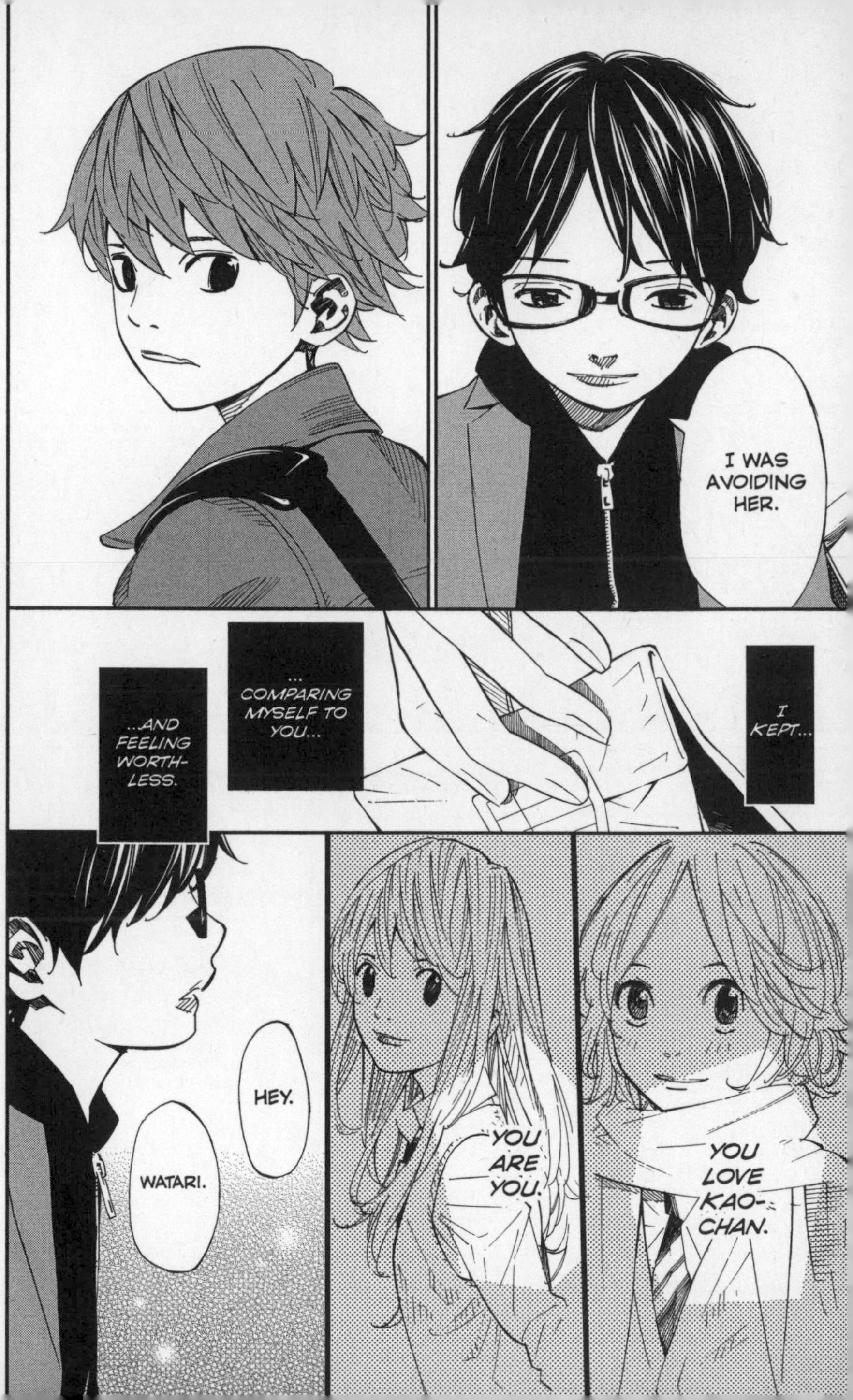
I WAS AVOIDING HER.
I KEPT...
... COMPARING MYSELF TO YOU...
...AND FEELING WORTH-LESS.
YOU LOVE KAO-CHAN.
YOU ARE YOU.
HEY.
WATARI.

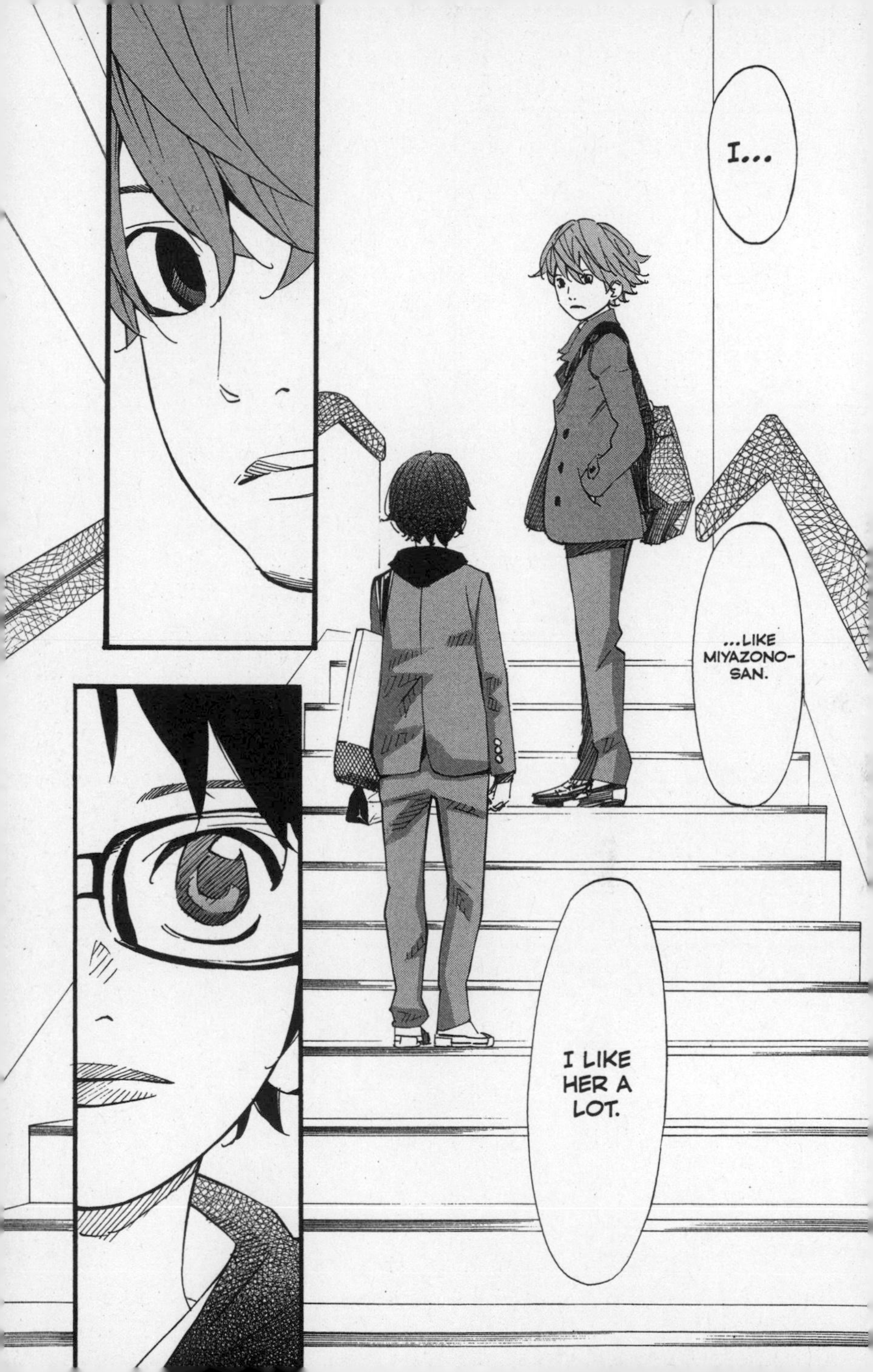
I...
...LIKE MIYAZONO-SAN.
I LIKE HER A LOT.

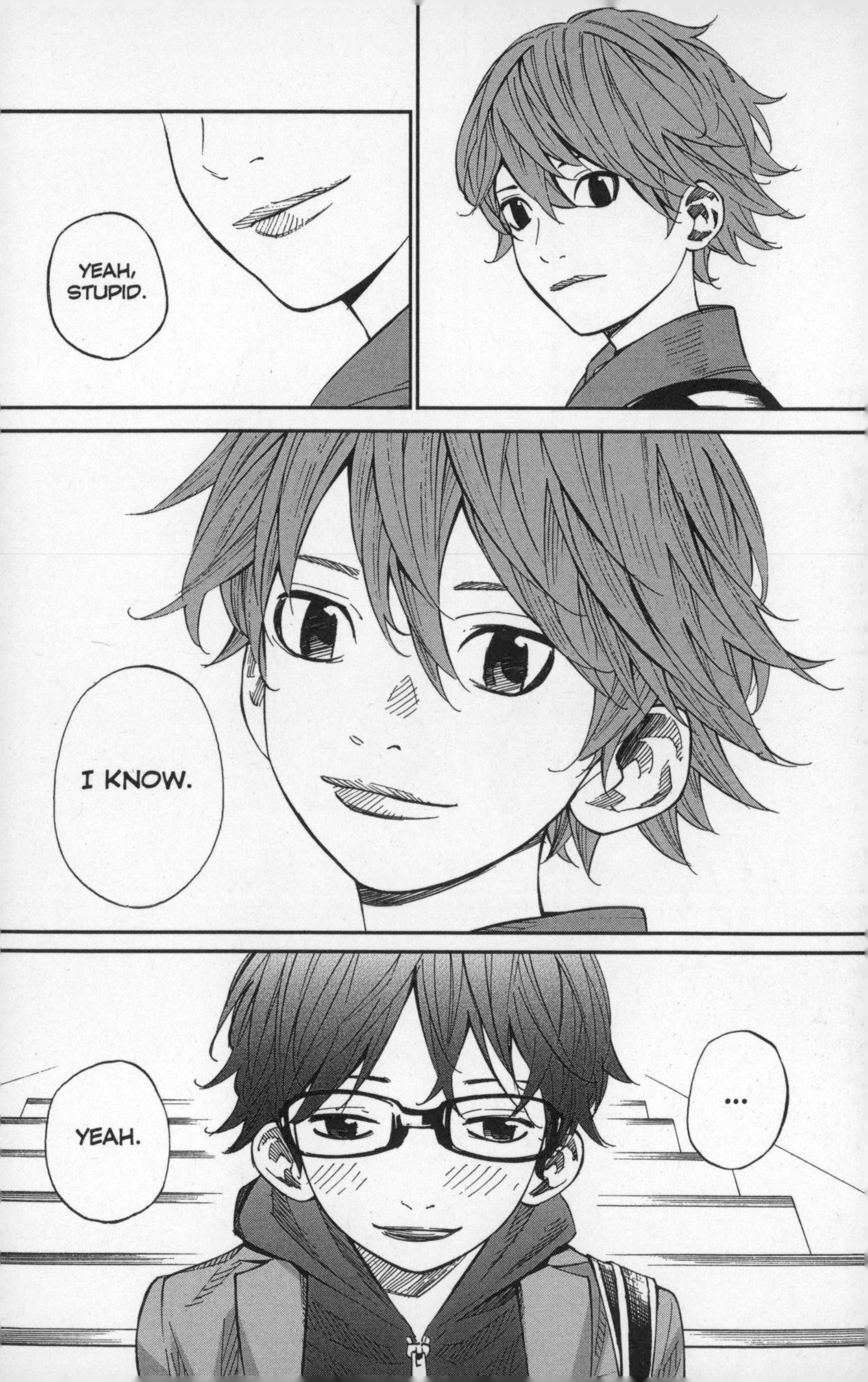
YEAH, STUPID.
I KNOW.
...
YEAH.

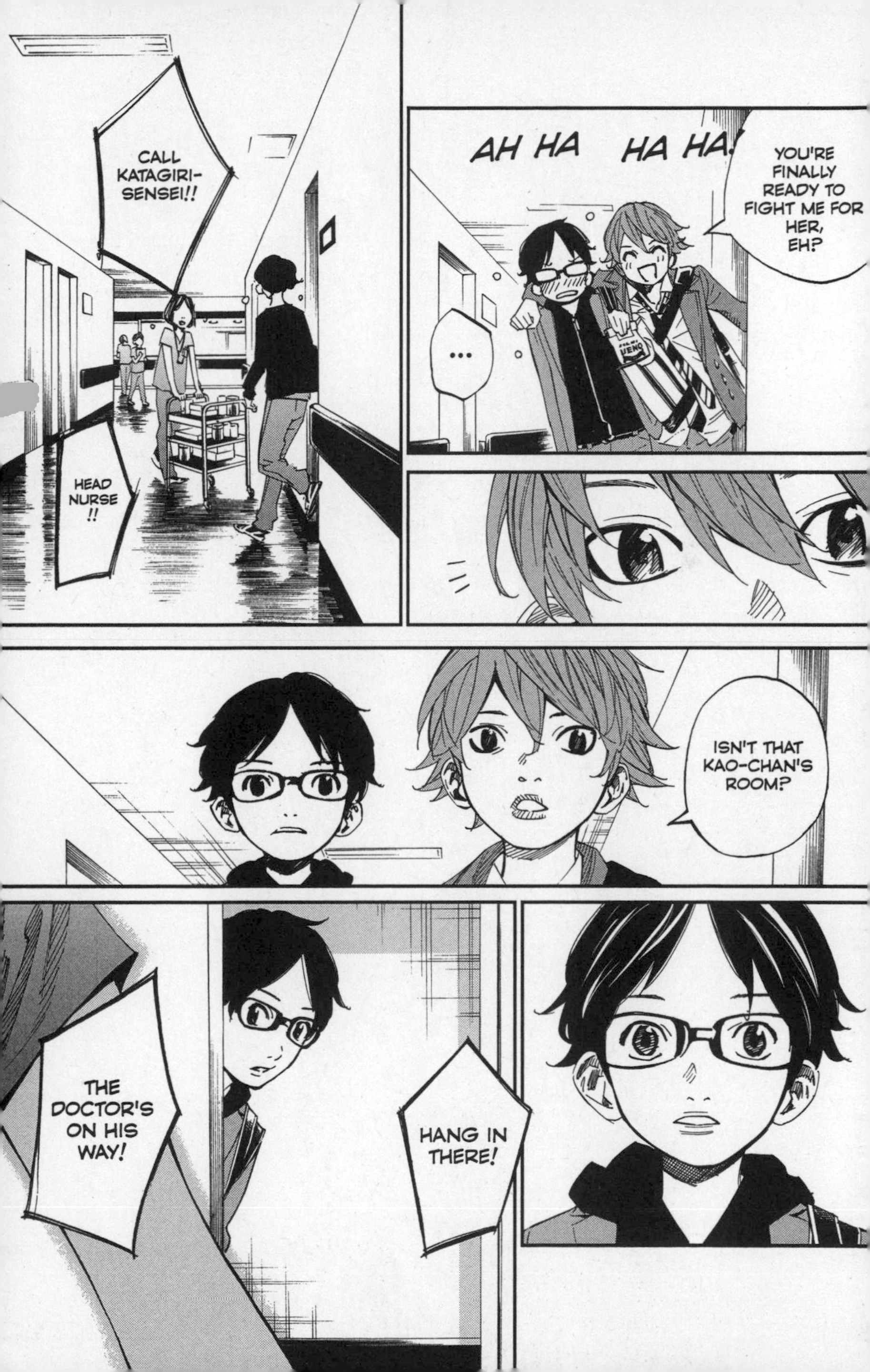
AH HA HA HA!
YOU'RE FINALLY READY TO FIGHT ME FOR HER, EH?
...
CALL KATAGIRI-SENSEI!!
HEAD NURSE!!
ISN'T THAT KAO-CHAN'S ROOM?
HANG IN THERE!
THE DOCTOR'S ON HIS WAY!

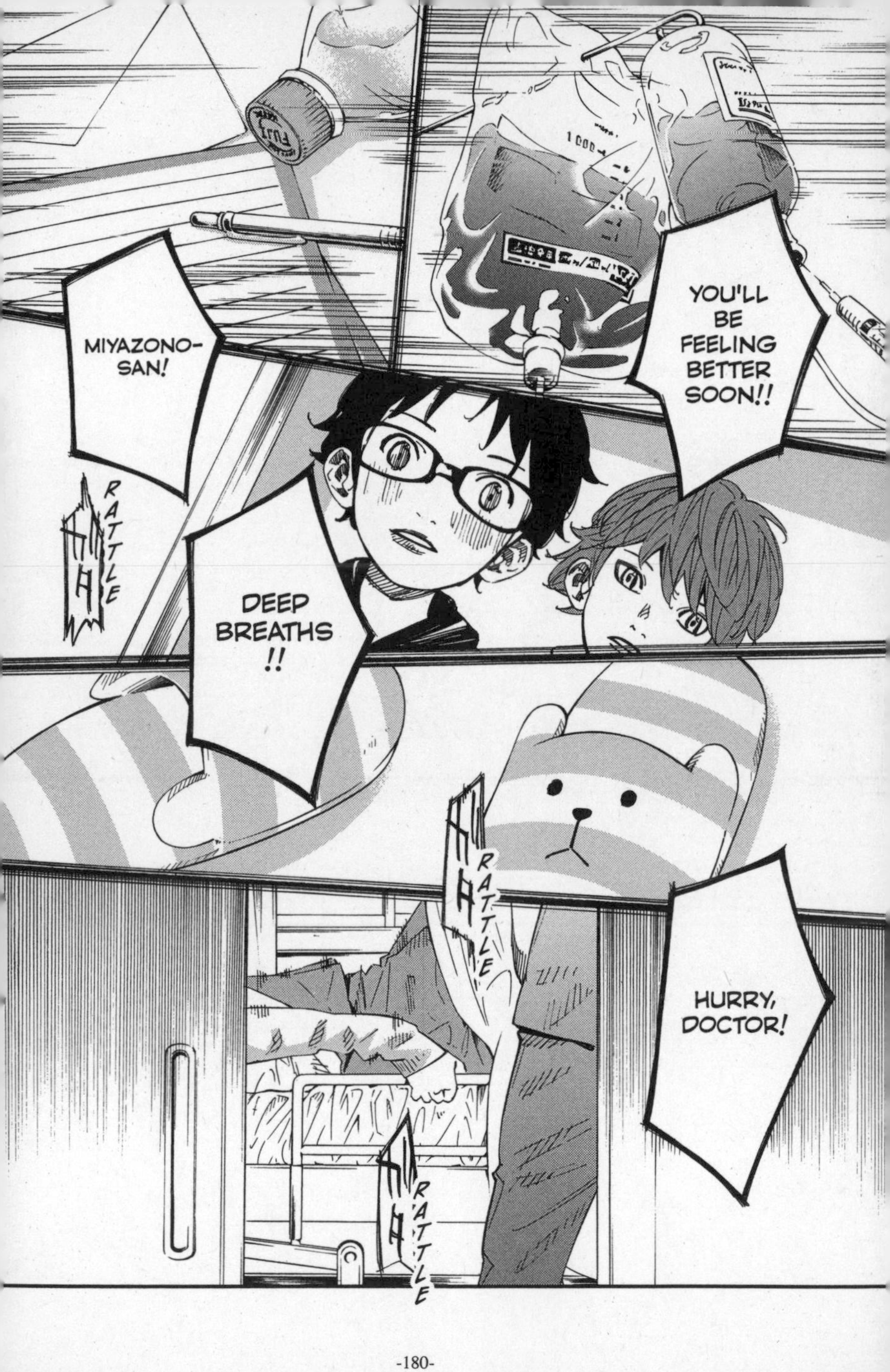
YOU'LL BE FEELING BETTER SOON!!
MIYAZONO-SAN!
RATTLE
DEEP BREATHS!!
RATTLE
HURRY, DOCTOR!
RATTLE

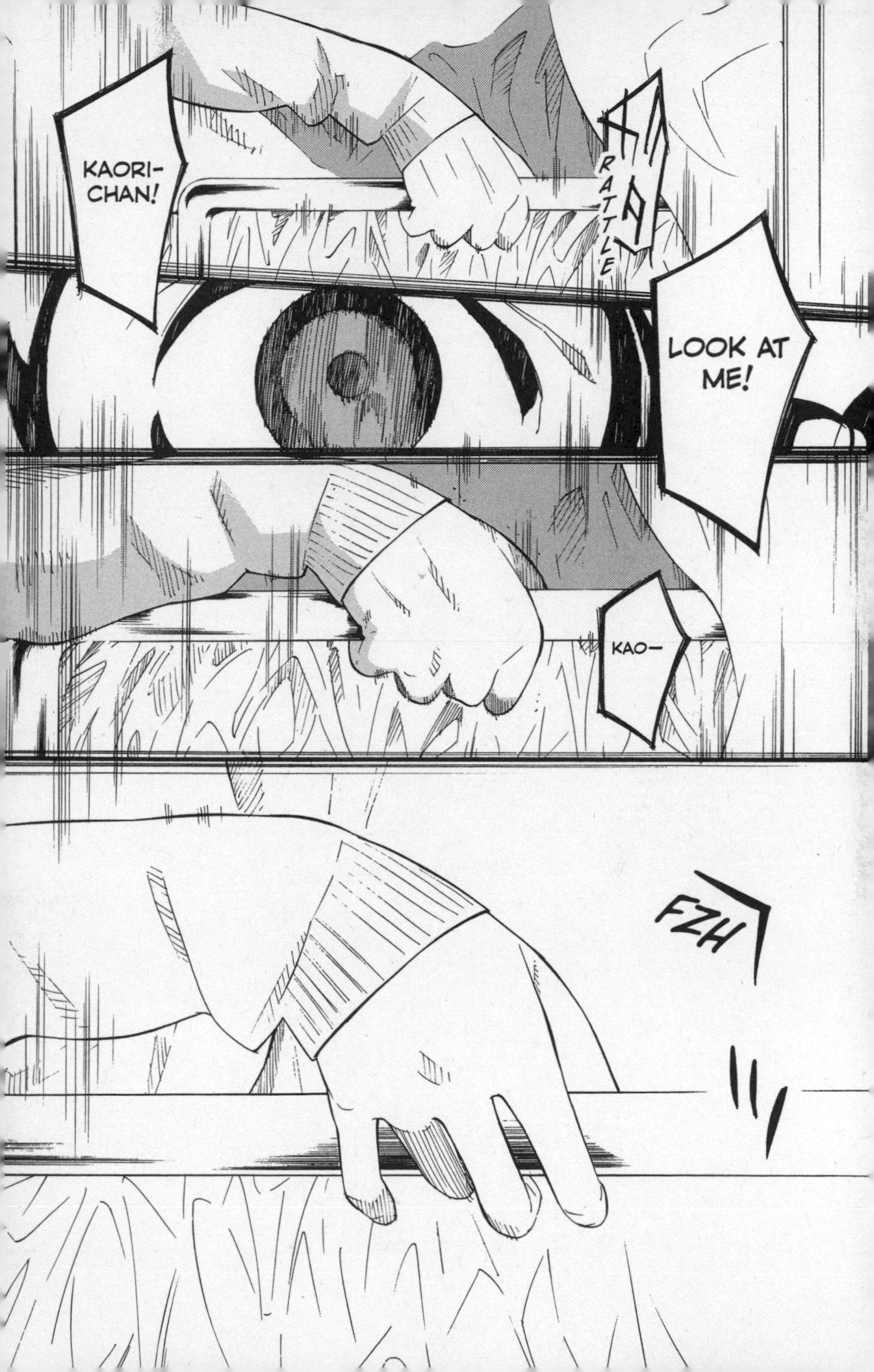
RATTLE
KAORI-CHAN!
LOOK AT ME!
KAO—
FZH

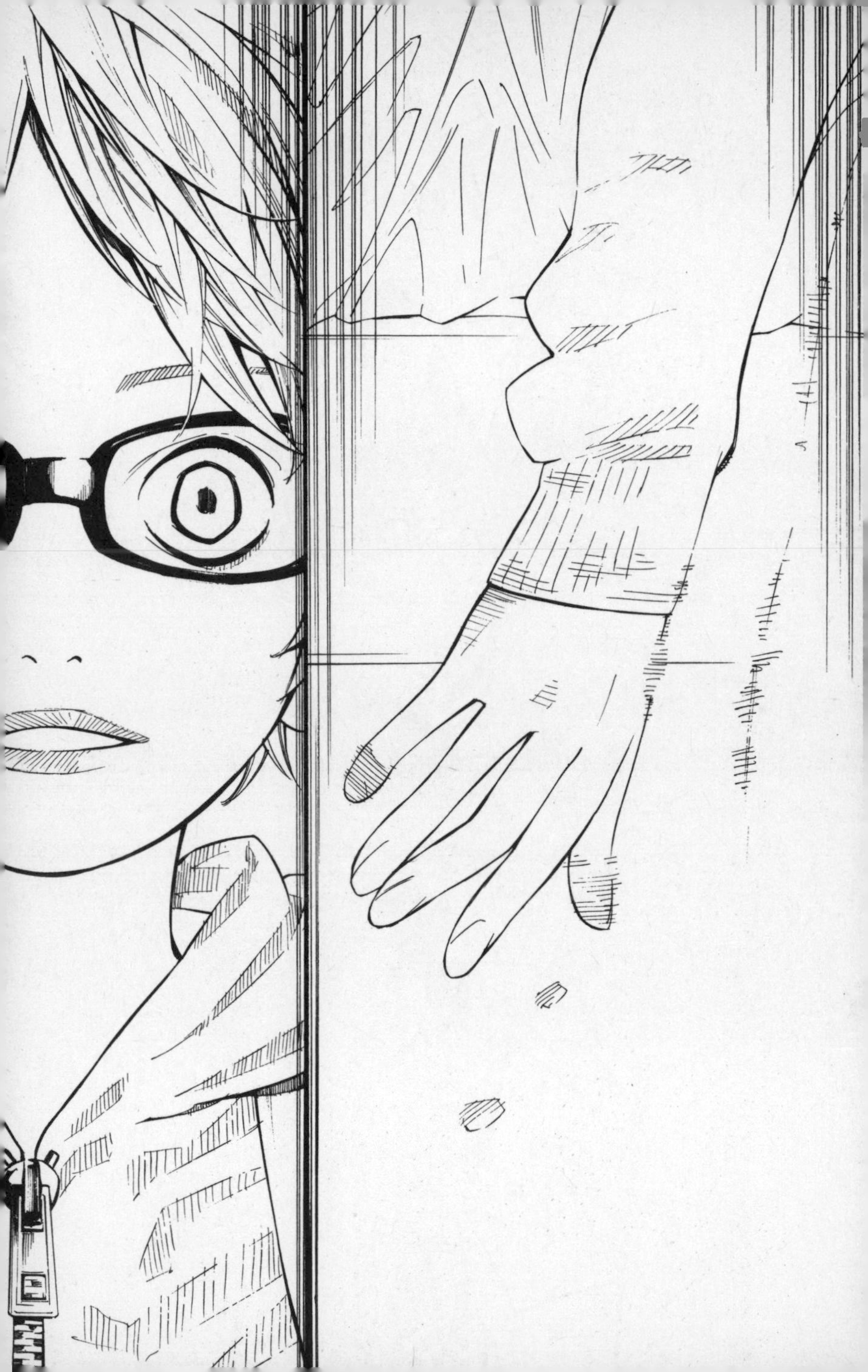

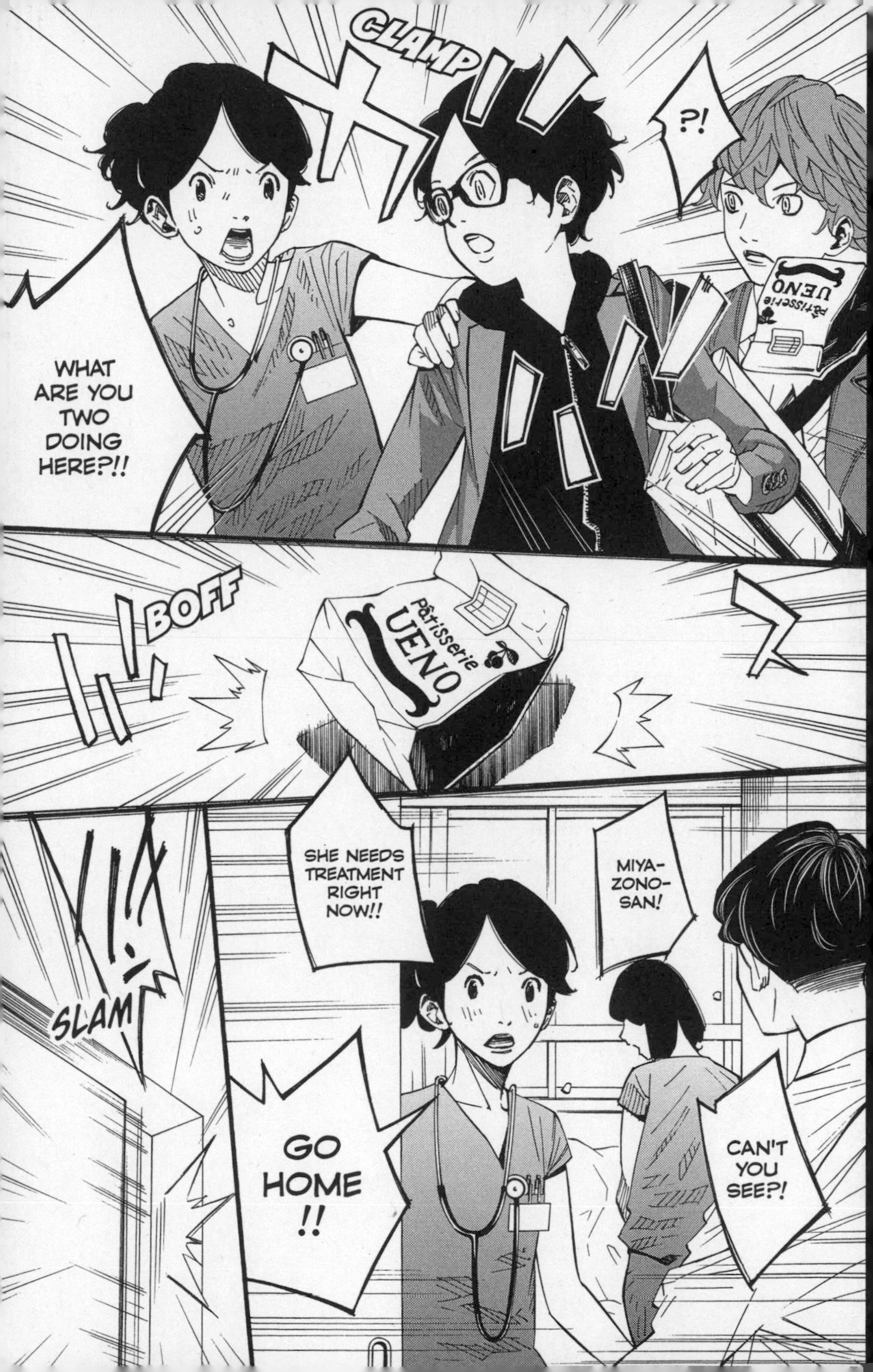
?!
CLAMP
WHAT ARE YOU TWO DOING HERE?!!
BOFF
Pâtisserie UENO
MIYA-ZONO-SAN!
SHE NEEDS TREATMENT RIGHT NOW!!
CAN'T YOU SEE?!
GO HOME!!
SLAM

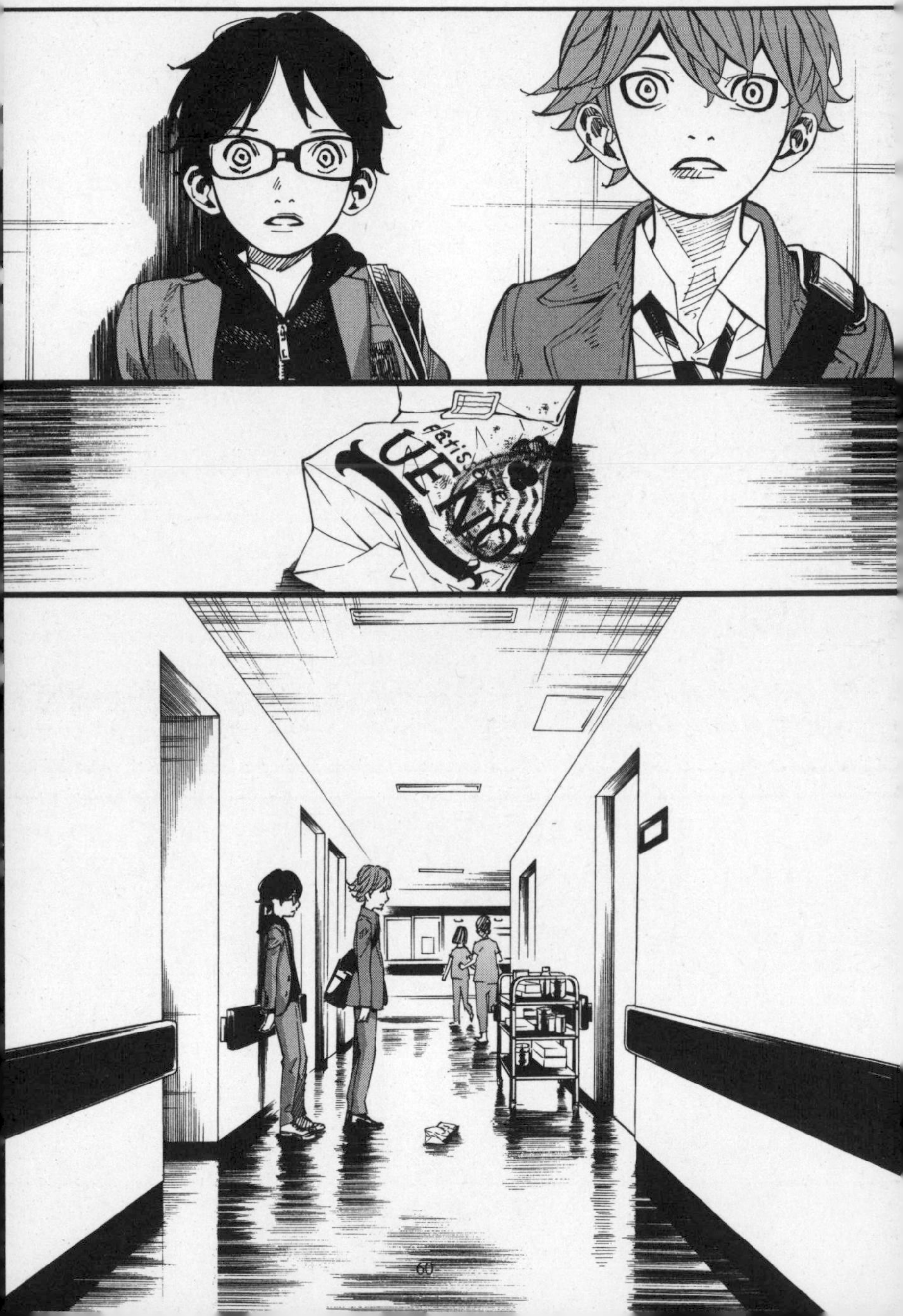
UENO

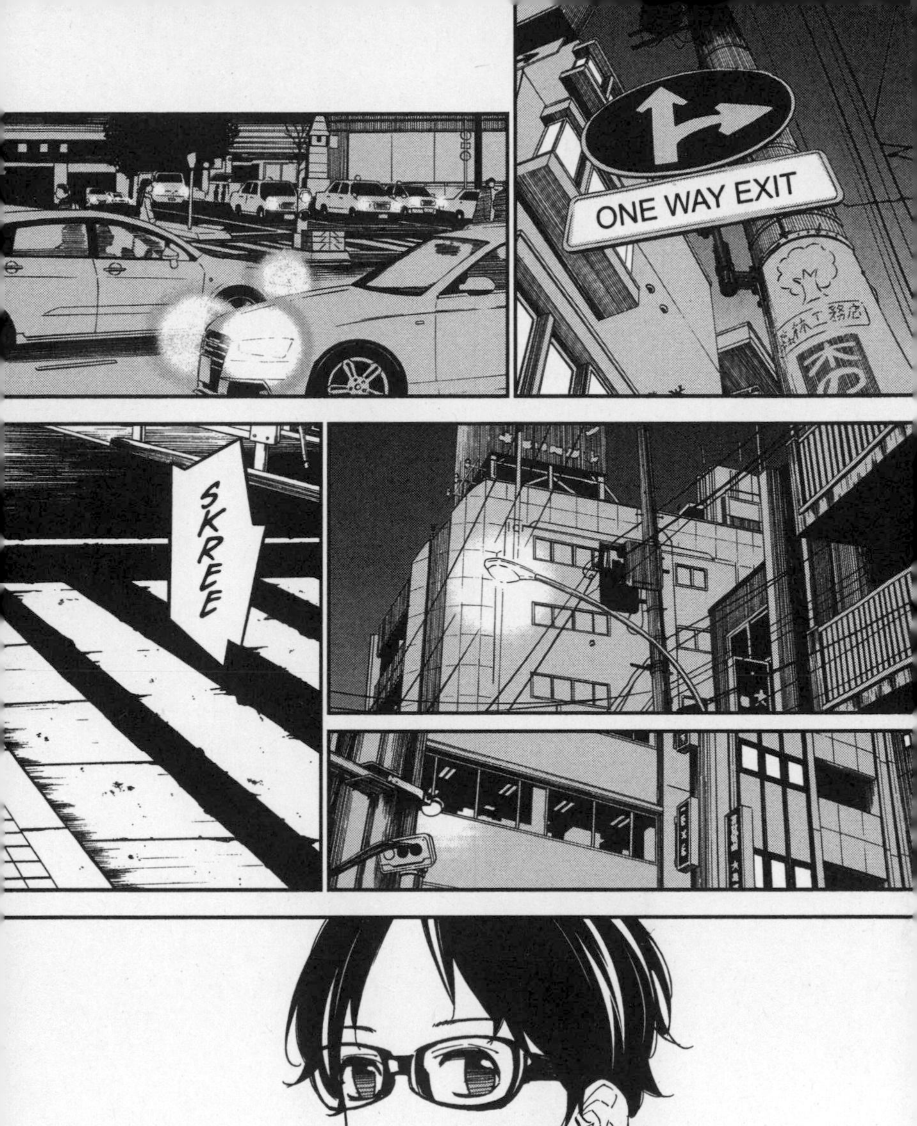
ONE WAY EXIT
SKREE

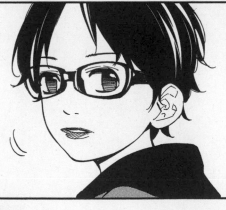

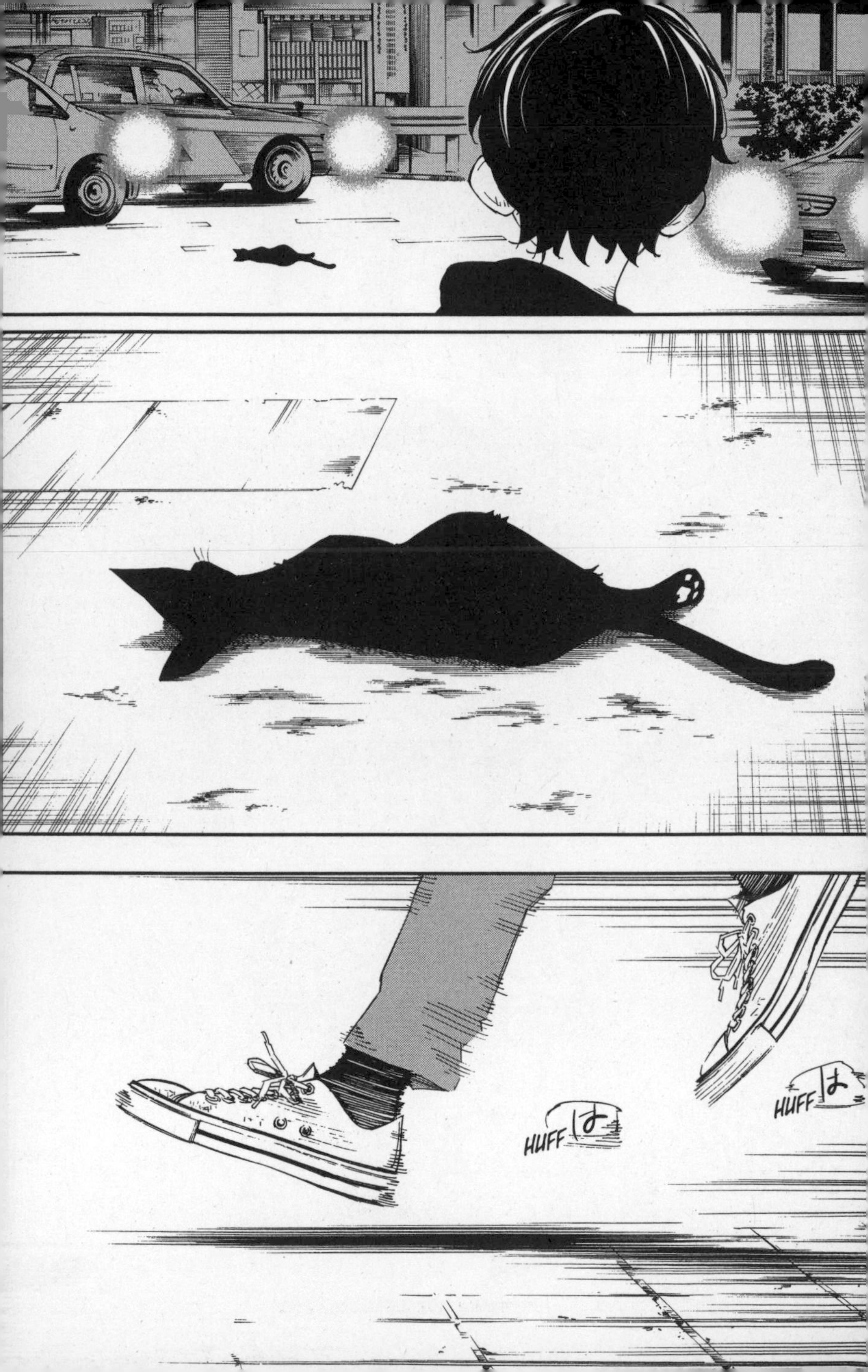
HUFF は
HUFF は

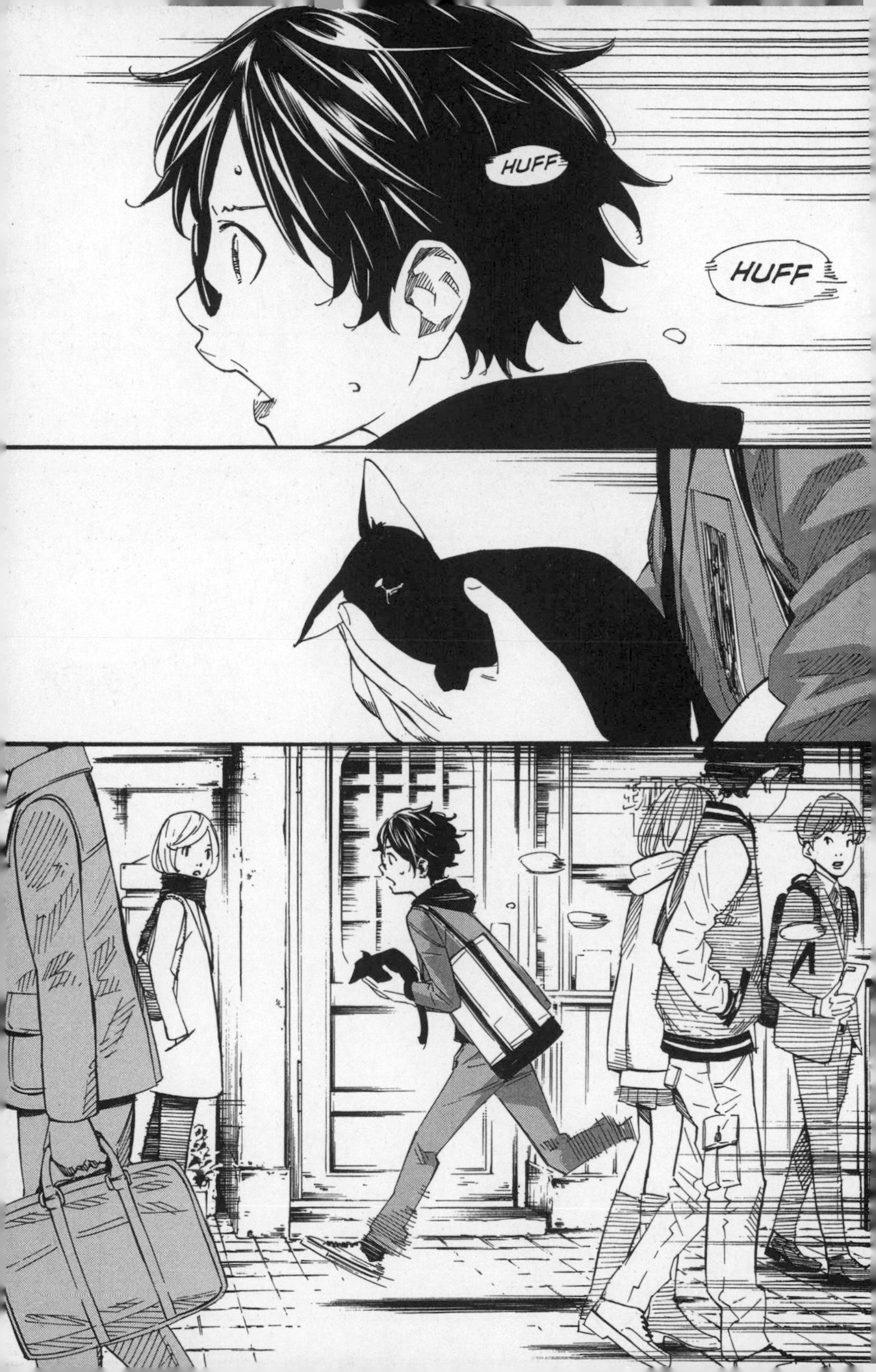
HUFF
HUFF

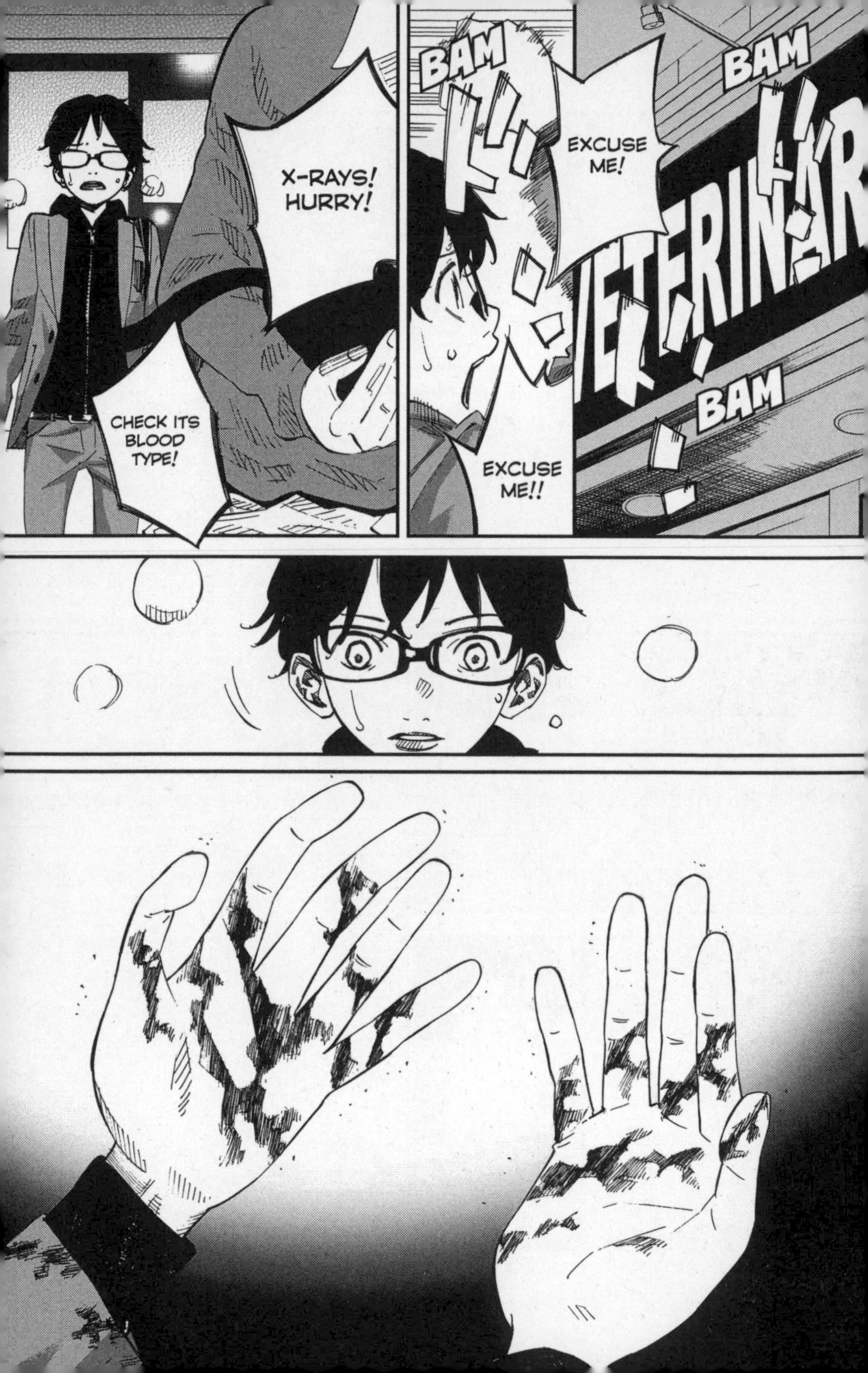
BAM
BAM
EXCUSE ME!
BAM
EXCUSE ME!!
X-RAYS! HURRY!
CHECK ITS BLOOD TYPE!

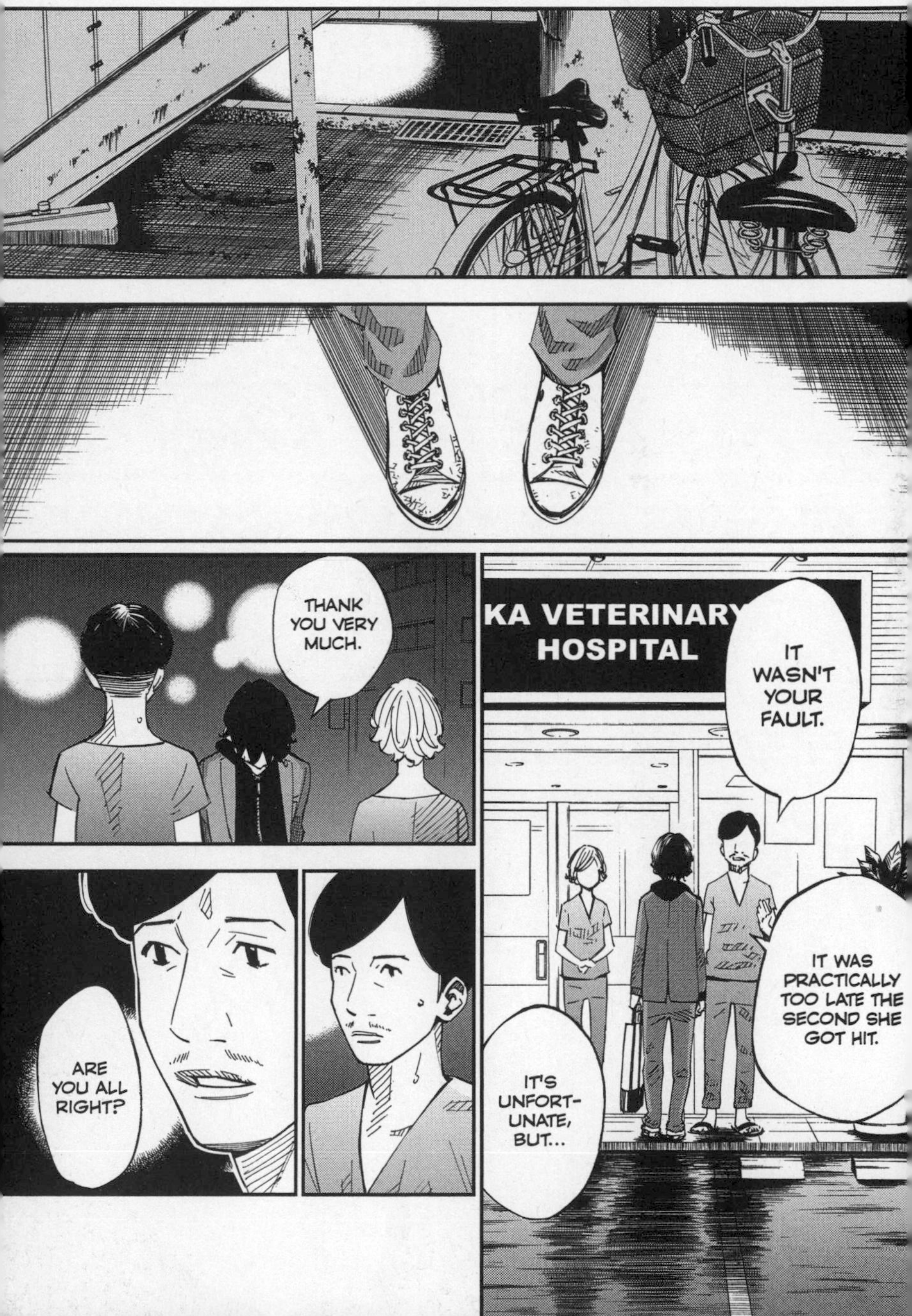
KA VETERINARY HOSPITAL
IT WASN'T YOUR FAULT.
IT WAS PRACTICALLY TOO LATE THE SECOND SHE GOT HIT.
IT'S UNFORT-UNATE, BUT...
THANK YOU VERY MUCH.
ARE YOU ALL RIGHT?

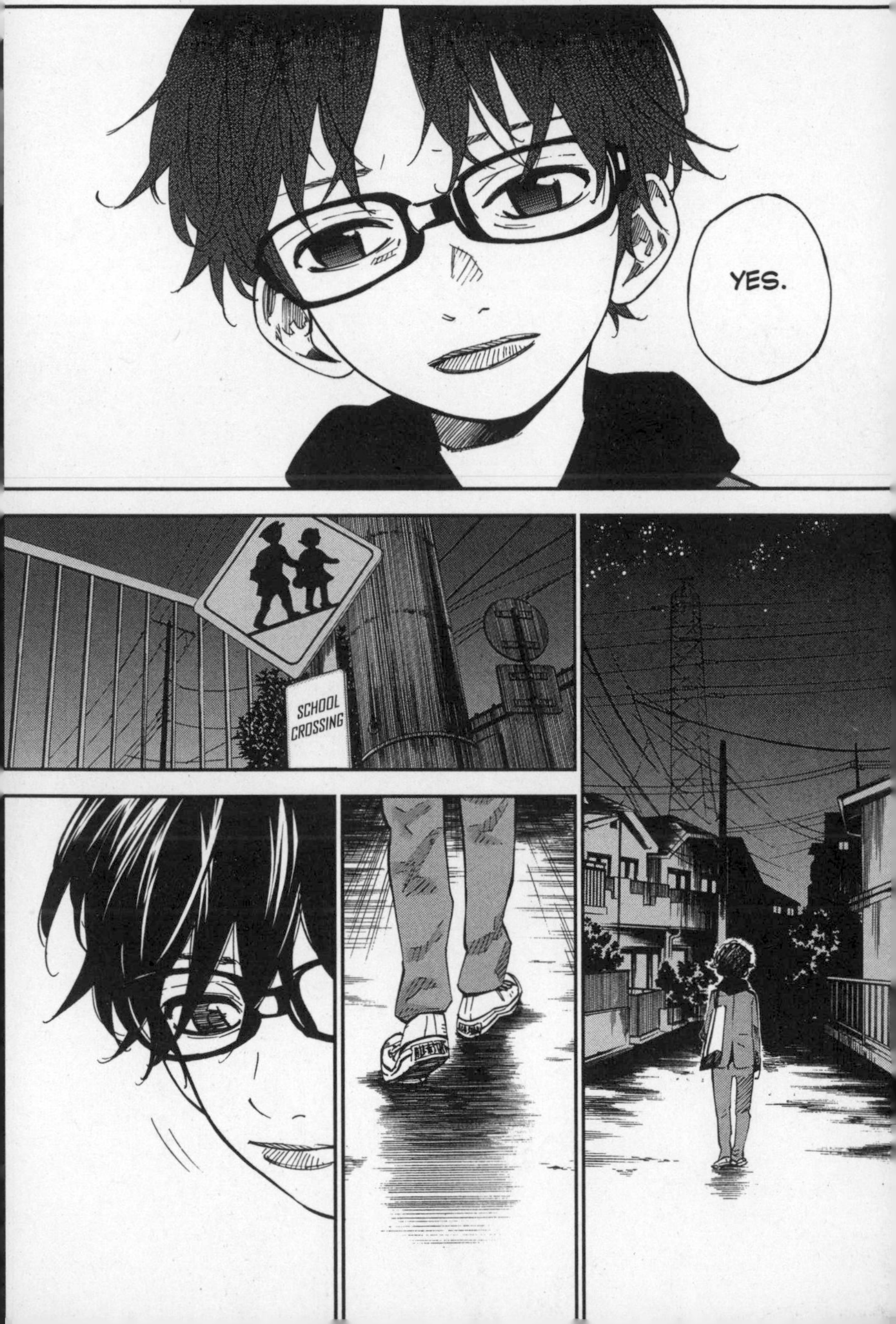
YES.
SCHOOL CROSSING

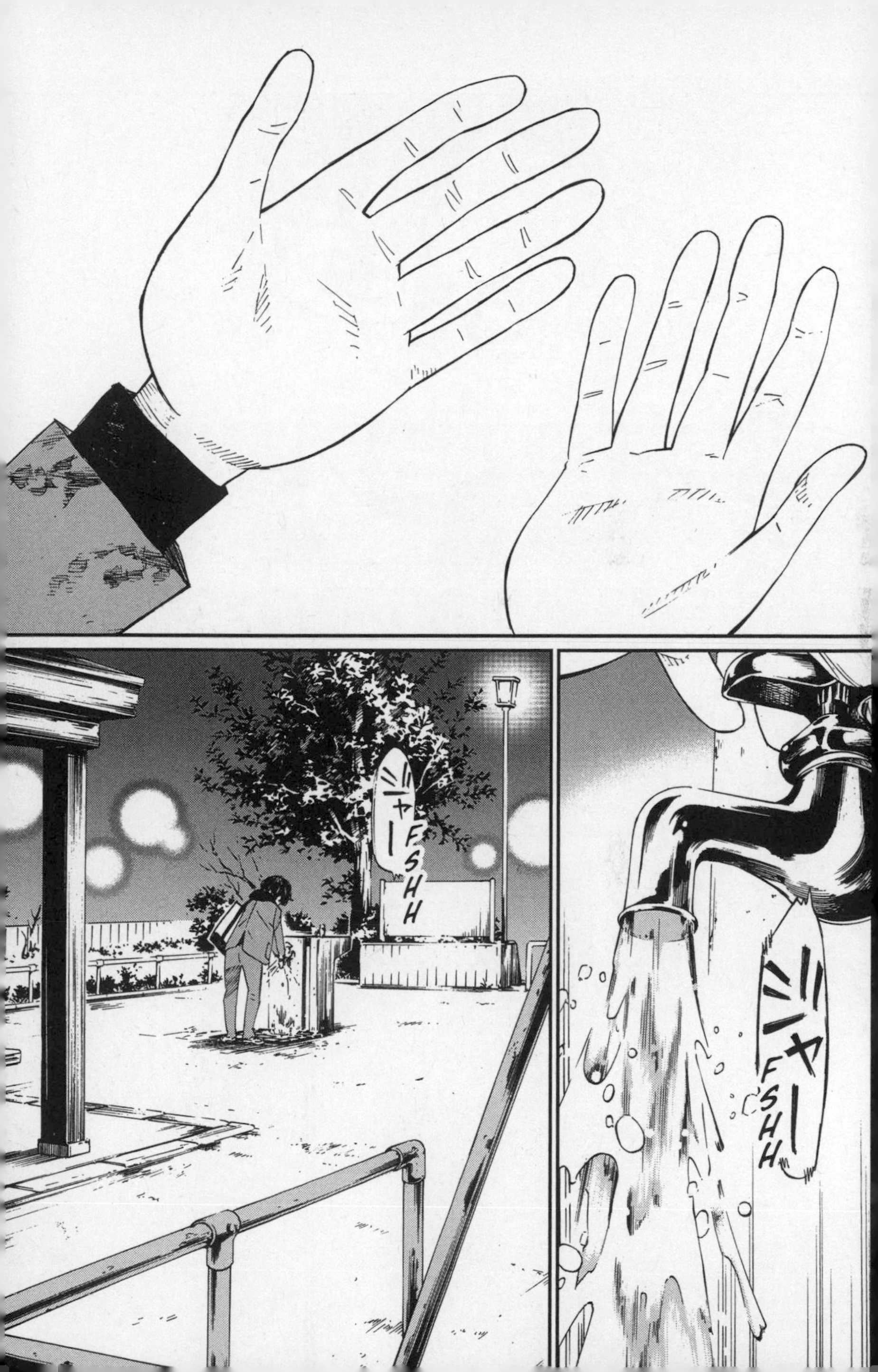
ジャー
FSHH
ジャー
FSHH

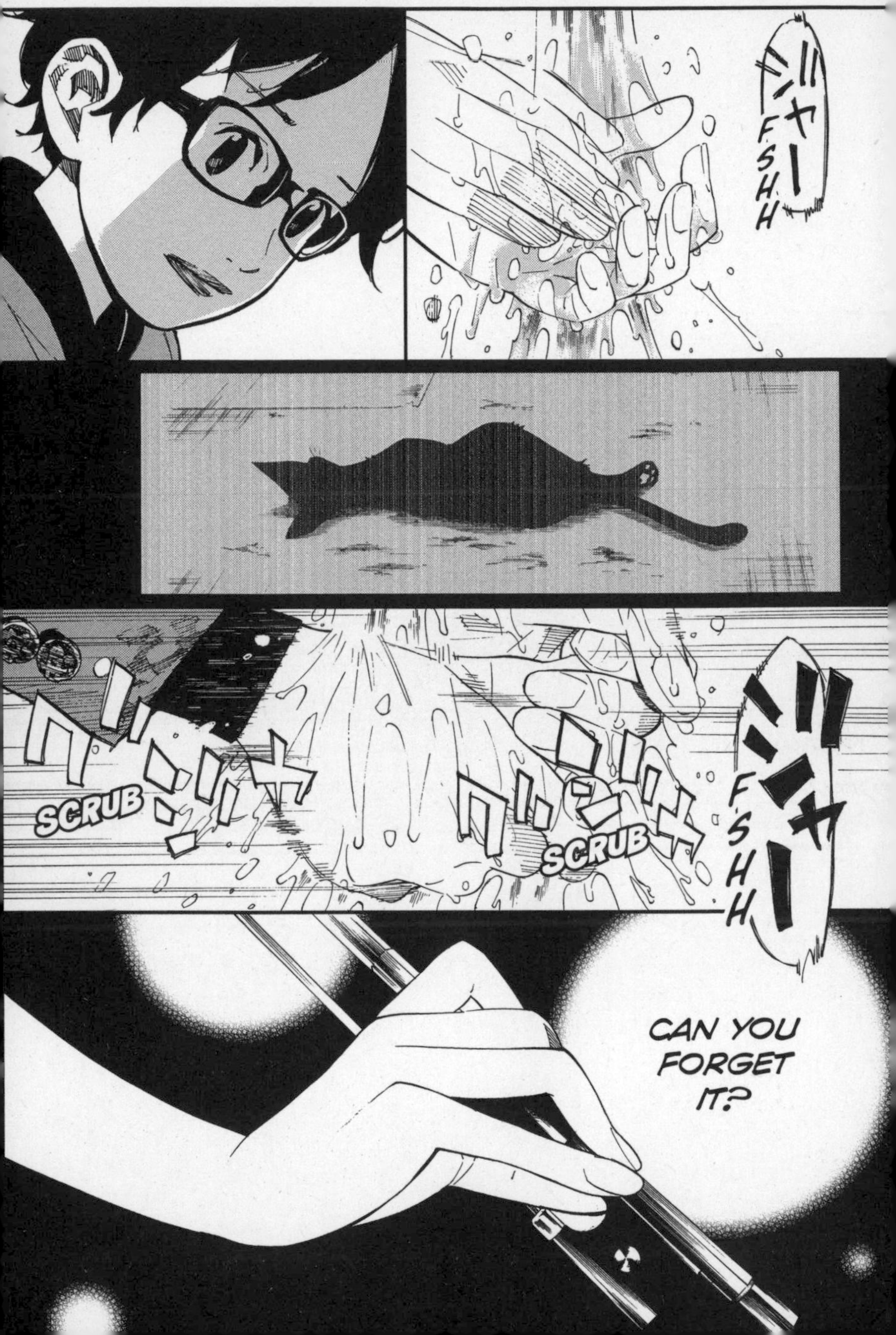
ジャー
F.S.H.H
ジャー
F.S.H.H
SCRUB
SCRUB
CAN YOU FORGET IT?

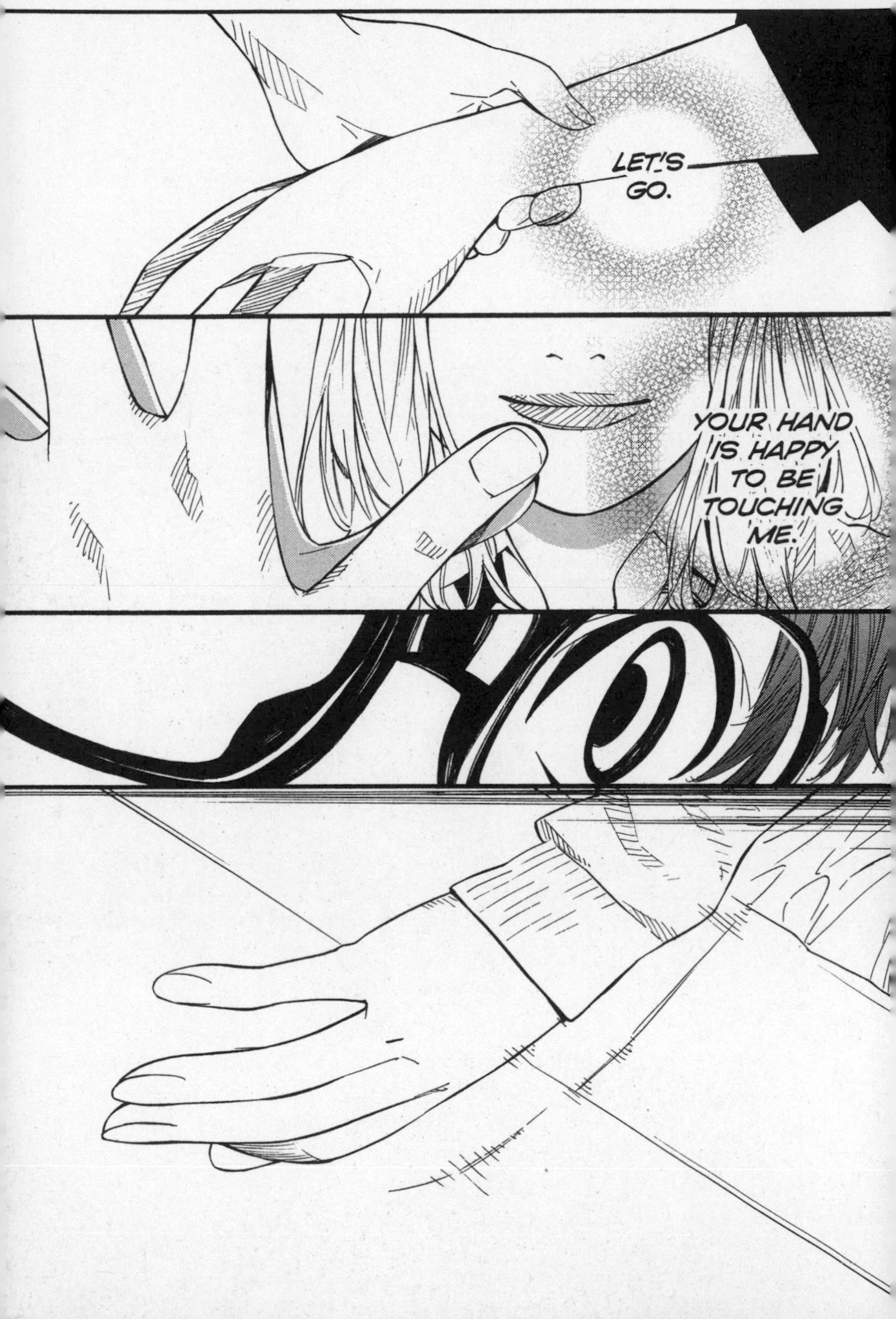
LET'S GO.
YOUR HAND IS HAPPY TO BE TOUCHING ME.

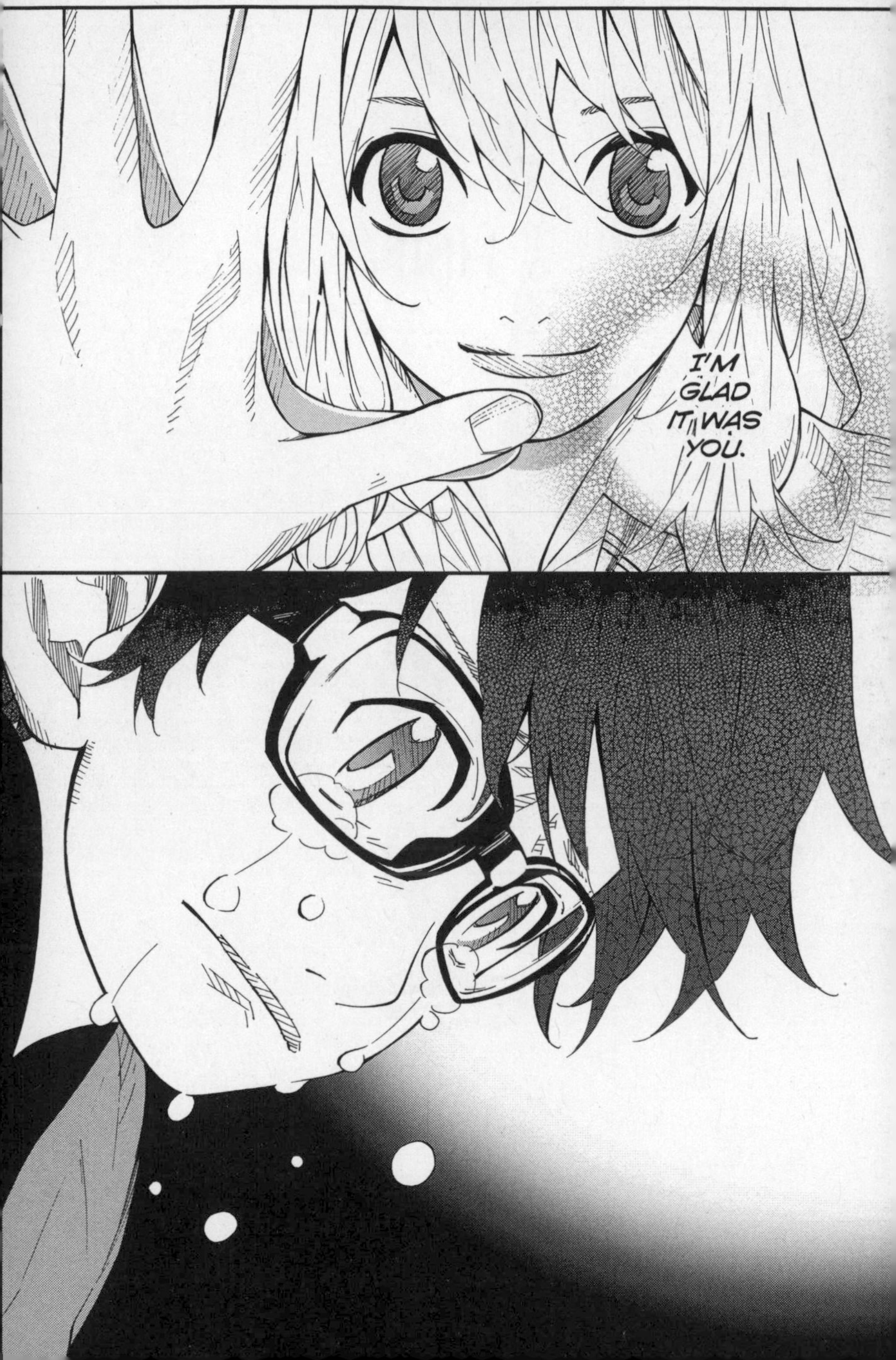
I'M GLAD IT WAS YOU.

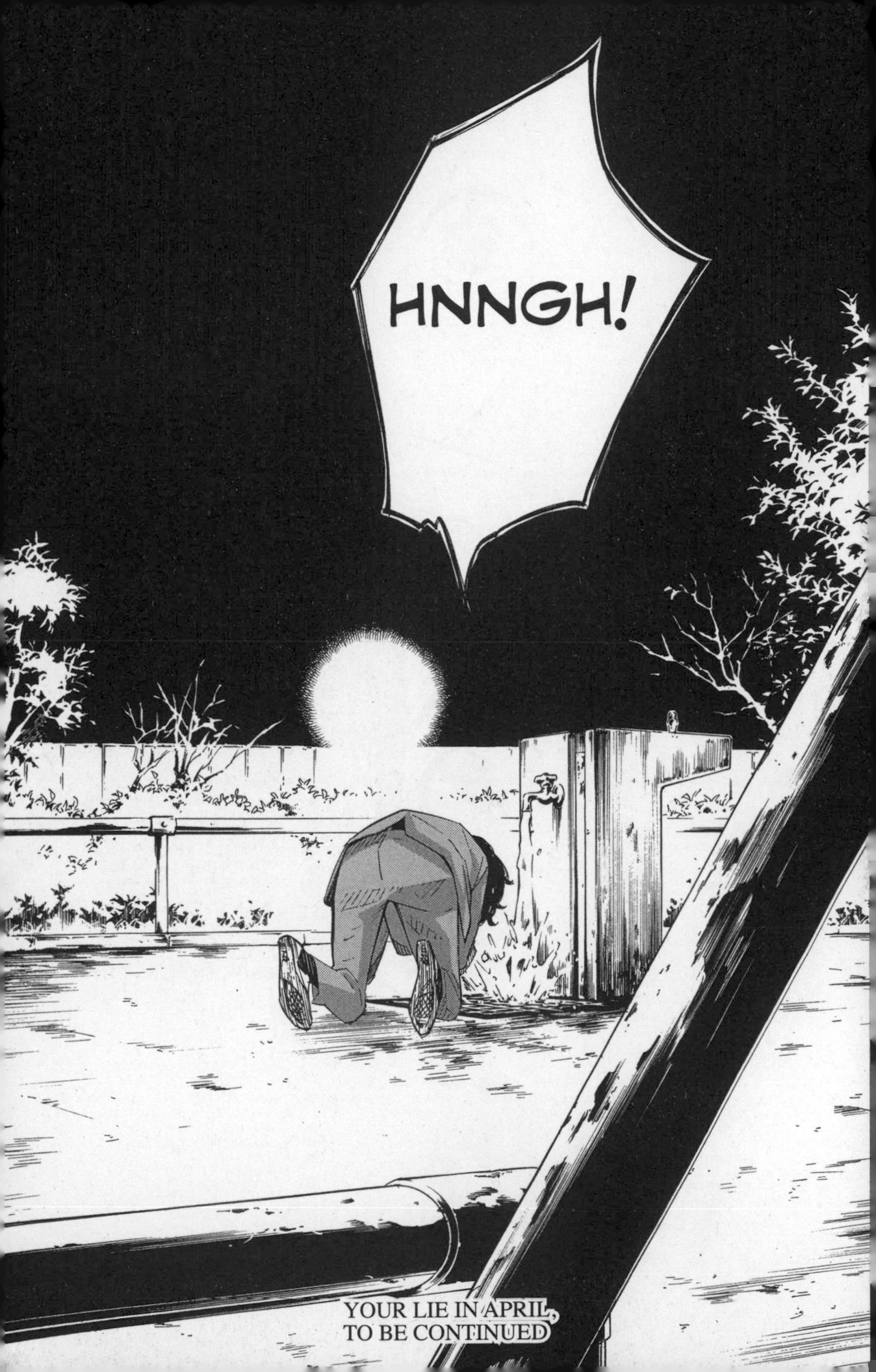
HNNGH!
YOUR LIE IN APRIL, TO BE CONTINUED

Special Thanks:

AKINORI ŌSAWA

MASANORI SUGANO

KAAI SUGANO

RIEKO IKEDA

KAORI YAMAZAKI

YOSHIHIRO KAMIYA

TOPPAN HALL

KAWAGUCHI LILIA

MUSIC HALL ANOANO

KING SEKIGUCHIDAI STUDIO

YOKOHAMA MINATO MIRAI HALL

UONUMA KOIDEGO CULTURAL HALL

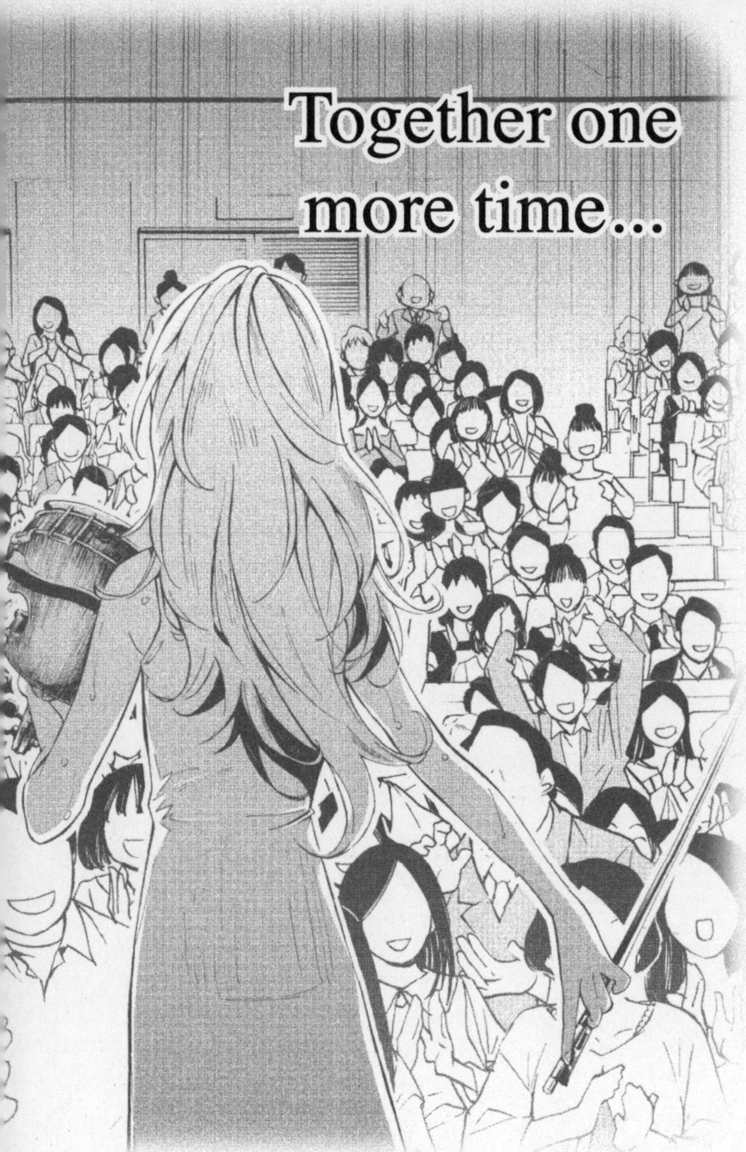
Together one more time...

I met the girl under cherry blossoms in full bloom, and my fate began to change.

Kōsei puts his feelings for Kaori into words, admitting that he is in love. Kaori continues her physical therapy so she can play the violin again. But their hopes and dreams are vain...the girl's condition worsens... With his competition looming on the horizon, can the boy make the piano sing?

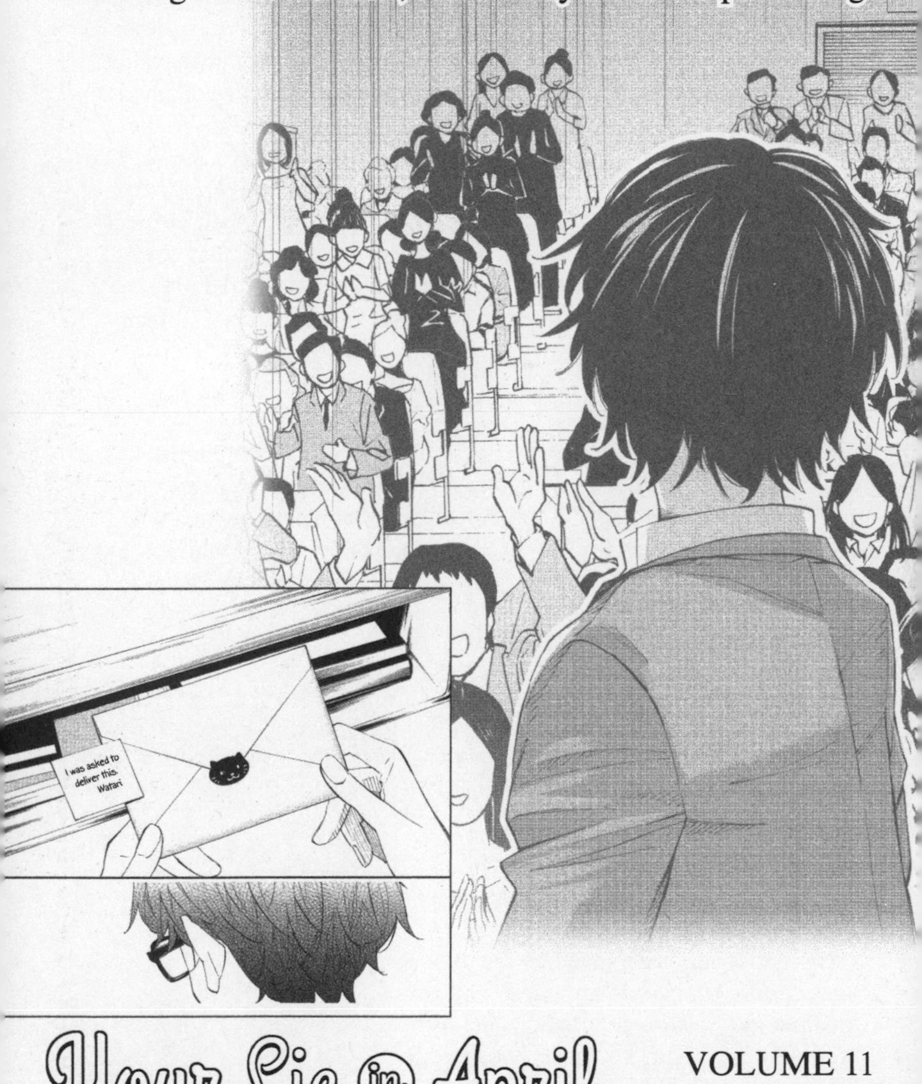
I was asked to deliver this. Watari

Your Lie in April

VOLUME 11
(FINAL VOLUME)

Your Lie in April 10 Translation Notes

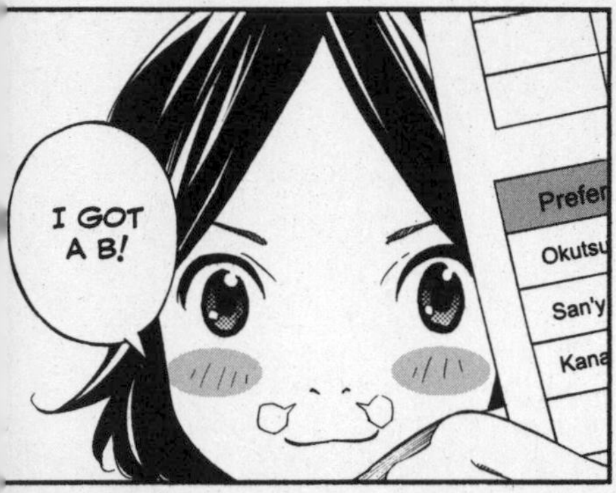
I GOT A B!

I got a B, page 13

While these grades are somewhat similar to standard grading system in the United States, they mean a bit more in this situation. The students have all taken mock exams in preparation for the entrance exams to the high schools of their choice. The letter grades given represent a rough estimate of their chances of passing the real test for each school. If one were to get an A, that would indicate a very high likelihood of getting into the student's desired high school. Tsubaki's B grade means she has a decent chance, especially if she keeps studying.

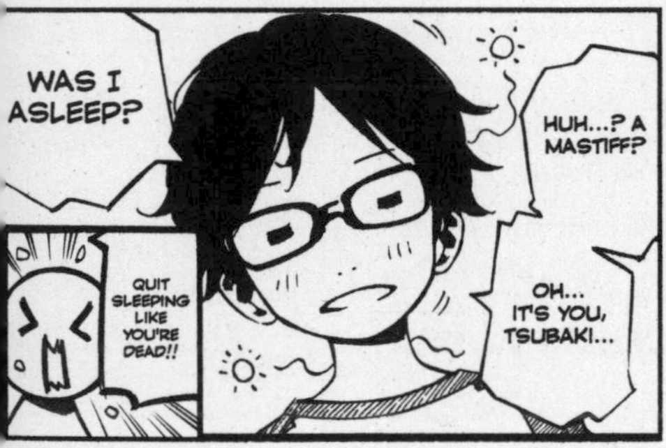
HUH...? A MASTIFF?
WAS I ASLEEP?
OH... IT'S YOU, TSUBAKI...
QUIT SLEEPING LIKE YOU'RE DEAD!!

A mastiff?, page 34

To be specific, Kōsei mistakes Tsubaki for a *Tosa Inu*, or Japanese mastiff, which is a large breed of dog that was originally bred for dog fights.

Katsudon and Florentines, page 49

Katsudon is bowl (*don*) of rice topped with cutlets (*katsu*) of breaded pork, which also happens to be the stereotypical dish given to people who are being interrogated by the police in Japanese police dramas. It is unclear whether or not this has any relation to it being a manly meal. A Florentine biscuit is a pastry made with nuts and fruit.

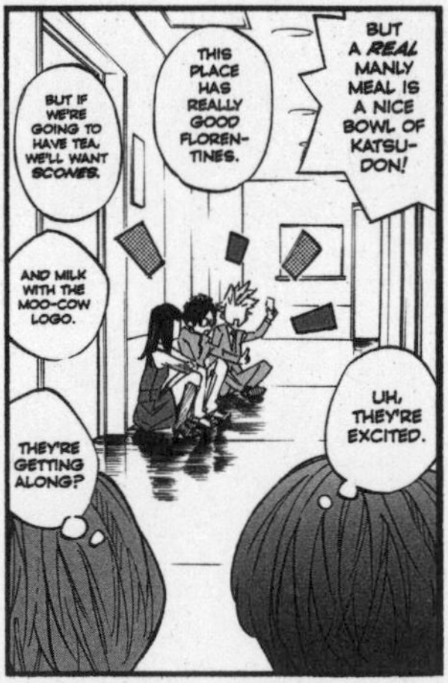
BUT A *REAL* MANLY MEAL IS A NICE BOWL OF KATSU-DON!
THIS PLACE HAS REALLY GOOD FLOREN-TINES.
BUT IF WE'RE GOING TO HAVE TEA, WE'LL WANT SCONES.
AND MILK WITH THE MOO-COW LOGO.
UH, THEY'RE EXCITED.
THEY'RE GETTING ALONG?

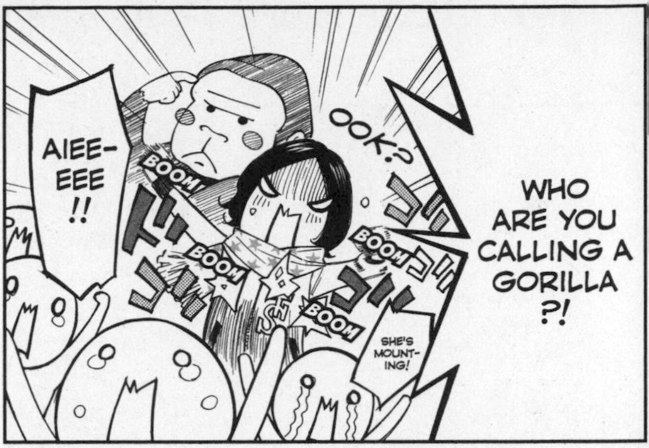
WHO ARE YOU CALLING A GORILLA?!
OOK?
BOOM
BOOM
BOOM
BOOM
SHE'S MOUNTING!
AIEE-EEE!!

She's mounting, page 106

These children seem to think they know something about animal behaviors, but they may be somewhat confused. While Tsubaki's action of pounding her chest can be a gorilla display of dominance, it's not the same thing as "mounting," which is when the male gorilla climbs on a female during mating.

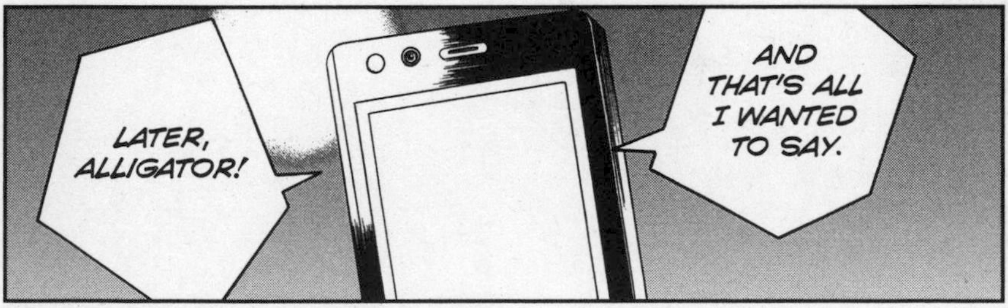
AND THAT'S ALL I WANTED TO SAY.
LATER, ALLIGATOR!

Later, alligator, page 166

The Japanese version of this farewell expression is *bai-baikin*, which is a combination of the English "bye-bye" and the Japanese *baikin*, which means "germ." Its origin is in the classic Japanese cartoon *Anpanman*, where it's the signature line delivered by the villainous Baikinman—literally, "Germ Man."

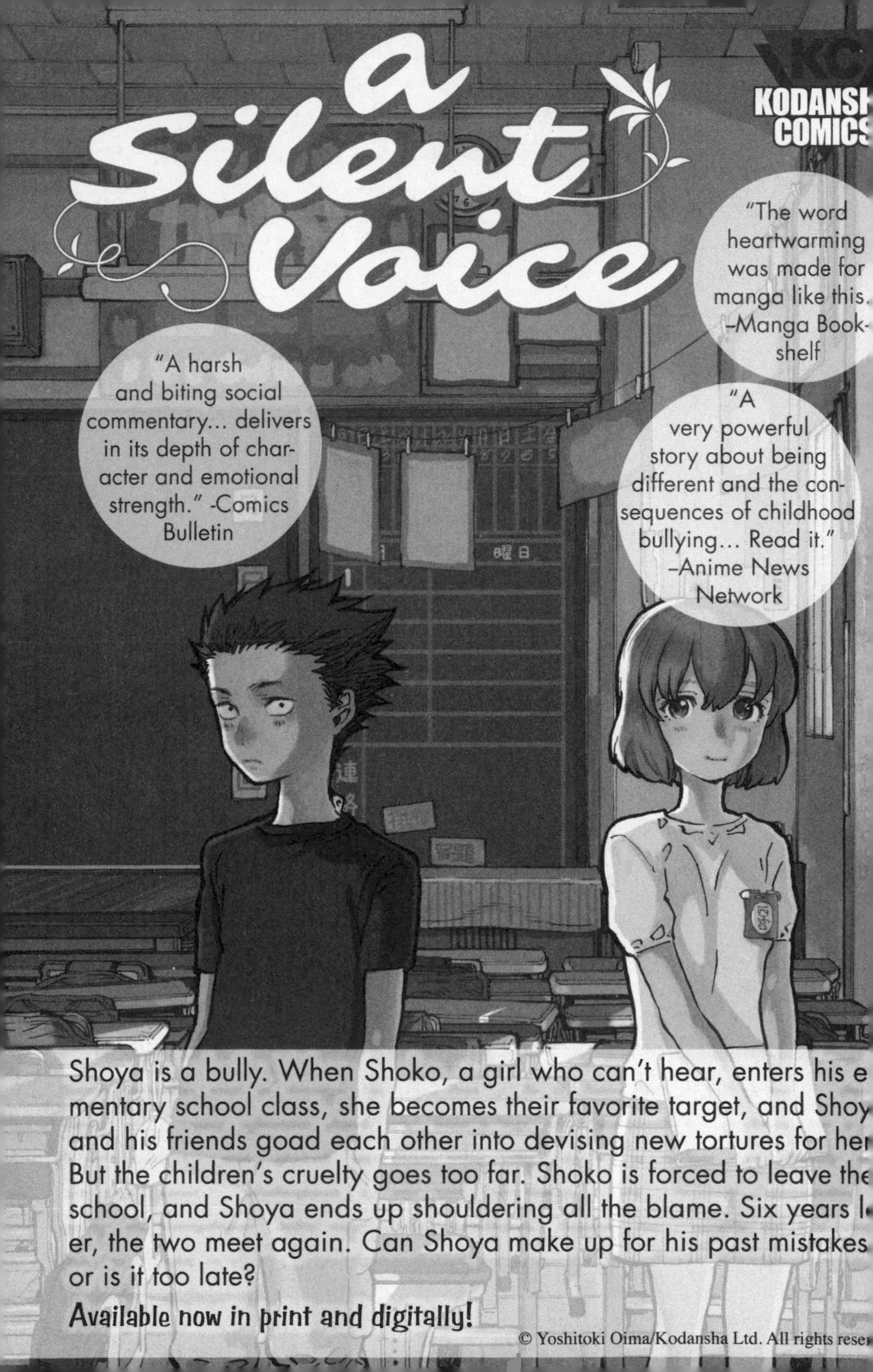
a Silent Voice
KODANSH
COMICS
"The word heartwarming was made for manga like this. –Manga Bookshelf
"A harsh and biting social commentary... delivers in its depth of character and emotional strength." -Comics Bulletin
"A very powerful story about being different and the consequences of childhood bullying... Read it." –Anime News Network
Shoya is a bully. When Shoko, a girl who can't hear, enters his e
mentary school class, she becomes their favorite target, and Shoy
and his friends goad each other into devising new tortures for her
But the children's cruelty goes too far. Shoko is forced to leave the
school, and Shoya ends up shouldering all the blame. Six years l
er, the two meet again. Can Shoya make up for his past mistakes
or is it too late?
Available now in print and digitally!
© Yoshitoki Oima/Kodansha Ltd. All rights reser

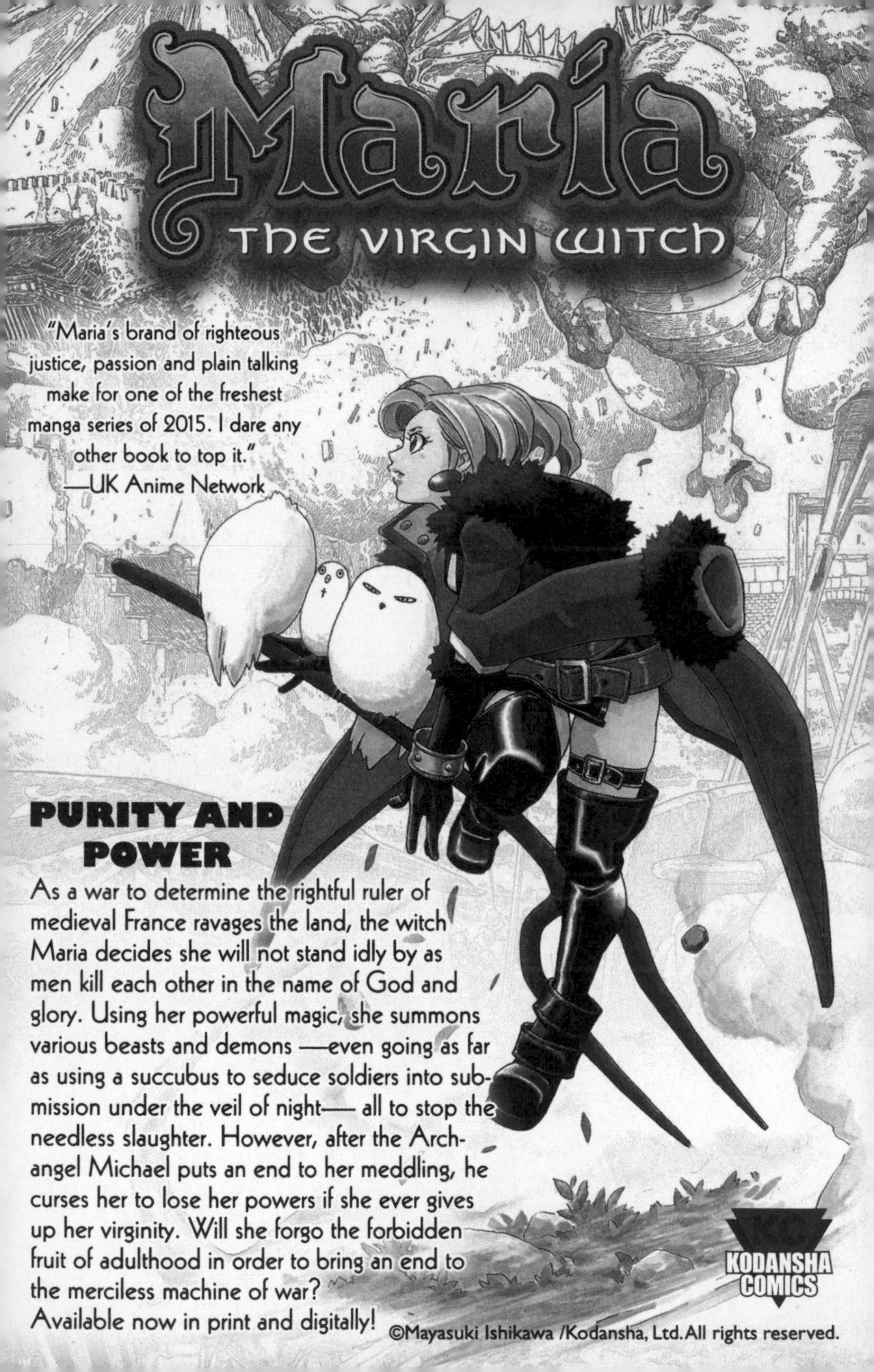
Maria
THE VIRGIN WITCH
"Maria's brand of righteous justice, passion and plain talking make for one of the freshest manga series of 2015. I dare any other book to top it."
—UK Anime Network
PURITY AND POWER
As a war to determine the rightful ruler of medieval France ravages the land, the witch Maria decides she will not stand idly by as men kill each other in the name of God and glory. Using her powerful magic, she summons various beasts and demons —even going as far as using a succubus to seduce soldiers into submission under the veil of night— all to stop the needless slaughter. However, after the Archangel Michael puts an end to her meddling, he curses her to lose her powers if she ever gives up her virginity. Will she forgo the forbidden fruit of adulthood in order to bring an end to the merciless machine of war?
Available now in print and digitally!
KODANSHA COMICS
©Mayasuki Ishikawa /Kodansha, Ltd. All rights reserved.

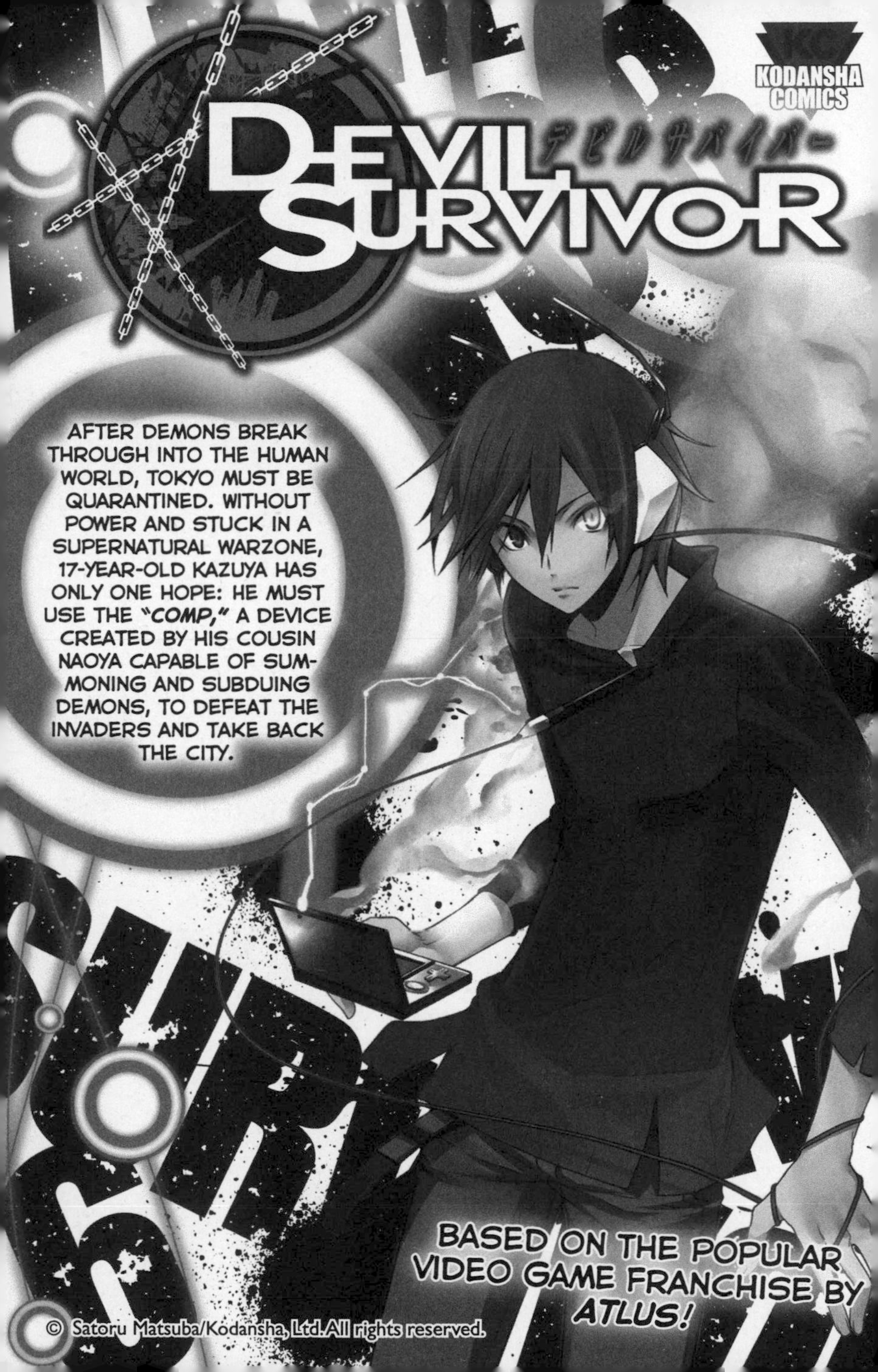
KODANSHA COMICS
DEVIL SURVIVOR
デビルサバイバー
AFTER DEMONS BREAK THROUGH INTO THE HUMAN WORLD, TOKYO MUST BE QUARANTINED. WITHOUT POWER AND STUCK IN A SUPERNATURAL WARZONE, 17-YEAR-OLD KAZUYA HAS ONLY ONE HOPE: HE MUST USE THE "COMP," A DEVICE CREATED BY HIS COUSIN NAOYA CAPABLE OF SUMMONING AND SUBDUING DEMONS, TO DEFEAT THE INVADERS AND TAKE BACK THE CITY.
BASED ON THE POPULAR VIDEO GAME FRANCHISE BY ATLUS!
© Satoru Matsuba/Kodansha, Ltd. All rights reserved.

Yamada-kun AND THE Seven Witches

"A very funny manga with a lot of heart and character."
—Adventures in Poor Taste

SWAPPED WITH A KISS?!

Class troublemaker Ryu Yamada is already having a bad day when he stumbles down a staircase along with star student Urara Shiraishi. When he wakes up, he realizes they have switched bodies—and that Ryu has the power to trade places with anyone just by kissing them! Ryu and Urara take full advantage of the situation to improve their lives, but with such an oddly amazing power, just how long will they be able to keep their secret under wraps?

Available now in print and digitally!

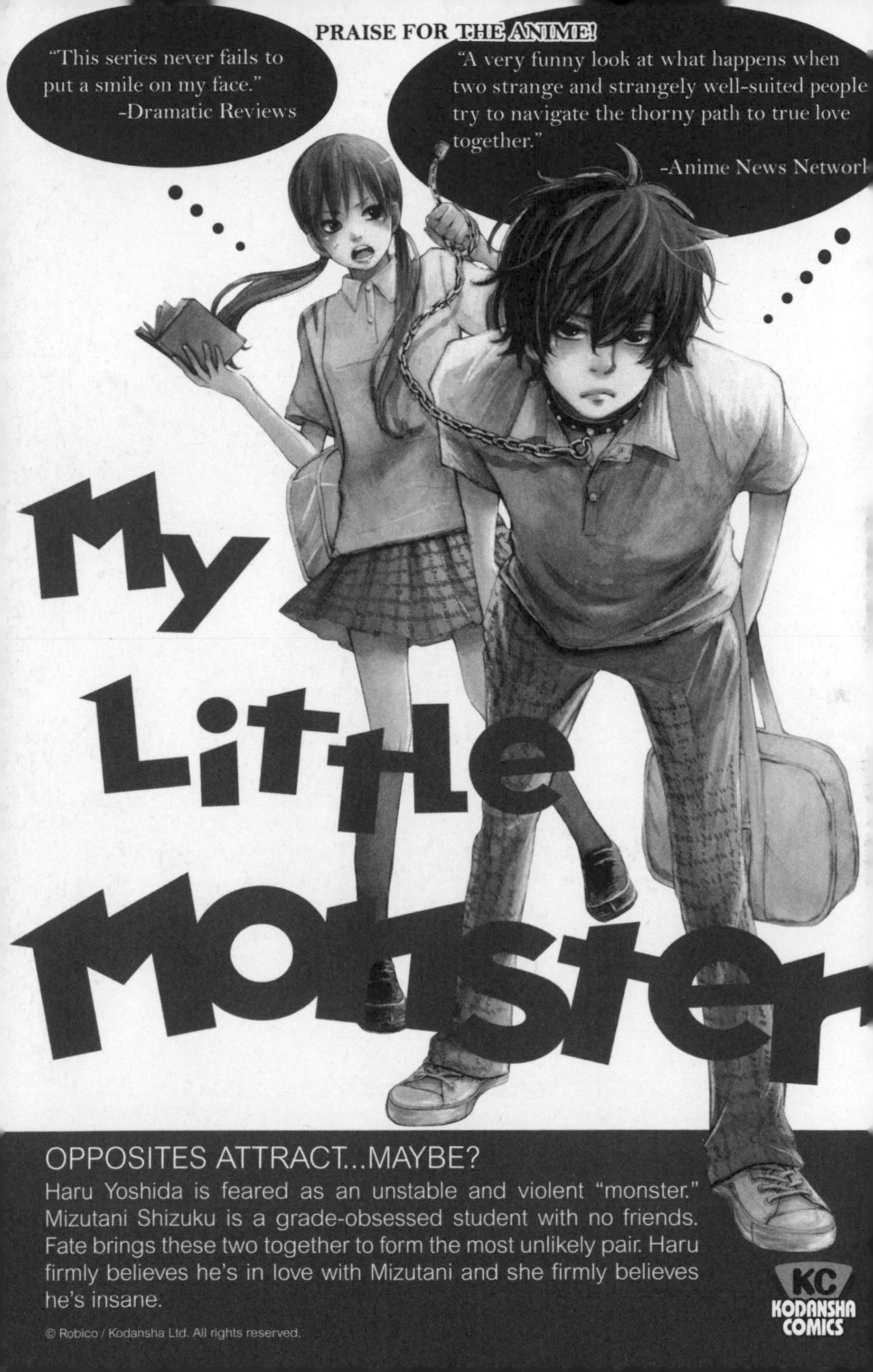
My Little Monster

Your Lie in April volume 10 is a work of fiction. Names, characters, places, and incidents are the products of the author's imagination or are used fictitiously. Any resemblance to actual events, locales, or persons, living or dead, is entirely coincidental.

A Kodansha Comics Trade Paperback Original

Published in the United States by Kodansha Comics, an imprint of Kodansha USA Publishing, LLC, New York.

Publication rights for this English edition arranged through Kodansha Ltd, Tokyo.

ISBN 978-1-63236-180-6

Special thanks:
Akinori Osawa, Rieko Ikeda, and Kaori Yamazaki

Printed in the United States of America.

www.kodanshacomics.com

9 8 7 6 5 4 3 2 1
Translation: Alethea and Athena Nibley
Lettering: Paige Pumphrey
Editing: Paul Starr
Kodansha Comics edition cover design by Phil Balsman